# Maritime Security and MET

# Maritime Security and MET

The International Association of Maritime Universities (IAMU) was founded in 1999 by seven maritime universities representing the five continents of the world. Since then, six Annual General Assemblies have been held, hosted by Member Universities. In August 2005, the total number of the membership stands at 47 maritime universities or faculties plus the Nippon Foundation.

"Maritime Security and MET" is the main theme of the 6th Annual General Assembly (AGA) 2005 hosted by the World Maritime University from 24th till 26th October in Malmö, Sweden.

After being reviewed by relevant experts in the maritime fields, 40 academic papers and 7 project reports which were presented at the 6th Annual General Assembly of IAMU are included in this book. Half of the papers are related to Maritime Security and the others are related to IAMU's traditional topics, current issues in MET, shore-based management and marine simulators, to name a few topics. The project reports present the (interim) results of research projects funded in the FY 2004 by IAMU.

The Local Executive Committee trust this book will be useful to those who are involved with the issues of Maritime Security, Maritime Education and Training and all fields related to maritime affairs.

Takeshi Nakazawa
Professor of the World Maritime University
Head of Local Executive Committee of the 6th Annual General Assembly

# Organization of IAMU

## Honorary Chair

Dr. Yohei Sasakawa
*(Chairman of The Nippon Foundation)*

## International Executive Committee

Dr. Karl Laubstein, Chair
*(World Maritime University)*

Dr. Gamal El Din Ahmed Mokhtar, Vice Chair
*(Arab Academy for Science and Technology and Maritime Transport)*

Prof. Dr. Osman Kamil Sag, Vice Chair
*(Istanbul Technical University, Maritime Faculty)*

Prof. Dr. Kinzo Inoue, Vice Chair
*(Kobe University, Faculty of Maritime Sciences)*

R. Adm. Leonard H. Tyler, Vice Chair
*(Maine Maritime Academy)*

Prof. Dr. German De Melo, Vice Chair
*(Polytechnical University of Catalonia, Faculty of Nautical Studies)*

Mr. Masazumi Nagamitsu, Vice Chair
*(The Nippon Foundation)*

Prof. Dr. Kyung-kun Kim
(Korea Maritime University)

Prof. Dr. Ivan I. Kostylev
*(Admiral Makarov State Maritime Academy)*

Dr. William Eisenhardt
*(The California Maritime Academy)*

Prof. Dr. Zuwen Wang
*(Dalian Maritime University)*

Prof. Dr. Jozef Lisowski
*(Gdynia Maritime University)*

Prof. Dr. Mykhaylo V. Miyusov
*(Odessa National Maritime Academy)*

V. Adm. John Craine
*(State University of New York, Maritime College)*

Prof. Dr. Kohei Ohtsu
*(Tokyo University of Marine Science and Technology, Faculty of Marine Technology)*

## Steering Board

Dr. Karl Laubstein
Dr. Gamal El Din Ahmed Mokhtar
Prof. Dr. Osman Kamil Sag
Prof. Dr. Kinzo Inoue
R. Adm. Leonard H. Tyler
Prof. Dr. German De Melo
Mr. Masazumi Nagamitsu
Dr. Hisashi Yamamoto

## IAMU Secretariat

Dr. Hisashi Yamamoto, Secretary
Ms. Shoko Yoshihara, Coordinator

# Maritime Security and MET

Editor:

**Detlef Nielsen**
*World Maritime University*

WIT*PRESS* Southampton, Boston

**Editor:**

**Detlef Nielsen**
*World Maritime University*

Published by

**WIT Press**
Ashurst Lodge, Ashurst, Southampton, SO40 7AA, UK
Tel: 44 (0) 238 029 3223; Fax: 44 (0) 238 029 2853
E-Mail: witpress@witpress.com
http://www.witpress.com

For USA, Canada and Mexico

**WIT Press**
25 Bridge Street, Billerica, MA 01821, USA
Tel: 978 667 5841; Fax: 978 667 7582
E-Mail: infousa@witpress.com
http://www.witpress.com

British Library Cataloguing-in-Publication Data

A Catalogue record for this book is available
from the British Library

ISBN: 1-84564-058-6
Library of Congress Catalog Card Number: 2005933487

*The texts of the papers in this volume were set individually by the authors or under their supervision. Only minor corrections to the text may have been carried out by the publisher.*



Printed in Great Britain by Cambridge Printing.

# $6^{th}$ IAMU Annual General Assembly at the World Maritime University, Malmö, Sweden

---

# Foreword to the Proceedings

In today's world, in addition to meeting high standards of safety, environmental protection and efficiency, the international maritime industry has to address the demands of enhanced security. The theme of this year's IAMU Annual General Assembly: "Maritime Security and Maritime Education and Training" is, therefore, most timely as it provides participating Maritime Education and Training (MET) Institutions the opportunity to explore together one of the major challenges facing the maritime industry today. IMO, for its part, has developed a comprehensive security regime for international shipping, which entered into force in July 2004, and our challenge now is to ensure its wide and effective implementation as well as continued vigilance over security risks. For MET, the issue should be how to provide the human element with the skills and competence required to achieve the set goals through education, training and research.

When IAMU met for the first time in 2000, one of its highest priorities was "to pursue tangible results". With the generous support of the Nippon Foundation, maritime institutions, under the IAMU umbrella, are wonderfully placed to do just that. We are all aware that ours is an industry that relies heavily on the professionalism of its people. Similarly, we are conscious of the challenges posed by the international nature of this most global of pursuits. What could be more relevant, therefore, than representatives from MET institutions all over the world coming together to discuss the best possible ways of preparing staff at sea, in shipping companies, ports and maritime administrations to meet these challenges? Hosted by the World Maritime University – itself a gem of international co-operation – there could be no better forum for stimulating interesting and fruitful contributions to discussion of maritime security issues and for developing strategies to address them through maritime education and training.

If we are to uphold and improve standards and ensure continued vigilance, nothing could be of greater importance than the training of the maritime professionals of the future. The papers presented at the $6^{th}$ IAMU Annual General Assembly cover a full range of topics, from operations, management and organization to engineering and sciences. These Proceedings are set to become a source of inspiration and reference for maritime institutions worldwide and are of relevance to all who are involved in the maritime industry.

In my role as Chancellor of the World Maritime University, I am pleased to have been invited to provide this foreword and take this opportunity to commend the work and achievements of IAMU to date and look forward to its continuing success and contribution in the future.

Efthimios E. Mitropoulos
IMO Secretary-General

# Contents

**Section 2: Maritime security and MET**

# Section 1
# Project reports

# Identification and formulation of Maritime Security Management System from the shore side: an interim report

D. S. Grewal
*School of Maritime Management and Logistics,*
*Australian Maritime College, Launceston, Tasmania*

## Abstract

This interim report presents the main issues researched in the IAMU-funded project. The primary objective of this study is to identify and analyse all shore-based and near-shore activities which are associated with maritime operations and to formulate them into a Maritime Security Management System. A curriculum development for maritime security studies will also be analysed and proposed as part of the project. The study involves two main stages. A focus group survey is conducted first to explore ideas and perceptions of experts in the field on different facets of research objectives. Based on the findings of this survey, a postal survey will be conducted to empirically examine the perception of the international shipping community on research objectives.
*Keywords: ISPS code, Maritime Security Management System.*

## 1 Introduction

In recent years, the issue of maritime security has become a major concern on the international maritime agenda. In fact, maritime security dates back to early maritime history under the themes of piracy and cargo theft and has more recently covered issues, such as stowaways, people and drug trafficking. There have been growing fears that terrorists can also use ships or their cargo as weapons to attack vulnerable points in the maritime chain just as aircraft were used in the terrorist attack in the United States. Terrorism, thus, becomes the new dimension of maritime security.

There have been a number of responses to this issue. The International Maritime Organisation (IMO) has recently adopted the International Ship and

Port Facility Security (ISPS) Code which came into force on 1st July 2004, aiming at the establishment of an international framework so that "ships and port facilities can co-operate to deter and detect acts which threaten security in the maritime transport sector". The Code establishes a number of requirements on contracting governments, ships, port facilities, and relevant maritime industry participants to carry out risk assessment, establish roles and responsibilities, work out security plans as well as assigning security officers both on board the ships and ashore (in the shipping companies and port facilities).

Although there has been some research done to address the issues of maritime security from different angles, there are some gaps that need to be taken into consideration:

- First of all, the coverage of the ISPS Code is basically within the traditional interactions and relationships between ships and port facilities. In addition, only port facilities serving ships engaged on international voyages are covered in the scope of the Code, while other dimensions of security such as cargo theft, stowaways, drug trafficking or people smuggling can exist in all ports no matter what type of ships they serve.
- Secondly, security threats can come from activities on the shore side. These have not been sufficiently addressed. In the transportation chain, however, maritime security also involves other shore-based activities which can provoke the critical issue of security management connected to maritime transport and operations. For instance, the links with stevedoring companies, road and rail transport companies, freight forwarders, etc and the relationships among them need to be explored. These are some examples of shore-based activities which are associated with maritime transport and have important implications in the establishment and implementation of security management system.

A lack of security management policy and, on the top of it, a "security culture", of such shore-based activities will certainly have direct and induced impacts on maritime transport as a whole. A formal research on this aspcct is, therefore, considered necessary and useful both from academic and practical perspectives.

## 2 Research objectives

The primary objective of this study is to identify and analyse all shore-based and near shore activities which are associated with maritime operations and to formulate them into a Maritime Security Management System. A curriculum development for maritime security studies will also be analysed and proposed as part of the project. This is an attempt to extend the coverage of the security net in the maritime industry, covering all dimensions of the issue.

## 3 Methodological framework

Different research methodologies were deployed to achieve the set objectives of this project:

- Literature review and secondary data analysis: this method was applied to review aspects of maritime security management in general and security management of shore-based activities associated with maritime operations in particular.
- Survey research by questionnaires and Focus group interview: in order to analyse the current practice of security management policies and systems in sea-based and shore-based activities in the industry and propose standard working procedures and requirements from academic perspective, these methods are needed as efficient tools to collect necessary data for analysis.

Based on this framework as shown in Figure 1, it is intended to conduct the following tasks:

- Identify all shore-based and near shore activities which are associated with maritime security management system (Action Plan 1).
- Identify key players in the identified activities and analyse their security-related relationships (Action Plan 2).
- Analyse the vital components and involved security risks in the Maritime Security Management System (Action Plan 3).
- Formulate the standards formats of components in the Maritime Security Management System (Action Plan 4).
- Formulate the necessary contents for maritime security courses (Action Plan 5).

The study involves two main stages: A focus group survey is conducted first to explore ideas and perception of expert in the field on different facets of research objectives.

Based on the findings of this survey, a postal survey will be conducted to empirically examine the perception of the international shipping community on research objectives.

## 4 Work done so far – a brief description

The first stage of this research is currently being conducted. Several maritime experts in Australia and New Zealand, employed in shipping companies, port operation companies, port authorities, as harbour masters and as administrative legislators, were asked to join the focus group survey and to provide their comments on the following questions:

1. In your opinion, have the current security initiatives, such as ISPS Code, covered all shore-based and near shore activities as far as security management is concerned? If not, please identify the omissions.
2. How would you assess the capability and effectiveness of these current security initiatives in helping to maintain and implement effective security management ashore in maritime transport industry?
3. Please identify the dimensions or security activities (e.g. access control, information security, etc.) that should be included in a holistic Maritime Security Management System.
4. Please describe the important inter-and intra organisational relationships which affect the management of maritime security.

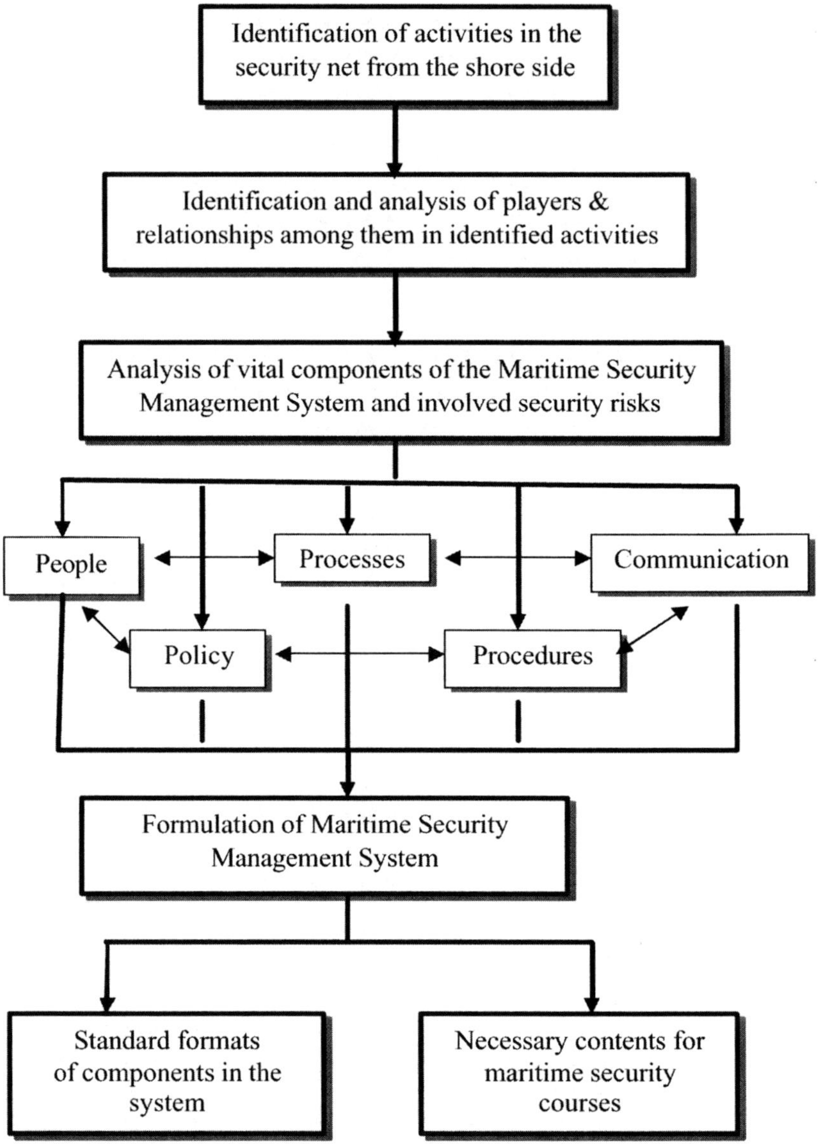


Figure 1: The study framework for the project.

5. In your opinion, what are the key criteria of a good/effective Maritime Security Management System?
6. It is said that a good/effective Maritime Security Management System should include the following: policy, processes, procedures, people, communication and technology. To what extent do you agree with this statement?

7. Do you see the need for further legislative changes to facilitate or enable the development and implementation of an effective security system that is able to deal with the challenges of a complex maritime security environment?
8. In your opinion, what should be included in the current curriculum of maritime universities so as to provide education and training of vital components of a good/effective Maritime Security Management System?
9. Are there any other factors which you would consider important to the success of a Maritime Security Management System?
10. Should security become a part of a wider safety management system?

Responses from focus group members were collated with author-related links removed, then synthesised and analysed into a single document. This was then sent around to all participants for their comments and additional inputs before being finalised.

The analysis and finalisation of this survey is currently under way.

# The influence of resources on the implementation of quality procedures in MET systems and safety at sea (IRMETS)

V. A. Loginovsky, A. P. Gorobtsov & V. E. Kuzmin
*Navigation Department, Admiral Makarov State Maritime Academy, St Petersburg, The Russian Federation*

## Abstract

The intensive development of various types of very important and useful regulations and standards in the shipping industry in recent years, in a lot of cases, is not sufficiently coordinated with the quantity and quality of resources to meet them and ensure their proper implementation. This paper presents the project sponsored by the Nippon Foundation describing some formal approaches in analysis of Human Element impact on safety and security in the shipping industry and MET efficiency.
*Keywords: crew resources, fuzzy logic, Bayesian nets, safety, security.*

## 1 Introduction

Application of such "catalysts of efficiency and safety" as ISO and ISM Code standards without granting the appropriate resources to meet their provisions has led to the emergence of some negative tendencies in which new terms and concepts are generated. These include "paper safety", "paper audit", "paper quality", etc. But the carrying out of many of such bureaucratic "paper procedures" to keep the "paper image" of the MET institution, shipping company or vessel, wastes the same resources and, in many cases, reduces the level of quality and safety. So, there is a vicious circle, and to escape from it, i.e. to raise the efficiency of the regulations and standards, we have only one possibility and that is finding the optimum balance between requirements and resources through the reasonable compromise between safety and economic efficiency of the industry. The shipping industry and MET field are linked in one system and in this Project we have tried to research such links using FIS and Bayesian nets.

# 2 Crew resources analysis

## 2.1 Fuzzy Inference System (FIS) application to regulation and crew resources analysis

The theory of Fuzzy sets, which basic ideas have been offered by American mathematician Lofty Zadeh, describe a qualitative, fuzzy concepts and knowledge of the world around and to operate with this knowledge and openly receiving new information. The methods of construction of information models based on this theory essentially expand traditional areas of computer applications and form an independent direction. Scientifically applied research has received the special name - Fuzzy modelling. The technique of modelling is described in [1]. The FIS flow-chart is presented on Figure 1. To make an FIS we used Gaussian membership functions distributed at regular intervals. These intervals and sets of linguistic variables are shown in brackets below. Input linguistic variables:

- manning (0-2; reduced, standard, increased);
- skill (0-2; low, medium, standard, high, excellent);
- regulations (0-4; lack, sufficient, functionally redundant, overlap, overregulation).

Output linguistic variables:

- workload (0-2; low, medium, standard, overload, extremely overload);
- task (0-2; not solved, almost not solved, almost solved, solved, little better solution, more better solution, the best solution).

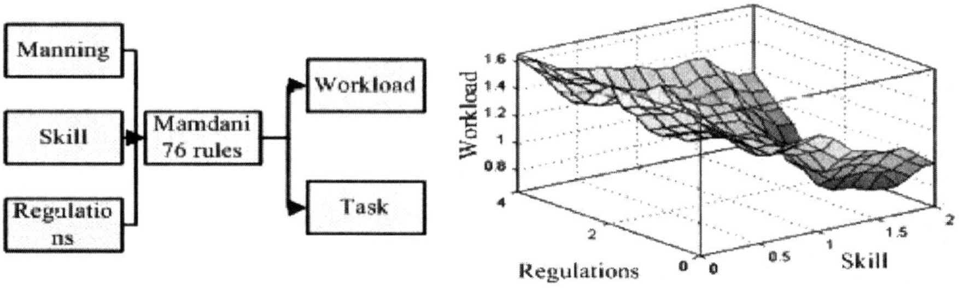


Figure 1: FIS and Workload surface.

All the standard (conventional) values in this model are equal to 1. So, if the value of workload is 1 it means that hours of rest meet the requirements of STCW 78, as amended and ILO 180 etc.

We used an adjustable model consisting of a set of 76 fuzzy *if-then rules* of the following type:

1. If (manning is standard) and (skill is standard) and (number of regulations is sufficient) then (workload is standard) and (level of task solution is standard)…76. If (manning is reduced) and (skill is low) and (there is an

overregulation) then (the crew is extremely overloaded) and (the task is not solved).

Some formal findings and results within the model frames are given below:

a) If even the number of regulations is functionally sufficient and manning and skill of the crew is conventional, then to make the 0.9 of conventional work the probable crew overload of 0.12 is a common thing.
b) If in “a” conditions the crew is reduced to 0.8 then the workload increases to 0.24, and crew performance falls to 0.85.
c) If the qualification of crew leaves much to be desired then it practically means that workload is at the same level as in result “b” and in this case the crew performance level is reduced to 0.71.
d) If there is a functional lack of regulations then even with the complete crew and their standard qualification, the crew performance level is 0.7.
e) The overregulation impact is very similar to the situation “d”. Overregulation is dangerous, as it distracts seafarers from performance of their direct official duties frequently to please the ship inspectors. This is the main reason of «paper image».
f) Overregulation is catastrophic for ship (company) when there is a shortage of crew especially if the crew is low qualified. In this case crew performance is only 0.58. It is accompanied by an enormous overload. Overregulation, unskilled seafarers and overload go together and they create the vicious circle to increase regulation even more.
g) Improvement of crew skill by 0.1 enables to give standard level of crew performance with its possible insignificant overload of 0.1.

The results "a-e" show low crew performance. In other words, in these cases there is a *constant hazardous atmosphere* originating with the high probability of incidents, accidents or catastrophes.

Analyzing the output linguistic variables, Workload and Task (Crew performance), we received some findings and results, which are partially submitted below:

h) Even in conditions of keen competition, the overregulation in the shipping industry could be avoided or its negative impact could be reduced by educating and training of highly qualified seafarers and the company’s shore based staff and ship inspectors.
i) Decrease in seafarer’s qualification is equal to increasing of his/her workload. It means an increase in the fatigue and reducing the level of safety as well as the attractiveness of shipping industry.
j) Non-compliance with the rest-hours required by STCW 78 and ILO 180, as well as the level of safety and security, is originated in MET institutions. For example, wrong and very formal implementation of ISO standards in MET institutions in lack of human resources could result in increasing of paper work and promote the outflow of teaching personnel from this bureaucratic work. In its turn this promotes the possible non-compliance with the MET

standards, and further such hazards block to meet the STCW, ISM, ISPS, … provisions.

k) One of the reasons of overregulation in shipping industry is cheap, low qualified and often multinational crews. Using non-native language for communication on board ship and while training and educating promotes a decrease in professional skill level of seafarers, at least in the very beginning of his/her maritime career.
l) Situational awareness is impossible without serious education, training and maritime experience.
m) Functional overlap in regulations (in a context of model) gives essentially a smaller workload on a qualified crew, than overregulation.
n) The functional redundancy in regulations (we use the term in a sense of functional integration of regulations) operates to improve the reliability and consistency of them if the crew resources are not lower than standard. If functional redundancy reaches the level not appropriate to crew resources (manning, skill) then there comes the situation similar to impact of overregulation.
o) Education and training of highly skilled seafarers, shore based company’s personnel and ship inspectors using an identical system of high standards will reduce the burden on seafarers and raise the level of safety and industry attractiveness as well.
p) The high absolute value of workload gradient (Figure 2) or task complexity gradient (short transitional periods) are most dangerous to the safety and security of the ship. These include the handover of the watch, the change of a crew, reducing or even increasing the number of crew, new regulations entering into force, approaching and leaving port, increasing or reducing the security level… etc.

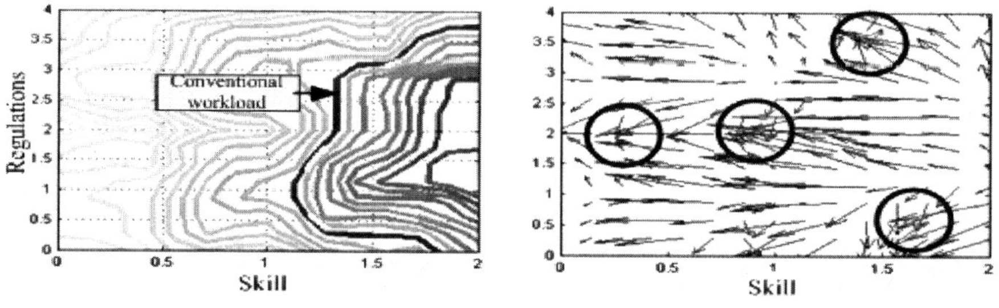


Figure 2: Workload contours and gradients.

q) Circles cover gradient variation areas. They show the lack of coordination in different activities in industry, for example when new regulations entering into force, the ship owner reduces the number of crew and degrades its skill; it may be the security drill while loading the ship, etc.
r) Increasing the complexity of the task is equivalent to degrading the crew skill.

s) The conventional (standard) workload level contour is marked on Figure 2. We can observe the area where "the unit workload" is not possible even if the crew is super qualified.

## 2.2 Efficiency of ISO, ISM and similar quality management systems applied according to STCW as amended in MET institutions

The process approach had been used in creating of the questionnaire distributed at the 2004 IMLA Conference in St. Petersburg. It was based on an 11 point Likert scale from 0 (fully not sufficient) to 10 (fully sufficient). We understood that return could not be greater than 10% of a total number. There were 70 questionnaires spread among participants. Nineteen questionnaires were returned. We can extend other projects results from ISM implementation in the shipping industry to QS implementation in MET institutions. The main weak points found in shipping have to be rigorously surveyed in the marine education field. Such extrapolation being not so theoretically pure may lead researchers directly to crucial points. Some of the negative considerations found in ISM implementation:

1. too much paperwork;
2. voluminous procedures manuals;
3. irrelevant procedures;
4. bought off-the-shelf systems;
5. no feeling of involvement in the system;
6. ticking boxes in checklists (without actually carrying out the required task);
7. not enough people to undertake all the extra work involved;
8. not enough time to undertake all the extra work involved;
9. inadequately trained people;
10. inadequately motivated people;
11. no support from the company;
12. no perceived benefit compared with the input required;
13. ism is just a paperwork exercise;
14. no respect for external auditors;
15. no respect for classification societies;
16. no respect for port state control inspectors;
17. no respect for the shore management by the seafarers;
18. no respect for the seafarers by the shore management.

What lessons could be learned from those negative findings?

To answer it we have to organize them into groups and remove items, which are not directly tied with MET quality processes.

The result of grouping is the following:

- procedures and manuals unsatisfactory (1–4, 13);
- overload of personnel (often without extra payment) (1, 7, 8, 9);
- lack of pre-training and quality ideas dissemination throughout (5 ,6, 9–11);
- lack of adequate resources (financial, technical, etc) (11, 12).

All the following items were found in literature laid down in random order without any consecutive explanations.

- Port state control statistics already shows a steady trend of crew related deficiencies, many of which are based on previous training experience (or lack of it).
- General decline of marine education in Western Europe may lead to shift of education "centre of gravity" to countries with insufficient adherence to efficient quality systems [2].
- Lack of MET financial support in EU countries [2].
- Lack of benchmark data to compare QS results.
- Absence of the experience and knowledge of quality assurance system [3].
- Lack of commitment from the top [3].
- Negative attitude due to hazardous thoughts like "we've always done it this way – why changing" or "I am the expert – I need no control" [3].
- Measurement of service is completely new for MET [3].
- A difference in academic and marine proficiency standards lead to potential problems due to partial inconsistency [5].
- Inadequate facilities and shortage of qualified teaching staff to cope with the increased demand of competence standards had an obvious damaging effect on the quality of maritime education and training [4].
- Quality standards system itself does not guarantee the depth and the width of knowledge, understanding and proficiency required by the internationally binding regulations [4].

Considering the ISM implementation process and areas of difficulty of the shipping industry similar to those experienced by MET institutions, we have to make some remarks:

*Remark 1.* Insufficient resources and inadequacy of resource management is a common place elsewhere.

*Remark 2.* Traditional education and training are main processes of MET. All support processes are often considered of less importance.

*Remark 3.* QS certification is sometimes more important for a market achievement than the actual quality of MET.

*Remark 4.* As in the shipping industry, there should be resistance against what is perceived as another regulatory and paper burden. It may lead to wrong perception of ways to MET quality achievement, wrong resources dissemination and keeping areas of required improvement out of attention if they are positioned within supportive items.

Independent evaluation and self-evaluation results made by expert groups in the Russian Federation confirmed our assumptions both qualitatively and quantitatively.

## 2.3 Questionnaire

An extensive survey among seafarers was given to serve as a base for modelling. Questionnaire "Sufficiency of resources for performing conventional duties" with 86 questions was produced within the frame of this research. More than 150 people took part in this survey; all of them are Masters, Chief Officers or OOW. Some of the results are given below in diagrams.

These diagrams prove that reduced crews are common nowadays, as most of the participants emphasize that the number of crewmembers is insufficient for safe operation. Additional workload, such as security duties under ISPS code, makes the situation even worse. Very often these additional duties result in distraction of OOW from his navigational duties, compromising safety (Figure 3A). Overall workload affects maintenance of the ship too, as the more time is spent for different duties less time is left for maintenance of the ship (Figure 4B).

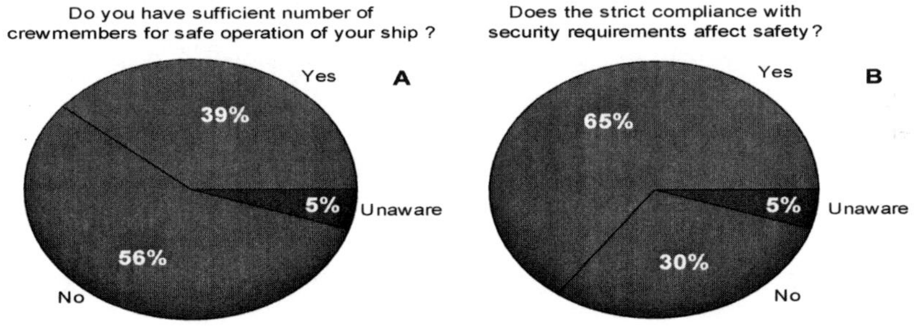


Figure 3: A. Safe ship operation B. Security and safety.

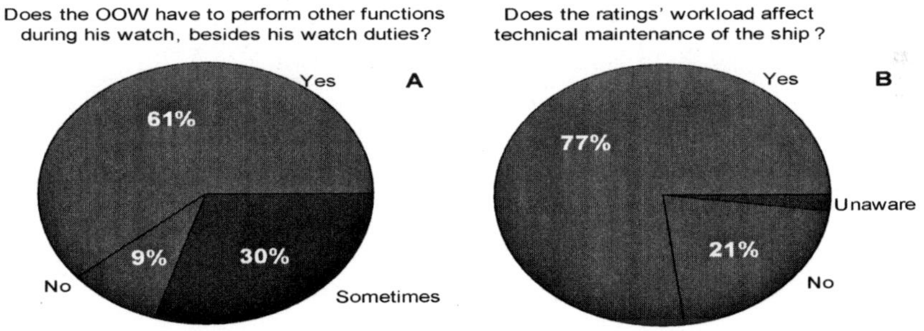


Figure 4: A. OOW distraction B. Ship maintenance.

The introduction of ISM and ISPS Code led to increased bureaucracy, extra paper work.

One of the most intriguing questions was about the factors preventing crew from complying with conventional requirements (Figure 5). The most common answers were: "Priority of records over actual compliance" and "under manning".

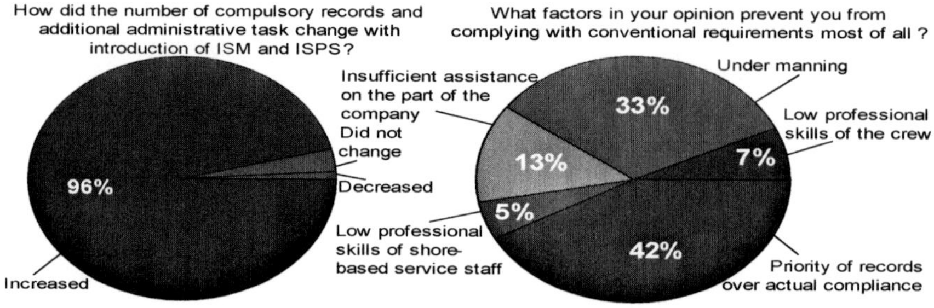


Figure 5: A. ISM and ISPS Code B. Crew performance.

## 2.4 IT Implementation onboard Vessels: crew resource study

This part of the project is devoted to analysis of modern navigational IT influence on crew workload and on the level of environmental protection and safety at sea. Bayesian networks are used as a formal background for the Research. New technologies in general have the most effect on the number of crewmembers, the job profiles, the workload, the work organization on board a ship, the safety on board the ship and the necessity of training. Safety aspects of new technologies appear to have counter effects. First of all, new technologies improve the safety of shipping. On the other hand, the different job functions require more technical people with less operational shipping knowledge. They might not respond adequately in an emergency situation. Indirect relationships between costs and new technologies, via human element, could appear in three different ways [6]:

- new technology resulting in a lower number of crew members;
- new technology resulting in a different composition of the crew with other wage levels;
- new technology resulting in a change of (overtime) working hours.

It needs to be evaluated by specific instruments during their implementation in the overall maritime sector. There have been specific tools based on Bayesian networks developed for assessing human factors' impacts on the implementation of new technologies. The results of analyzing the effects of IT on the human element, the main effects seem to be caused by navigation and communication related technologies.

Increased automation on board the ship has resulted in a shift from physical work demand towards mental work demand. Mental work demand is related to the perceptual-cognitive demands of monitoring the technical systems. Too much mental work demand may result in fatigue and stress for the seafarer.

The use of new technologies on board ships results in extra training needs for the crewmembers that have to work with these new systems. This means that with regular intervals the seafarer will be asked to take a course/training in working with new technological systems.

Automation reduces the number of repetitive tasks in a job, and makes it possible to perform the same tasks with fewer people. Because of the implementation of new technologies on board a ship, different functions are increasingly being integrated. This means that crewmembers must be able to perform different jobs on board. To be able to perform different tasks, the crewmember has to be multi-skilled.

## 2.5 Impact of international, regional and national instruments on navigational safety in restricted waters: Baltic Straits as particularly sensitive sea area – Case Study including crew resources

This part of the project is devoted to crew resources influence on navigational safety in the Baltic Straits. The increase in international shipping activity stimulates the development of new Associated Protective Measures (APMs). Only the complex of measures could produce desired tangible results. The following Crew Resources APMs were emphasized in the project:

**Safety culture** – Introduction of a safety culture on board ships should be a long-term goal of any shipping company. This not only enhances safety of navigation but also reduces risk of overall negligence and poor maintenance at a rather low cost. Moreover, it gives a good motivation for crew members to take an active part in SMS on board ship.

**Simulator training** – The training as required by STCW is a minimum, and it is further assessed that improved navigator training would have positive effect on the safety level of the vessel. An example of improved navigator training is advanced ship manoeuvring, including training of crisis situations, which can only be done safely in simulators. The training should be done with simulators to give a real life and **area-specific experience** of the given situations and thus prepare the navigators in case they face a similar incident. For example, Masters' training for Baltic Straits passage with appropriate certification, renewed at regular intervals.

**BRM/BTM/CRM** – BRM is designed to reduce errors and omissions in bridge operations through a simple system of checks and delegation of duties. BRM system emphasizes a coordinated effort among bridge personnel to ensure smooth, efficient and safe operation of the vessel. Similarly, Crew Resource Management (CRM) is designed to ensure teamwork and cooperation in emergency situations of the deck and engine crews. For communication and other responsibilities that are connected to the shore personnel, such training should also include key shore personnel.

The second group of APMs deals with shore based activities, such as VTMIS, pilots, DGPS, and buoyage. The main idea of this group is to facilitate ship handling process, either remotely via VTMIS or directly, by the pilot (compulsory pilotage), enhanced positioning accuracy, facilitate position control – DGPS, additional navigational marks, buoys, TSS, extra routeing measures, etc. In other words, this is a kind of outsourcing of some ship duties to shore.

## 2.6 ISPS code as a Bayesian node in general crew workload structure

Resources in this study were defined as available human power on board vessels. Detailed model descriptions could be found in proceedings of the same conference named "ISPS code as component of onboard resources in Bayesian Analysis". The main finding is that it is hardly possible nowadays to find one or two new effective measures, which allow us to raise the level of safety and security considerably and therefore, only the most complex of such measures could produce tangible results. The crew is limited in number as well as in other resources; to cope with numerous duties officers should be more competent and to be able to do more things within allocated time. For example, to keep ship's charts folios updated, an experienced Navigation Officer needs less time than his less experienced colleague. With unchanged crew, any increase in workload implies higher competency of crews to be able to complete their duties in time. The better the education, the better is the situational awareness. In other words, here we have a direct link between ISPS Code and MET. Crew competency is the measure of ship safety and security.

## 3 Conclusion

The part of findings and results of the Project is shown in the corresponding paragraphs and because of economy of a paper the authors do not see any sense in their recurrence. However we would like to emphasize the important idea, which has been clearly realized while executing the Project:

A globalized shipping industry is a very complicated system consisting of many interconnected active and passive components, of which activity could result in its stable or unstable state. To study and 'tune' the system by rules and regulations we need tools and models. To implement all the instruments we need resources, otherwise the high goals will never be achieved. The seafarer is the most important active component in this system, which is why the role of IAMU in MET field cannot be overestimated.

## References

[1] Loginovsky V., *Fuzzy Inference as an Approach to Safety Management System (SMS) analysis*, IAMU, AGA 5 Proceedings, pp. 194–197, 2004.

[2] Pourzanjani M., Schroder J.-U. & Zade G. *Maritime education and training (MET) in the European Union: how can maritime administrations support MET.* IAMU Journal December 2002, Vol.2, No.2.

[3] Dauwe M., *Quality assurance in MET's: burdens and proofs.* 13th International Conference on Maritime Education and Training IMLA 13 Proceedings. St. Petersburg, 2004.

[4] Prasad R., *Quality standards versus MET standards.* 13th International Conference on Maritime Education and Training IMLA 13 Proceedings. St. Petersburg 2004.

[5] Mejia M., *Performance Criteria for the International Safety Management (ISM) Code.* Proceedings of the 2nd General Assembly of IAMU. Kobe, Japan 2001.

[6] *THALASSES*, WA-97-SC-2108, Final Report, June 2000.

# Study in standardizing marine engineering curriculum

B. Butman
*U.S. Merchant Marine Academy, Kings Point, New York, USA*

## Abstract

This paper presents the preliminary results of an ongoing research study. In spite of the substantial efforts of the IMO and the maritime community aimed at developing standardized curriculum for training ship officers, the educational programs in different institutions vary quite substantially. Undergraduate marine engineering programs offered in various countries differ in their duration, content, onboard training, specific requirements, etc. For instance, the average length of a license/degree program, which leads to the Third Assistant (or just Fourth Engineer) license and a bachelor degree, is four years, including about a year of sailing. However, there are three-year programs on one side, and five-plus-year programs on the other side. Composition of the marine engineering programs varies. First is the share of the sea portion, which normally takes one year. However, there are exceptions when the cadets spent much more time at sea. Second, every program might be looked upon as a combination of building blocks. The distribution of time among the above portions of a program and the list of academic courses varies quite substantially from country to country, and even among different schools from the same country.
*Keywords: marine engineering education, curriculum, programs, license and degree components of programs.*

## 1 Introduction

The research project content is analysis and assessment of undergraduate marine engineering programs in various countries for possible standardization. The following are the principal objectives of the research as it is understood at this stage of study:

a. Classification of marine engineering programs being offered by the members of IAMU, as well as by non-member institutions based of the program academic and practical content, duration and final assignment (license, certificate, diploma, etc.).
b. Analysis of time distribution among the principal program components, such as:
   - mathematics and basic science;
   - humanities - language, history and culture;
   - basic engineering science (mechanics, materials, thermodynamics, electricity, etc.);
   - special engineering – propulsion and power plant, systems and machinery, etc.
c. Study of the sea-going training component in various programs (content, duration, specifics)
d. Assessment of program components regarding:
   - value for the future career;
   - response to maritime regulations and standards;
   - meeting licensing requirements;
   - meeting customer requirements;
   - meeting accreditation institution requirements (IME, ABET, etc.).

Not many publications have been devoted to the subject. In this research conference proceedings and magazine articles, and also the Government maritime and licensing institution materials have been reviewed. Substantial information has been found on the Internet. The pace of the research has been drastically slowed down for some unexpected circumstances. A very limited response of the IAMU members to the survey which has been initiated at the commencement of the project appeared to be the principal problem.

## 2 Survey of marine engineering programs

A survey questionnaire has been prepared and emailed to practically all IAMU member institutions. Unfortunately, only seven institutions have responded, and only four curriculum have been received and analyzed.

Websites of maritime institutions became the principal source of information. To date the curricula of about thirty institutions has been studied. The list of the institutions is presented in Table 3. There are still some clarification with the institutions is required. The most detailed information has been collected from the principal maritime universities and academies in the US, Canada, Australia, Philippines, Japan, India, Singapore, Taiwan, Egypt, Turkey, Croatia, Norway, Denmark, United Kingdom, Netherlands, Poland, Belgium, Estonia, Ukraine and Russia. This list makes an adequate representation of the variety of marine engineering programs.

# 3 Classification of marine engineering programs

## 3.1 Types of educational institutions

Several hundred educational institutions in the world provide various types of maritime education. All of them might be subdivided into four groups:

a. Maritime academies offering complete program leading to a license of a marine engineering officer.
b. Maritime academies and universities offering programs leading to an engineering license and to an academic degree.
c. Maritime schools, union schools and training centres offering individual marine engineering courses. There is a wide variety of such courses:
   - advanced courses intended for upgrading the license;
   - various certificate courses, such as ISM, security, new engine/equipment operation, etc;
   - re-training courses, etc.
d. Vocational maritime schools (sail boats, motor boats, etc.).

The two first groups of the educational institutions are the subjects of this study.

## 3.2 Types of program orientation

Maritime academies and universities are offering two distinct types of marine engineering programs:

a. mariner license oriented programs;
b. mariner license and academic degree oriented programs.

According to STCW, the first engineering license is officer in charge of an engineering watch. Some school curriculum identify the first license as Engineering Officer Class 4. American maritime institutions, in accordance with the Code of Federal Regulations CFR 46 identify the first license as Third Assistant Engineer. Other schools and academies offer shorter programs leading to a Junior Engineer or Assistant Engineering Officer certificate. Normally, after a certain at sea training, the former cadet sits for a full scale first engineering license. Therefore, this type of a program should be considered in assessment of the college type license curriculum.

Obviously, the two types of programs, license oriented, and degree/license oriented, differ in content and duration. However, the core of license related courses should be identical, or at least similar. The main difference should be in the scope and content of academic subjects.

# 4 An analysis of marine engineering programs

## 4.1 Program duration

The average length of a program, which leads to the officer in charge of an engineering watch or Third Assistant (or just Forth Engineer) license, is four years, including about a year of sailing. However, there are three-year programs, on one side, and five-plus-year programs, on the other side, like in Russia, Ukraine, Egypt and other countries. Figure 1 presents an approximate distribution of the duration of the marine engineering programs among 60 maritime schools. The program at U.S.M.M.A., Kings Point, represents a typical example of a four-year curriculum. Therefore, in the discussion below, this program is accepted as a basic one (see Table 1).

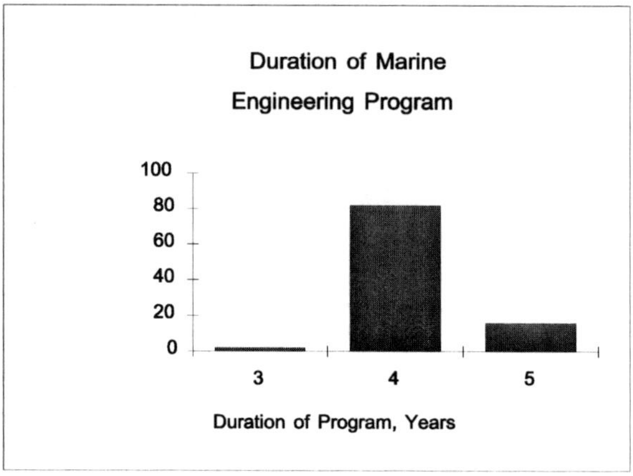


Figure 1: Distribution of program duration.

In the final report a detailed analysis of the program duration will be presented with identification of the time required for license related component, academic subjects and the at sea training.

### 4.2 Program structure

Composition of marine engineering programs varies. First to mention is the share of the sea portion, which normally takes one year. However, there are exceptions, when the cadets spent substantially less or more time at sea. Secondly, every program might be looked upon as a combination of the building blocks. In most of the marine engineering programs the following blocks or components might be found:

a. Mathematics and basic science.
b. Humanities - language, history and culture. Social science and economic courses, if offered, normally belong to this portion of the program.
c. Engineering science - mechanics, materials, thermodynamics, fluids, basic electricity, etc.
d. Special engineering - propulsion plant, power plant, systems and machinery, naval architecture, etc.
e. Physical fitness - offered either as mandatory classes, or as activities beyond the scheduled hours.

Table 1: U.S. Merchant Marine Academy, Basic-Level Curriculum.

**Marine Engineering Systems Program**

| Year; Semester or Quarter | Course (Department, Number, Title) | Category (Credit Hours) | | | |
|---|---|---|---|---|---|
| | | Math & Basic Sciences | Engineering Topics | General Education | Other |
| **4th Class** | DN 110 Basic Fire Fighting | | | | 2.0 |
| | HE101 English 1 | | | 3.0 | |
| | KP100 Maritime Prof. Studies | | | | 4.0 |
| Term 1 | MM101 Calculus 1 | 3.0 | | | |
| | MP101 Physics 1 | 4.0 | | | |
| | PE 110 Swimming/First Aid | | | | 1.0 |
| | EE120 Intro to Electrical Engr. | | 2.5 | | |
| | EG111 Engineering Shop 1 | | | | 1.0 |
| | ES110 Computer Engineering | | 2.0 | | |
| Term 2 | MC100 General Chemistry | 4.0 | | | |
| | MM130 Calculus 2 (Eng.) | 4.0 | | | |
| | NS120 Intro to MMNR | | | | 1.0 |
| | PE101 Self Defence | | | | 1.0 |
| | EG100 Engineering Graphics | | | | 2.0 |
| | EM100 Intro to Marine Engr. | | 2.0 | | 1.5 |
| Term 3 | ES100 Engr. Mechanics | | 3.0 | | |
| | HH100 History of Seapower | | | 3.0 | |
| | MP130 Physics 2 | 4.0 | | | |
| | PE120 Aquatic Survival | | | | 1.0 |
| **2nd & 3rd Class** | DN100 Safety of Life at Sea | | | | 2.0 |
| | ES200 Intro. To Materials Engr. | | 2.0 | | |
| | ES210 Transport Processes 1 | | 3.5 | | |
| Term 1 | HE202 English 2 | | | 3.0 | |
| | MM232 Math for Engr. 1 | 4.0 | | | |
| | NS 220 MMNR Officer | | | | 2.0 |
| | DB210 Economics | | | 3.0 | |
| | EE300 Electric Circuits | | 2.5 | | |
| | EG211 Engineering Shop 2 | | | | 1.0 |
| Term 2 | EM200 Marine Engineering 1 | | 3.5 | | |
| | ES301 Strength of Materials | | 2.0 | | |
| | ES305 Materials Engr. Lab | | 2.0 | | |
| | MM332 Math for Engr. 2 | 3.0 | | | |
| | PE Elective 1 | | | | 0.5 |
| | PE Elective 2 | | | | 0.5 |

Table 1: Continued.

| Year; Semester or Quarter | Course (Department, Number, Title) | Category (Credit Hours) | | | |
|---|---|---|---|---|---|
| | | Math & Basic Sciences | Engineering Topics | General Education | Other |
| Term 3 | Mxxxx Math/Science Elective | 3.0 | | | |
| | EM301 Naval Architecture | | 3.0 | | |
| | ES310 Transport Processes 2 | | 3.5 | | |
| | HC400 Topics in History | | | 3.0 | |
| | MC300 Engineering Chemistry | 3.0 | | | |
| | NS402 Naval Leadership/Ethics | | | | 2.0 |
| | PE200 Ships Medicine | | | | 1.0 |
| Sea Term 1 | Sea Projects | | | | 6.0 |
| Sea Term 2/3 | Sea Projects | | | | 16.0 |
| **1st Class** Term 1 | EE400 Electrical. Machines | | 3.5 | | |
| | EM415 Internal Comb. Engines | | 3.5 | | |
| | EM420 Diesel Simulator | | 1.0 | | |
| | EM480 ME Systems Design | | 3.5 | | |
| | EM481 MES Design Project 1 | | 0.5 | | |
| | HH310 Modern World | | | 3.0 | |
| | Exxxx MES Option 1 | | 3.0 | | |
| | PE Elective 3 | | | | 0.5 |
| | PE Elective 4 | | | | 0.5 |
| Term 2 | DB230 Management | | | 3.0 | |
| | EM400 Marine Engineering 2 | | 3.5 | | |
| | EM410 Marine Refrigeration | | 3.5 | | |
| | EM482 MES Design Project 2 | | 0.5 | | |
| | HH360 Modern Am. History | | | 3.0 | |
| | Exxxx MES Option 2 | | 3.0 | | |
| | NS412 Adv. MMNR Officer | | | | 2.0 |
| Term 3 | DN410 Advanced Firefighting | | | | 1.5 |
| | EE401 Electronics | | 2.5 | | |
| | EM470 License Seminar | | | | 1.0 |
| | EM483 MES Design Project 3 | | 1.0 | | |
| | Exxxx MES Option 3 | | 3.0 | | |
| | Exxxx MES Option 4 | | 3.0 | | |
| TOTAL CURRICULUM (173.5 credits) | | 32 | 66.5 | 25 | 50 |

f. Naval reserve training - offered by some schools as an integral part of the program.
g. Navigation and ship handling - several introductory courses are normally offered in a plain marine engineering curriculum and a special core of courses is provided for the integrated officers training.

h. Others, such as safety, medicine, operational procedures related to specialized ships.

The distribution of time among the above portions of a program and the list of academic courses vary quite substantially from country to country, and even among different schools of the same contra. Table 2 presents the comparison of marine engineering programs at the U.S. Merchant Marine Academy and the St. Petersburg State Maritime Academy of Russia

Table 2: Comparison of program components.

| School | Share of the Program Component, % | | | | |
|---|---|---|---|---|---|
| | Math. and Science | Humanities | Basic Engineering Science | Special Engineering | Others (Physical Ed., Navigation, Naval, etc.) |
| U.S. Merchant Marine Academy | 20 | 13 | 20 | 26 | 21 |
| St. Petersburg State Maritime Academy | 16 | 18 | 18 | 35 | 13 |

The two principal components of a license/degree program are the license courses and the academic courses. Another subdivision is found in the strict license oriented programs – by the license courses and the general education courses.

### 4.3 Content and scope of subjects in marine engineering license component

STCW requirements are a base for the analysis of the license component of the marine engineering program. Column 2 of Table 3 provides the minimum required list of subjects (knowledge, understanding and proficiency) needed for marine engineering function on the operational level.

Another guidance document for assessing the required training is the IMO Module Course 7.04 developed for IMO by the Norwegian Maritime Directorate. Yet one more guidance material, specific for the American maritime academies, is the list of subjects for engineering licenses which is included in the Code of Federal Regulations 46 CFR Ch. 1 #10.950.

In continuation of the research project, it is intended to evaluate the surveyed marine engineering program relative to the above guidance documents.

Table 3: Subject areas for specific learning outcomes expected from BEng degrees.

| No | Subject Area |
|---|---|
| 1 | Mathematics and Science |
| 2 | Engineering Analysis |
| 3 | Design |
| 4 | Economic, social, and environmental context |
| 5 | Marine Engineering Practice |
| 6 | Economic, social and environmental context |
| 7 | Engineering Practice |

### 4.4 Content and scope of subjects in academic degree component

The IMO Module Course 7.04, and also the American 46 CFR identify certain subjects which belong to the academic degree component of the program. However, while the license component might be easily standardized based on the above mentioned guidance documents, the academic component allows a much wider variation in the content and scope. The only feasible way of building a uniform academic component is statistical analysis of a large number of programs. The results of the analysis of the curricula of over twenty educational institutions will be presented in the final report.

An important factor in setting the academic component of a marine engineering program is the requirements of the accrediting institutions. Even if the program is not intended for accreditation, many of the requirements should be evaluated and incorporated based on the available time space in the curriculum. As an example of the requirements, Table 3 contains the subject areas considered by the UK Institute of Marine Engineers in their accreditation of the marine engineering programs. Other accreditation bodies include Classification Societies, like DNV and Lloyd, American Accreditation Board for Engineering and Technology (ABET), National Educational Authorities, and others. In the final report the results of evaluation of the accreditation requirements as a factor in the development of the uniform academic component of marine engineering curricula will be presented.

### 4.5 Sailing component

As it was mentioned before, the average time to be spent onboard for a first engineering officer license is one year. However, actual requirements by different countries vary substantially. It is reflected in the career paths accepted by the national authorities. Two examples of a career path are presented in Figure 2 (a career path in India) and in Figure 3 (in the USA).

The statistical analysis of the information related to the required duration of the sea time will be continued in the project study.

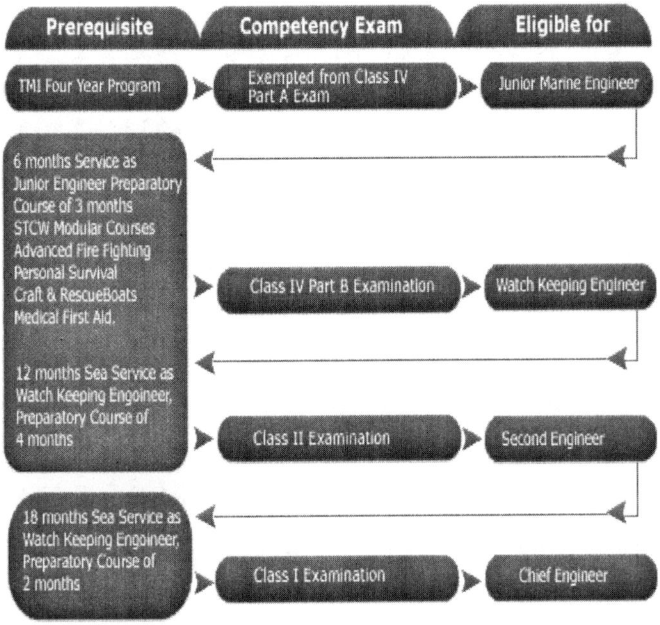


Figure 2: Career path as per Tolani Maritime Institute, India.

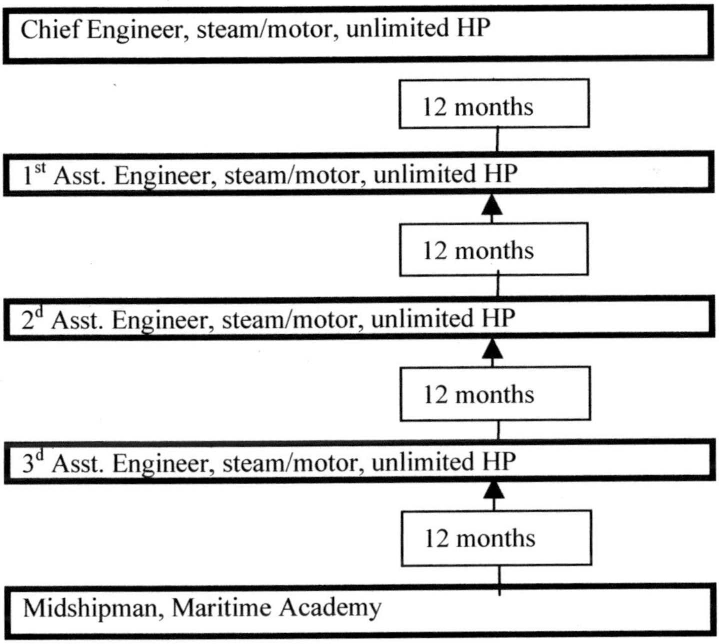


Figure 3: USA engineering license structure as per 46 CFR, #10.505.

## 5 Conclusion

In the process of preparation of the final report the following activities are intended to be carried out:

a. Some additional information will hopefully be collected. Another attempt to survey the member institutions will be undertaken.

b. Analysis of the programs will be finalized and working version of classification developed.

c. Available information and survey data re customer requirements will be assessed and the results incorporated into the curriculum proposals.

d. Analysis of program components will be finalized and draft versions of the sea-going license components developed.

e. Analysis of college related program components will be finalized, and draft versions of a BS curriculum identified.

# Maritime terrorism and developing case studies for teaching and analysis: an interim report

D. J. Nincic
*California Maritime Academy, California State University, USA*

## Abstract

Maritime terrorism is emerging as a significant issue in global trade and national security. However, very few maritime institutions offer a formal study of maritime terrorism. Students preparing for the maritime professions would be well served in their future careers by having studied theories and typologies of maritime terrorism, and having participated in active discussions of how these threats and challenges will affect them in their future careers. The use of case studies dealing with maritime terrorist incidents would provide a valuable teaching tool in courses dealing with maritime security and/or as stand-alones for workshops outside the formal curriculum.
*Keywords: maritime terrorism, hijacking, hostage taking, dirty bomb, LNG.*

## 1 Introduction

The goals and objectives of the project are to: (a) provide students with an understanding of maritime terrorism (including the sources of maritime terrorism), and the likely forms maritime terrorism may take in the future; (b) provide future mariners and maritime business and policy professionals with an understanding of the procedures and conventions in place to prevent maritime terrorist events, and he importance of international cooperation in preventing these events.

The case study is a widely used classroom tool, using "real life" events and "past lessons learned" to shed light on existing issues and problems. In this project, students using the case studies will gain a deeper appreciation of the risks of maritime terrorism, and the importance of domestic and international codes and conventions, and cooperation, to prevent terrorist events.

The case study provides unique opportunities for students. It emphasizes student-led learning, allowing participants to adopt "role playing" techniques, leading to active classroom discussions and group problem solving. The *Maritime Terrorism* cases developed as part of this project may be embedded in existing classes, or used as "stand alones," in whole or in part, as seminars.

## 2 Work completed to date (July 2005)

The five general cases proposed in the original grant are:

- hijacking and hostage taking;
- attacks on ships;
- the use of a ship as a "vector";
- the use of the ship as a weapon;
- sinking or disabling a vessel to block a chokepoint/port.

Each of these cases has been further refined, as described below. The status of each case (or components of each case) is noted.

### 2.1 Case 1: hijacking and hostage taking (status: completed)

Specific hijacking incidents have been identified for study:

- *Santa Maria* (1961);
- *Vory* (1974);
- *Mayaguez* (1975);
- *Achille Lauro* (1985);
- *Penrider* (2003).

The following has been provided for each of these incidents: (a) detailed description of event; (b) how event was resolved; (c) specific lessons learned; (d) general lessons learned; and e) preventing future events.

The objective in this case is to compare and contrast each of the hostage incidents, and to draw lessons applicable to today's environment.

Case 1 focuses primarily on the Achille Lauro hijacking incident. The case has been completed, and test run in my *Ocean Politics* class in Spring 2005. The students were given the case for study, and then presented with questions to answer during class sessions. Students worked in groups, taking the roles of (a) the hostage takers, (b) the ship captain and crew, and (c) the international negotiators and key actors. Students presented their findings and analysis to the class. Further details of the outcome of this case will be presented to the IAMU meeting in Malmö, Sweden.

## 2.2 Case 2: attacks on ships (status: in progress)

The following terrorist attacks have been selected for study:

- *USS Cole* (2000);
- *Lady Mediatrix* (2000);
- *Silk Pride* (2001);
- *Limburg* (2002).

The following will be provided for each of these incidents: (a) Description of event; (b) specific lessons learned; (c) general lessons learned; and (d) preventing future events.

The objective in this case is to compare and contrast each of these terrorist attacks on ships, and not only to arrive at an understanding of how to prevent such attacks in the future, but also to understand how difficult it can be to prevent such attacks.

This case will be test run during my Fall 2005 *Maritime Security* class.

## 2.3 Case 3: the use of the ship as a "vector" (status: in progress)

The following have been identified as ways terrorist groups have used innocent merchant vessels:

- stowaways, with suspected ties to terrorist groups, have been found on several ships in recent years;
- suspected terrorists posing as mariners by using false papers have been identified on at least two occasions in the Mediterranean;
- in the 1998 bombings of the US Embassies in Kenya and Tanzania, it is widely suspected that the materials used for the attacks were brought into the country by ship;
- Al Qaeda is believed to charter vessels for its money-making operations (trade in sesame seeds, etc), and in support of its terrorist activities.

The following will be provided for each incident: (a) description of event; (b) how the incidents were discovered, (c) how to prevent similar future events.

The objective of this case is to provide students with an understanding of how easy it can be for terrorist groups to use vulnerabilities in the global shipping industry for their ends; and to understand not only the proposals in place to deal with these possibilities (biometric IDs, etc.), but also how important enforcement of these proposals will be.

This case will be test run during my Fall 2005 *Maritime Security* class.

### 2.4 Case 4: the use of the ship as a weapon (status: in progress)

Unlike the first three cases, Case 4 involves hypothetical scenarios – ways innocent vessels could be used to attack vital ports or densely populated cities. Here the emphasis is on the “nightmare scenarios”, the “iconic attacks” that not only create significant human and economic damage but, because of their sheer size and audacity, truly terrorize both the target population and the international community as a whole.

The following scenarios best represent these forms of terrorist attack:

- A radioactive device placed in a shipping container, primed to detonate when the ship (or container) arrives at its target destination.
- A chemical or LNG tanker attacked near a port facility or populated urban area, with its cargo released into the atmosphere. Chemical tankers may carry hazardous materials which, if released, could be deadly. LNG tankers have the potential, if attacked, to create superheated “fireballs”.

The following will be provided for each scenario:

- description of event (Status: In progress);
- plans and procedures in place to prevent these scenarios (Status: In progress);
- how well these plans and procedures are working (Status: In progress);
- the costs of these plans and procedures (Status: In progress).

This case will be test run during my Fall 2005 *Maritime Security* class.

### 2.5 Case 5: sinking or disabling a vessel to block a chokepoint/port

Like Case 4, Case 5 represents hypothetical scenarios of current concern to the maritime industry. Here, the objective of the terrorist group is to create economic damage by impeding access to vital chokepoints or ports.

The following scenarios will be used to illustrate this potential form of maritime terrorist attack:

- Sinking or disabling a vessel to impede access to the port of Singapore. In this case, the links between maritime pirate groups and maritime terrorist groups will be explored.
- Sinking or disabling a vessel in the Strait of Hormuz.

The following will be provided for each scenario:

- feasibility and likelihood of event;
- economic impact analysis;
- preventing event (e.g., *Regional Security Initiative*).

The case will be run during my Fall 2005 *Maritime Security* class.

# 3 Remaining schedule

All research has been completed – all that remains is for the write-ups of the cases to be finished, and for the test runs of the cases to occur on the CMA campus. Dry runs will occur during my Fall 2005 Maritime Security class for the four cases noted above. Time and scheduling permitting, a run will also occur on the campus allowing for the opportunity for all interested students and faculty to become involved.

Results of all case study runs will be presented in Malmö, along with CDs of the cases (including teaching instructions, power point slides, etc).

# 4 6$^{th}$ AGA in Malmö, Sweden

Due to the delay in funding approval, the project is not yet complete. As kindly allowed in Mr. Tyler's letter of 8 April 2005, I will complete the final project in time for a full presentation of results to the 6$^{th}$ AGA.

The final report will include:

- the project objective and outcomes;
- how the outcomes are of value to the IAMU member universities;
- the results of how the project has been used at Cal Maritime;;
- all deliverables outlined in the project proposal, available in print and/or on CD.

# IAMU model course on ECDIS

A. Weintrit
*Gdynia Maritime University, Poland*

## Abstract

The revision of SOLAS, Chapter V, which entered into force on 1 July 2002, has firmly established the electronic navigational chart as part of the international maritime safety system. Its possible recognition as a paper chart equivalent confirms the considerable safety benefits provided by the official Electronic Chart Display and Information Systems (ECDIS). Elaborated by the Author IAMU Model Course on operational use of ECDIS (IAMU research project FY 2003) aims to provide answers to some of the most commonly asked questions regarding various types of electronic charts (ENC, RNC, DNC) and electronic chart systems (ECDIS, RCDS, ECS). Following the earlier adoption of the International Convention STCW 78/95 and IMO model training courses to assist in the implementation of the Convention and the associated IMO Assembly resolutions, a number of IAMU Member Universities had suggested that IAMU should develop model-training courses on a higher academic level. This would assist in achieving a more rapid transfer of information and skills regarding new developments in marine technology. The provision of model courses could help instructors improve the quality of their existing courses and enhance their effectiveness in meeting the requirements of the IAMU. In the paper, the author presents the results of IAMU research project FY2004 sponsored by the Nippon Foundation, entitled "IAMU Handbook on ECDIS".
*Keywords: navigation, GIS, ECDIS, ECS, electronic navigational charts, safety at sea, simulator, model course, training, MET, IAMU, IMO, STCW.*

## 1 Introduction

The main objective of the International Association of Maritime Universities (IAMU) Working Group III is to promote the global maritime excellence. WG-III is directed towards the establishment of the global standardization of the maritime education system. To achieve this purpose, academic discussions should be carried out regarding with the improvement of the existing education and certification system. To initiate the newly developed international system IAMU members should analyse and assess existing education systems offered by maritime universities/faculties, including proposed model courses and academic handbooks.

The major role of the navigational departments of IAMU member universities/faculties is to provide their students with effective and highly levelled maritime education and training. With this point of view, the Author would like to consider in this paper the effective training methods for navigators in compliance with STCW'95 convention and the set of IMO model courses. In addition, he would like to consider additional training programs, which aim at higher competencies than the minimum requirements for the competencies shown in the STCW.

Electronic navigation, although still relatively new and unfamiliar, is becoming increasingly more commonplace, particularly onboard commercial vessels.

The International Maritime Organization published in 2000 *IMO Model Course 1.27: the Operational Use of the Electronic Chart Display and Information System (ECDIS)* [2]. In the Author's opinion, IAMU members on a higher level could arrange this model course program.

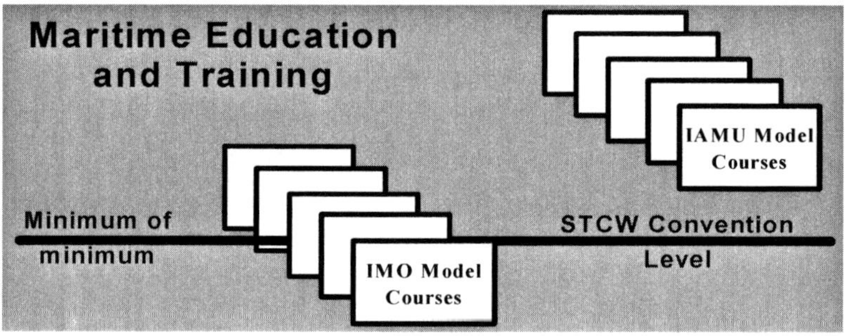


Figure 1: The first step – the set of IAMU model courses on the academic level, higher than STCW.

In 2003, the Author has worked out the IAMU Model Course: *The Operational Use of the Electronic Chart Display and Information System (ECDIS)* [7] - the first IAMU Model Course, intended to be on higher level than STCW. Now the Author has made one more step forward, he had prepared to publish the first IAMU handbook on the base of elaborated IAMU Model Course on ECDIS [5]. Presentation of new approach to the maritime education and training MET in the field of ECDIS is the main subject of this handbook.

In the opinion of the Author IAMU should consider and make a decision to start forward with series of IAMU Model Courses on a higher (academic) level than STCW convention which seems to be for maritime universities the "minimum of minimum" only. IAMU model course on training in the operational use of the Electronic Chart Display and Information System (ECDIS) as a sample is the first on the long list of IAMU model courses to be elaborated in the near future.

## 2 Relevance to the work of IAMU and IMO

Proposed Handbook is based on IAMU model course on training in the operational use of the Electronic Chart Display and Information System (ECDIS) and the results of IAMU research grant FY2003, sponsored by Nippon Foundation, received by the Author in 2003 (www.ecdis.am.gdynia.pl/iamu [7]). The Author presented an IAMU model course on training in the operational use of the ECDIS based on simulators in written consolidated form.

In the handbook, the Author presents his point of view on maritime navigation, simulation and technology in maritime education and training and the methods of maritime pedagogy, especially in the electronic chart systems field to be adopted by the IAMU member universities/faculties.

Research work was based on the results of the Polish Working Group on ECDIS chaired by the Author. The Author presented Gdynia Maritime University (GMU) model course on training in the operational use of the Electronic Chart Display and Information System (ECDIS) based on simulators. He is the head of the electronic chart and ECDIS laboratory in Navigational Department of Gdynia Maritime University, with 20 years experience in the field of electronic charts.

The IMO's Sub-Committee on Standards of Training and Watch keeping at its thirty-second session (2001) developed Interim Guidance on Training and Assessment in the Operational Use of the Electronic Chart Display and Information System (ECDIS) Simulators prepared on the base of Polish document STW 32/9. The Author was the father of this document. He was the chairperson of the Polish Working Group, which prepared a Polish document submitted to the IMO forum. He was the speaker of the Polish delegation at the 32 session and next the chairman of STW Sub-Committee Drafting Group on Development of Guidance which reviewed Polish documentation taking into account discussions in the plenary session. The drafting group expanded document STW 32/WP.7, which was approved at the NAV plenary. The Maritime Safety Committee, at its seventy-fourth session approved this interim guidance [3]. For the past few years, the Author has regularly represented Poland at the IMO Sub-Committee on Safety of Navigation (NAV), usually as a member of the Technical Working Group on Navigational Aids and Related Matters. Between sessions, he is active as a member of correspondence groups. Previously he was a member of Correspondence Groups on ECDIS established in 2004 during the 50th session of NAV Sub-Committee in order to prepare a proposal for revision of IMO Performance Standards (PS) for ECDIS. He was also a member of the Correspondence Groups on INS and IBS established during the same session of the NAV Sub-Committee to elaborate a proposal for revision of INS PS and IBS PS and a development of a PS for a Bridge Alarm Management System. A year before, he was a member of the IMO Correspondence Group on Radar Performance Standards (2003/2004) and the

IMO Correspondence Group on Presentation of Navigation Related Information (2003/2004).

The IAMU model course on training in the operational use of the Electronic Chart Display and Information System (ECDIS), as a pioneer sample, is the first on the list of IAMU model courses. The IAMU handbook on ECDIS based on IAMU model course on training in the operational use of the Electronic Chart Display and Information System (ECDIS), as a pioneer sample, by analogy, is the first on the list of IAMU handbooks [5].

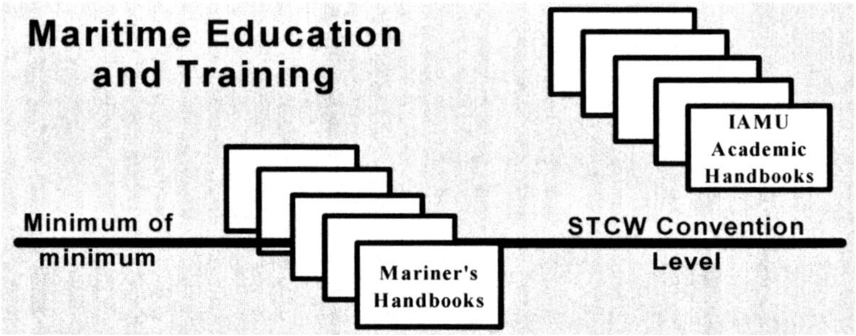


Figure 2: The second step – the set of IAMU handbooks on the academic level, higher than STCW.

## 3 ECDIS training requirements

With the increasing use of Electronic Chart Systems (ECS), there is an increasing number of Officers who require training. Given the flexibility of the labour market, it is highly likely that officers may arrive on board a ship without experience or training. The officer of the Watch (OOW) who has received recognised, formal training in the use of the bridge equipment at his disposal is, potentially, a safer OOW than his counterpart who has not received training.

A number of National Administrations have recognised the possible need for "type training". Common sense and maritime expertise combined with the rules of the ISM Code clearly indicates that familiarisation training on such vital navigational equipment as an ECDIS is a necessity, especially when bearing in mind that incompetent operation of ECDIS could influence adversely on the safety of life and protection of the marine environment.

In response to a UKHO Questionnaire on the use of vector charts, the following questions and their responses were noted:

- *Have you received training on using the ECDIS?*
- *Do you think training on the ECDIS and ENC's is necessary?*

Two-thirds of the respondents had received specific ECDIS and ENC training but only one mariner responded that he did not think that training was necessary.

This emphatic endorsement of the need for specific training reflects the mariner's viewpoint that, in order to keep up with improving technology, it is essential to be trained in the use of new equipment. With the increasing use of ECS, there will be an increasing number of Officers requiring training. Given the flexibility of the labour market, it is highly likely that officers may arrive on board a ship without experience or training and Masters are rightly concerned over this matter.

The provisions of STCW'95 are vague with respect to ECDIS although Table A-II/1, ***Navigation at the operational level*** requires:

*"Thorough knowledge of and ability to use navigational charts and publications. NOTE: ECDIS systems are considered to be included under the term "charts"."*

In Table A-II/2, ***Navigation at the management level*** requires:

".3 *using modern electronic navigational aids, with specific knowledge of their operating principles, limitations, sources of error, detection of misrepresentation of information and methods of correction to obtain accurate position fixing".*

While undoubtedly, training should be the principal concern of the shipowner, there needs to be some consideration given by Flag State administrations, Hydrographic Offices and others to the level of minimum training, which should be undertaken before an Officer, is permitted to keep a watch with an electronic chart system. The IMO have produced a "model course" but, as far as is known, its availability is limited. It is envisaged that, in the absence of international agreement, Flag States may introduce their own national requirements for training in the use of ECS.

The maritime education and training (MET) institutions agree that they are able to provide training programmes for the shipowners' staff but they do not appear to be willing to provide this without cost to the shipowner. At the same time, the shipowner appears to be reluctant to invest in training, adopting the attitude of *"you'll be trained by using the equipment"*. This is unsatisfactory and grossly inadequate. Where a system is fitted in a new building, the cost of training can, in many instances, be absorbed into the capital cost but it appears that where the equipment is to be retro-fitted, additional costs for training are unacceptable (the Hailwood Report [1]).

The majority of officers and masters interviewed are in favour of the development of CBT programmes to cope with this lack of experience or training. In particular, and until such time as statutory training requirements are introduced and enforced, CBT has significant potential for Officers joining the vessel for the first time with no previous experience in the use of ECS.

In the expectation that, in the near future, officers on ships fitted with ECDIS will be required, under possible amendments to STCW95 or under Flag State requirements, to complete an ECDIS training programme, the IMO ECDIS Model Course will serve as an ideal platform for such training. CBT has significant potential to deliver an appropriate training programme, in particular for Officers with little or no previous experience in the use of ECS.

Members of the discussion group are invited to comment on these observations. They are also invited to suggest what should be incorporated into any revision of STCW95 and to suggest ways in which CBT can be developed to the benefit of all parties.

## 4 Course outline

The course outline for the ECDIS training course is specified as follows:

- a list of the principal ECDIS subjects (training areas) including the area objectives and syllabus outline;
- a flowchart to illustrate the interrelationships between the principal ECDIS subjects;
- a suggested weekly course timetable (a few options for different groups of trainees/users).

### 4.1 List of principal ECDIS subjects (training areas)

The area objectives for the principal ECDIS subjects (written in italics) are understood to be prefixed by the words:
*"The expected learning outcome is that the trainee is able to".*

Teaching staff should note that the timetables are suggestions only regarding sequence and length of time allocated to each objective. These factors may be adopted by lecturers to suit individual groups of trainees depending on their experience, specific character of their job, ability, equipment and staff availability for training.

Teaching staff should note that some Training Areas should be carried out on professional navigation and ECDIS simulators about practical use in Route Planning and Route Monitoring processes.

### 4.2 Description

This course will give the trainee guidance and practice on the operational use of Electronic Chart Display and Information Systems (ECDIS) equipment in accordance with the requirements of the STCW Convention '78 as amended in 1995. The general objective of the ECDIS training course is to enhance navigational safety by the safe operation of ECDIS equipment; proper use of ECDIS related information and knowledge of the limitations of ECDIS equipment.

**Course outline:**

- History of ECDIS and process of international standardization.
- ECDIS - maritime application of GIS (Geographical Information System).
- Description of the structure of ECDIS and the ENC.
- Description of the structure of RCDS and the RNC.
- Description of the formats used for the Database S-57.

- Description of digital vectorized charts.
- Description of the projections used for ENC.
- Performance standards for ECDIS (IMO Resolution 817(19)).
- Revision of Chapter V SOLAS.
- Raster Charts - limitations and comparisons.
- Cycle of operation of ECDIS.
- Correction of ENC and methods used (updating system).
- Worldwide Electronic Navigational Chart Database (WEND).
- Use of the chart catalogue.
- Possible errors in displayed data.
- Requirements for the carriage of ECDIS.
- Requirements for the carriage of back up systems.
- Appropriate Portfolio of Paper Chart.
- Description of GPS / GLONASS / DGPS systems and their use in ECDIS.
- Input sensors to ECDIS.
- Description of the Radar and ARPA interface.
- Description of the AIS Transponders.

Practical exercises will involve hands on use of real ECDIS equipment with a variety of ENC's and sensors connected to bridge simulator equipment.

The ECDIS course should be open to masters, deck officers and trainee deck officers. The aim of the course is to enhance navigation safety and efficiency by training the Watch-keeping Officer in the safe operation of ECDIS. This will be achieved by developing an understanding of the generic principles of ECDIS and other electronic chart systems, and by understanding the capabilities and limitations of ECDIS. The course should also cover awareness of the potential errors and risk of over reliance on ECDIS, and understanding the regulatory requirements of the system. The updating regimes and differences between various systems will all be covered allowing future operators to fully appreciate the value of ECDIS and maximise its numerous safety benefits.

### 4.3 Entry standards

With the development of modern and faster ships and a need to run them more economically, by reducing the work force, the number of marine casualties has increased in the recent past. These casualties can mainly be attributed to a human failure on the Bridge of a vessel. The need to reduce such casualties is being felt by the entire maritime industry.

An ECDIS is one such navigational tool on the bridge, which would help the Master and the Officer of the Watch to navigate his ship safely and economically. The ECDIS with inputs from various sources like GPS/GNSS, Radar/ARPA, AIS, Echo Sounder, Log, Gyro, etc. would be ideal equipment providing all the data on one screen. This equipment amongst various other facilities would help in Route Planning, Monitoring and Executing, with voyage recording capabilities and anti-grounding functions.

### 4.4 Course objective and contents

Upon completion of this course, the participant will be able to:

- Get an overview of the ECDIS and understand the difference between a raster & vector chart;
- Appreciate the capabilities and limitations of an ECDIS;
- Operate an ECDIS and use its functions for safe navigation.

Key training factors for the use of the ECDIS:

- Guidance regarding ECDIS Simulators and ECDIS simulation equipment,
- Operational use of the ECDIS,
- Inclusion of the STCW Code (A + B1-12),
- Requirement for a prior completion of ARPA courses,
- Real-time operating environment,
- Creation of a realistic visual scenario,
- Simulation of "Own Ship" dynamics.

Course contents:

- Theory of ECDIS;
- International regulations and requirements governing the use of ECDIS;
- Knowledge of Raster and Vector Charts;
- Capabilities and limitations of ECDIS equipment;
- Capabilities and limitations of ECS equipment;
- Practical knowledge of the various features of the ECDIS;
- Practical passage planning on the ECDIS;
- Practical route monitoring on the ECDIS;
- Simulator exercises using the ECDIS.

## 5 IAMU model course 1.00 on operational use of ECDIS

The model course presented provides training in the basic theory and use of ECDIS. The theoretical aspects like all major characteristics of ECDIS data such as data contents and all major characteristics of the display of ECDIS data will be covered in sufficient depth.

For capabilities and skills, exercises are performed which will provide practice in setting up and maintaining an ECDIS display, in planning and monitoring a route, in using basic navigational functions and equipment in a real time navigational environment, in activating updates and in performing proper actions which are necessary for a safe navigational watch. This course is specially aimed for navigating officers of operation and management level. On successful completion of this course, the trainees will be able to use ECDIS on their navigational watch. They will be able to operate ECDIS equipment, use the navigational functions of ECDIS, select, assess all relevant information, and take proper action. Trainees will acquire and develop a knowledge and understanding of the basic principles governing the safe operation of ECDIS, including ECDIS data and their presentation, as well as system related limitations and potential dangers.

Table 1: IAMU model course on operational use of ECDIS (FY2004).

| No. | Training Area | Lessons | including: L | D | E |
|---|---|---|---|---|---|
| 1. | Legal Aspects, Requirements and International Standards | 1½ | 1½ | - | - |
| 2. | Principal Types of ECS and Electronic Charts | 2 | 1 | 1 | - |
| 3. | ECDIS Data | 2 | 1 | ½ | ½ |
| 4. | Presentation of ENC/SENC Data | 3½ | 1 | 1½ | 1 |
| 5. | Main Functions of ECDIS | 3 | ½ | ½ | 2 |
| 6. | Route planning and special functions | 7½ | ½ | 1 | 6 |
| 7. | Route monitoring and special functions | 7½ | ½ | 1 | 6 |
| 8. | Data updating system | 2½ | ½ | 1 | 1 |
| 9. | Additional navigation-related information sensors, display and functions | 3 | 1 | 1 | 1 |
| 10. | Voyage data recording (documentation) | 1½ | ½ | ½ | ½ |
| 11. | Errors, status indications, warnings and alarms | 3 | 1 | 1 | 1 |
| 12. | Operational requirements | 3 | 1 | 1 | 1 |
| | **Total** | **40** | **10** | **10** | **20** |

Trainees will be able to generate and maintain displays, to operate all basic navigational functions and all specific functions for route planning as well as route monitoring, to use and select proper navigational data and to display the data in the appropriate manner. They will also be able to perform updating.

Trainees will be able to analyze nautical alarms during route planning and route monitoring as well as sensor alarms. They will be able to assess the impact of the performance limits of sensors on the safe use of ECDIS and to appreciate that the back-up system is only of limited performance. They will be able to assess errors, inaccuracies and ambiguities caused by improper data management. Thus, they will be aware of errors in displayed data, errors of interpretation and the risk of over-reliance on ECDIS and be able to take proper action.

This paper presented the model course on training in the operational use of ECDIS, the first IAMU model course, may be used by staff and students of any maritime university, navigational faculty and training institution as an alternative or supplement to the IMO Model Course. "*IAMU handbook on ECDIS*" and can assist in the training process.

## References

[1] Hailwood P.: Barriers to the adoption of ECDIS. The United Kingdom Hydrographic Office. Admiralty World, Issue 1, 2005.

[2] IMO Model Course 1.27. The Operational Use of Electronic Chart Display and Information Systems (ECDIS). International Maritime Organization, London 2000.
[3] IMO. STCW.7/Circ.10. Interim Guidance on Training and Assessment in the Operational Use of The Electronic Chart display and Information Systems (ECDIS) Simulators. International Maritime Organization, London, 11 June 2001.
[4] Weintrit A.: Training and Assessment in the Operational Use of the Electronic Chart Display and Information Systems (ECDIS). Guidance regarding the use of ECDIS simulators. *IAMU News*, Publication of International Association of Maritime Universities, Issue 9, May 2003.
[5] Weintrit A.: Introduction to IAMU Model Course on operational Use of Electronic Chart Display and information System (ECDIS). Proceedings of 6th International Symposium on Navigation organised by Faculty of Navigation of Gdynia Maritime University and The Nautical Institute, Gdynia 30 June - 1 July 2005.
[6] Weintrit A.: IAMU Handbook on ECDIS. International Association of Maritime Universities, Tokyo - Maine - Gdynia 2005 (manuscript).
[7] Weintrit A.: IAMU Model Course on operational use of ECDIS. IAMU research project FY2003 sponsored by Nippon Foundation. http://ecdis.am.gdynia.pl/iamu.

# Study on accreditation of marine engineering programs

B. Butman & J. Harbach
*US Merchant Marine Academy, USA*

## Abstract

The intermediate results of a research study on accreditation of marine engineering programs are presented in this paper. Similar to other higher education curricula, undergraduate marine engineering programs are routinely accredited by national accreditation bodies. Various methods of program approval and accreditation are analyzed in this ongoing project, but the program assessment by a specialized accreditation board or panel is the principal objective of the study. This accreditation of an engineering program is intended to improve its quality on one side, and to bring it on the level with other engineering specialties like mechanical, civil, aeronautical, and others. Obviously, only the programs that offer an engineering degree together with or without a maritime license are the subjects of the study. Yet the project recommendations might contain conditions and requirements for converting a strictly license program into a combined license/degree engineering curriculum.
*Keywords: accreditation, marine engineering program, accreditation institution, conditions of accreditation.*

## 1 Introduction

Due to the specifics of marine engineering programs, some of them undergo a triple tier accreditation:

1. as college level programs - by the National Higher Education Body, like a Ministry of Higher Education in many countries, or the Middle States Association of Colleges and Schools, like in the case of the US Merchant Marine Academy in New York.

2. as a marine engineering license programs – by the STCW associated Government Body, like the US Coast Guard in the USA, Technical Panel for Maritime Education in the Philippines, or Russian Ministry of Transport.
3. as an engineering program – by a Government or non-Government Accreditation institution, like American Accreditation Board for Engineering and Technology (ABET), or the UK Engineering Council.

## 2 Survey of existing methods and institutions

The survey of IAMU member institutions has not produced sufficient data for the project. Internet sources have been used and provided substantial data on maritime educational institutions. Various publications have been also analyzed, including those of the Conferences dealing with maritime education.

### 2.1 Certification of license component of programs

The component of the marine engineering program which contains the subject courses and other educational activities required for a mariner's license is a subject of a substantial scrutiny by national and international organizations. First of all, it has to comply with the regulations and requirements of the National Maritime Authority, like Ministry of Transport in some European countries, USCG and similar Government bodies in other countries. These authorities approve the programs (and individual courses, when required, mainly for the continuing education), initiate and conduct the license examinations, set the requirements for training institutions.

For instance the Commission on Higher Education of the Republic of Philippines has created a Technical Panel for Maritime Education which in turn formed several inspection teams to evaluate the compliance of maritime schools with the new policies and standards for maritime education programs.

Another type of certification, which has become quite popular, is provided by the Classification Societies. For instance, DNV has developed a standard for certification of Maritime Academies. This standard has been developed in close co-operation with several institutions. According to DNV "*the standard will ensure that all educational aspects are carried out under controlled conditions and in a consistent way, also that the Maritime Academy is operated according to established practices and specific requirements. It can be applied to all Maritime Academies offering education and training up to mandatory certificate level and to the industry in general. The standard supports the requirements and objectives of the ISM code and the revised STCW-95 Convention.*"

The international certification of the license component of marine engineering programs has been initiated by IMO. The International Maritime Organization (IMO) as a specialized Agency of the United Nations prescribes the international standards concerning maritime and environmental safety. The IMO has developed a comprehensive series of conventions to establish a framework of international law covering the subject. Bearing in mind that the most important element in the safe operation of any ship is the competence and experience of its crew, a key component of this legal framework is the International Convention on Standards of Training, Certification and Watchkeeping for Seafarers (STCW), which was adopted in 1978 by the IMO. The Convention lays down minimum standards of competence for all ranks of seafarers. In 1995 the STCW Convention was substantially revised and updated to clarify the standards of competence required and provide effective mechanisms for enforcement of its provisions.

The STCW Convention prescribes minimum mandatory requirements for training, vocational qualifications, assessment and certification of seafarers. It sets the minimum levels of proficiency to be achieved by candidates, for the proper performance of functions on board ship, in order to obtain certificates of competency. These requirements apply to all officers and ratings. The international maritime training and certification requirements of the STCW Convention were introduced into legislations of all maritime countries, setting the minimum level of training of seafarers.

Realizing that the demand for competent seafarers will grow in the years to come, structured education and training are vital elements to meet this demand and expectations to the shipping industry. This has also been acknowledged in the revised STCW 95 Convention, which incorporates requirements to quality assurance principles in all mandatory maritime education and training and in the operation of related facilities. The need for a uniform standard within the area is essential. The standard has been developed to meet this need, and become a foundation of certification of the license component of a marine engineering program. The current list of STCW certified maritime academies includes 53 institutions, including 36 from the Philippines and 8 from Norway.

## 2.2 Accreditation of degree oriented component of programs

The principal method of accreditation, or rather certification, common for most maritime academies and schools is the mandatory approval of a program by the Governmental or non-government accreditation agency. In most of the countries a Ministry or a Department of Higher Education evaluates programs for compliance with the set requirements and allows their implementation.

In the U.S. a non-government body assesses the engineering programs. Actually, there are several such bodies formed base on the territorial principle. The U.S. Merchant Marine Academy, for instance, is accredited by the Middle States Association of Colleges and Schools. This accreditation is founded on the program outcome assessment, and in this regard it is similar to the process carried out by the engineering accreditation boards and/or councils in some countries.

Engineering programs in the U.K. are accredited by the Engineering Council (ECUK) through 36 engineering Institutions (Licensed Members), who are licensed to put suitably qualified candidates on the ECUK's list of accredited engineering programs. The Institute of Marine Engineering, Science and Technology (IMarEST) is one of the most active members. IMarEST is accrediting marine engineering academic programs in the United Kingdom, as well as in other countries.

Accreditation Board for Engineering and Technology (ABET) is the American counterpart of ECUK. ABET is the organization that accredits engineering, engineering technology, applied science and computer science programs in the United States. ABET is not an agency of the U.S. government, but a private organization made of members from over 20 professional societies. Society of Naval Architects and Marine Engineers (SNAME) is the one that is responsible for accreditation of marine engineering programs. ABET publishes a set of criteria developed by representatives from the member societies that programs must satisfy. Accreditation by ABET involves periodic (not less than every six years) audits that include preparation of documentation by the institution and an on-site visit by a team of volunteers from the member societies. There are over 30 marine engineering programs which are ABET accredited in the U.S.

## 3 Content and advantages of engineering accreditation

Accreditation in engineering education is a mechanism to certify a degree the programs are meeting a certain set of standards. Globalization has increased the tendency of engineering practice to be international in scope. Accreditation of engineering education programs had evolved as the primary basis upon which mutual recognition across national borders is based – both for educational equivalency, and increasingly for practice mobility.

Accreditation is also increasingly seen as an appropriate means of enhancing the quality of engineering education in countries where major changes in the education pattern are occurring, and in developing countries where improvement in the quality of engineering graduates is seen as a major way of building an indigenous technological base upon which economic growth in the world marketplace can be achieved. A quick review of developments in engineering accreditation in several countries around the world can illustrate various ways in which it is having major impacts upon engineering education.

a. In Germany, in response to declining interest in engineering study and to pressures to harmonize its programs with those of other developed countries, universities are developing new engineering education systems in the bachelors plus masters pattern. To assist in the development of these new programs, and to evaluate and certify their quality, a new Accreditation Agency for Programs in Engineering and Computer Science (ASII) has been established.
b. The economic downturn in Japan in recent years has made job security a thing of the past, and globalization has made it imperative that Japanese engineering graduates are prepared for more self directed career development. A new Japan Accreditation Board for Engineering Education has been established to provide quality assurance as new engineering programs are developed and implemented.

c. The Accreditation Board for Engineering and Technology (ABET) has been the major quality assurance mechanism for engineering education in the US since the 1930's. It also has served as a model for engineering accreditation developments in other countries, and it has developed major international thrusts such as substantial equivalency reviews of engineering programs in foreign countries where it has been invited. In the past several years, ABET has made a major change in its evaluation criteria – moving from technique specifications to outcomes assessment. Its 'Criteria 2000' is based upon institutional self study and goal setting against which it will be evaluated, continuous improvement requirements for accredited programs, and detailed assessment of the outcomes of the engineering programs as the fundamental criterion for accreditation.
d. As engineering programs have developed in Latin American countries, several countries have moved toward the establishment of accreditation programs. Both ABET and the Canadian Engineering Accreditation Board (CEAB) have conducted workshops and training efforts in Latin America to assist in the development of engineering accreditation systems there.

## 4 Comparison and analysis of accreditation process

Accreditation is a process in which degree programs are reviewed by independent and knowledgeable evaluators on a regular multi-year cycle. As an example, the accreditation by ABET is discussed below. The criteria required for programs to be accredited are defined by the Engineering Accreditation Commission – EAC – which is an elected body of volunteers representing each of the engineering professional societies. ABET evaluators are appropriately trained volunteers who are typically professors and practicing engineers. They review the self-study reports submitted by the program under review. Then the evaluators come to the university or college whose engineering programs are being reviewed. Following this site visit, the evaluators report their recommendations to the Engineering Accreditation Commission. At their annual meeting, EAC reviews the recommendations from all the evaluators for all the programs being reviewed that year and makes a decision on each program regarding its accreditation. Accreditation is for a designated period after which the program must be reviewed for re-accreditation. The maximum term of accreditation is six years. If there are severe shortcomings – and that is rare – evaluators will recommend that the program not be reaccredited. For programs to be reaccredited, terms of less than six years can be recommended to synchronize the next evaluation of several programs at that institution. If evaluators determine there are shortcomings that are not severe, they may recommend an accreditation term shorter than six years so that the institution's progress at remedying those shortcomings can be evaluated sooner.

To be accredited programs must have defined *Program Educational Objectives* developed with input from their key constituents (typically current students, alumni, and employers); they must regularly evaluate their progress at achieving those objectives; and must continuously improve their educational program based on that evaluation.

# 5 International engineering accreditation

## 5.1 General comments

Engineering education has become an international enterprise, following the major internationalization trend in engineering practice itself over recent decades. Graduates of an engineering program in any given country practice across national borders. This situation has especially deep impact on the maritime industry. This international mobility of marine engineering graduates has enhanced interest in the accreditation of the institutions and programs, which educate them. Employers, maritime schools, and licensing boards all have a keen interest in the quality of education received by marine engineering graduates who are looking for an employment in another country.

In the engineering professions where, like in marine engineering, professional licensure is required for engineering practice, the credentials of engineering graduates who want to practice engineering in a country other than their home country become extremely important. The engineering education which such engineers have obtained is subject to scrutiny by foreign licensure boards, and any assurance that the school or education system from which the foreign engineer has graduated has been subjected to accreditation makes acceptance of the foreign education credential much more likely.

Aside from improving the program quality, engineering colleges accredit their programs for some other reasons, like making the program more attractive for the candidates, as well as for the employers. Accreditation might be a useful tool for a general assessment of the program and its outcome.

## 5.2 International agreements on engineering accreditation

International agreements on engineering education and practice have been developed in recent years, based upon engineering accreditation. One such agreement, establishing full reciprocity for engineering graduates between ABET in the US and the CEAB in Canada, has been in place for several decades. A much broader mutual recognition agreement, the Washington Accord, was developed several years ago among several developed countries. While there are significant differences in the engineering accreditation systems in these countries, it was agreed – after extensive reciprocal visits – that the resulting engineering graduates were essentially equivalent. Thus graduates from each of the Washington Accord countries are accepted in all of the other countries as equivalent, for purposes such as graduate study and licensure applications.

The Accord applies only to accreditations conducted by the signatories within their respective national or territorial boundaries: Australia, Canada, Hong Kong, Ireland, Japan, New Zealand, South Africa, United Kingdom and USA. The admission of new signatories to the Accord requires the unanimous approval of the existing signatories. Admission is preceded by a period of provisional status during which the applicants accreditation criteria and procedures are examined. Applicants must be nominated by two of the existing signatories and are accepted by a positive vote of at least two-thirds of the existing signatories. Germany, Malaysia, and Singapore currently have provisional status.

Educational equivalency agreements can be the basis for cross-border practice agreements, and the group of countries involved in the Washington Accord have set in motion a parallel effort – the Engineers Mobility Forum – which is developing an international register of engineers approach. In Europe, the European Federation of National Engineering Associations (FEANI) has established an international practice system, based upon a seven year formation process for engineers, which leads to EurIng status. In North America, the three countries which have entered into the North American Free Trade Agreement (NAFTA) have attempted to develop a mechanism for the mobility of practicing engineers across their borders. Canada and Mexico have agreed on such a system of mobility, but efforts to include the United States have been stymied by licensure issues controlled at the state level by 55 separate jurisdictions. In the Asia-Pacific area, several countries have developed an agreement on engineering practice mobility, the APEC Engineer Register.

Accreditation is a valuable mechanism for effecting and assuring ongoing quality in engineering programs within a given country. When the quality of engineering programs in two or more countries has led to similar results in graduates, accreditation programs can provide the basis for mutual recognition of graduates across national borders.

## 5.3 ABET international activities

While ABET does not directly accredit programs in countries other than the United States, it does recognize the equivalency of some non-US programs in two ways: through mutual recognition agreements such as the Washington Accord and through a program termed Substantial Equivalency.

Programs that are not included in the Washington Accord can request that ABET conduct a review for "substantial equivalency". ABET defines substantial equivalency as comparable in program content and educational experience, but such programs may not be absolutely identical in format or method of delivery. It implies reasonable confidence that the graduates possess the competencies needed to begin professional practice at the entry level. While these evaluations follow similar policies and procedures used for accreditation, no accreditation action is taken, nor is there any inference that a program is undergoing accreditation or will be accredited as a result of such review. The activity is an evaluation (program review) in which ABET, through selected representatives, acts on a consultancy basis, and leads to an assessment of "substantial equivalency" of the program under review with accredited programs in the United States.

Substantial equivalency evaluations are conducted with the current ABET criteria used to accredit equivalent US programs. Current ABET criteria are outcomes-based and require evaluation of program objectives and outcomes.

ABET provides a Consultation Report with suggestions for improvement shortly after the visit. It is not uncommon for the institution to be asked to prepare a focused report regarding any recommendations made in the report. Based on positive results from the initial consultancy review, the institution will be provided with the full evaluation package and asked to prepare the complete self-study reports. After an on-site visit a "preliminary statement" is prepared by ABET and submitted to the institution for comment. The institution has 30 days to report back to ABET on errors of fact or other reported observations pertaining to the items addressed in the statement. All the available information will be reviewed by INTAC and the final recommendation approved at its annual meeting. "Substantial Equivalency" will be granted to programs that meet or exceed the minimum requirements. Term of the equivalency status is usually two to six years. A return visit and review is necessary before the term expires to extend the equivalency status.

### 5.4 IMarEST accreditation procedures and international activities

The IMarEST as a licensed member of the Engineering Council (UK) and the UK Science Council is required to establish education and professional development standards and procedures in compliance with the national standards set by EC(UK). Accreditation is undertaken by the Institute's Professional Affairs and Education Committee (PAEC) who initially scrutinize the applications from academic establishments against IMarEST's standards and requirements. If a prima facie case is perceived a Visiting Panel is appointed to visit the establishment. During the visit, the Panel's focus is on aspects of the program where they need clarification. The institution's facilities including workshops, laboratories, and library are visited, and examination papers and scripts, and also project reports are examined and assessed against the Institute's standards.

The visit report is first submitted to the academic establishment to check for accuracy and then considered by the PAEC in committee who make the final decision on the outcome and any recommendations or conditions to be made. The Institute then formally informs the EC(UK) and the academic establishment of the outcome.

The EC(UK) is a signatory to the Washington Accord, Sydney Accord and Dublin Accord, the Engineers Mobility Forum (EMF) and the Engineer Technologist Forum (ETMF) international agreements, and programs that the IMarEST accredits are therefore accepted internationally as meeting the academic and/or professional development standards for the three categories of professional engineer.

## 6 Analysis of impact of accreditation requirements on academic process and core curriculum

In order to have a marine engineering program accredited by either a national accreditation board, or by any International Institution, a very substantial changes should be made. Compliance with all requirements might require adding new courses and projects, repackaging existing courses, and dropping certain subjects and courses. Table 1 presents the excerpts of the requirements of the IMarEST to a marine engineering program.

Table 1: Specific learning outcomes expected from BEng degrees.

| Subject Area | Specific Outcomes |
|---|---|
| Mathematics and Science | Knowledge and understanding of:<br>- scientific principles and methodology necessary to underpin their education in their engineering discipline;<br>- mathematical principles necessary to underpin their education in their engineering discipline;<br>- other engineering disciplines to support study of their own engineering discipline. |
| Engineering Analysis | Understanding and ability to apply:<br>- engineering principles;<br>- the performance of systems and components through the use of analytical methods and modelling techniques;<br>- quantitative methods and computer software relevant to their engineering discipline, in order to solve engineering problems;<br>- a systems' approach to engineering problems. |
| Design | Knowledge, understanding and skills to:<br>- Investigate and define a problem and identify constraints;<br>- Understand customer and user needs;<br>- Identify and manage cost drivers;<br>- Use creativity to establish innovative solutions. |
| Economic, social, and environmental context | Knowledge and understanding of commercial and economic context:<br>- management techniques to achieve engineering objectives;<br>- requirement for engineering activities for sustainable development;<br>- potential impact of marine engineering on the marine environment;<br>- framework of relevant legal requirements;<br>- high level of professional and ethical conduct in engineering. |
| Marine Engineering Practice | Knowledge and understanding of:<br>- particular materials, equipment, processes, or products;<br>- operations, maintenance, technology development, etc;<br>- use of technical literature and other information sources;<br>- awareness of nature of intellectual property and contractual issues;<br>- appropriate codes of practice and industry standards;<br>- awareness of quality issues;<br>- design processes and methodologies. |

Engineering education as a whole, particularly in developed countries, has in recent years focused on outcomes assessment for quality assurance and evaluation of educational programs. This trend has been driven both by educators and by publics interested in quality education – parents, legislators, funding agencies, etc. ABET has been a leader in moving to outcomes assessment as the primary mechanism for accreditation of engineering programs, in its "Criteria 2000".

The following statement of outcomes from the ABET criteria was developed with substantial input from employers of engineering graduates, and other organizations concerned with quality assurance in engineering education:

"Engineering programs must demonstrate that their graduates have:
a) an ability to apply knowledge of mathematics, science and engineering;
b) an ability to design and conduct experiments, analyze and interpret data;
c) an ability to design a system, component, or process to meet desired needs;
d) an ability to function on multi-disciplinary teams;
e) an ability to identify, formulate, and solve engineering problems;
f) an understanding of professional and ethical responsibility;
g) an ability to communicate effectively;
h) the broad education necessary to understand the impact of engineering solutions in a global and societal context;
i) a recognition of the need for, and an ability to engage in life-long learning;
j) a knowledge of contemporary issues;
k) an ability to use the techniques, skills, and modern engineering tools".

## 7 Conclusion

This is an ongoing study. The specific recommendations related to preparation of the marine engineering program for engineering accreditation will be developed on the final stage of the project.

# Internet-based integration of multiple ship-handling simulators: an interim report

C. Shi & Q. Hu
*Shanghai Maritime University, China*

## 1 Background

The research team members of the project include: Shi Chaojian, Hu Qinyou, Huang Zhenmin, Zhang Yi and Yu Lili from Shanghai Maritime University; Adam Weintrit, Przemyslaw Dzuila and Andrzej Bomba from Gdynia Maritime University; Chae-Uk Song from Korea Maritime University; Gyei-Kark Park from Mokpo National Maritime University.

Due to the high expense and risk for the ship handling practice on a real ship, most MET institutions implement ship-handling (SHS) training. With the development of the technology in recent years, SHS has been improved greatly on ship handling model and scene image. However, most of the SHSs are stand-alone facilities and the trainees in the programs usually come from the same country or the same company, which differs from the reality. Navigation is an international activity, and there may be many ships from different countries sailing in the same sea area. Some training institutes having seafarers from different countries or regions trained together as a team, although this method proves to be costly. Integrating SHSs internationally through the Internet is an effective way to solve the problem. On integrated SHSs, cadets and seafarers trained on local SHS can do ship handling and communication practice together with trainees at SHSs in other countries or regions. The integrated training will create a realistic scenario for the trainees and can be performed economically and effectively. The reasons why we need to integrate multiple SHSs internationally are evident:

- To close the gaps between the technical, operational level and methodology between IAMU member universities. It benefits global standardization of simulator training and promotes the exchange and sharing of training experiences.
- To enhance mutual understanding of navigational procedures between cadets and seafarers from different countries. It provides a good platform of intercommunion among cadets with an international background.

- To facilitate communication and Maritime English training. Through the Internet based VHF cadets and seafarers can communicate (using IMO Standard Marine Communication Phrases) in more realistic and diverse situations.
- To extend the application of SHSs. Integrated SHSs provides an excellent training opportunity in virtual twenty-four hour watch-keeping practice for a complete voyage including shift watches. In addition, it is a good supplement to the training on real ships.

Therefore, the internationalization of SHS training will greatly enhance seafarers' technical and operational abilities.

The project "Internet Based Integration of Multiple Ship Handling Simulators" NetSHSs in short, focuses on solving technical problems and developing necessary software and hardware for integrating multiple simulators on the Internet. The necessity of integration of multiple SHSs and its application has being discussed at AGA4 of IAMU 2003, Egypt and the project was granted by IAMU in July 2004.

In this project, we design and realize the platform to integrate multiple SHSs, and compose the relative technology standard. We will describe the relevant specification for the integration of multiple SHSs, and establish the infrastructure for the integration of multiple SHSs according to the technological specification. Standardized guidelines will be provided for the integration of multiple SHSs in IAMU member institutions. A management centre will be set up for managing and coordinating the complete integrated system and a prototype will be built to implement the integration of two or three SHSs from different counties.

## 2 Methodology

The system is based on a Multi-Agent System (MAS) technology to implement the integration of the multiple SHSs from different countries or regions. MAS are one of the mainstream technologies in distributed computing and Computer Supported Collaborating Work (CSCW) area.

There are three advantages in using the MAS to realize the integration of multiple SHSs, they are:

- only small changes on existing SHSs are required;
- the MAS platform can be used as the foundation for the integration of multiple SHSs;
- the integrating SHSs can be easily expanded.

To realize the integration of the SHSs by using MAS technology, we set up a Management Centre as a Server. Five Agents run in the Server: (1) Name Server Agent which is in charge of recording the names of the active SHSs and their Network addresses, (2) Facilitator Agent which records information of each Virtual Sea Area (VSA in short) and the SHSs joining it. (3) Visualizer Agent by which the administrators can visually manage the cooperation among several SHSs, (4) Judge Agent which is responsible for deciding whether a SHS can enter or quit a VSA, and (5) Time Agent which records the current time of each VSA and synchronizes the time of a SHS when the SHS want to enter a VSA.

To implement the interaction between existing SHS and the above Management Centre, a SHS Agent will be built for each SHS. A SHS Agent will take an intermediate role between the SHS and Server. A SHS Agent collects relevant information from the SHS and sends it to the Server, as well as receiving information from the Server and forwarding it to the SHS. Both are in real time.

To realize VHF communication on the Internet, a VHF Agent was built for each VHF terminal. A VHF Agent receives all voice data and channel information, and then forwards them to the SHS Agent. When the VHF Agent receives any voice data from the SHS Agent, it will forward the voice data to the VHF terminal. The communication between the SHS Agent and the Server is taken by IoMSHSs (Integration of Multiple Ship Handling Simulators) protocol. This protocol enables several SHSs to exchange VSA data, ship feature data, voyage information and VHF audio data, etc, through the Server. The IoMSHSs protocol is built on the HTTP protocol. Therefore, IoMSHSs messages can pass through the firewall of the LAN. Figure 1 shows the architecture of the whole system.

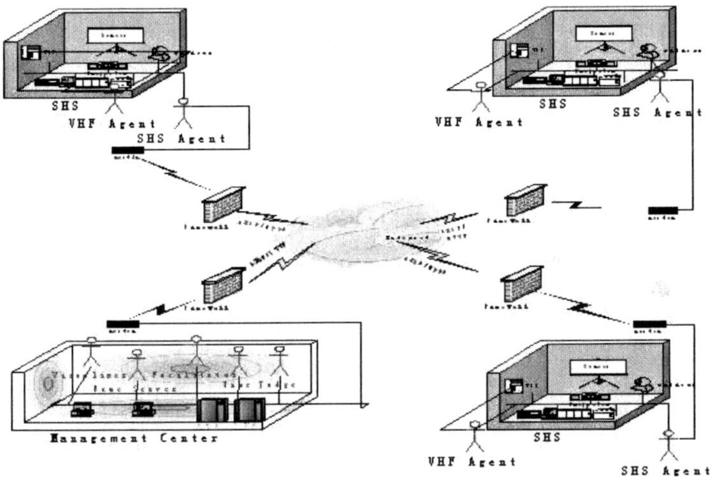


Figure 1: System architecture.

When an SHS starts up, its Agent will register related information to Name Server Agent, such as the SHS name and its network address, the instructor can then select an existing VSA or create a new one. When an SHS enters a VSA, it can exchange its own ship data and VHF audio data with other SHSs in the same VSA through the Server. According to the information received, the SHS will create the ship's model and display its movement in the virtual scene.

After the connection between Agents was established, seafarers can handle the ship, perform watch keeping, and communicate with the trainee at remote SHSs. Moreover, they can communicate via the Internet Based VHF system.

The whole system is mainly composed of two function modules: A Simulator Agent for local ship handling simulator stations and the Management Agent for a central coordinating station. Each agent can respond to the administration/user's inputs through its GUI interface and perform the corresponding tasks. Figure 2 shows the implementation chart of the system.

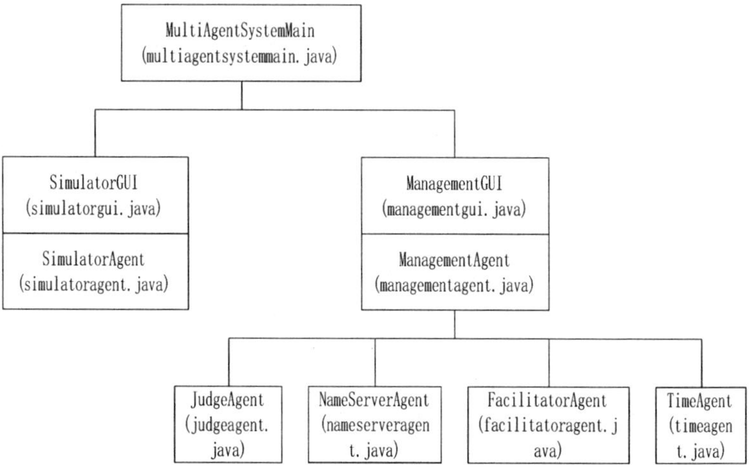


Figure 2: Chart of the system implementation.

# 3 Implementation of the modules

At present, the frameworks of the SHS Agent, desktop simulator and VHF terminal design have been completed. The work on SHS-Linker Web Server is on going.

## 3.1 SHS agent

A simulator agent, who has the function of communicating with the system simulator, contacts the simulator. During the runtime of the system, a simulator agent forwards the simulator's data to the Management agent, and then forwards the updated data received from the Management Agent to the simulator, and responds to the Instructor/User's control through its GUI.

As an "Agent" of the simulator, the SHS Agent is in charge of communicating with the Server and delivering relative information.

- Information exchange with the simulator: Collecting the simulator's runtime data, informing the local simulator when remote SHSs enter or exit the current Virtual Sea Area (*VSA*), forwarding the update information of *VSA* to its simulator.

- Interacting with the Server through the Internet: Acquiring the VSA list from the Server; requesting connection/quitting VSA on the Server or for opening/closing a VSA and receiving the feedback of the Server; receiving and processing the data from the Server.

Supplying an Operating Interface (GUI) for Instructor/User: Through the GUI, Instructor/User could control the Simulator Agent, send commands, get information, and manage local own ships (add or delete own ships).

Through SimulatorGui, a SimulatorAgent can respond to local Instructor's command to connect the system/Internet, register, enquire interactive area list, add or delete the ship, etc. There are two function modules in Simulator Agent Class: the Simulator Manager implements the function that administers the local simulator and communicates with it; and the Management Agent Connector, which implements all interactive action with the Management Agent. Figure 3 shows the block diagram of Simulator Agent.

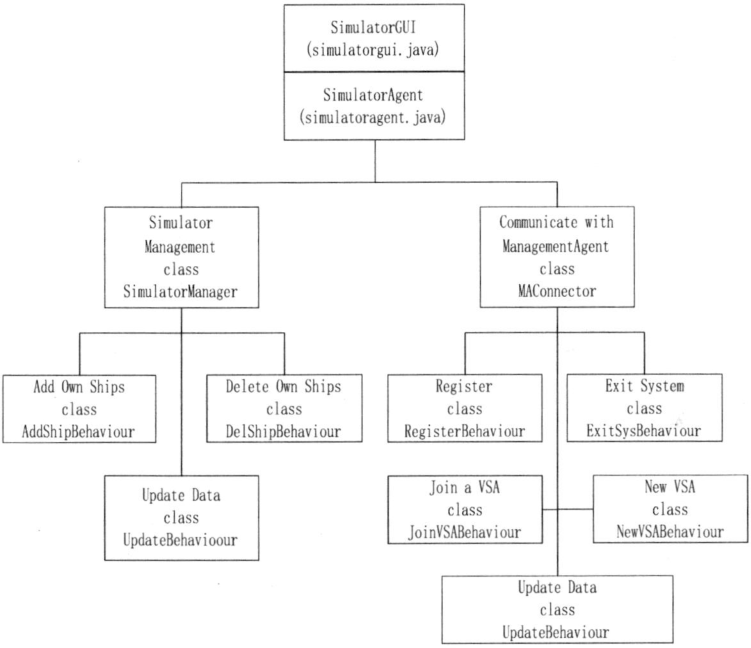


Figure 3: Block diagram of Simulator Agent.

### 3.2 Desktop simulator

The project focuses on solving technical problems and developing necessary software and hardware for integrating multiple simulators on the Internet. Usually, the real SHS is a complicated facility and the availability is limited, it is inconvenient to test and debug our program if we use the real SHS directly. On the other hand, we need multiple standalone simulators to set up the multiple SHS environment. It is necessary to develop a simple desktop SHS, which can be used to test or debug the whole system.

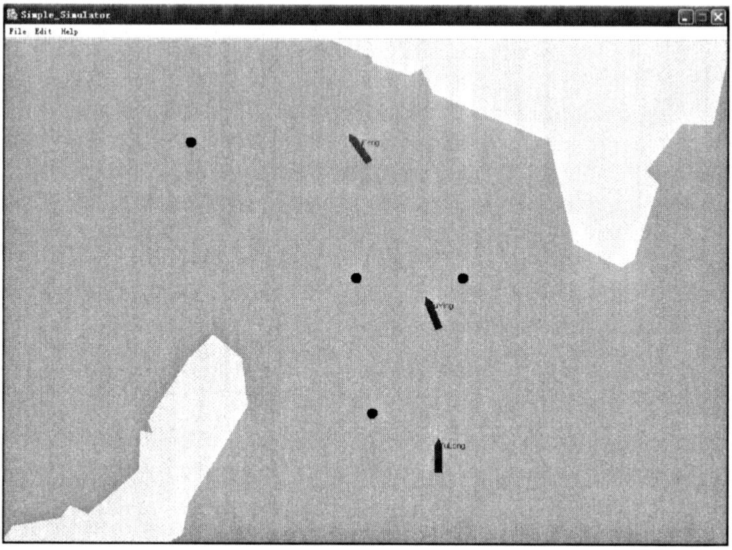


Figure 4: Desk top SHS.

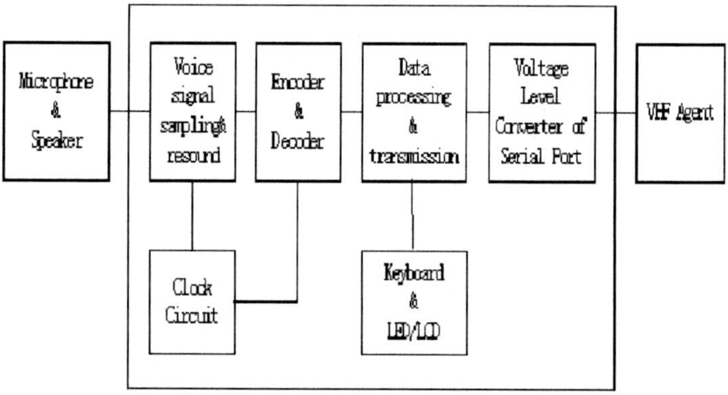


Figure 5: VHF Terminal Architecture.

In order to achieve the aim of substituting the real SHS when testing and debugging, the desktop SHS should include the following functions:

- Showing 2D simulative maritime space based on input data (islands, obstacles) showing 2D ships based on input data.
- Using keyboard control to respond to the user's operation to control the ships speed and course.
- Receiving ship's data from the other SHS in the same virtual maritime space and displaying their movement.
- Calculating and deciding whether there exists any risk of collision among ships, islands, and obstacles. If so, taking suitable action to avoid a collision.

The following modules are included in the desktop SHS:

- Virtual sea area including islands and obstacles;
- Mathematical model of the ship's movement;
- Display panel of simple desktop SHS Context classes.

Figure 4 shows the runtime interface of a simple desktop SHS. This simple desktop SHS has implemented the essential functions of real Ship Handling Simulator.

### 3.3 VHF terminal

In order to realize a more lifelike simulative environment, the ship-handling simulator should have the function to interact and communicate between multinational ships. The real-time voice communication with the VHF simulation system is an important part of this project.

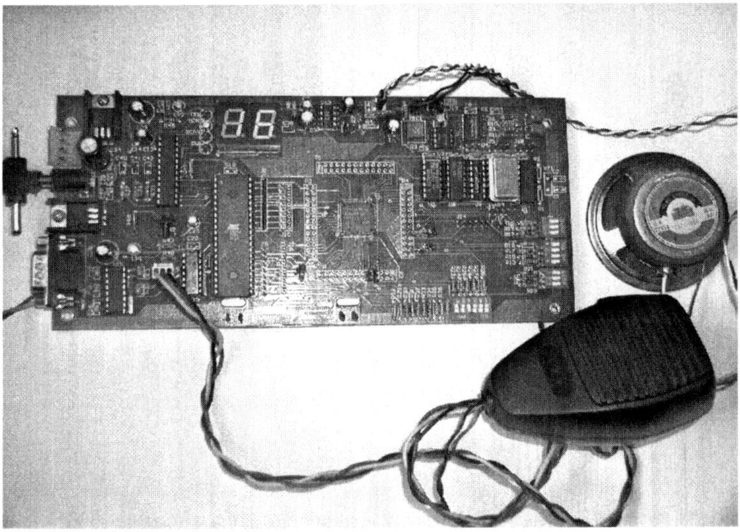

Figure 6: VHF circuit board connection.

The VHF simulation system is based on DSP. The research is focused on the study, selection and experimentation of speech coding algorithms, the design of a hardware circuit, the development of embedded control software, the programming and debugging of the PC's interface and network transmission.

There are two parts of the research work: software design and hardware design of the system. The software design includes PC and microcontroller embedded programming. The hardware design includes the speech data sampling and reconstruction unit, encoder and decoder unit, data processing and transmission unit, clock synchronous unit, keyboard and display unit, and RS-232 converter unit. Figure 5 shows the VHF Terminal Architecture and Figure 6, the VHF circuit board connection

### 3.4 SHSLinker Web Server

The main purpose of the SHSLinker Web Server is to manage and coordinate the integrated simulators in the system. It also displays the necessary information and provides general functions for monitoring and controlling the running system.

Figure 7 shows a display of administration tools of the SHSLinker Web Server.

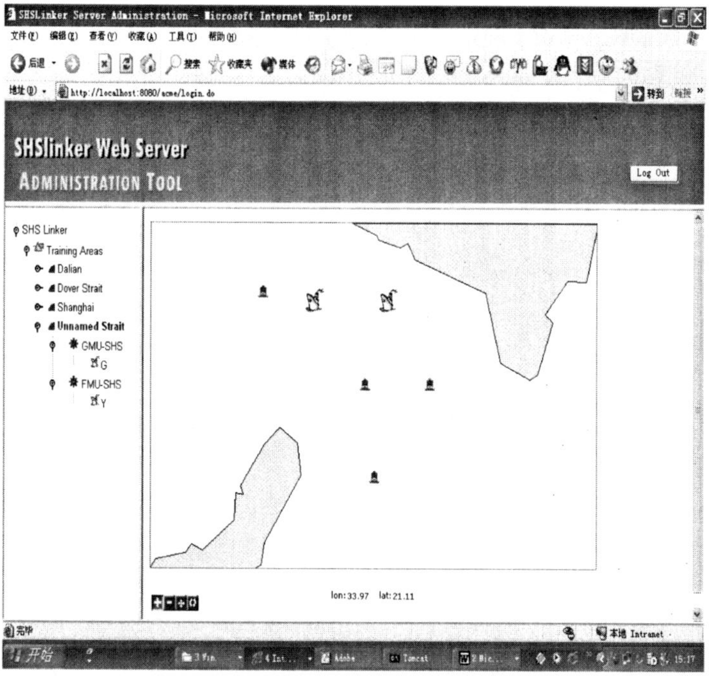


Figure 7: SHSLinker Web Server.

# 4 Summary

Apart from the Management Agent, all major module frames have been completed, although further refinements are necessary. Interface standards also need further consideration. The status of the project is summarized in the table to the appendix.

# Appendix: progress status of the project

| Time | Module | Sub-modules | status | Documentation | Participants |
|---|---|---|---|---|---|
| Apr.1, 05~ Oct.1, 05 | VHF terminal | Voice signal sampling &resound | Finished | General Design for NetSHSs.doc<br>*Implementation report,* N/A | Shi Chaojian Hu Qinyou Huang Zhenmin Zhang Yi Yu Lili Adam Weintrit Przemyslaw Dzuila Andrzej Bomba Chae-Uk Song Gyei-Kark Park |
| | | Encoder &Decoder | Finished | | |
| | | Data processing & transmission | Finished | | |
| | | Voltage level converter of serial port | Finished | | |
| | | Clock Circuit | Finished | | |
| | | Keyboard & LED/LCD | Finished | | |
| | VHF agent | Receive Module | Finished | General Design for NetSHSs.doc<br>*Implementation report,* N/A | |
| | | Forward Module | Finished | | |
| | Simple Desktop SHS | Maritime Space Module | Finished | Design & Implementation of Simple Desktop SHS.doc | |
| | | Ship's Movement Calculating Model Module | Finished | | |
| | | Ship's Movement Displaying Model Module | Finished | | |
| | | Display Panel Module | Finished | | |
| | | Context Module | Finished | | |
| | NetSHSs Server | Facilitator Module | Finished | General Design for NetSHSs.doc<br>*Implementation report,* N/A | |
| | | Name Server | Finished | | |
| | | Time Module | Under development | | |
| | | Judgement Module | Under development | | |

| Time | Module | Sub-modules | status | Documentation | Participants |
|---|---|---|---|---|---|
| Apr.1, 05~ Oct.1, 05 | SHS agent | SHS Agent Gui Module | Finished | General Design for NetSHSs.doc<br><br>Design and Implementation of SHS Agent.doc | Shi Chaojian<br>Hu Qinyou<br>Huang Zhenmin<br>Zhang Yi<br>Yu Lili<br>Adam Weintrit<br>Przemyslaw Dzuila<br>Andrzej Bomba<br>Chae-Uk Song<br>Gyei-Kark Park |
| | | SHS Agent Ontology | Finished | | |
| | | SHS Agent Interface | Finished | | |
| | | Ship Adding Module | Finished | | |
| | | Ship Reset Module | Finished | | |
| | | Ship Delete Module | Finished | | |
| | | Register Module | Finished | | |
| | | Deregister Module | Finished | | |
| | | New VSA Module | Finished | | |
| | | Join-in VSA Module | Finished | | |
| | | Data Update Module | Finished | | |
| | | Quit VSA Module | Finished | | |
| | NetSHS Website | Index Page | Finished | Introduction to SHSLinker Administration Web Server.doc | |
| | | Log in/out Module | Finished | | |
| | | Administer Module | Finished | | |
| | | Database Module | Finished | | |
| | SHS Integration | SMU | Under development | N/A | |
| | | GMU | Not start | | |
| | | KMU | Not start | | |
| | | MMU | Not start | | |

# The Professional Profile of a Maritime English Instructor (PROFS): an interim report

C. Cole[1], B. Pritchard[2] & P. Trenkner[3]
[1]*World Maritime University, Sweden*
[2]*Faculty of Maritime Studies, University of Rijeka, Croatia*
[3]*Hochschule Wismar, Fachbereich Seefahrt, Germany*

## Abstract

That communication within the maritime industry in general, and at sea in particular, requires a high level of competency is axiomatic. For international employees today, this inevitably means communicative competency in the English language, especially the variety commonly referred to as Maritime English. Gradually Maritime English is becoming recognised as a fully-fledged subject and the need to establish standards is an issue receiving widespread attention. In the shipping industry the increased global need to use English due to the new demands imposed by technological and commercial developments, together with high profile misdemeanours at sea causing loss of life, damage to property and environmental pollution, have resulted in the legal requirements (i.e., STCW/SOLAS) regarding communicative competency in the English language for professional purposes being considerably sharpened. The authors have observed the rise in interest and concern of maritime organisations as to how they should best accommodate these new demands. Maritime Education and Training institutions, often reluctant to recognise Maritime English on an equal footing to Navigation or Marine Engineering, or to dedicate more instruction hours in an already tight programme, have been keen to find more effective strategies. Often this is attempted by paying little or no attention to the amorphous global body of Maritime English instructors at their disposal. The Professional Profile of a Maritime English Instructor (PROFS) project aims on the one hand to create generally accepted guidelines/recommendations for MET institution management on how to qualify teachers of general English and other persons of substandard maritime-technical qualifications currently teaching English to navigational/marine engineering university students to become lecturers/instructors in Maritime English, meeting at least the requirements of the relevant legislation, and on the other hand to provide prospective candidates to the Maritime English teaching profession with an idea of what will be expected from them should they wish to instruct navigational/marine engineering students at university level. This report presents the activities and preliminary observations of the PROFS team's ongoing research.

*Keywords: Maritime English (instructors), communicative competency, PROFS, profiling, twinning, typology.*

# 1 Project aims and objectives

Various conferences, seminars and workshops have revealed that there is an urgent need to establish a sound, well-structured profile of a qualified Maritime English instructor for higher MET institutions in order both to satisfy the demands of the current legislation, as well as the requirements of today's maritime industry. Put simply, instructors of Maritime English, just like all other instructors involved in the education and training of seafarers, have to comply with Section A-I/6(3) of the STCW 1978/95 which requires, that "all instructors... are appropriately qualified for the particular types and levels of training... of seafarers either on board or ashore."

The *Professional Profile of a Maritime English Instructor (PROFS)* project aims on the one hand to create generally accepted guidelines/recommendations for MET institution management on how to qualify teachers of general English and other persons of substandard maritime-technical qualifications currently teaching English to navigational/marine engineering university students to become lecturers in Maritime English, meeting at least the requirements of the relevant legislation, and on the other hand to provide prospective candidates to a Maritime English teaching profession with an idea of what will be expected from them (both in terms of the necessary maritime background knowledge and the appropriate methodical qualification) should they wish to instruct navigational/marine engineering students at university level.

The initial idea for PROFS was hatched in discussions resulting from the researchers' own experience in combination with previous research. Two papers were prepared (Cole, Trenkner) for IAMU's AGA4 in Alexandria (September 27-October 01, 2003) and for IMLA's IMEC15 in St Petersburg (October 07-10, 2003) where the authors presented a typology of Maritime English instructors. As a result of the encouraging response, a research proposal application was made to IAMU in November 2003; the PROFS project was approved on July 12, 2004 with a time line beginning on October 01, 2004. The final outcome, to be delivered by the end of 2005, will be seven work packages and a final report including an executive summary.

# 2 Relevance to the work of IAMU

It is well reported that more than three in ten accidents occurring at sea or in ports can be attributed to communication deficiencies, primarily due to an insufficient command among seafarers or other maritime personnel of what is called Maritime English. As a result, the legal requirements regarding communicative competency, as mentioned above, have been considerably sharpened in recent years to promote safety at sea and in ports. Coincidently, as the percentage of seafarers in the shipping industry shrinks and the number of internationally employed shore-based personnel increases, Maritime English has become an essential career tool, permitting mobility, flexibility and competitiveness.

The authors, having worked extensively in this field, have observed the rise in interest and concern of maritime organisations as to how they should best accommodate these new demands. Maritime Education and Training institutions, often reluctant to recognise Maritime English on an equal footing to Navigation or Marine Engineering, or to dedicate more instruction hours in an already tight programme, have been keen to find more effective strategies. Often this is attempted by paying little or no attention to the amorphous global body of Maritime English instructors at their disposal and the various qualifications and skills individual instructors possess, or do not possess, in meeting the legal requirements. Thus, the results and findings of this project, i.e. the guidelines and recommendations to be developed and suggested, should have a direct impact upon the urgently required improvement of the Maritime English communication competence of the graduates of maritime institutions via a solidly based professional profile of the instructors teaching navigational and marine engineering students at IAMU affiliated institutions.

## 3 Research questions

The key questions being considered by the PROFS project team are:

- What types of Maritime English instructors are currently employed at MET institutions? What is the usefulness and limitations of each type?
- What are the linguistic and methodical requirements of a "qualified" Maritime English instructor? How can these requirements be met?
- What is the minimum maritime background knowledge required? How can this be best acquired?
- What further qualification measures for Maritime English instructors in the maritime field and in language teaching/acquisition methodology can be identified?
- Which professional organisation or affiliation would best assist Maritime English instructors in meeting the requirements of STCW 1978/95?
- Is there a suitable body to oversee developments and advise IAMU on progress?

## 4 Methodology and preliminary observations

Both deductive and inductive reasoning processes were considered to be appropriate for this type of research. The deductive element consists primarily of academic desktop research based on the researchers' own experience in combination with previous research, whereas the inductive element involves the evaluation of the response to a specially designed questionnaire, the evaluation of round-table discussions, personal interviews, and brainstorming sessions with international MET students and graduates as well as with representatives of the maritime industry.

### 4.1 Deductive element

The deductive element, based on the team's collective experience and previous research, was largely arrived at in the papers noted in section 1 above and refined, with the third member of the team's inclusion (Pritchard), at the kick-off meeting in Warnemünde (September 29-30, 2004) and through follow-up communications.

#### 4.1.1 Typology

The typology proposed for consideration includes 4 categories of Maritime English instructors typically employed at MET institutions, namely:

1. Career Specialists, recognised as they:
   a. are Graduates/Qualified Teachers;
   b. have become "marinated" – have seafaring credibility;
   c. have a reasonable institutional standing;
   d. may (or may not) be "qualified" to teach Maritime English.
2. English Language and Literature Graduates, recognised as they:
   a. are lovers of English;
   b. are not necessarily interested in applied linguistics;
   c. prefer to teach general English;
   d. are often asked to teach Maritime English but fail to meet the STCW standards.
3. Former Seafarers, recognised as they:
   a. are technical experts but ...
      i. not necessarily skilled at English;
      ii. not necessarily skilled at teaching;
      iii. often over-challenge their students.
   b. could deliver technical subjects in English.
4. "Native" English Speaking Persons ("backpackers/nomads", housewives, spouses, retirees, etc), recognised as they:
   a. are often employed to motivate students to listen/speak in English but...
      i. not necessarily skilled at English;
      ii. not necessarily skilled at teaching;
      iii. rarely knowledgeable in maritime matters.

A fifth category has been considered, namely those instructors at MET institutions who are encouraged or ordered to use English (as a foreign language) when teaching technical subjects. Such persons are not regarded by the PROFS team as Maritime English instructors but are increasingly seen by management as a/the source of supplying students with the perceived dosage of Maritime English required. The team recognises that this approach could play a supporting role but has yet to see an institution providing a considered list of the intended learning outcomes, suggesting that standards have yet to be established. Instead, the team much prefers the so-called "twinning" approach (the essence of which involves partnering technical subject instructors with Maritime English instructors). However, the temptation for institutional managers, in financially stretched situations, to do away with the Maritime English instructor altogether, hoping that the English competency of the remaining technical teaching staff will be sufficient compensation, cannot be ignored. The pros and cons of the "fifth category" and twinning will receive further attention in the Final Report.

### 4.2 Inductive element

The inductive element consisted of a specially designed questionnaire that was produced, trialled, amended and finalised during the first quarter of the project's time frame. In addition, a discussion/interview paper was devised in much the same way for use at round-table discussions and during personal interviews. It is reassuring to note the respondents and participants have unanimously regarded the tenor and strategic aims of the questionnaire and round table discussions as appropriate, and the objectives as highly relevant for promoting/ensuring the quality of Maritime English instruction.

#### 4.2.1 Questionnaire

The questionnaire contained a brief introductory description of the aims of the Project, and four parts.

- Part 1: Ways to Maritime Background Knowledge - to be completed by Maritime English instructors
    - 4 subsections containing in total 16 "questions"
- Part 2: Ways to Maritime Background Knowledge - to be completed by mariners teaching or expecting to teach Maritime English
    - 4 subsections containing in total 10 "questions"
- Part 3: Maritime English Management - to be completed by managers responsible for, but not teaching, Maritime English
    - 4 subsections containing in total 17 "questions"
- Part 4. Opinion – to be completed by all respondents
    - 20 statements to be ranked on a scale from 1 ("strong no") to 6 ("strong yes")
- Room was provided for additional comments.

The questionnaire was distributed extensively throughout the world, primarily at meetings and conferences, through email and websites, as well as at maritime institutions and via personal contacts. Using such methods of distribution means that it is impossible to calculate the distribution/return ratio.

The end of the second quarter (March 31) marked the deadline for including the questionnaire responses into the statistical summary. At this point 129 responses had been received; the initial target of 100 replies, having been well surpassed, suggests that the outcome in general terms will be statistically representative. It should be noted, however, that the majority of respondents represented Maritime English instructors, 80%, with mariners teaching or expecting to teach Maritime English, and managers responsible for, but not teaching Maritime English, sharing equally the remaining 20%. Also worth noting, has been the limited response from IAMU members.

The task of collating and summarising the responses to the questionnaire was completed during the third quarter and the documentation (including the raw data) has been deposited with the IAMU Secretariat. At the time of writing an evaluation of the responses is underway and this will be reported and reflected upon in the deliverables and the final executive summary.

### 4.2.2 Structured round table discussions and interviews

The PROFS team members are fully aware that questionnaires do not always "tell the truth". In order to offset this problem the team's methodology has included structured round table discussions and personal interviews. The structural element has consisted of a specially designed, in-depth round-table question sheet for use on appropriate occasions during the first three quarters of the project period. Among others, three specific gatherings were targeted, giving most satisfactory results:

- the International Maritime English Conference IMEC16 (international but primarily Asian participation) held in Manila, Philippines, October 26-29, 2004;
- the mid-project team meeting at World Maritime University, Malmö, Sweden (international participation: MET Masters degree students), April 06, 2005;
- the IMO Maritime English Instructor's Training Course, Szczecin, Poland, (eastern European participation), May 30-June 10, 2005.

Unfortunately none of the team was able to attend IAMU's AGA5 in Tasmania, Australia, however, it is understood that at the team's request an announcement was made to promote the project and the questionnaire was distributed.

The questions for discussion as presented in the question sheet reflect the project's research questions and were as follows:

- What types of Maritime English instructors are currently employed at MET institutions? What is the usefulness and limitations of each type?
- How, based on your experience, can MET institutions improve Maritime English instruction?
- What is the minimum maritime background knowledge necessary for a Maritime English instructor to adequately perform his/her job? How can this be best acquired?
- Can/could a Maritime English instructor become "qualified"? If so, what are/would be the language and teaching requirements? How can these requirements be met?
- Which professional institution, organisation or affiliation would best assist Maritime English instructors in meeting the requirements of STCW 1978/95?

The task of recording and summarising the results of the round table discussions and personal interviews was completed during the third quarter and the documentation (including the raw data) has been deposited with the IAMU Secretariat. At the time of writing an evaluation of the responses is underway and this will be reported and reflected upon in the deliverables and the final executive summary.

# 5 The AGA6 presentation

On the occasion of AGA6 the project will be nearing its completion. It is thus the intention of the team to report to the participants on the general progress and specific findings of the project whilst providing recommendations for the IAMU membership to consider. The completed research element (raw data) will become available to members only at the discretion of the IAMU Board.

# 6 Conclusion

The results of the research and the deliberations of the PROFS project team will be presented in eight deliverables (work packages) as follows:

WP 0: Introduction to the project, including a description of the methodology employed.
WP 1: Categorising the profiles of the various types of currently employed Maritime English (ME) instructors, clarifying the usefulness and limitations of each.
WP 2: Identifying the linguistic and methodical requirements of a qualified ME instructor and the ways of meeting them.
WP 3: Identifying the horizontal/vertical maritime background knowledge (scope/depth) to be expected of a ME instructor and the ways of acquiring such.
WP 4: Identifying adequate, appropriate and practicable further qualification measures for ME instructors in the maritime field, in language teaching/acquisition methodology and course development.
WP 5: Proposing an appropriate affiliation of the ME teaching staff within the structures of MET institutions in order to guarantee their involvement in the overall MET conception of the latter.
WP 6: Proposing a suitable body to oversee developments and advise IAMU and other relevant authorities on progress and probably certify that the requirements of STCW 1978/95 & SOLAS 1992/02 are met.
WP 7: Final report with executive summary.

The PROFS project will conclude by the end of 2005.

# Section 2
# Maritime security and MET

# Potential consequences of imprecise security assessments

J. U. Schröder[1], M. Q. Mejia Jr.[1], P. K. Mukherjee[1], F. M. Manolis[1] & S. Dreeßen[2]
[1]*World Maritime University, Sweden*
[2]*Scandlines, Germany*

## Abstract

The recently implemented International Shipboard and Port Facility Security (ISPS) Code requires security assessments for ships and port facilities. Although Part B provides elaborate guidance on issues to be observed and included into such risk assessments, a generally accepted methodology to carry out such risk assessments is not prescribed in the Code. This allows for subjective expert judgement as the basis for security risk assessments. However, subjective risk assessment will vary in scope and results. This is a normal feature of any risk assessment involving opinions of different individuals. This would, in principle, not cause any harm if legal consequences would not be involved in case a ship or its cargo was subject to a security incident. Legal experts voiced opinions that in such a situation they would challenge the security risk assessment. In the case that an issue connected to the security incident in question that harmed ship or cargo was not addressed properly in the security assessment they would question the seaworthiness of the ship. This would, of course, have far-reaching liability consequences for ship owners. The question, therefore, is how ship owners can be protected against uncertainty resulting from imprecise standards for security-risk assessment of the ISPS Code.
*Keywords: maritime security, security risk assessment, seaworthiness.*

## 1 Introduction

The ISPS Code [1] requires in its Part A Sec. 8 a shipboard security risk assessment to be carried out as "an essential and integral part of the process of developing and updating the ship security plan." Guidance is given in the non-mandatory Part B of the Code in the corresponding Para. 8. A comprehensive list of issues to be considered when such a security risk assessment is carried is provided in this regulation. Apart from this non-binding list of issues no methodology is suggested. Only brief and general advise is given in paragraph 8.2, where the Company Security Officer (CSO) is referred to "any specific guidance offered by the Contracting Governments". To the knowledge of the authors only one country, the United States, has specified such guidance [2]. This leaves it up to the CSO to define a suitable methodology. Principally there is nothing wrong with such an approach. In fact it is used widely throughout various approaches to the assessment of safety and security related matters. One aspect of concern is, however, that such an approach involves a certain degree of deviation and comparability of the results provided by different risk assessment teams. The resulting question could therefore be why to discuss this issue any further.

The answer to this is relatively simple. The security risk assessment forms the basis of the ship security plan, which creates the security system on board a ship. A plan not addressing all relevant maritime security areas of concern could therefore be considered as not sufficient and subsequently open up the opportunity to challenge the seaworthiness of the ship in question. This would clearly result in far reaching liability issues for the ship owner. Although no case is yet known in the above-mentioned security context, attempts have been undertaken to challenge the seaworthiness in court with respect to the International Safety Management (ISM) Code [3], a Code bearing many similarities to the ISPS Code. Prominent examples were *Eurasian Dream*, *Torepo*, and *Patraikos II* [4]. The question therefore remains if a cargo owner could challenge a ship owner for lacking due diligence with respect to the scope of a security risk assessment if this risk assessment has not addressed areas of concern which led to cargo damage in a security incident. If this is the case would it not be desirable to have stricter guidelines for ship security risk assessment, which would limit the liability of ship owners?

This paper is intended to investigate the issues mentioned above and to highlight potential consequences. It will furthermore outline a framework intended to safeguard sufficient security risk assessment and discuss advantages and disadvantages linked to minimum standards for security risk assessment.

## 2 What can ship crews do against maritime security threats?

The options available to ship's crews when dealing with maritime security threats are very limited. To begin with, ship crews are neither trained nor attuned to responding to security threats. Seafarers are only beginning today to train, as a result of ISPS Code implementation, to deter and prevent threats and to mitigate the effects of security incidents. Nevertheless, their security tasks are only collateral to their primary functions as navigators and engineers. They cannot be expected to react to a security threat in the same manner as security professionals who are trained to detect, intercept, delay, or neutralize targets [5]. Indeed, the proposed security-related amendments to the International Convention on

Standards of Training, Certification and Watchkeeping for Seafarers (STCW) concentrate on the integration of ship security officer (SSO) training within the curriculum and not combat or weapons training [6]. This complements the long-standing policy of various maritime organizations against the arming of seafarers in spite of rapidly rising levels of maritime violence in the past two decades.

Prevailing manning levels and the demanding nature of shipboard life are also factors that limit the options available to ship crews in dealing with security threats. Crews have simply become "too small and too busy to offer any sort of realistic protection against a human intelligence actively seeking to subvert the ship to its wicked purpose" [7].

The most prevalent security threats facing ships today are piracy and armed robbery. The groups that commit these unlawful acts come in different levels of organization and sophistication and employ varieties of *modi operandi*. One variety that is popular in the waters of Malacca Straits and Indonesia is one where a rubber boat carrying the attackers would come alongside the merchant vessel, climb on board using grappling hooks, bind the crew with rope, collect all personal valuables, and raid the ship's safe. Many attacks result in some sort of injury to the crew. In a few attacks where the vessel and its entire cargo were hijacked, crew members have been killed or seriously injured either as a direct result of violence from the attackers or while trying to flee or escape. According to statistics collected by the International Chamber of Commerce-International Maritime Bureau (ICC-IMB) for the year 2004, a total of 325 attacks were reported by ships, of which 197 involved pirates and armed robbers who were armed with guns, knives, or other weapons. During this period, 234 persons were either kidnapped or taken hostage, 59 were injured, 30 were killed, and 30 are still missing. 226 ships were boarded, 12 ships were fired upon, and 11 ships were hijacked [8].

The threat of maritime terrorism, on the other hand, remains largely a potential one. Compared to piracy and armed robbery against ships, there are relatively fewer incidents of maritime terrorism. The *Santa Maria* (1961), *Achille Lauro* (1985), *City of Poros* (1988), *Our Lady of Mediatrix* (2000), *USS Cole* (2000), *Limburg* (2002), *Superferry 14* (2004), and *Doña Ramona* (2005) are some of the few that readily come to mind. Also, a security threat involving terrorism carries with it a potential for much greater damage and injury. While pirates and armed robbers aim to escape with their lives and the stolen items, terrorists do not seek the cargo or personal valuables. Terrorists are highly trained in the use of violence and stand ready, if need be, to kill others or to give up their own lives [9].

There are other threats to the security of ship's crews aside from piracy, armed robbery, and terrorism. One threat for which the ISPS Code was also developed is the problem of stowaways. According to IMO statistics, 265 cases were reported in 2002 and 185 in 2003 [10]. The discovery of stowaways is a serious violation of the integrity and security of the vessel, and stowaways who find themselves in desperate situations could resort to violence against the crew. By the same token, there have been incidents [11] where stowaways have been abused and even killed by the crew.

It is too early to determine what specific effect the ISPS Code has had in terms of the risk profile of ships. One can only assume that the conscientious implementation of the Code would increase deterrence against criminal attacks and therefore result in a lower risk profile. It is now more than a year after the Code entered into force and a number of organizations have issued positive comments on the shipping industry's compliance. The United States Coast Guard (USCG) praised the international maritime community for having "demonstrated a significant level of compliance with the ISPS Code on the July 1st (2004) implementation date" [12, p.2]. The USCG also reported a continuing downward trend in the overall rate of ISPS-related major control actions (MCA), that is, denial of entry into port, expulsion from port, and ship detention. In July 2004, the rate was 2.5%. By year end, the MCA rate had dropped to 1.5% or 92 out of 6,087 inspections [12, pp.6, 25]. Similar praise was given by the secretariats of both the Paris and Tokyo Memoranda of Understanding on Port State Control. The Paris MoU reported a 1.46% ISPS-related detention rate [13] while the Tokyo MoU reported 1% [14]. However, even in the face of such positive comments it is important to note that the question of whether significant ISPS compliance – as determined during port state control – translates to more secure ships and seafarers, is a complicated one.

After the passage of time and the accumulation of sufficient data, it might eventually be feasible to measure the level of success of the Code. As regards the threats of piracy and armed robbery, IMB statistics show a decrease in the number of attacks reported between the years 2003 (445 attacks) and 2004 (325 attacks) [8, p.6]. They also show a significant decrease in the number of attacks according to type of attack (attempted boarding, detention, firing, hijack, robbery, etc.), type of violence employed (hostage-taking/kidnapping, assault, injury, killing), and type of arms used (guns, knives, other weapons) for the first quarter of 2005 compared to the same period of the previous five years [15]. It would be interesting to see whether in a few years this turns out to be the beginning of a discernable decrease in reported incidents. As far as the threat of terrorism is concerned, the lack of critical mass in statistical data will prove the task of determining success to be even more challenging.

To measure the ISPS Code's success would be to determine whether ship crews are able to achieve the Code's objectives of effectively deterring and preventing unlawful acts and mitigating the consequences of an actual security incident. As mentioned earlier, ship crews are already at a disadvantage because of low manning levels and heavy workloads. Also, attention to security is not innate in the seafarer in the same way that safety has come to be. In addition, because an offensive capability is inconsistent with the objectives of the ISPS Code, the only "weapons" available to ship's crew are safety equipment such as fire hoses and signal flares. In other words, the answer to the question *Can ship crews effectively react to security incidents?* is a qualified "yes," that is, to the extent that training and proficiency in deterrence and other security tasks are required by the ISPS Code. Once deterrence and prevention have failed and a security incident is imminent or underway, the actions available to the crew are basically limited to activating the ship security alarm system (SSAS), calling emergency stations, evacuating the ship, and acting on instructions from the contracting government.

There is not much a ship's crew can do once an armed robber or terrorist has decided to strike in spite of the ship's ISPS-compliant security system. Merchant ships are not equipped with either an active defence or offence capability. In fact as the *USS Cole* incident so clearly demonstrated, even a technologically advanced guided missile destroyer manned by professional naval warriors could be limited in its response options once the watercraft, its lethal cargo, and its crew of suicide bombers have already blown up in a thousand pieces. In the case of merchant vessels, security risk management (in many cases, risk avoidance) through the ISPS Code is offered as the optimum solution.

# 3 Liability for unseaworthiness in the context of maritime security

The central issue here is whether non-compliance with the ISPS Code constitutes a failure of seaworthiness which in turn can lead to potential liability on the part of the carrier or shipowner. An affirmative conclusion may arguably be attributed to a dubious ship security plan based on deficient or inadequate risk assessment. The problem, of course, is that there are neither any decided cases on this point in relation to the ISPS Code, nor is there any authoritative or scholarly legal literature. (See, however, [16, p. 370] where the authors refer to deficiency in ISPS compliance, in particular, lack of crew security training, deficient ISPS documentation and master or crew negligence as possibly constituting unseaworthiness.) At best an analogy can be drawn with liability implications for failure of seaworthiness in relation to the ISM Code in the context of which some views have been expressed and some tangential references have been made judicially. These will be examined in the following text.

## 3.1 What is seaworthiness?

For the discussion to be meaningful, it must obviously begin with a review of what is the legal concept of seaworthiness. This is a notion peculiar to maritime law and exists mainly within the domain of commercial maritime law; to be precise, in contracts of carriage under bills of lading, in charterparties and in marine insurance contracts tempered by relevant statutory provisions. Judicially, a seaworthy ship has been described as one that is "...in a fit state as to repairs, equipment, crew and in all other respects, to encounter the ordinary perils of the sea of the voyage" (*Dixon* v. *Sadler* [17]). A question that arises is whether a security risk is an ordinary peril. Another judicial definition describes a seaworthy ship as "...one which is reasonably fit for its intended purpose" (*Phipps* v. *ss Santa Maria* [18]). If without ISPS Code certification a vessel cannot be insured or utilised to transport cargo internationally, can it be argued that it is not "fit for its intended purpose" [19, p. 1601]? The classic definition of "seaworthiness" in the case of *F.C. Bradley & Sons Ltd.* v. *Federal Steam Navigation Co.* [20, p. 454] where approving a statement on *Carver on Carriage by Sae* the court held that "[T]he ship must have that degree of fitness which an ordinary careful owner would require his vessel to have at the commencement of her voyage having regard to all probable circumstances of it."

"Seaworthiness is not an absolute concept; it is relative to the nature of the ship, to the particular voyage or even to the particular stage of the voyage on which the ship is engaged", ([21 p. 315], approved by [22 p. 197]; see [23 para. 126]).

### 3.2 Seaworthiness in carriage law: application of Hague-Visby rules

Article III, Rule 1 requires a carrier to exercise due diligence before and at the beginning of the voyage to make the ship seaworthy and cargoworthy. The duty pertains to "all reasonably foreseeable eventualities" but in "normal circumstances" [24, p. 19]. This raises the question of whether a security incident is a reasonably foreseeable eventuality in normal circumstances. In legal terms the test is an objective one, no doubt, but its application may be fraught with confusion.

In *The Eurasian Dream* [23, para. 123] decision, the court identified the following steps in terms of the application of the Hague-Visby Rules:

First, the claimant must carry the burden of proving unseaworthiness. Second, the claimant must prove causation, i.e., that the loss or damage was proximately caused by unseaworthiness. (See [19 p. 8], for what constitutes "proximate cause"). Third, the defendant must carry burden of proof to invoke the defence of due diligence; [25, p. 5]. Fourth, if the defendant fails to discharge the burden, he would not be entitled to rely on any of the Art. IV, r. 2 exceptions.

This brings us to the fundamental question of whether a failure to comply with the ISPS Code per se is a breach of the requirement to exercise due diligence to make a ship seaworthy. In *The Eurasian Dream* the failure to have adequate documentation (Fire Manual in) may have been a consideration in the mind of the court. Support in the affirmative for this proposition is doubtful given the paucity of authority. A better proposition is that compliance with the ISPS Code is indicative of due diligence exercised by the defendant [19, p. 1601].

It is perhaps a fair conclusion that compliance with the ISPS Code on balance has better evidentiary use as defence of due diligence than non-compliance as a positive indicator of unseaworthiness in respect of Hague-Visby Rules. (For the same conclusion in respect of the ISM Code, see [26 pp. 11-12]). At any rate, a judicial pronouncement on liability arising out of unseaworthiness, whether it is in the affirmative or in the negative, will surely impact, or at least raise some serious questions relating to security risk assessment.

## 4 Maritime security assessment as a risk control option for the protection of the ship owner

Following the discussions of the earlier sections of this paper it can be concluded that ship crews can prevent or mitigate security incidents only to a certain extent. Security incidents can result from a number of sources and involve a wide range of methodologies. It is therefore very difficult to consider all potential security threats appropriately. At the same time ship owners would benefit from a stricter definition of the scope of maritime security assessments, as they cannot foresee all potential sources of such incidents. The question to be raised is how this can be achieved taking all the aforementioned aspects into consideration.

The ISPS Code [1] apart from its Sec. 8 in parts A and B does not provide any more specific guidance on how to carry out shipboard security risk assessments. Part A (refer in particular to 8.4) refers to the identification of existing security measures, the evaluation of key shipboard operations to be protected, the identification of threats to these operations and the identification of weaknesses resulting from infrastructure, policies, etc. Part B is more elaborate and provides a number of issues to be considered in shipboard security risk assessments (refer to Part B Sec. 8.7 – 8.10). Although this list is not very long it is specific guidance for risk assessments. The only problem involved is that Part B is not mandatory. One could of course say that in the absence of other guidelines one has to observe the issues mentioned in Part B. However, not all maritime stakeholders are of this opinion. Recognized organizations (RO's) provide different guidelines for shipboard security risk assessments. A majority, such as the American Bureau of Shipping (ABS) or Lloyd's Register favours the risk assessment guidelines provided by the United Sates Coast Guard (USCG) [2]. The USCG guidelines, however, do not specifically relate to the ISPS Code. They have been developed for security risk assessments in general and are lacking therefore specific cross-references to the relevant ISPS Code requirements. Two RO's, Det Norske Veritas (DNV) [27] and Germanischer Lloyd (GL) [28], have developed guidelines based on checklists which have a very close relationship to the ISPS Code. Both approaches apart from varying methodologies have another significant difference. The USCG guidelines do not include any statements about likelihoods of security threats, whereas the DNV-GL approach allows for a consideration of likely threats only. This means that on the one hand shipowners who follow the USCG approach strictly have to document any potential security threat and develop mitigation strategies of those issues which can result in severe consequences. If one would follow this approach one has to provide for a number of costly measures. On the other hand shipowners following the DNV-GL approach have to update their security assessments frequently depending on the latest security information available. Potential disputes about the validity and appropriateness of the security information are not likely to be avoided. To make it even more confusing the USCG requires all ships calling US ports to comply with both parts of the ISPS Code – A and B. The result therefore will to a certain degree most likely be frustration by a shipowner who is confronted with the task of arranging for security risk assessments on board his ships. What could therefore be suggestions to overcome this problem?

## 5 Conclusions and summary

Any suggestions regarding solutions for the above-mentioned problems have to consider the following three issues:

- Ship crews have limited capabilities to mitigate security attacks against their ships.
- Motives/reasons for security incidents result from a large variety of sources.
- Shipowners need certainty about scope and applicable requirements for the shipboard security as far as their liability is concerned.

In this respect it is remarkable to see that a number of IMO instruments or documents issued within the IMO framework focussing on risk assessment in general or maritime security in a wider sense have taken some of the above mentioned points into consideration. They provide for more guidelines on the contents of risk assessment on their area of interest.

One example, to be mentioned in this context, is the guideline on Formal Safety Assessment (FSA) [29]. The 2002 extended guidelines include not only "technical" risk assessment, but also human reliability assessment with detailed descriptions of methodologies. Another example is the guideline on places of refuge [30]. In order to assist maritime administrations the IMO provided for these guidelines where in section 3 a dedicated part deals with risk assessment only. Although no specific methodologies are described at least a number of issues to be considered during the risk assessment is listed. It is hoped that the place of refuge guidelines will be extended and updated similar to the FSA guidelines.

Most recently another remarkable example was given through the IMO/ILO Code of Practice on Security in Ports [31]. These guidelines provide for a much more defined framework for a number of issues around port security. The risk assessment part was given special attention in this code. A full methodology is suggested here. This goes significantly beyond the ISPS Code requirements. This example is not the only one. The European Commission (EC) recently suggested a directive on enhancing port security [32]. Annex I deals with the port security assessment. Although the specifications made there do not go beyond the ISPS requirements it is at least remarkable that the EC found it necessary to address this subject.

The question still remains why is special attention only paid to port security and not to ship security as well? Although ships are the weaker link in the security chain they still have an important part to play in the security framework. The lack of more specific guidelines disadvantages shipowners. Therefore more detailed guidelines should be designed for ships security assessments. These guidelines should address the following points:

- List of security incidents that ship crews can respond to depending on:
  - type of the ship;
  - type of the cargo;
  - size of the crew;
  - trading area.
- List of key shipboard operations (incl. safety measures) which have to be protected.

- List of restricted areas where special security measures should be introduced.

The above listed issues are just only a very general outline of key issues to be observed in more detailed guidelines. These guidelines would be in line with current developments on other maritime security related issues, i.e. port security. More communication of the different stakeholders in politics, shipping and research is needed to develop and implement such elaborate guidelines in shipping.

## Disclaimer

The views expressed in this paper are the personal views of the authors and not necessarily those of the employers of the authors.

## References

[1] International Ship and Port Facility Security Code; IMO Doc. SOLAS/CONF.5/34, 17 December 2002.

[2] NVIC. 10-02, Security Guidelines for Vessels; United States Coast Guard, 21 October 2002. http://www.uscg.mil/hq/g-m/nvic/02/10-02.pdf

[3] International Management Code for the Safe Operation of Ships and for Pollution Prevention (International Safety Management (ISM) Code); IMO Doc. A. 18/Res. 741, 17 November 1993.

[4] North of England P&I Club, The Exercise of Due Diligence in Employing Crew. *Signals – the Loss Prevention Newsletter for North of England Members*, Issue 50, p. 6, January 2003. http://195.173.17.24/risk/publications/newsletters/pdf/signals50.pdf

[5] Emerson, S.D. & Nadeau, J., A Coastal Perspective on Security. *Journal of Hazardous Materials*, 104, p. 4, 2003.

[6] Measures to Enhance Maritime Security, Training and Certification Requirements for Company and Port Facility Security Officers, Report of the Working Group; IMO Doc. STW 36/WP. 2, 12 January 2005.

[7] Insight and Opinion; Lloyd's List, 7 May 2003.

[8] International Maritime Bureau, *Piracy and Armed Robbery against Ships: Annual Report 1 January-31 December 2004*, ICC-IMB: Essex, 2005.

[9] Mejia, M., Maritime Gerrymandering: Dilemmas in Defining Piracy, Terrorism, and other Acts of maritime Violence. *Journal of International Commercial Law*, 2(2), p. 165, 2003.

[10] Reports on Stowaway Incidents: Annual Statistics for the Years 2002 and 2003; IMO Doc. FAL. 2/Circ. 83, p. 11, 12 July 2004.

[11] Eales, B., Getting away with Murder? *Fairplay*, pp. 16-18, 18 November 2004; also Moore, A., Crime on the high Seas. *Fairplay*, pp. 18-19, 18 November 2004.

[12] United States Coast Guard (USCG), *Port State Control in the United States: annual report 2004*, USCG: Washington, 2005.

[13] The Paris Memorandum of Understanding on Port State Control, *Annual Report 2004: Changing Course*, Paris MoU on PSC: Rotterdam, p. 46, 2005.

[14] Memorandum of Understanding on Port State Control in the Asia-Pacific Region, *Annual Report on Port State Control in the Asia- Pacific Region 2004*, Tokyo MoU on PSC: Tokyo, p. 3, 2005.

[15] International Maritime Bureau, *Piracy and Armed Robbery against Ships: Report for the Period 1 January-31 March 2005*, ICC-IMB: Essex, pp. 8-9, 2005.

[16] Andrewatha, A. & Stone, Z., English Maritime Law Update. 35 *J. of Mar. L. & Com.* 369.

[17] Dixon v. Sadler (1839), 5 *M & W* 414.

[18] Phipps v. ss Santa Maria, 418 *F.*2d 615-617 (5th. Cir. 1969).

[19] Rodriguez, A.J. & Hubbard, M.C., The International Safety Management (ISM) Code: A New Level of Uniformity, 73 *Tul. L. Rev.* 1585.

[20] F.C. Bradley & Sons Ltd. v. Federal Steam Navigation Co. (1926), 24 *Ll.L.Rep.* 446.

[21] Moor-Bick, J., The Fjord Wind (1999), 1 *Lloyd's Rep.* 307.

[22] Clark, J. (2000), 2 *Lloyd's Rep.* 191.

[23] Cresswell, M.R., The Eurasian Dream (2000), 1 *Lloyd's Rep.* 719.

[24] LLP, *A Guide to the Hague and Hague-Visby Rules*, LLP: London, 1985.

[25] The Toledo (1995), 1 *Lloyd's Rep.* 40.

[26] Hill, Taylor, Dickinson, *"ISM Code What if..." Shipping at a Glance, Guide: 4*, Hill Taylor, Dickinson: London, 2003.

[27] Norwegian Shipowners' Association (NSA), *Guideline for Performing Ship Security Assessment*, NSA: Oslo, 2003.

[28] Germanischer Lloyd, *Development and Implementation of a Methodology for the Performance of a Ship Security Assessment,* GL, Hamburg, 2003.

[29] Guidelines for Formal Safety Assessment (FSA) for Use in the IMO Rule-Making Process; IMO Doc. MSC/Circ. 1023, MEPC/Circ. 392, 5 April 2002.

[30] Guidelines on Places of Refuge for Ships in Need of Assistance; IMO Doc. A23/Res. 949, 5 March 2004.

[31] Code of Practice on Security in Ports; IMO/ILO, 2005. http://www.imo.org/includes/blastDataOnly.asp/data_id%3D8557/ILOIMOCODEDRAFTmesshp-cp-aEnglish.pdf

[32] Proposal for a Directive of the European Parliament and if the Council on enhancing Port Security; European Commission, 2004. http://europa.eu.int/eur-lex/en/com/pdf/2004/com2004_0076en01.pdf

# Estimation and allocation of security costs at the Port of Boston

T. Campbell, R. V. Cellucci & T. Wellman
*Massachusetts Maritime Academy*

## Abstract

Several studies have been undertaken to assess the economic implications of ISPS with emphasis on risk management and cost control in shipping. Attempts have been made to explore the information management issues that relate to compliance with ISPS code and other related regulatory requirements. According to an OECD estimate, implementation of the ISPS Code will cost vessel operators $1.28 billion in the first year and $730 million a year thereafter. Our paper attempts to identify all costs associated with implementing the ISPS code in the port of Boston, while at the same time it focuses on distributing those monetary amounts in a fair and efficient manner to all parties involved in supporting the location's maritime sector. The security costs will be estimated with the aid of surveys, available data and econometric techniques. We also will estimate the adverse economic impact that will occur to various stakeholders should a major breach of security occur. Based on these figures, the paper will attempt to build a game theoretical model to calculate how the implementation costs are to be allocated to the parties concerned. The possibility of extending the model to other ports both in the USA, and in other countries will also be addressed.
*Keywords: ISPS code, compliance, implementation costs, ports.*

## References

[1] Khalid Bichou The ISPS Code and The Cost of Port Compliance: *'An Initial Logistics and Supply Chain Framework for Port Security Assessment and Management'* Maritime Economics & Logistics (2004) 6, pp. 322–348.
[2] http://www.oecd.org/dataoecd/19/61/18521672.pdf

*Paper not available at time of going to press.*

# Critical success factors of effective security management: a survey of Vietnamese maritime transport service providers

T.-V. Vinh & D. Grewal
*School of Maritime Management and Logistics,*
*Australian Maritime College, Tasmania, Australia*

## Abstract

In this study, based on the analysis of the nature of security threats, we place the three corner stones for the effective management of security in maritime transport: quality management (QM), risk management (RM), and business continuity management (BCM). A conceptual model of critical success factors of effective security management is devised following this reasoning. The model is further analysed and discussed following the analysis of a survey conducted among three main groups of maritime transport service providers in Vietnam: shipping companies, port operators, and freight forwarders/NVOCCs towards this research issue. Findings from the survey proved that all proposed 24 critical success factors are valid and should be used as critical factors for success in effectively managing security in maritime transport, so as to satisfy security requirements while enhancing other business objectives. The confirmed implication of this research is that effective security management can be achieved by employing critical success factors derived from the fundamental principles of quality, risk and business continuity management.
*Keywords: critical success factor, quality management, risk management, business continuity management, effective security management.*

## 1 Introduction

In recent years, the issue of maritime security has become a major concern on the international maritime agenda. Maritime security dates back to early maritime history under the themes of piracy and cargo theft and now includes also stowaways, people and drug trafficking, information security and, of course, maritime terrorism after the September 11$^{th}$ event. There have been some arguments elsewhere that heightened security measures would hamper international trade and have negative impacts on business results. However, from the management point of view, security threats in maritime transport should be viewed as one of the risks in the organisation's risk profile. The objective of security management is to support the organisations in achieving their business goals and objectives. The management of security in maritime transport is therefore, in fact, a management and business issue rather than the compliance with international security conventions. With this background, one of the fundamental questions in security management is how to achieve effective security management, e.g. satisfying security requirements while enhancing other business objectives, such as service quality or operational efficiency. In other words, it is important to identify and comprehend the critical success factors (CSFs) for the effective management of security in maritime transport. In this paper, we aim to seek the answer to that question. The remainder of this paper is organised as follows. First, the fundamental background for this research is presented in that three approaches to effective security management are analysed and discussed. Based on this, the critical success factors (CSFs) of effective security management are identified. Empirical validation of these CFSs is presented next with the research methodology described and findings discussed. The paper concludes with recommendations for future extension of this research.

## 2 Fundamental background

### 2.1 The QM approach to effective security management

#### 2.1.1 Security design and process control

In quality management, in-process quality control and management is needed as a supplementary philosophy to prevent it from the source so as to ensure that variability during the process is driven out. Similarly, the prevention from the source in security management must be followed by in-process control in order to monitor shipments while they are in transit and thus significantly reduce the risks of a shipment being tampered with, creating security breaches. In this respect, the primary objective of process control in the management of supply chains and maritime transport security is to have a better visible control of shipments while they are en route, so as to ensure the integrity of physical shipments and their associated information. A quality system like Poka-Yoke can be effectively applied to security management so that operating processes of shipment movements can be controlled and managed for security purposes. These processes must be designed and built in so that any tampering of the shipments has to be detected, and mitigation measures are immediately deployed in due time. Like quality, security should be built in from a project inception. Besides, security should be integrated into the overall business policy and plans and should not be conducted as a separate issue. This approach to security management will help make security accepted as part of the daily business operations.

#### 2.1.2 Total organisational focus in security management

In quality management, it is seen that the total organisational focus in terms of the commitment and leadership of senior management, and the involvement, empowerment and training of employees is crucial so as to inspire a quality culture throughout the organisation, thus contributing to improved quality. The bottom line in this respect is that senior management realises that the long-term benefits of quality far exceed the costs of conformance. Security, as it is traditionally defined in organisations, is one of the most pervasive problems that an organisation must address. Since security is a problem for the whole organisation, it simply is no longer effective or acceptable to manage it from a security department. Quality initiatives such as the Six Sigma process emphasise the awareness, focus, and dedication of everyone in the organisation to identifying and fixing quality problems, and such a total approach is what is needed in addressing security problems; Lee and Whang [1]. In fact, since the support by senior management for improving the quality of products and services is already in place in many organisations, what is important is that management executives realise the eventual return on their security investment in the form of greater efficiencies, better contingency planning against disruptions and improved levels of customer service Doak [2]. Like quality, the key to success in implementing security measures is the commitment and support from senior management so as to inspire the security culture throughout an organisation, thus promoting the involvement and empowerment of all employees in security matters. In this respect, teamwork is also critical, and people must work together to get security work done since no one person can secure a business. Like in quality management, the total organisational focus in security management is vital for the success of any security program. This total approach must start with the commitment of senior management and their security leadership, followed by the empowerment and involvement of all employees, supported by sufficient training in security matters.

### 2.1.3 Continuous security improvement cycle

Continuous improvement has been proved to be fundamental for success in quality management, especially in TQM. Since quality improvement is a process, organisations should strive for continuous efforts so as to drive all the variables out of the process and achieve a 'zero defect' quality goal. Together with the Six Sigma cycle, the PDCA (Plan-Do-Check-Act) cycle, commonly known as the Deming cycle, forms the conceptual basis of continuous improvement activities in many companies; Deming [3]. Since security is a process and not a product, the same approach should also be taken to effectively manage security, meaning that organisations have to strive for continuous security improvement (CSI).

This is based on the fact that security threats are not static, and therefore all necessary activities prepared to cope with them should also be dynamic. The CSI cycle begins with the planning, in which security threats are identified and their criticality and likelihood are determined, vulnerability is assessed and priority is assigned. The next stage is to develop, evaluate, and implement security policy, strategies, and plans to prevent and mitigate the effects of security breaches. As some security breaches may occur, the next step is to verify whether policy, strategies and plans implemented have successfully prevented or mitigated the impacts of successful security incidents, as well as collect additional information from these incidents for further adjustment in the security risk assessment. The next stage of the cycle is to take action, meaning that proper adjustments are conducted so as to complete the security management cycle. From this moment, a new management cycle is taking place, taking into consideration all new inputs from the previous steps. The cycle will thus continue and become more and more finely-tuned for better security management. The CSI cycle is illustrated in Figure 1.

Figure 1: The Continuous Security Improvement (CSI) cycle.

## 2.2 Risk-based security management and its connection with Business Continuity Management (BCM)

There is an interrelationship between risk management and BCM. Since security risk is a component of the organisation's risk portfolio, it is argued that the management of security should be based on sound risk management, and business continuity should also be one of the expected outcomes of security management. Indeed, the literature review has suggested that security management must be based on risk management in order to be effective, and the steps of the risk management process can be applied to address security risks. Broder [4] emphasises the benefits of risk-based security management, especially highlighting areas where greater (or lesser) security is needed through security risk identification, analysis and evaluation. ESPO [5] emphasises that a stable and reliable port brings risks under control, and believes that policies aimed at fighting terrorism should be clearly linked with other and existing initiatives aimed at fighting organised crime, piracy, fraud, smuggling and illegal immigration. Any measures and policies should furthermore be based on a serious assessment of the actual risks involved.

The steps of the risk management process have been woven into the security management process, in which security risks need to be identified, analysed and evaluated in order to provide the grounding for risk control strategies. Furthermore, the organisation also needs to develop a contingency plan as part of the process to help the organisation return its resilience, and this is clearly the expected outcome of security management in connection with BCM. The application of risk management in security risk management has been emphasised by many scholars and practitioners, especially the risk assessment to provide the background for risk control. A detailed study of vulnerability, criticality (consequence) and threat is necessary to formulate a security risk profile. It is argued that such a security risk assessment is the key to making IMO's ISPS Code effective. A risk-based security management process should also consist of four core elements: threat identification, risk assessment, acceptance criteria, and the implementation process of risk control. These are clearly the necessary steps of the risk management process so as to effectively manage security risks in transportation and maritime transport. Specifically, Iarossi [6] and Nolan [7] argue that an effective risk based security management process must take a holistic approach. There are three phases that must be considered within such an integrated process. First, it is necessary to identify all possible threat scenarios. Then the risk of each scenario must be characterised (the threat of each scenario must be assessed, the vulnerability must be analysed, the possible consequences of each scenario must be determined). Finally, the information gained from this security risk assessment must be used to adjust the planned risk management controls that are already in place or that should be developed to address normal operation risks. A prioritised, risk-based approach to security management is a critical element in determining practical and affordable solutions. Once the risks are identified, assessed, and prioritised, action plans can be developed to mitigate the risks.

In short, it can be seen that the management of security, as an element of the organisation's risk portfolio, should be based on a sound risk management approach and be closely related to BCM in order to be effective. In this regard, security management should adopt and integrate the fundamentals of RM into its management process. Security threats, vulnerability and criticality must be examined and the security acceptance level must be set so as to provide a firm background for the implementation of any security optimisation strategy. The organisation, in conducting these management processes, should also communicate and consult with its internal and external stakeholders. Moreover, these processes need to be continuously monitored and reviewed so as to provide new inputs to keep security management abreast of changing security threats and their probability of occurrence, and therefore, be valid and effective. In addition, the organisation should also address business continuity management as an integral part of its security management, and have in place the necessary processes and procedures so that it can return to resilience once a security breach is successful. With all of these in mind, one can argue that the RM approach to security management and consideration of its relationship with BCM would be powerful management weapons for the organisation in the quest of achieving its goals and objectives.

## 3 Identification of CSFs of effective security management

Security management is effective only when it helps the organisation to achieve its goals and objectives by facilitating efficient business operations while protecting the organisation's resources from security threats. In this connection, it has been argued that the QM and RM approaches to security management

(SM) can contribute valuable inputs. QM philosophies and principles are now adopted in not only SM but also RM and BCM, while both RM and BCM not only have an interrelationship with each other but also affect the good/effective SM. Today, many organisations are adopting a risk-based approach to security, and the move to a risk-based paradigm is a catalyst for moving security from a technical specialty to an organisational competency. Moreover, since modern organisations must continually adapt to their environment and emerging risks – risks that perhaps unknown until the organisation is impacted by them, it is critical that the organisation view security in the context of the larger picture - security as one of organisational or enterprise resilience. A resilience approach transforms the basic premise of security – that of 'locking down' an asset so that it is free from harm or attack – to one that positions security as a contributor to strengthening the organisation's ability to adapt to new risk environments and accomplish its missions. The three approaches of QM, RM and BCM to security management as discussed above lead to the following proposed critical success factors (CSFs) for the effective management of security in any organisation, including maritime transport service providers as summarised in Table 1.

# 4 Empirical validation of CSFs

## 4.1 Research methodology

In order to empirically validate the 24 CSFs as identified previously a survey instrument was developed. This instrument was developed on the basis of an exhaustive review of the literature and the subsequent research model. It has been refined several times based on the pilot study findings and on the comments and suggestions of the experts in the field. The instrument has been so developed in order to maximally capture all the CSFs of effective security management. The questionnaire begins with the guidelines in which the concept of effective security management is carefully explained, and the confidentiality of respondents is assured. The questions with respect to the various CSFs were jumbled and arranged in a random order in the instrument so as to avoid order bias. The respondents were asked to indicate their perception of the importance of each critical success factor of ESM on a five-point scale (from 1 indicating not at all important to 5 indicating very important). Since the unit of analysis is the maritime transport service providing organisations, the target population in this research is, therefore, encompassing the groups of shipping companies, port operators and freight forwarders/NVOCCs which are providing maritime transport services in Vietnam. The sampling frame for this research is constructed from the directory of shipping companies, port operators and freight forwarders/NVOCCs in Vietnam listed in the Visaba Times – Vietnam Shipping and Logistics Review. This publication is a well-known and prestigious source of specialised information on maritime transport and the logistics business in Vietnam, and recognised by both professionals and governmental officials in the field. A list of 197 maritime transport service providing organisations from the directory in this publication, including 66 shipping companies, 49 port operators and 82 freight forwarders/NVOCCs, was used as the mailing list for this research. By the cut-off date, there were 119 returned questionnaires, including 42 from shipping companies, 43 from port operators, and 34 from freight forwarders. This represents a 60% response rate. The high response rate is due to the personal contact approach used followed by periodic follow-ups over telephone and also personal visits.

Table 1: CSFs of effective security management.

| No. | Critical success factor | Code |
|---|---|---|
| 01 | Well-defined and clear security accountability and responsibility at all levels of the organisation | CSF1 |
| 02 | Documented security processes and procedures | CSF2 |
| 03 | Security threats, critical resources to be secured and impacts of security threats identified, analysed and evaluated | CSF3 |
| 04 | Minimum security requirements for resources identified and risk acceptance level established | CSF4 |
| 05 | Security risk levels clearly defined | CSF5 |
| 06 | Security risk mitigation strategies and plans in place and clearly understood by operators | CSF6 |
| 07 | Resource allocation plan to mitigate security risks based on defined security risk levels | CSF7 |
| 08 | Contributions of employees, business partners and related agencies to security policy, strategies, and plans, including their changes if any, taken as essential inputs | CSF8 |
| 09 | Emphasis on monitoring and reviewing all security processes and procedures, at all organisational levels | CSF9 |
| 10 | Continuous review and improvement of security policy, strategies, plans, processes and procedures | CSF10 |
| 11 | Use of specific organisational structures (security improvement committee, work teams, etc) to support security improvement | CSF11 |
| 12 | Long-term benefits of security recognised by senior management executives | CSF12 |
| 13 | Security policy, strategies and plans actively directed by senior management executives | CSF13 |
| 14 | Allocation of adequate resources to security improvement efforts, including training | CSF14 |
| 15 | Preparedness of the senior management executives to remove the root causes of security problems | CSF15 |
| 16 | Employees encouraged to find and provide feedback on security problems | CSF16 |
| 17 | Employee involvement in the design and planning of the security policy, strategies and plans | CSF17 |
| 18 | Security training viewed as a long-term investment and service quality improvement facilitator | CSF18 |
| 19 | Security policy, strategies and plans integrated in overall business policy, strategies and plans | CSF19 |
| 20 | Security processes and procedures integrated in daily operation processes and procedures | CSF20 |
| 21 | Technology-based solutions to security problems understood by senior management as not the only answer | CSF21 |
| 22 | Security of information viewed as important as security of physical resources (assets, people, etc) | CSF22 |
| 23 | Availability of detailed contingency plans to follow in the event of security breaches or incidents, continuously reviewed and updated | CSF23 |
| 24 | Availability of detailed recovery plans to maintain business resilience after security breaches or incidents | CSF24 |

The following hypothesis was subsequently formulated:
*The CSFs of effective security management in maritime transport are the 24 identified items stated above.*

## 4.2 Analysis of findings

In order to test the hypothesis and validate the research CSFs, a number of statistical analyses have been conducted using the SPSS version 11.0 software. The descriptive statistics provide an overview concerning the variables (here are the critical success factors) in the survey. In this respect, the mean and standard deviation of each variable are calculated to see whether the variable could be accepted by the respondents and exist as a critical success factor in question. Based on the mean scores of all variables, a ranking order is established accordingly to reveal the magnitude of importance of each factor. Table 2 illustrates these descriptive statistics.

Table 2: Perceived importance of critical success factors.

| Critical success factor | Mean | Std. Deviation | Rank | Critical success factor | Mean | Std. Deviation | Rank |
|---|---|---|---|---|---|---|---|
| CSF23 | 4.66 | 0.56 | 1 | CSF6 | 4.15 | 0.48 | 13 |
| CSF2 | 4.58 | 0.57 | 2 | CSF19 | 4.15 | 0.73 | 14 |
| CSF24 | 4.56 | 0.62 | 3 | CSF8 | 4.13 | 0.50 | 15 |
| CSF5 | 4.44 | 0.58 | 4 | CSF22 | 4.02 | 0.64 | 16 |
| CSF14 | 4.42 | 0.54 | 5 | CSF15 | 4.02 | 0.68 | 17 |
| CSF1 | 4.42 | 0.60 | 6 | CSF16 | 3.99 | 0.56 | 18 |
| CSF13 | 4.39 | 0.55 | 7 | CSF10 | 3.87 | 0.62 | 19 |
| CSF7 | 4.34 | 0.57 | 8 | CSF9 | 3.85 | 0.63 | 20 |
| CSF4 | 4.28 | 0.52 | 9 | CSF21 | 3.73 | 0.65 | 21 |
| CSF3 | 4.25 | 0.52 | 10 | CSF18 | 3.64 | 0.62 | 22 |
| CSF12 | 4.21 | 0.69 | 11 | CSF11 | 3.52 | 0.57 | 23 |
| CSF20 | 4.16 | 0.74 | 12 | CSF17 | 3.34 | 0.78 | 24 |

The standard deviation in response to each CSF is seen as quite small. It is seen that all the CSFs of the effective security management proposed are accepted by the respondents, in which CSF17 (Employee involvement in design and planning of security policy, strategies and plans) with the lowest mean score of 3.34 is still above the measurement scale with 3 being neutral. The most important CSF is CSF23 (availability of detailed contingency plans to follow in the event of security breaches or incidents, continuously reviewed and updated), followed by CSF2 (documented security processes and procedures), and CSF24 (availability of detailed recovery plans to maintain business resilience after security breaches or incidents). Among these three most important critical success factors, two (CSF23 and CSF24) are related to incident handling and response within the scope of business continuity management. Moreover, it is emphasised that these factors are closely connected to quality management, as the contingency and recovery plans should be continuously reviewed and updated.

The respondents also highly rated documented security processes and procedures, and well-defined and clear security accountability and responsibility at all levels of the organisation (CSF1 and CSF2) are ranked as the second and sixth most important factors. Factors related to security risk assessment and risk-based security mitigation strategies and plans are also perceived among the most important critical success factors of effective security management in this survey. Specifically, respondents view the security risk levels clearly defined (CSF5) as the fourth most important factor, while other factors involving risk management (CSF3, CSF4, CSF6, CSF7) are also ranked as the eighth, ninth, tenth and thirteenth most important factors. It is noted that respondents view these as critically important ones since security risks should be clearly identified, analysed and assessed and these assessment should be the foundation upon which strategies and plans are based.

Factors related to the senior management's commitment and leadership are also highly appreciated by the respondents in that CSF14 and CSF13 are ranked as the fifth and seventh most important factors. It can be seen that effective security management requires not only the involvement and leadership of the senior management, but more importantly, that they should provide adequate resources for security improvement, including training as well. As anticipated, factors related to security design and process control (CSF20 and CSF19) are also highly ranked by the respondents being the twelfth and fourteenth most important critical success factors with mean scores of 4.16 and 4.15 respectively. In this respect, it is confirmed through the survey that effective security management is attributed by the security policy, strategies, plans, processes and procedures integrated in the overall business ones and should not be designed separately from the overall picture of business operations. Other factors involving communication and consultation with stakeholders, holistic approach and employee empowerment (CSF8, CSF22 and CSF16) also received relatively high ranking as critical success factors of effective security management. The survey also reveals that the quality principle of continuous improvement is recommended in security management, in that security policy, strategies, plans, processes and procedures should be continuously reviewed and improved. This factor received a mean score of 3.87 and was ranked in nineteenth place. The least important CSF, as ranked by the respondents, was CSF17, employee involvement in design and planning of security policy, strategies and plans, although its mean score was still higher than the average consensus level in the scale. This magnitude of importance may be explained as, although employees should be encouraged to find and provide feedback on security problems (CSF16), the designs and planning of security policy, strategies and plans require the expertise and skills of specialised staff so that not all normal employees can be qualified and involved. Nevertheless, it can be seen from table 3 above that all these 24 CSFs are essential so that security in maritime transport can be effectively managed. In short, the hypothesis has been empirically tested and the critical success factors of effective security management have also been validated.

## 5 Conclusion

In summary, the proposed hypothesis has been empirically tested. The statistical analysis conducted in the survey has proved that this hypothesis is accepted in the context of Vietnamese maritime transport service providers. All 24 proposed factors are accepted as CSFs of effective security management in maritime transport with the lowest mean score of 3.34, which is above the average score of the scale. These CSFs are derived from the QM, RM and BCM approaches to security management. Among the most important factors, ones related to incident handling and response (CSF23 and CSF24) are perceived as the most and the third important factors, and have higher rankings than those involving security risk assessment and risk-based security mitigation strategies and plans (CSF3, CSF4, CSF5, CSF6 and CSF7). This finding more or less indicates that Vietnamese maritime transport service providers currently focus on 'situational' and short-term factors. Among the identified CSFs, the five most important ones are the following:

- Availability of detailed contingency plans to follow in the event of security breaches or incidents, continuously reviewed and updated (mean 4.66)
- Documented security processes and procedures (mean 4.58)
- Availability of detailed recovery plans to maintain business resilience after security breaches or incidents (mean 4.56)
- Security risk levels clearly defined (mean 4.44)
- Allocation of adequate resources to security improvement efforts, including training (mean 4.42)

In short, it has been empirically tested that all proposed 24 CSFs are valid and should be used as critical factors for success in effectively managing security in maritime transport, so as to satisfy security requirements while enhancing other business objectives. The confirmed implication of this research is that effective security management can be achieved by employing critical success factors derived from the fundamental principles of quality, risk and business continuity management. This research can also be extended by being conducted in various other social contexts in order to maximise its generalisability.

## References

[1] Lee, H. L. and Whang, S., Higher supply chain security with lower cost: lessons from Total Quality Management, http://gobi.stanford.edu /ResearchPapers/Library/RP1824.pdf, 2003.

[2] Doak, R., Security measures & growing quality logistics practices, *Logistics quarterly*, **9(1)**, http://www.lq.ca/issues/spring2003/articles/article04.html, 2003.

[3] Deming, W. E., *Out of the crisis*, MIT Technology Center for Advanced Engineering Study: Cambridge, MA, 1986.

[4] Broder, J. F., *Risk analysis and the security survey*, Butterworth Publishers: USA, 1984.

[5] ESPO, Port and maritime security, www.espo.be/policy/initialviewsFINAL.pdf, 2002.

[6] Iarossi, F, J., Creating a safe and secure environment for the marine transportation of energy, http://www.absconsulting.com/news/fji-nov 182002.html, 2002.

[7] Nolan, T. M., Security and safety: real responses to maritime security threats, www.socp.org/archive/3-5-03/presentation-3-5-03/tn_abs.ppt, 2003.

# EU Phare Twinning project "strengthening enforcement of maritime safety"

D. Heering
*Estonian Maritime Academy, Estonia*

## Abstract

During the year 2000, about 6 million passengers and around 35 million tons of cargo was handled by Estonian ports. Twenty million tons of it was oil products, which can be defined as a dangerous cargo. It has been estimated that the maritime traffic will increase two-fold in 2010–2015. In addition to vessels visiting Estonian ports, a large number of tankers visiting new Russian ports sail along the Estonian coastline. The risk of accidents is high due to the high concentration of traffic, the number of substandard vessels and the difficult navigational conditions, especially in winter. Twenty seven casualties or incidents occurred in Estonian waters or involved vessels under the Estonian flag in 2000. These indicate the importance of making Flag State Control (FSC) and Port State Control (PSC) more efficient.

Estonian Maritime Administration (MA) and Estonian Maritime Academy (EMA) prepared and carried out the EU Phare Twinning project "Strengthening Enforcement of Maritime Safety". The duration of the project was 24 months and it included 9 sub-projects and an investment component, which included the procurement of a VTS simulator. The objective of the project was to improve the skills of the personnel of the Ministry of Economic Affairs and Communications, the Estonian Maritime Administration and the Estonia Maritime Academy. The main partners in the project were the Finnish Maritime Administration (FMA) and the Centre for Maritime Studies (CMS) at the University of Turku. The junior partner of the project was the Maritime and Coastguard Agency (MCA) of the United Kingdom. In addition to experts from FMA, CMS and MCA, experts from Denmark, Germany and Sweden took part in the project. The budget of the project amounted to €1.7 million.

*Keywords: Phare Twinning, maritime safety, VTS, GOFREP, flag state control, port state control, ism, winter navigation, continual training, simulator.*

# 1 Introduction

Estonia has a very long maritime tradition. After the Soviets won their long-lasting control of this region in 1944, they proceeded to shut down the region's domestic maritime industry. The closure of the sea affected the entire region's way of life. Before the Red regime, Estonia's merchant fleet had 340 boats with total capacity of nearly a quarter-million tons. Two hundred sixty-three registered shipping companies were operating out of 26 international ports. On a per capita basis, Estonia was the third-largest commercial marine power on the Baltic Sea. Sweden and Denmark were ahead of Estonia, Germany, Poland and USSR were well behind.

During the occupation time, hundreds of fishing boats were nationalised, almost all international ports were closed, with only three remaining open, ship owners, captains and many seamen were deported to Siberia. The islands of Saaremaa and Hiiumaa were cleared of people and made closed regions. It has been calculated, that about 12 million dollars (calculated in 1940 dollars) in marine assets were confiscated.

On December 31, 1940, the Waterways Department (name of the Maritime Administration that time) had to conclude its work when the Ministry of Defence of the Soviet Union assumed the responsibility. The hydrography and aids to navigation sector was subordinated to the Hydrography Service of the Soviet Union Navy. Cartography and navigational information was subordinated to the Navy's central administrative board.

On December 1, 1989, the Estonian Maritime Administration took over full responsibility for maritime issues. It was the time to start building up the system again.

Traffic on the Gulf of Finland has been increasing every year since. In year 2000 about 6 million passengers were handled by the Port of Tallinn alone. Thirty-five million tons of cargo was handled by Estonian ports and 20 million tons of it was oil products, which can be defined as dangerous cargo. There were 8400 port visits to Estonian ports that year, which makes over 23 visits per day. There were around 50 arrivals/departures of passenger vessels per day during the peak season. Today there are 40 departures from Tallinn alone. The average number of tanker calls was 3-4 per day. By the years 2010-2015, the maritime traffic will increase almost two times to about 105000 vessels. The will be about 290 vessels transiting the Gulf per day. During the summer period the number can be even higher.

Do these numbers scare you? I am scared... It is only a matter of time before something big happens. Are we prepared to act quickly and efficiently? Do we have enough resources; are we trained properly to respond quickly?

# 2 Preparation of the project

Estonian Maritime Academy and Estonian Maritime Administration decided to start with the EU Phare Twinning project to improve the maritime safety in Estonia by improving the skills of the personnel of the Ministry of Economic

Affairs and Communications, Estonian Maritime Administration. Additionally was decided to purchase a simulator for training of the VTS operators and future GOFREP (Gulf of Finland Reporting) operators. There were numerous objectives and they were very ambitious. The duration of the project was 2 years and during that time 9 components or sub-projects were planned to be carried out.

I joined the project in autumn 2002, when the project was already approved by the European Commission. It was time to choose the partner(s) with whom to implement the idea. I have maritime background – 2 years of sailing worldwide as a mate on Dutch-flagged ships. I graduated Estonian Maritime Academy in year 2000 and had decided to bind myself with the sea and the maritime sector. It was very challenging to start working as an Estonian project leader of this big project.

There were 5 proposals from the “older” EU member states: Sweden, Denmark, Germany, Spain and Finland together with United Kingdom. We met with all the delegations from each country at the Ministry of Transport and Communications in Tallinn and later at the Delegation of the European Commission to Estonia. It was a difficult decision to make, as the proposals were all good and the people in the key organisations were involved in the future project implementation. Finally, the consortium of Finland and United Kingdom was selected as the partner of the project. From Finland two institutions were taking part: Finnish Maritime Administration and Centre for Maritime Studies of the University of Turku. From United Kingdom Maritime and Coastguard Agency was the junior partner. Additionally experts from Denmark, Sweden and Germany were invited to participate in the project.

It took almost 9 months to prepare the Twinning Covenant. It included details of the administrations and departments involved, officials responsible for different components and tasks, the availability of the appropriate office space and logistics, the budgetary resources and the timetable for the work to be carried out. It was the contractual framework for implementing the project and specified the obligations both the Member State and the Candidate Country. On July 25, 2003 we got the notification from the EU Commission to start with the implementation of the project and on the August 3, 2003 the Pre-Accession Adviser (now Resident Twinning Adviser) moved to Tallinn, Estonia to live for two years. This was the starting point.

## 3 Implementation of the project

### 3.1 Objectives of the project

The project had as its overall objective the improvement of maritime safety. This called for the following:

1) Analysis of national maritime safety legislation and assistance in harmonising it with EC Directives. Adaptation process initiated by Estonian authorities;

2) Reviews and recommendations concerning operational procedures & management structure of the Maritime Administration (MA) for monitoring enforcement of maritime safety standards being finalized and delivered to the Maritime Administration (in particular with regard to vessel traffic service, Flag State Control, International Safety Management Code, Port State Control, quality management issues). Implementation process started by the MA;
3) Training of Estonian Maritime Administration's staff through Twinning, seminars and study-visits completed, with about 80 certificates issued. Process of implementing new procedures and methods of work initiated by the MA;
4) Reviews and recommendations concerning national winter navigation policy. Additional investment needs completed and delivered to the MA. Implementation process initiated by the MA;
5) Preparation of four new continual training course curricula for the MA staff completed and delivered to the MA and the Estonian Maritime Academy. Preparation of new training activities, based on the new curricula started by the Estonian Maritime Academy;
6) Support concerning establishment of a sustainable and continual training capacity at the Maritime Academy, for delivering training to the MA on basis of a new HRD plan, finalized. Enhancement of the continual training capacity initiated by the Estonian Maritime Academy.

### 3.2 Components of the project

Project consisted of 2 different contracts: the Twinning project and investment in infrastructure. The Twinning part includes 9 components: vessel traffic service, winter navigation, quality management, human resource development, maritime legislation, Flag State Control, Port State Control and the carriage of dangerous goods, International Safety Management code and training organisation. For every component, there was a responsible person for the topic from the Member State as well from the Estonian side. An exact timetable was drawn for every component and agreed with by all involved persons from the administrations. All components consisted of a detailed work plan, with expert names involved and a budget.

### 3.3 The budget of the project

Total budget of the Twinning part was, by the Covenant, 1,135,700€ (Phare contribution) and 130,000€ (Estonian co-financing). Phare financing for the investment part was 280,000€ and Estonian part was 115,000€. Altogether it amounted to 1,660,700€. Estonian co-financing was divided between the Estonian Maritime Administration and the Estonian Maritime Academy.

### 3.4 Project management

The main reason why the project was so successful is the very good and open cooperation among the Member States, the Estonian project leaders and the administrations. Each Twinning project has a Resident Twinning Adviser (RTA), who worked full-time in the candidate country or in new member state to implement the project and along with a senior Project Leader responsible for the overall coordination of the project. Very useful tool of project management appeared to be weekly RTA meetings with beneficiary contact persons from Estonian Maritime Administration and Estonian Maritime Academy. On those meetings the visits of the short-term experts (STE) and management issues were discussed. The full commitment of both Estonian and foreign experts involved was very high, e.g. the Director General of the Maritime Administration, Rector of the Maritime Academy and several Deputy Secretary Generals from the Ministry of Economic Affairs and Communications were participating on a regular basis.

On the Estonian side, the Programme Officer representing the Ministry of Economic Affairs and Communications was responsible for the overall project coordination, implementation management and local monitoring. There was an established Steering Committee (SC) by the MoEA&C to support the Estonian project leader on issues connected with monitoring the project activities and approving reports and the budget on Estonian side. The members of the committee were from Ministry of Finance, Delegation of the European Commission in Estonia, Ministry of Education and Research, Ministry of Economic Affairs and Communications, Estonian Maritime Administration and Estonian Maritime Academy. Meetings were held once every three months.

### 3.5 Work carried out

Altogether 29 experts from 5 "old" EU Member States took part in the implementation of the project. They carried out nearly 300 visits to Estonia during the 24 months. There were four maritime administrations involved: Finnish Maritime Administration, Maritime and Coastguard Agency of the United Kingdom, Danish Maritime Authority and Swedish Maritime Administration.

Twinning is the principal tool of pre-accession assistance for Institution Building. It aims to help the candidate countries in their development of modern and efficient administrations, with organizational structure, human resources and management skills needed to implement the *acquis communautaire* to the same standards as Member States. The Estonian Maritime Administration and Finnish Maritime Administration were acting like "twins". Everyday there was close cooperation between the experts of the two administrations, an exchange of expertise and experiences. Within 5 project components, 8 study visits to the EU Member State administrations and training centres were carried out. A considerably higher amount of workshops were carried out by the short-term experts than was planned in the Covenant. All involved persons from the beneficiary administrations were working on this project in addition to their everyday work. But everybody knew the importance of the project and was fully committed. By the Covenant 106 workshops were planned. The actual number of the workshops was 257. It means that the colleagues from the EU Member State countries and Estonia were willing to work more and gain more.

### 3.6 Results

The results of the Phare project can be divided into two groups: planned and additional values. By the end of the project, 100% all guaranteed results were achieved. The main results achieved of the nine components were as follows:

#### 3.6.1 Vessel Traffic Service – VTS

Finnish VTS experts delivered and introduced the Finnish legislative acts concerning the VTS and GOFREP (Gulf of Finland Reporting). During the project, a Document of Joint Procedures (DJP) was developed and introduced to both Finnish and Estonian operators. Coverage of the Automatic Identification Systems (AIS) was determined in order to avoid duplication by Estonian and Finnish equipment. Three study visits were made to Finland, of which two visits were additional to the Covenant plan. A preliminary study was prepared by the short-term experts concerning the VTS activity, including a short-term study of the Estonian traffic profile and maritime traffic in ports and fairways. Staff of the VTS department was given advice on the preparation of qualification requirements and manuals for VTS operators, in conformity with IMO. Other requirements were carried out by the STE's in workshops dealing with training and certification of VTS personnel and a joint test of the GOFREP system was carried out.

An additional and very important result is the effective cooperation now present between Finnish and Estonian VTS operators. Additionally, the Estonian side succeeded to finish contract 2 of the project: investment in infrastructure. A VTS simulator was procured before the end of the project and 4 new VTS operators were trained in Estonian Maritime Academy on the new simulator supplied by Transas Eurasia Ltd. and based on the new curriculum developed during the project in component 4 (human resource development).

#### 3.6.2 Winter navigation

Analysis and a preliminary study of the current situation of winter navigation services and the connecting infrastructure was carried out by the Finnish STE′s during workshops and field visits with Estonian colleagues. A training programme for the ice-breaker managers, operators, masters and mates of the Maritime Administration was drafted. A winter navigation concept for Estonia was drafted in cooperation with staff of Estonian Maritime Administration and Ministry of Economic Affairs and Communications. Additional results of a winter navigation component were practice for a period of 10 days by the Mater of I/B Tarmo in Finland onboard I/B Fennica. Together with Finnish STE's, the first ice-breaking seminar (Ice Day) for ports, operators, ship owners and civil servants was planned and arranged. This began the start of the regular seminars with the purpose to inform all parties about the icebreaking services in Estonia. For the first time, the information about the icebreaking services in Estonia for the coming season were published free of charge in the Finnish Maritime Administration's information booklet for the shipping industry.

### 3.6.3 Quality management system and development of organisational structure

In cooperation with German short-term experts, quality management indicators were established for the Maritime Administration in preparation for the upcoming external audit of the quality management system by the Lloyd's Register Quality Assurance Ltd. The indicators were fully approved during the audit. Many good proposals were given to the MA as to how to improve the work of auditors and how to delegate the different tasks among civil servants of the MA. Together with MA, colleagues STE's visited maritime training units in Estonia to assess the present situation and to develop possible recommendations. Based on the visits, a preliminary study was drafted with recommendations and conclusions.

### 3.6.4 Human resource development

Four training curricula were developed: a 10-day course curriculum for VTS operators, a 3-day continual training course curriculum in ISM relates issues, a 5-day course curriculum in flag state control and port state control, and a 3-day quality management training course curriculum for STCW purposes. "Training Need Analysis" was prepared and introduced to the Maritime Administration. Examples of Finnish and British solutions on drafting the human resource development plan and training policy were introduced in the workshops. Maritime Administration's quality management document, "Simplified Procurement Proceedings", was prepared which laid down the procedures for buying training services.

### 3.6.5 Legislation preparation

Principles and relevant practice on the regulative mechanism and the requirements of the *acquis communautaire* concerning maritime transport and safety, casualty investigation and common maritime rules was introduced by the STE during joint workshops with the staff of Maritime Administration, Ministry of Economic Affairs and Communications and Estonian Maritime Academy. British STE prepared an interim report on the current state of the implementation of EC legislation. The work of STE was completed before the accession of Estonia in EU.

### 3.6.6 Flag State Control (FSC)

Preliminary study about the current organisation of the flag state control services and the skills of inspectors was drafted by the STE's. The inspection procedures were evaluated and advice was given concerning development of ship inspection methods and manuals. Some recommendations made by the experts have been considered in the amendments to the Maritime Safety Act, which entered into force on June 3, 2005. One study visit was carried out to the Finnish Maritime Administration Headquarters concerning FSC issues and the plan approval services of the FMA.

### 3.6.7 Port State Control (PSC)

The staff of Dangerous Goods Section of the Maritime Administration was advised by the Finnish and British short-term experts concerning the EC legislative requirements, including the corresponding preparation of methods and manuals for inspection of ships carrying dangerous goods. Information databases used in the Finnish Maritime Administration and the Maritime and Coastguard Agency (MCA) were introduced. Two study visits were organised for the Estonian civil servants to Finland and to UK.

### 3.6.8 International safety management

The Finnish and British experts evaluated the current situation and skills of the inspectors and advised the staff on the development of ship inspection methods and manuals.

One ISM auditor of the Maritime Administration spent 2 periods with the Maritime and Coastguard Agency auditors in British shipping companies (five days) and onboard ships (10 days). It was an additional benefit not planned in the Covenant.

### 3.6.9 Organisation of continual training

A preliminary study of the current situation was drafted by the Finnish experts. During the joint workshops, topics were introduced and given advice on multimedia delivered training (MMDT) solutions and possibilities of e-Learning. Also, on organisation and management issues, on the continual training courses as well as on budgeting and cost calculation and planning a course and seminar. Additionally, a study visit for training staff from the Estonian Maritime Academy and the Estonian Maritime Administration was organised to Turku University in Finland.

## 4 Conclusions

During these two years, all objectives set up in the Twinning Covenant were fulfilled along with many additional results. Very good and strong cooperation among Finnish, British, Danish, German, Swedish and Estonian colleagues took place. From this Phare Twinning project, not only Estonia benefited, but every administration taking part in it got something important: good relationship with others administrations in EU member states.

In every component short-term experts have made many recommendations on how to improve the work of the administrations and training units. Already during project lifetime, the Estonian Maritime Administration and the Estonian Maritime Academy have started actively implementing some recommendations. For an example, when preparing the seminars of the Twinning project, the Estonian Maritime Administration and the Estonian Maritime Academy applied new methods introduced by the STE's. Quality management indicators were established and implemented and approved by the Lloyd's Register Quality Assurance Ltd. All results, conclusions and recommendations are pointed put in the Final Report of the project.

Phare Twinning project did not just improve the cooperation among the administrations and colleagues from the EU member states, but also internally among the Maritime Administration, the Estonian Maritime Academy and the ministries. Good personal and working relationships were developed during those years when working on the project.

## References

[1] Mylly, M., Siltanen, M., Heering, D., Ots, T., *Strengthening Enforcement of Maritime Safety, Final Report,* 2005

# The potential implications of radio frequency identification technology on marine security

B. Way
*School of Maritime Studies, Fisheries and Marine Institute of Memorial University of Newfoundland, Canada*

## Abstract

In the past, knowledge of the exact whereabouts of members of a ship's crew was generally beyond the capability of any ship's master. However, RFID (Radio Frequency Identification) tags are an emerging technology that may provide just such information within the proximity of a ship. An RFID tag is similar to a barcode containing a unique identifier for an asset, except that it contains a small integrated circuit chip with limited memory and a small antenna. This allows the RFID tag to be read or programmed at a distance using wireless signals. Driven by retailers such as Wal-Mart, RFID technology has rapidly evolved to allow for the accurate tracking of all types of physical assets through the supply chain. This escalating adoption of RFID technology has driven its cost down to the point where other spin-off applications are becoming feasible. In the post 9/11 marine world of the ISPS code, people are beginning to realize that RFID tags can be used to track mobile human assets, or ships' crews, just like others track physical assets. Apart from the obvious security applications, RFID technology can also alert that an emergency situation has arisen - for instance, if a member of the crew can no longer be located by the RFID system, it may be that he or she has fallen overboard. The challenge for marine industries will be how to best leverage this emerging technology within the world of the ISPS code so that it benefits seafarers without impinging on their rights and freedoms. This article will begin by examining RFID technology to reveal its implementation issues and technological limitations, along with current applications. Then before concluding, the paper will consider potential applications of RFID technology in marine security and safety.
*Keywords: RFID, radio frequency identification, ship's personnel, person tracking, maritime security.*

## 1 Introduction

Although described as "the first important technology of the twenty-first century," [1] radio frequency identification (RFID) technology originated during World War II when the British Air Force used it to identify bombers that were returning from night-time raids in Germany. Before RFID came along, there was no easy way to differentiate between British and German, or friend and foe, bombers in the dark, but by fitting each British bomber with a powered RF transmitter, it allowed British ground gunners to recognize them and not shoot them down [2]. Then, in 1948, Harry Stockman realized that the transmitter on the object being identified could be powered from the energy it received from the identifying device [3], and his findings formed the basis of passive RFID, which will be explained in more detail presently. Since that time, the technology has evolved significantly, with many uses of the technology prevalent in society. From mundane applications such as garage door openers to futuristic applications such as chic nightclubs implanting RFID tags under the skin of their VIP patrons, many predict that the application of RFID technology is about to explode as the price of the technology continues to fall.

This paper will begin with a brief introduction to RFID technology, followed by current implementations of the technology and some issues and limitations. Next, the paper will examine potential applications of the technology with respect to maritime security and safety before discussing some of the non-technical issues associated with this technology. A literature review is omitted due to the scant academic literature available on this topic.

## 2 RFID Technology

Much of the discussion in this section of the paper is based on Chapter 2 of *RFID – Applications, Security, and Privacy* [4]. RFID technology requires three elements – an RFID tag attached to the object being identified, an RFID reader that collects data from the RFID tag using radio waves, and an information processing unit, typically a computer, that can process the information received from the tag via the reader.

The tag itself consists of an antenna and an integrated circuit chip that contains a small amount of memory. Some tags are read-only and some are read-write. The simplest tags store data in the form of a 64- or 96-bit serial number, which is returned to the reader when the reader queries the tag. Some authors have compared RFID tags to barcodes, in that each can store data that can be read by a reader. However, the information storage capacity of a barcode is far less than that of an RFID tag. Also, barcodes must have a close and direct line of sight to a barcode reader, whereas RFID tags can be read at some distance and do not have to be "seen" by an RFID reader to be successfully read.

To contrast the difference, with a barcode each can of Campbell's chicken soup produced will have the same barcode, which identifies two things – the fact that it is made by Campbell's and the fact that it is chicken soup. If RFID tags were used instead, each can could have a unique serial number that identified not only that it was Campbell's chicken soup, but also when and where it was manufactured and how long it had been sitting on the shelf. That is the level of sophistication that differentiates RFID technology from barcode technology. It is like comparing a computer made in the 1970's, when barcodes became widespread, to a computer made today, when RFID is beginning to spread.

The mode of operation for RFID technology is a call and response system whereby the reader sends out frequent queries, basically polling all tags within its radio range and asking "are you there?" to which any tag that receives the signal will respond with the data contained in its memory. If a tag does not respond, then it is not within the zone that is defined by the range of the reader in question. Of course, just because the tag receives a query from a reader, it does not mean that the reader will receive a response. In order for that to occur, each tag would have to possess the same transmitting power of the reader, making the tags bulky and impractical.

The range that a tag can transmit its data back to the reader depends on a number of factors, including the frequency in use and the size of the antenna. However, the most relevant factor is whether the RFID tag contains its own power source that it can use to transmit. There are two main types of RFID tags in use today – passive and active. Passive tags contain no internal power source and must use the energy received in the query signal from the reader in order to generate a response signal, thus limiting their useful range. Active tags, on the other hand, contain a battery that powers the transmitter in the RFID tag, which allows for a much longer transmission range – meaning they can be read from a much longer distance than passive tags. Crawford and Goldman [5] state that the maximum range of passive tags ranges from a few inches up to 20 feet, and the maximum range for active tags ranges from 25 to 100 feet.

Passive tags are much smaller and cheaper than active tags, and they have become the tag of choice for most RFID applications in use today. To give the reader an idea of how small passive RFID tags have become, there are tags so thin that they can be inserted into a piece of paper and used to track documents; in the United States, the FDA has approved an RFID tag the size of a grain of rice that can be implanted subcutaneously in a human. On the other hand, active tags can be large compared to passive tags, mainly because active tags contain more powerful transmitters that require the active tags to carry a power source. An active tag is typically the length and width of a standard sized credit card, but roughly five times as thick [6].

Of course, once a tag is queried and responds with its data, which is nothing more than a binary number, then the data processing component of the system must take that data and use it to find further information on the object being identified. Using the Campbell's soup example given earlier, a reader might query a can on a grocery store shelf. The can would return its serial number, which would then be passed on to the store's stocking computer to determine when the can had entered the store. If the product was out of date, an alert could then be raised to remove the can from the shelf.

### 2.1 Issues with RFID implementation

Problems associated with RFID technology in its current state fall into two broad categories – technical and ethical. On the technical side, each manufacturer of RFID equipment is using proprietary standards, meaning that equipment and tags made by one company are not compatible with those of other companies. Until industry standards are developed and adopted, each RFID system purchased will be proprietary in nature, which could have costly implications for a purchaser if the manufacturer went out of business or if the product purchased was incompatible with an existing system. Also, while the adoption of RFID technology has been increasing, economies of scale are eventually expected to lower the prices of tags and equipment much further [7]. Furthermore, the resolution of the technology, or how precise the system can be in determining the exact location of an object, is currently limited. Basically, systems use geographic zones with one RFID reader per zone; the system can only tell the user in which zone, if any, an object is currently located. With technological advances, it may be possible to be much more precise in tracking assets [8].

On the ethical side of the equation, opponents of RFID technology cite privacy issues as one of their main concerns. In particular, they do not like the possibility that the products and clothes they buy may contain RFID tags that allow them to be tracked and identified without their knowledge [9]. In their current stage of development, RFID tags cannot be turned off, or 'killed' in RFID-speak, meaning that when Mr. Jones buys a pair of shoes containing an RFID tag, anyone with the appropriate reader can know when he walks into their store, and perhaps store it in a database. How this data is collected and used is another point of contention; will employers, for example, be able to subpoena information contained in such databases and use it to prove Mr. Smith was out shopping when he called in sick? In the extreme, privacy advocates argue that RFID is a technology that can lead to a 'Big Brother' type of society, where everyone can be monitored constantly. Finally, if/when RFID transaction devices, such as the Exxon Speedpass, are compromised, users of the technology could be vulnerable to significant financial losses.

## 3 Current applications of RFID technology

As mentioned above, one application for RFID technology is the Speedpass that is being used by Exxon gas stations. With his or her Speedpass in hand, an Exxon customer simply pulls up to a gas pump, waves the Speedpass in front of an RFID reader located in the gas pump, and then proceeds to fuel the car, take the printed receipt, and then drive away – it is the ultimate in gas station convenience. The RFID reader recognizes the serial number of the user's pass, and the transaction information is then fed to a database that contains the patron's credit card number, which is automatically charged the purchase price of the gasoline. While a novel application, opponents of RFID will point out that the system could be compromised, potentially leading to fraudulent purchases. This, in fact, is not an unlikely scenario given that several students at Johns

Hopkins University did crack the Speedpass and were successfully able to steal customers' Speedpass information without the customers' knowledge, and then purchase goods that were charged to the unsuspecting customers' accounts [10]. However, proponents of RFID technology might point out that RFID has been used in remote control garage door openers for many years, and that any vulnerability would long since have been exposed by enterprising thieves.

Along the lines of using RFID to activate a garage door for entry into a home, many offices and buildings are secured with electronic key access systems. Many of these systems use RFID technology to identify an electronic key holder and provide him or her access to only designated areas. These systems have been in use for many years and essentially use technology to replace a mechanical lock and key system. More recent applications, however, are harnessing the power of RFID to track and locate objects such as library books and luggage [11, 12]. A library book that has been placed on the wrong shelf could take a long time to locate using traditional means. The use of an RFID system to tag books would make locating a missing book much easier. Likewise, at some airports, luggage is now being tagged with RFID tags to aid in processing and tracking baggage.

### 3.1 RFID used to track people

A more controversial use of RFID technology is tracking people and their whereabouts. There are varying levels of tracking employed in different systems. For example, at one end of the spectrum, inmates in many prisons have now been fitted with non-removable bracelets that contain RFID tags [13]. This makes it possible to track the whereabouts of each inmate in the prison, and, more importantly, to ensure that no prisoners have left the premises prematurely. Another example of RFID used to track people is being employed in the nursery wards of hospitals. The 'Hugs' infant protection system sees every newborn fitted with an RFID bracelet to prevent infant abductions and parent-child mismatches. In fact, in July 2005, the system proved its worth by thwarting an abduction attempt at the Presbyterian Hospital in Charlotte, North Carolina [14]. In a different attempt at using RFID to monitor children's whereabouts, however, parents objected. A trial project saw a school in California issue mandatory ID badges to students that, unbeknown to students and parents, contained RFID tags. Tag readers were installed in each classroom to help teachers with attendance, but parents were not impressed when they learned that scanners had been placed in some washrooms as well. Due to protests, the project was cancelled [15].

## 4 Maritime security and safety

Given the current political state of affairs in the world, maritime security has never been more important. The regulatory environment of marine industries is likely to become more restrictive as governments look for new and better measures to counter terrorism; the implementation of the ISPS code is one step in that direction. What role RFID can and should play is an interesting question.

Very little work has been done in this area, meaning this section will deal mostly with what could be done, rather than what is being done today because there is very little RFID technology in use for the purposes of maritime security. With the current level of RFID technology, it would be possible to outfit every member of a ship's crew with an RFID tag that could be used to track his or her location on the ship. Given the limited range of passive tags, active tags would have to be utilized for the system to have any practical value. The current size and cost of active tags might make deploying such a system impractical at this time; however, that is likely to change over time. While this author does not necessarily advocate implementing such a system, even if it was practical today, some potential applications for security and safety at sea are apparent. From a safety perspective, if a crew member falls overboard, the RFID system would know instantly and sound an alert. Also, crew could be tracked to ensure that they are not entering areas for which they do not have security clearance, or an incapacitated crew member could be located during an emergency. Also, when it comes to getting ship's personnel on shore, passports containing RFID tags can help expedite the process. Such a system is currently being implemented by the United States [16].

## 4.1 Ethical issues with RFID technology

Tagging prisoners, infants, and children for the purpose of tracking them is one thing, but tagging free adults is a different matter. Whereas the former group has limited rights and privileges, the latter have come to expect a certain level of privacy and freedom. However, it is generally accepted that adults must forfeit some of that when they go to their place of work. For a person working on land, one might argue that the employer would have the right to monitor the movement of an employee while he or she is being paid to be at work, but that right would expire at the end of the work day when the employee goes home. In fact a company in the United States has developed a system that tracks restaurant employees to ensure that they wash their hands after visiting the washroom [17]. While the employee may not appreciate being monitored at work, is it unreasonable to expect employees to endure such monitoring on company time? This is one issue that must be resolved as RFID technologies become more widespread.

To extend the discussion to what occurs on a ship is more complicated, considering ships' crews do not leave to go home at the end of the work day. Members of a crew generally spend extended periods of time on the ship, which is split between being on or off duty. So, some would question whether the captain has the right to monitor crew members when they are off duty, or at all for that matter. As well, while a prisoner can be forced to wear a non-removable RFID bracelet, it is questionable whether members of a ships crew would willingly wear a tracking device at all times. If they were forced to do so, they might resent being treated in the same manner as common criminals, but if crew members have the option to not wear the RFID tag, it could defeat the whole purpose for which the system was implemented.

# 5 Conclusions

RFID has the potential to become a very powerful and pervasive technology. While some technological challenges persist, it is the non-technical issues that likely pose the biggest problems for RFID systems. A question that has been asked before about technological innovations is this: just because it can be done, does that mean that it should be done? This question is a valid one in this case because the technology is approaching the point where things that people never considered possible will soon become a reality.

On the technical side, standardization of the technology is a significant issue. Other than that, the true technical challenges will be to increase the range of passive tags while keeping their size small, or decreasing the size of the active tags while maintaining their long range capabilities. As well, developing systems that are more affordable and that can track people and things with greater resolution will be some of the technical challenges that the RFID industry will face.

With respect to the shipboard environment in particular, attenuation of the signal through, and reflection of the signal off metal walls on steel ships might also be an area worthy of further technical research. As the state of RFID technology stands right now, person tracking on board of a ship might not be practical given the size of active tags and the question of whether members of a ship's crew would voluntarily wear them or legally be forced to do so.

On the ethical side, societies and lawmakers must decide the amount of privacy to which employees, both on land and at sea, should be entitled. This is not an easy question at the best of times, but it becomes even more difficult to answer in a political climate that stresses increased maritime security measures. The challenge with RFID technology, as has been the case with all new technologies, will be to best reap its benefits while avoiding the pitfalls.

# References


[1] Ashton, K. in Garfinkel, S. and Rosenberg. B., eds., *RFID – Applications, security, and privacy*, Addison-Wesley: Upper Saddle River, New Jersey, p. xxi, 2006.

[2] Garfinkel, S. and Rosenberg. B., eds., *RFID – Applications, security, and privacy*, Addison-Wesley: Upper Saddle River, New Jersey, p. 5, 2006.

[3] Stockman, H., Communication by means of reflected power. *Proceedings of the IRE*, pp. 1196-1204, October 1948.

[4] Garfinkel, S. and Holtzman, H.. in Garfinkel, S. and Rosenberg. B., eds., *RFID – Applications, security, and privacy*, Addison-Wesley: Upper Saddle River, New Jersey, pp. 15-36, 2006.

[5] Crawford, K. and Goldman, A., RFID Primer: Where the WLAN hits the RFID fan, December 23, 2003, www.isp-planet.com/fixed_wireless/technology/2003/rfid_primer.html.

[6] Taylor, S. Personal communication, 15 July 2005, President, Cathexis Innovations, St. John's, Canada.

[7] Kopakchick, J. III and Monk, C., RFID risk management. *Internal Auditor,* **62(2),** pp. 66-72, April 2005.
[8] Taylor, S. Personal communication, 15 July 2005, President, Cathexis Innovations, St. John's, Canada.
[9] Archer, Q. and Salazar, G., RFID: a threat to privacy? *Computer Weekly,* p. B, 5 April 2005.
[10] Bono, S. et al, Security analysis of a cryptographically-enabled RFID device, 28 January 2005, http://rfid-analysis.org/DSTbreak.pdf.
[11] library books
[12] Security friend and foe, *Industrial Engineer,* **35(11),** pp. 39-40, November 2003.
[13] Financing for RFID prison systems, *RFID Journal*, 31 December 2002, www.rfidjournal.com/article/articleprint/241/-1/1.
[14] RFID prevents infant abduction at North Carolina hospital, *Wireless IQ*, 19 July 2005. www.wirelessiq.info/content/topstories/745.html.
[15] Smith, L., RFID report, *The Humanist*, **65(3)**. pp. 37-38,46, May/June 2005.
[16] Smith, L., RFID report, *The Humanist*, **65(3)**. pp. 37-38,46, May/June 2005.
[17] Tagging toothpaste and toddlers, *Information Management Journal,* **38 (5),** p. 22, September/October 2004.

# The ship security officer - a new challenge for maritime education

E. Barsan
*Constantza Maritime University, Romania*

## Abstract

From the academic point of view, we have to determine if the training for this job is a matter for the maritime education system only or if we have to deal with a cooperation process between different institutions in order to obtain an interdisciplinary approach. The first question is "how much maritime background is necessary for this new type of on-board personnel?" Analyzing the tasks required by this job, this paper will try to present a conclusion for this dilemma. We also have to think if the new security responsibilities could be "attached" to the already existing duties of the watch officer or if we have to create a new distinctive job on board. It is also very important to define how much supplementary training will be required in order to familiarize the watch officer with specific onboard security tasks: stowaways, drug smuggling, robbery, violent attacks, terrorism, etc.
*Keywords: ship security officer, maritime security, SSO, ISPS Code, training, watch officer, designated person.*

## 1 Introduction

In respect of IAMU $4^{th}$ General Assembly goals regarding tasks and functions on board future ships and different aspects of Maritime Education and Training, we want to debate one of the last issues revealed by IMO regarding the Ship Security Officer (SSO).

From the academic point of view, we have to determine if the training for this job is a matter regarding the maritime education system only or we have to deal with a cooperation process between different institutions in order to obtain an interdisciplinary approach.

The first question is "how much maritime background is necessary for this new type of on-board personnel?"

To get an answer to this question we have two options:

- to "convert" an already certified deck or engine officer into a security officers.
- to "update" experienced security personnel in order to perform the new tasks as ship security officer.

For the first alternative we have to decide which type of maritime officer is more suitable for the new assignment: a deck officer or an engine officer. Analyzing the tasks required by this job, the paper would try to present a conclusion for this dilemma. We also had to think if the new security responsibilities could be "attached" to the already existing duties of a watch officer or if we have to create a new distinctive job on board. It is also very important to define how much supplementary training will be required in order to familiarize the watch officer with specific security onboard tasks: stowaways, drug smuggling, robbery, violent attacks, terrorism, etc.

For the second alternative, if we decide to hire specially trained security personnel in order to perform the ship security officer duties, this would mean that we have already taken the decision of having a special job on board for this purpose. After that we must decide the required amount of specific knowledge regarding maritime ships activities in order to perform the ship security tasks.

For a Navy Academy, the problem of the Ship Security Officer seams to be easier to solve, but for the major part of the IAMU members we think that it is a matter that must be debated in order to offer owners such type of personnel.

## 2 Pressure for meeting the deadline

World scale application of ISPS Code [1], imposed through SOLAS Chapter IX, with July 01 2004 as the deadline, was the most expedient implementation of an IMO decision. Owners and port users were confused for an appreciable period of time regarding the practical steps that must be undertaken in order to think out their own SSP or PFSP. Fortunately, some international organizations (IMO, ABS, Lloyd's Register, USCG) draw up guidelines [2] for ships and port facilities security plans and started training courses for CSOs, SSOs, and PFSOs. The ISPS put in difficulty also Maritime Administrations due to the necessity to create a board able to certify the SSPs or the PFSPs. This problem occurs mainly in countries where the Maritime Administration was not based on a military structure (as USCG or the Canadian CG), because they do not have specialized staff in maritime security.

In Romania, validation of the security plans was divided between the Romanian Maritime Authority for the SSPs and the Maritime Ports Administration (MPA) Constantza for the PFSPs. In order to do this job, both institutions had to create special departments and to send personnel abroad for training. These new departments became operational only at the beginning of 2004, and due to this delay, some of the Romanian owners who were already ready with the SSPs had their plans certified by foreign classification registers.

After the implementation of the maritime security department of Maritime Ports Administration Constantza, an unfair-play fight began for the accreditation of organizations that could draw up security plans for the port facilities. More questions arose after the auction organized by MPA Constantza for the assignment of overall security system contracts in the Constantza, Midia and Mangalia ports.

Because each port user was constrained to apply a PFSP, in Constanza Port there are no less than 78 approved PFSPs. Due to the hiring and leasing system for berths and storage facilities applied in the port of Constantza, we have now many security areas extended only along one or two berths. The result was a tissue of fences and checkpoints, a lot of access passes that must be obtained by the same person who has to go on board ships (agents, chandlers, and other representatives). Consequently, the transportation time needed to shift cargo by road inside the port increased by 25-30% and the number of foreign crew members leaving their ships to visit the town decreased by 50-55%, due to the required supplementary formalities and limitation of private transport means (cars, taxi).

In Figure 1 we have an example of a pier in Constantza Port (berth 35 to 44) divided between two port users and the security areas established in accordance with their PFSPs.

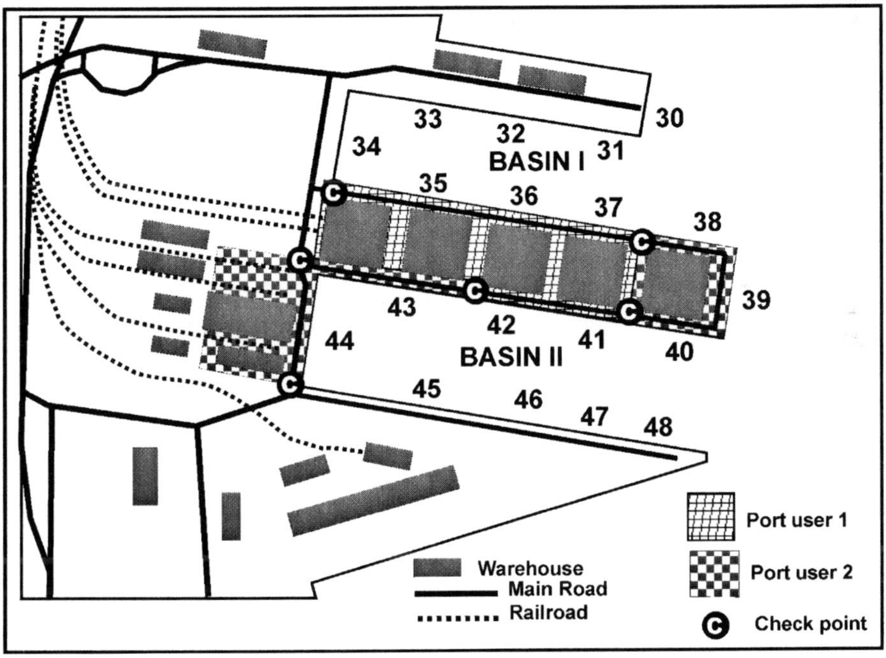


Figure 1: Pier in Constantza Port, divided between two port users.

## 3 Training of SSO

Since the first edition of the IMO model courses 3.19 ISPS-SSO, 3.20 ISPS-CSO, 3.21 ISPS-PSFO it was obvious that their aims get beyond the traditional problems related to maritime security with a great number of events, such as piracy, illegal immigration and smuggling. All the security risk evaluations, measures and actions included in the syllabus of these courses were mainly orientated towards prevention of terrorist and sabotage acts. From merchant ships officers' point of view, these new issues were not included in their basic training, field of activities and duties.

That is the reason why the first organizers of ISPS courses were firms specialized in protection and security and many of these delivered courses that were focused on inland prevention of terrorism and countermeasures, without an actual connection with the realities of the maritime transport activities. Such courses were mainly valuable for the port user, facilitating their knowledge concerning the drawing up of the port facilities security plans.

Meanwhile, the maritime training institutions, specialized in delivering IMO courses, have sent their own instructors to take train-the-trainer special maritime security courses. After that, these centres started to run their own IMO ISPS courses, but in most of the cases, such a course was delivered with a combination of 2 or 3 instructors with different backgrounds and qualifications (maritime, police, and/or secret service officers), in order to cover the syllabus of the SSO and PFSO courses as well as possible.

In Romania, the Maritime Training Centre CERONAV, started IMO model courses for SSO, CSO and PFSO in August 2003. By the end of 2004, 3300 SSOs, 80 CSOs and 180 PSOs were trained. In the first semester of 2005, CERONAV trained another 415 SSO, but the request for these courses has diminished very much.

Because the Ship Security Plans were drawn up only in respect of the ISPS Code provisions, without a real life feasibility test of this onboard measure, many of the owners decided to designate, as SSO, the on board officer with less responsibilities during the ship's operation in ports. As a result, we have second engineer officers, electrical officers or radio officers as SSOs. In other cases, the Master is also SSO, because the owner considered that he already has a long experience dealing with port authorities.

Duration of SSO training courses, organized by Maritime Centres or other certified institutions are very different, even if all these courses are sometimes certified by the same authorities. Average SSO training period was set to 2-3 days but longer periods of time could be found in courses organized by security companies. For example:

- Hudson Trident, US, duration 1,5 days, certified by DNV;
- Star Center, US, duration 2 days, certified by USCG;
- Aalesund University College, duration 2 days, NORWAY;
- AMC Search Limited, Australia, duration 2,5 days, certified by AMSA;
- ABS Consulting, US, duration 3 days, certified by ABS;
- Lloyd's Register, UK, duration 3 days, certified by Lloyd's Register;
- Lairdside Maritime Centre, UK, duration 3 days, certified by MCA;
- Ship and Port Security Services, UK, duration 3 days;
- Pacific Maritime Institute, US, duration 3 days, certified by USCG;

- Elkins Marine Training International, US, duration 2 days, certified by DNV;
- US Merchant Marine Academy, US, duration 3 days, certified by USCG;
- Port Maritime Security International Ltd, UK, duration 2-3 days, certified by DNV, MCA;
- Security Solutions International, US, 8 days.

Taking into account the goals of ISPS regarding the training and competences required for SSO, and the real background knowledge of maritime officers in terms of maritime security, we consider that a minimum period of 7 up to 10 days is required in order to achieve the declared objectives of the SSO course. We underline here some of the provisions of ISPS Code – Part B [1], that demonstrate the exaggerations of the ISPS Code expectations from the merchant marine officers designated as SSO:

- instruction techniques for security training and education, including security measures and procedures;
- handling sensitive security related information and security related communications;
- recognition and detection of weapons, dangerous substances and devices;
- recognition, on a non-discriminatory basis, of characteristics and behavioural patterns of persons who are likely to threaten security;
- methods of physical searches and non-intrusive inspections;
- crowd management and control techniques operations of security equipment and systems; and testing, calibration and maintenance of security equipment and systems while at sea;
- simulation of emergency situations.

More than that, the SSO is also responsible for the training of other crew members with specific security duties, in accordance with the SSP, in matters regarding:

- recognition & detection of weapons, dangerous substances & devices;
- recognition of characteristics and behavioural patterns of persons who are likely to threaten security;
- crowd management and control techniques;
- security related communications;
- methods of physical searches of persons, personal effects, baggage, cargo, and ship's stores.

In accordance with the ISPS provisions, there are no compulsory stages of training for the crew members with responsibilities in the SSP. That means that the only training regarding their specific security duties is made by the SSO or in very few occasions by the CSO. After a 12–20 hours course, the SSO must have enough knowledge regarding maritime security issues in order to deliver a credible training for the rest of the crew. In case of an inspection on security matters, these crew members must demonstrate their skills in order to satisfy the inspector's standards [3]. We consider that the initial training of SSO in accordance with the duration specified by the IMO model course, is totally insufficient for delivering an efficient training to other crew members subsequently. It is puzzling that the draft for the SSO IMO model course, in which the 12 hours duration was stipulated for the first time, was drawn up by the United States Merchant Marine Academy at Kings Point. We think that the authors of the draft believed that all merchant marine officers were trained as students in a Naval Academy [4].

The shipping companies that own passenger ships and ferries realized, before the entry of the ISPS, that the problems related to the security of their ships and passengers could be solved, in an efficient way, only by specially trained personnel, able to carry out the following procedures, routine tasks and checks:

- photo identification badges to employees [5];
- matching tags of luggage;
- visitors not allowed on board ship unless they have pre-arranged permits;
- passengers are provided with guest identification cards (also used for onboard purchases) that are electronically checked before each passenger is allowed to board the ship;
- hand-carried luggage is X-rayed and passengers pass through a walk-through security;
- screening system prior to embarkation;
- cabin baggage is x-rayed;
- canine search of stores for explosives ;
- all shoreside workers are credentialed;
- ship stores are security screened prior to loading;
- ship personnel security checks;
- access points to the ship are secured or manned.

As a result, on board these ships we have a well defined category of hired staff, leaded by a Chief of Security Officer with the following job description requirements:

- prevention and detection of crime and to maintain law and order on board the ship;
- ensure that the Company's rules and regulations are not breached by passengers or crew;
- ensure security measures when docked and be aware of the correct protocol and procedure in relation to local customs and immigration regulations;
- investigation of minor and serious crime;
- must have experience in the field of drug use, and know the signs, symptoms and effects of any particular type of drug;
- advise the Captain of any intelligence reports received and related threat assessments in any particular port or location;
- assess vulnerability of crew and/or passengers and formulate drug search patterns and procedures; provide training for such drills;
- be mindful as to what effects an act of terrorism would have on the ship;
- should have experience in bomb search techniques and provide training by means of regular drills on board the vessel;

- prevent stowaways from boarding the ship;
- have an idea of International Migration Law and procedures for handling stowaways caught.

It is obvious that the person able to comply with all these tasks must be a security and protection professional with enough land based experience, but also familiarized with the characteristics of passenger ships activities.

If we compare the imposed job description of a Security Officer onboard a passenger ship with the competences for tasks of all SSOs required by the ISPS, we will find no significant differences. This means that ISPS promoters had applied the standards used by passenger ships owners to all merchant ships [6]. Unfortunately this policy could not work in real life with the same expected results as for passenger ships and with only 12 to 20 hours of training for the merchant ship SSOs.

Taking into account the above mentioned issues, it is obvious that, from the practical point of view, an onboard security system for normal cargo ships similar with the one already existing for passenger vessels, could not be applied at the same standards. In our opinion, the role of the SSO of cargo ships must be limited to an active cooperation with PFSO and local authorities, in order to reduce the risk of incidents related to smuggling, stowaways, and maybe drugs traffic. Large-scale implementation of the onboard ISPS will have a very limited impact on risk reduction against terrorist assaults or other types of terrorist threats. More than that, even the piracy attacks against merchant ships will not decrease without an active, determined and in force measures from the national authorities, in the already known high risk maritime areas [7]. If we look at the graph from Figure 2, we can see that there are no major differences between the number of piracy incidents in 2001, 2002, 2004 and 2005.

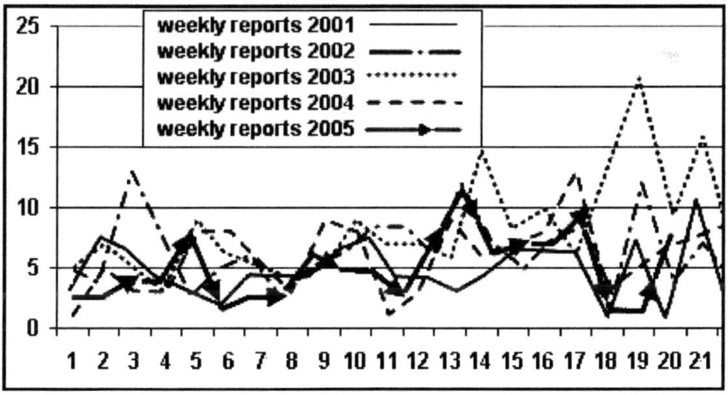


Figure 2: Piracy incidents between 2001-2005.

Reduction of potential terrorist threats in maritime transport could only be achieved with the help of security systems and measures implemented by port and local authorities [8], using specialized companies and personnel with upgraded training relating to antiterrorist measures. In these circumstances, the SSO and crew members, designated in the SSP from cargo ships, must ensure the onboard implementation of the procedures required by the PFSO, during the stay of their ship in port, and maintain an active communication with the PFSO, in order to report any incidents or suspicious events.

For the moment, the risk of violent acts against cargo ships remains focused on the piracy attacks. We consider that during the SSO training courses, the main security issues must be directed towards the practical measures that could prevent boarding the ship by pirates. Also, the SSO must be instructed on how to react and how to manage the emergency situation when pirates are already on board [9], when they have fire arms and/or have captured members of the crew. A lot of scenarios could be set on these matters based on real events reported and analyzed in the past years. Because the time to react is very limited in many cases, the SSO must have a clear knowledge about the risks involved and the best practice in these type of events.

Some of these practical actions were included in IMO circulars, but application of these measures is optional and responsibility for the consequences lies only on the Master or the SSO [7]. Here we can start another debate, regarding a potential conflict between the decisions of the Master and the SSO in such a specific case. Also a debate regarding possible legal prosecution against the SSO and his decisions must be brought to attention. It seams that the ISPS code had missed this aspect and majority of the designated SSOs, at the moment, is not aware of this possibility.

## 4 Maritime Universities' reaction

The Maritime Universities have a slower reaction concerning curricula update with new courses, due to the bureaucracy characteristics of the academic education system. With some exceptions, the situation regarding implementation of ISPS courses was the same, and today there are not many universities that have a special maritime safety course included in their regular teaching program. We are talking about a course that could assure the required competences for SSO or CSO. For Navy Academies it was easier to respond to this challenge because they already have their own staff that could teach such type of courses.

In many cases Maritime Universities organized SSO, CSO and even PFSO courses, based on IMO model courses, for the already certified maritime officers or port user's personnel, as requested by third parties. The issue of maritime security was also brought to attention in Master's courses, because the Master Program curriculum is more flexible and easy to update, especially in case of a modular system.

Now, taking into account the practical experience regarding the on board personnel designated as SSO, the question is which category of students must attend an SSO course, if we decide to introduce such a course in the basic curriculum.

Consequently we will have the following options:

- this course must be attended by the students from the deck department;

- the course must be taught to all the students, including the students from the engineering and electrical departments.

From the point of view of the Constantza Maritime University, the best solution is to keep such a dedicated course outside the basic curriculum because we do not have a teaching staff specially trained in these matters. If a SSO course is included in the curricula, the number of teaching hours will be not enough to allow for employment of a new full time teacher qualified to deliver this course. If the University does not intend to give to the graduates, an explicit certification as SSO, the maritime security training issues could be brought into the already running courses related to ship management and on board regular activities and officers' duties.

## 5 Conclusions

Taking into account the above mentioned issues we think that we can underline the following conclusions:

- the time available for implementing the provisions of the ISPS Code was very short and some of the solutions found, were improvised by ship owners and port operators;
- the training courses for SSO and CSO are very short, compared with the goals and competences that have to be achieved in accordance with the ISPS Code requirements;
- for most of the merchant ships, there is no practical justification to put into operation a security system similar to the security measures implemented for passenger vessels of ferries;
- the main role for the maritime security must be played by port authorities and port operators because they are the only ones who have the means to assure an efficient control of goods and persons into the port operational area;
- overdoing of security measures in ports have created a new stress factor for ship crews;
- for most of the ships, the main risk involving violent acts is represented by pirates attacks;
- the new equipment for sending distress alarms in case of any kind of attack against a ship are welcomed, but real help for the crews could come only if national authorities have the determination, expertise and means to solve such type of crises;
- efficient training for SSO could be done through specially tailored courses, starting from the framework of the IMO model courses, but using instructors with practical experience in the field of security and law enforcement;
- for ships at higher risk of terrorist targets, protection of the crew and passengers could be insured only by employing special security personnel, who are also trained for crowd management crises and are familiar with ships activities and characteristics.

We think that in the following years, application of ISPS provisions will be more pragmatic, with a more realistic evaluation of the practical possibilities to undertake security measures on board merchant ships and focused on the national maritime waters, ports and terminals security systems efficiency.

## References

[1] IMO, ISPS Code, London, 2003
[2] Germanischer Lloyd, Information on ISPS Code Certification, Hamburg, Germany, 2004
[3] UK Department for Transport, ISPS Code operational guidance, http://www.dft.gov.uk
[4] Cruise Job Line, http://www.cruisejobline.com
[5] United States Merchant Marine Academy at Kings Point, New York, Draft for IMO Model Course Ship Security Officer, 2003
[6] Dolby, I., ISPS (International Ship and Port Security), Webmaster of Seamania, 2004
[7] Reinhardt, C. J., Maritime Piracy: Sign of a Security, Mercer on Transport & Logistics, 2005
[8] Bichou, K., The ISPS Code and The Cost of Port Compliance: An Initial Logistics and Supply Chain Framework for Port Security Assessment and Management, Maritime Economics & Logistics, 2004
[9] Enders, S. Wimbush, S. E., Maritime Security in East Asia in 2025: Critical Uncertainties, Center for Strategic and International Studies, 2004

# Maritime security in a time of challenge: Admiral Makarov State Maritime Academy (SMA) facing the challenges with pride

I. I. Kostylev
*Admiral Makarov State Maritime University, Russia*

## 1 Introduction

The process for establishing a maritime security system in the Russian Federation began at the same time as the Inter-session working group of the IMO Maritime Safety Committee. Most of the process had been achieved by the time Chapter X1.2 of SOLAS-74 and the ISPSC Code were accepted. The implementation of the new regulations was difficult due to the considerable size of the country and the remoteness of many marine regions.

## 2 The beginning

In the beginning of 2003 SMA already had experience in the training of professionals in accordance with safety management systems in compliance with ISM Code, the analysis of operational risks and dealing with emergency circumstances. As a result, SMA formed a group to work out a methodical system for training professionals in the field of maritime security in Russia.
The Ministry of Transport assumed the responsibility for the compliance with the regulations of Clause XI-2 of SOLAS – 74 and ISPS Code in the Russian Federation.

"Maritime Security Service" Enterprise was commissioned as an executive organization. It accepted the SMA proposal as a concept basis for the unified training system of the personnel responsible for the security measures on board and ashore. In August of 2003, a national working seminar was held at SMA. It was held within the Global IMO Program for the Maritime safety and was devoted to the training of maritime transport security professionals. The instructors of "International maritime security" Ltd (UK) were involved in the work of the seminar as well as a wide range of other security and safety specialists. The professionals of these organizations contributed their experience and combined it with the knowledge of the experts in the field of maritime education and training.

The international experience has also been taken into consideration as well as the approaches used in other countries and leading maritime organizations, including some courses in foreign countries, the requirements of national Administrations, the recommendations of the classification societies, the requirements of the US Coast Guard and, of course, the IMO model courses.

## 3 The approaches selected

The major goal posed by the academy has been formed in the following way: to determine the general national requirements and the programs for the training of the professionals in compliance with the requirements of the ISPS Code. That is to be done with the obligatory consideration of the national experience in the field of the accident prevention with the application of modern approaches used in the national practice. An important decision was made to shorten the preliminary preparation period as well as for attracting the most experienced instructors and professionals: firstly to arrange the security familiarization training at the basis of higher maritime educational institutions.

As a result, this system became the basis for the national system of training in compliance with ISPS Code and was subsequently unified and standardized. Such an approach guaranteed a definite quality of the qualification levels in most of the regions of Russia.

The programs for 5 categories of trainees were designed in the Russian Federation in the autumn of 2003. Requirements for educational institutions providing the training in compliance with the ISPS Code were also formulated. The program training pack includes the following specialist categories:

- Ship Security Officer;
- Company Security Officer;
- Port State Control Security Inspector (Officer Duly Authorized for Security);
- Inspector in maritime security for the training centres.

It is important to note that all Russian instructors qualified to provide training in the ISPS Code have been trained at the Makarov Training centre of SMA.

So the unified system of training of the professionals for the security of ships and port facilities was established in the Russian Federation. The system of standard approaches has enabled us to provide the depth of the issue outlook exceeding the IMO Model Course, and to show the role of the safety and security measures at sea in the wider context of present maritime industry problems. At the first national seminar for Maritime Security, it was mentioned that an effective system of training and certifying of Maritime Security professionals had been created in Russia.

## 4 Today

Today the Academy is cooperating intensively with many international institutions. The main target of this cooperation is to formulate standard methods and procedures which can be implemented in training exercises targeted to port personnel in the areas of coast security.

To provide the unified national system for ISPS certification of personnel, the Academy has designed complex software toolkits for the knowledge assessment in the five categories of specialists ("Delta-ISPS"). It was approved by the Maritime Administration of Russia and Liberia for the worldwide usage in training centres and companies in-house seafarers' assessment. During 2004-2005 the instructors and examiners completed the final certification with the "Delta –ISPS" appliance at the Academy and all other training centers.

The total number of the professionals trained in Russia is approximately 5000 people (summer 2005). A large number, 2,700 to be precise, were trained at the Makarov training center of SMA. We have been assigned with the design of the programs, methods, examination standards, and with the very procedure of training and certification of the security professionals.

The level of training and assessment achieved at the Academy Courses on the Security of Ships and Port Facilities is confirmed by the appropriate certificates of Russian and Liberian maritime Administrations and is under the general quality system which is also accordingly confirmed by the Russian maritime register of shipping and IQNet.

## 5 What will be the second step?

Now when the preliminary stage of the ISPS Code application is completed, the goals of the educational institutions in every country are changing. They are:

- Firstly, the necessity to provide a smooth application of the Requirements for the Competency of the Ship Security Officer inputting into STCW-78/95;
- Secondly it is necessary to improve the practical component of the security training;
- And finally to develop the most acceptable methods of crew training.

It is necessary to organize a broad exchange of experience in the field of practical training and educational programs at an international level.

During the first months of Chapter XI-2 SOLAS -74 implementation revealed that only, the upper level of the problem is dealt with. Higher Maritime Educational Institutions, providing training in these fields, ought to become the centers of broader research for maritime security.

We shall concentrate our attention not only on such issues as the prevention of terrorism and piracy in marine transport, but also such problems as drug trafficking, illegal immigrants, cargo stealing, etc..

To define the area of the research issues, it is necessary to consider the opinion of Shipping Companies who definitely have a broader experience with regard to facing and solving problems in reality.

# Examining and promoting ISPS Code training for Chinese seafarers

X. M. Zhao[1], Y. Chun[2] & W. Ruan[2]
*[1]Seafarer Examination Centre of the Chinese Maritime Safety Administration, Beijing, People's Republic of China*
*[2]Shanghai Maritime University, People's Republic of China*

## Abstract

The effectiveness of implementing International Ship and Port Security Code (ISPS Code) relies greatly upon the awareness, knowledge and skills of maritime seafarers in respect of maritime security. For most of the seafarer training and certification systems in the world, the implementation of the code, compared with that of other maritime safety legislation, has limited flexibility in terms of time, and the subject thereof is new to many states. Therefore, the syllabus of ISPS Code training set down and the methods for training adopted in the first stage of implementation are becoming limited. It is worthwhile examining what has been done in terms of ISPS Code training and then how to promote it. Based on an introduction to Chinese ISPS Code training system and related facts, this paper analyzes major problems encountered in such training activities. Furthermore, it provides recommendations for possible solutions to achieve higher quality ISPS Code training, such as encouraging the use of Computer Based Training, the establishment of an ISPS Code information database and a co-operation with professional security companies.
*Keywords: seafarer, maritime training, ISPS Code, maritime security.*

## 1 Introduction

The UNCTAD's statistics show that China owned an ocean-going fleet with more than 2,300 vessels by the end of 2003. Together with the group of Chinese seafarers who are serving onboard foreign flag vessels which is about 40,000 – 50,000, of whom about 10,000 may need ISPS Code related training, examination and certification. In its home fleet, China has a huge group of seafarers and it is reported that about 160,000 seafarers are licensed [2]. There is obviously great potential need for ISPS Code related training activities.

Thanks to the capability of the maritime education and training system in China, the huge workload could be done in a relatively short time period. Taking the Shanghai Seafarer Training Centre as an example, which is the largest seafarer training centre in China, it has completed training courses for more than 2,000 Ship Security Officers (SSO) by 1st July 2005 [11]. Meanwhile, available statistics from the Maritime Safety Agency (MSA) China report that by 1st July 2005, more than 1,100 vessels engaged in international voyages have obtained their Ship Security Certificates (SSC) and that more than 10,000 SSOs and Company Security Officers (CSO) have been trained, examined and certificated [2].

Although the Chinese MSA has laid down rules for the implementation of the Code and has published comprehensive standards for training and examination, the code is quite new in its nature in a maritime context and the implementation thereof had to be done in a very short time. Arguably, deficiencies and problems may be found once the details of the training regime are critically examined, by industry organizations or individual shipping companies

## 2 Introduction to the Chinese ISPS Code training system

After accession to a particular piece international legislation, the typical way of the Chinese Central Government to implement it is to promulgate domestic legislation. For the ISPS Code, the same procedure was applied, and in this particular case the MSA China was appointed as the responsible Government Agency. To this effect, *"The Rules for the Chinese Seafarers' ISPS Code Training, Examination and Certification, 2003"* [8] were developed by the MSA China. The rules also define the responsibilities and functions of the local MSA, who should work within the framework of the authority delegated to them by the National MSA with regard to seafarers' professional training and examination. Therefore the organization, supervision and management of ISPS Code training and examination was under the supervision of the respective local MSA offices.

The existing Seafarer Training Centres, which are established in accordance with national laws and regulations and are operated and managed in compliance with the quality standards, can carry out ISPS Code training after filing an application with the local MSA. Such applications shall be approved by the local MSA and filed at the national MSA. Additionally, the following requirements shall be met for ISPS Code training [8]:

- All trainers and examiners involved in ISPS Code training activities shall receive special training provided by the national MSA. The local MSA shall be responsible for the organization of the training.
- The trainers shall demonstrate sufficient knowledge with respect to ship security, as laid down in the chapter XI-2 of the SOLAS convention and other international or national maritime legislation, and shall possess the necessary skills in handling security matters. The trainers should also be familiar with maritime professional teaching and training techniques.

- The training centres shall have the necessary facilities and infrastructure in place such as classrooms, workshops, audio and visual equipment, models and reading materials, as well as training plans and materials, including SOLAS Convention, training syllabus, etc.

Table 1: The framework of ISPS Code training set by "The Rules for the Chinese Seafarers' ISPS Code Training, Examination and Certification" [8].

| Contents for training | CONTACT HOURS | |
|---|---|---|
| | theoretical study | practical skill training |
| 1. Introduction: Background, purposes and requirements | 1 | |
| 2. The framework and contents of ISPS Code<br>2.1 The arrangement of the code<br>2.2 Definitions<br>2.3 Applications<br>2.4 The responsibilities of the member states<br>2.5 The over-riding authority of shipmasters for onboard safety and security<br>2.6 Declaration Of Security | 1 | |
| 3. Ship Security<br>3.1 The obligations and responsibilities of shipping companies<br>3.2 The ship security levels and measures<br>3.3 The deployment and duties of company security officers<br>3.4 The deployment and duties of ship security officers<br>3.5 The outlines of ship security<br>3.6 The training and drills of ship security | 4 | |
| 4. Ship Security Assessment and its implementation<br>4.1 Elements of ship security assessment<br>4.2 Contents of ship security assessment<br>4.3 Preparations, implementation and approval of ship security assessment<br>4.4 On-scene verification | 2 | 2 |
| 5. The meaning, formulation and implementation of ship security plan<br>5.1 Purposes, uses and approval of ship security plan<br>5.2 Contents, formulation and implementation of ship security plan<br>5.3 Document control, up-keeping and caring of ship security plan | 2 | 2 |
| 6. Training and Drills onboard<br>6.1 Security management<br>6.2 Applications of security evaluation methods<br>6.3 Security assessment and verification<br>6.4 Drills of ship security measures<br>6.5 Drills for the possible threats to ships, personnel and cargo<br>6.6 Applications of inspection, controlling and monitoring technologies<br>6.7 Identification of weapons, dangerous goods and installations<br>6.8 Briefing on the ship security alarming system<br>6.9 Use of ship-shore communication system<br>6.10 Use of ship security facilities | 6 | 4 |
| 7. Introduction to port security facilities | 1 | |
| 8. verification and certification of ship security | 1 | |

As described in Table 1, the Rule recommends a detailed framework of ISPS Code related training so as to ensure the quality of ISPS Code training [8]. The total length of an SSO training course shall not be less than 26 contact hours, of which at least 18 hours are devoted to theoretical studies and practical skills training last for at least 8 hours. The size of each SSO training class shall not exceed 40 participants. After attending the training course, all participants shall be examined by the local MSA in a written examination. Only those trainees who score more than 80 points can be certificated as SSO An analysis on the ISPS Code training in China.

## 2.1 A discussion of ISPS Code related training

Arguably, the subject of ISPS Code, maritime security is quite new to most seafarers. Before its introduction into the shipping industry, the Maritime Education and Training system focused primarily on maritime safety and pollution prevention, as well as maritime economics and maritime law. This is the challenge but also the opportunity for ISPS Code training regimes. The challenges not only apply to the trainees but also sometimes to the trainers.

Maritime security covers rather broad topics such as smuggling, stowaways and piracy, although the main aim of the code is the prevention of terrorist activities. In additionally, even though terrorism is the particular maritime security topic, there are many detailed but often differing regulations and practices in different ports and nations. For example in the United States and Western European countries where maritime security has right from the start been a particularly critical issue, various regulations have been developed and several measures have been taken for security reasons. There are a few differences between those regulations and practices and the ISPS Code. The United States, for example, have made it compulsory to implement part A and B of the ISPS Code while in many other countries this is not the case. Meanwhile, the United States expanded the ISPS Code in its territory through the Maritime Transportation Security Act 2002 (MTSA), which means that all vessels calling at US ports shall not only meet the requirements as set down in part A and B of the ISPS Code, but also the MTSA. Inspections by US Government Agencies relating to maritime security are thus becoming wider and stricter. For example, the MTSA requires the US Coast Guard to carry out a "Detailed Vulnerability Assessment" for those vessels which have visited ports with poor port security facilities prior to calling at a US port [4,10,12]

Moreover, the ISPS Code covers not only maritime security aspects, but also some issues of criminal law nature. The relevant topics of the ISPS Code such as terrorism, smuggling and stowaways are all closely linked to the criminal laws. For example, Japan passed a Law with the intention to secure the security of her ports and ocean-going vessels, which mandates the observation of maritime security rules by shipowners and port facility managers, and stipulates that a shipmaster will be sentenced to prison not exceeding one year or be levied with 0.5 Million Yen if he files makes fraudulent reports on maritime security [2].

All of these laws, regulations, procedures and practices affect the operational procedures onboard ships. They may be of great help should a maritime security incident onboard occur if properly incorporated into the training regime. However, the systematic introduction of these various laws may be difficult to achieve.

Lastly, maritime security issues have to be updated from time to time since the ISPS Code itself, the detailed practices and regulations, the legal system and procedures in different nations and ports are subject to change. This will make the coverage of ISPS Code training quite dynamic.

High quality ISPS Code training should seek to achieve the full coverage of the above. However, more efforts need to be made, because the prerequisite of reaching the goal is to have timely, sufficient and correct ISPS Code information. Although some entities or individuals are collecting the information, this may in some cases be incomplete or even limited data. For example, the MSA China currently does not have a formal way of collecting such detailed information. The shipping companies presumably collect such information focusing on only those routes or voyages that their vessels are sailing regularly. Therefore the information collected by the CSO may not always be reliable or broad enough and could in fact be quite limited with respect of maritime security.

Recognised Organizations (e.g. Classification Societies) or even Protection & Indemnity (P&I) Clubs might collect more reliable and professional information but they would normally circulates this only to their member ships [9]. In the above three scenarios, ISPS Code training centres would not benefit too much, since normally they would not have access to the information collated by the above organizations, but they are the organizers of every step of ISPS Code training! It would appear that a key problem, from a higher quality ISPS Code training viewpoint is the fact, that China has not yet established a specific "platform" to collect and exchange various reports and information.

## 2.2 The training facilities and trainers

There are other problems and difficulties in ISPS Code training, for instance the facilities available for ISPS Code training. The reality is that those security facilities are difficult to obtain in the existing Chinese criminal law system even for teaching purposes, and operating such facilities for training purposes is only permitted after an approval from the public security authority has been received. Therefore it is comparatively difficult for the training centres to have real security facilities and systems for demonstration or briefing during the training course. This is a formidable barrier to develop practical skills and in an effort to overcome this obstacle many training centres use multimedia facilities and materials during for the training courses.

Another problem may exist with respect to the ISPS Code trainers. The ISPS Code is not only new to most trainees but also to many trainers. An experienced and qualified ISPS Code trainer should ideally possess knowledge and experience of both maritime and security aspects. Private security companies or the National Public Security Authority are specialized in security matters but they need to expand their knowledge of maritime operational matters. Arguably, most of them can only provide some sort of support rather than being "trainers".

The Recognised Organizations, such as China Classification Society (CCS) are professionally very well qualified in this regard, but it is unrealistic to expect that the implementation of ISPS Code training can rely to a large extent on the trainers from CCS since the group of trainees to be trained is so huge. So ultimately the responsibility for the improvement of the quality of training goes back to the trainers.

### 2.3 The training hours

The 18 plus 8 hours is workable in the present framework of ISPS Code training, but will be not enough for higher quality training. Using multimedia technologies to improve the efficiency of lecturing and demonstration can solve part of problems in the regard. 18/8 is also a quite reasonable rate for the distribution of theoretical study and practical skill training. However, the reality and then a pity is that some training centres may cut down a few hours from the practical training hours and increase the hours for theoretical teaching due to the inadequate real security training facilities and the limitations of the trainers, while keeping the total hours the same. The cutting-down will of course affect adversely the quality of training.

## 3 Feedback on the ISPS Code training regime

Feedback received from different sectors of the shipping and port industry is useful for an assessment of present the ISPS Code training regime and for the further improvement of such training. The Paris Memorandum of Understanding reported in March, 2005 that the new code was satisfactorily observed onboard after the member states had conducted three months of intensive inspections on board ships focussing on ISPS Code compliance. Only 72 vessels among 4681 inspections were detained due to deficiencies relating to maritime security [4,5]. Meanwhile the Tokyo Memorandum of Understanding (of which China is a member) reports in its 2004 annual report details on ISPS Code compliance inspections carried in the second half of 2004 (see Table 2). The data shows that the ISPS Code compliant Security Systems were well implemented onboard. Finally, the 2004 annual report from the Chinese MSA indicates that the MSA inspected 1,008 vessels from the 1st July 2004 to 30th September 2004 specifically to assess ISPS Code compliance. A total of 255 vessels with about 586 deficiencies relating to ISPS Code compliance were identified. Altogether 17 vessels were detained (2.9%) [2]. It seems arguable to say that the quality of ISPS Code training is acceptable on the whole.

This is of course good news. However, the key problems mentioned before still exist. Some training centres reported that the trainees did acquire their practical knowledge on maritime security only after completion of the training course, and stated that they needed more opportunities for practical operations with real security facilities. One shipmaster, who is serving in an international shipping company engaging in the carriage of chemical goods, stated that there are many minor operational deficiencies onboard such as: poor gangway watch, unfamiliarity with the execution of security plans, improper ways to dispose of suspect article such as packages and unfamiliarity with the restricted areas onboard. Partly, this may be due of the attitude or awareness of the seafarers onboard, but other reasons might be: insufficient training; over-stressing on theoretical teaching and neglecting practical operations; and inadequate knowledge on the regulations and practices of main shipping nations with respect to ISPS Code compliance.

Table 2: Port State Inspections on maritime security - TOKYO MOU, 2004 [3].

| Authority | No. of inspections | No. of inspections with security related deficiencies | No. of security related deficiencies | No. of security related detentions | Detention percentage (%) |
|---|---|---|---|---|---|
| Australia | 1,589 | 0 | 0 | 0 | 0 |
| Canada | 140 | 2 | 3 | 0 | 0 |
| Chile | 265 | 19 | 28 | 0 | 0 |
| China | 2,222 | 261 | 356 | 15 | 0.68 |
| Fiji | 3 | 0 | 0 | 0 | 0 |
| Hong Kong, China | 352 | 32 | 48 | 22 | 6.25 |
| Indonesia | 23 | 0 | 0 | 0 | 0 |
| Japan | 2,503 | 355 | 495 | 5 | 0.20 |
| Republic of Korea | 2,452 | 422 | 609 | 10 | 0.41 |
| Malaysia | 164 | 27 | 38 | 2 | 1.22 |
| New Zealand | 236 | 14 | 18 | 1 | 0.42 |
| Papua New Guinea | 0 | 0 | 0 | 0 | 0 |
| Philippines | 197 | 6 | 8 | 0 | 0 |
| Russian Federation | 487 | 26 | 32 | 4 | 0.82 |
| Singapore | 954 | 204 | 220 | 25 | 2.62 |
| Thailand | 73 | 1 | 1 | 0 | 0 |
| Vanuatu | 3 | 1 | 1 | 0 | 0 |
| Vietnam | 176 | 6 | 8 | 0 | 0 |
| Total | 11,839 | 1,376 | 1,865 | 84 | Regional 0.71% |

# 4 The future prospects for high quality ISPS Code training

Watching-keeping on the bridge seems easy if the ship runs smoothly. However, it will be never enough to have knowledge, skills and experience in case of being involved in maritime accidents or emergency operations. Maritime security as a part of maritime professional operations has this feature as well. The high quality ISPS Code training aims to develop the seafarers' capabilities or skills in actively and correctly responding in instances of breaches of security. But the present ISPS Code training is organized mainly to cope with the challenges faced through the implementation of the ISPS Code. The industry faced the enormous task of to organizing and completing training courses for a large number of seafarers. It is to be hoped that the quality of ISPS Code training could be improved in a long run.

The ISPS Code contains both theoretical study and practical skills training. For the former, high quality means full coverage of ISPS Code rules and regulations, including the regulations and practices adopted by major maritime nations with respect of maritime security. With respect to skills training, high quality implies the development of practical skills for ISPS Code emergency handling by means of modern technologies and demonstration of real security facilities.

# 5 The solutions

## 5.1 Establishing an efficient way of reporting security information and constructing an ISPS Code information platform

It will be very useful to have such means and a platform to solve the above mentioned problems. In fact, it will be beneficial for the whole industry to enable it to disseminate available information on maritime security aspects. A good example is the way in which BIMCO is collecting ISPS Code information mainly through collecting ISPS Code information from and circulating it back to its member ships. The International Maritime Bureau (IMB) is also a good example, which focuses on the collection on piracy information.

The suggested platform not only aims to simply disseminate information available, but also should be equipped with more functions. Such an information platform could be established in a maritime administration, a certain maritime research centre or in one of the maritime universities. In detail, the nature of such a platform is a web-based dynamic information database, collecting the latest security information on the regulations and practices and notices of different maritime nations, with respect to maritime security, piracy, and stowaways. With advanced computer technologies, the functions of such a platform could expand further to include information processing and analysis. The proposed structure is shown in Figure 1.

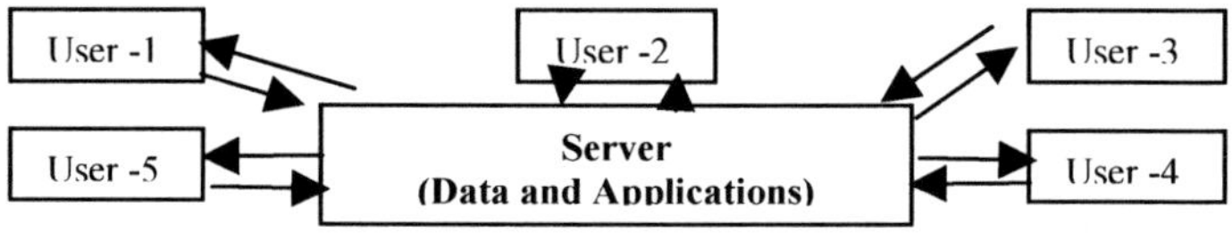


Figure 1: A possible framework of a proposed ISPS Code information database.

Table 3: Main items for ISPS Code reports [6].

| | |
|---|---|
| ➢ | ISSC acceptance, additional information demands from port state inspector (e.g. Security plan, disclosure, problems in respect of the Continuous Synopsis Record, records of training, drills, exercises). |
| ➢ | Port State Control attitudes - Crew interrogation, availability of ID, use/display of firearms, aggressive attitude, abuse of powers, integrity, placing armed guards, refusal of access to shore facilities/shore leave, problems with specific crew nationalities. |
| ➢ | Problems over agreement on a Declaration of Security. |
| ➢ | Excessive information demands before entering port, current and historical information (e.g. Port, Customs, Immigration). |
| ➢ | Problems caused by trading history (previous calls at non-compliant port facilities, previous ownership or flag). |
| ➢ | Access control issues – identification, manning access points, searching visitors, accompanying visitors, securing waterside access, access to ships for essential visitors. |
| ➢ | Perceived port and ship security deficiencies. |
| ➢ | Problems caused (delay, detention, refusal of entry or departure, additional inspections). |

The sources of the information intended to be collected, which are always the critical issue when establishing and operating such a platform, could be the information shared with other organizations or associations, the IMB or MSA for instance, and various reports sent by the shipmasters, pilots, companies, individuals, or maritime researchers. In case of maritime research, Table 3 shows a matrix used by the ICS/ISF

### 5.2 Up-grading computer based maritime security training and drills

The difficulties or restrictions for maritime training centres to obtain real security facilities or installation will remain for quite long period. But the requests for higher ISPS Code training or stricter security inspections are continuously presented to the industry. Alternatives must be found. Multimedia technologies are still an important alternative. But Power Point materials are not enough to demonstrate the security responses onboard since in many cases they are still pictures. More advanced technologies such as Flash and professional computer software shall be produced and employed, by which the trainees can have more opportunities for interacting exercises.

### 5.3 Co-operating with professional security companies or public security authority

Also for the same reasons, attempts shall be made to co-operate with professional security companies or public security authority although they are not professional in maritime. They are established in compliance with laws and regulations, owning legally certain security facilities and much experience in security responses. With their participations and rich expertise in the ISPS Code training, trainees and trainers can be both benefited, and hopefully, the possibilities of seeing or operating some real security facilities may increase as well.

## References

[1] Ai-guo He, personal communication, 25, July, 2005, General Master of the Stolt Chemical Transportation Company, Shanghai Branch, China.

[2] Annual Report of the China Maritime Safety Administration Maritime Safety Administration , 2004.

[3] Annual Report on Port State Control in the Asia-Pacific Region, Tokyo Memorandum of Understanding, 2004.

[4] China Classification Society (CCS) http://www.ccs.org.cn/

[5] Annual report of the Paris Memorandum of Understanding, 2004.

[6] Feedback Report of International Chamber of Shipping / International Shipowners Federation (ICS/ISF), ICS/ISF, London, http://www.marisec.org/isps/

[7] Grey, M. The ISPS Code - its first year, Bimco Bulletin, vol. 100, No.2, pp. 58, 2005.

[8] Rules for the Chinese Seafarers' ISPS Code Training, Examination and Certification", the Maritime Safety Administration of China, 2003.
[9] UK P&I club loss prevention on maritime security, website, London, http://www.ukpandi.com/ukpandi/Infopool.nsf/HTML/LP_Init_Maritime Security.
[10] United States Coast Guard, Office of maritime safety, website, Washington DC, http://www.uscg.mil/hq/g-m/pscweb/index.htm
[11] Yong-yu Pan, personal communication, 25 July, 2005, Deputy Director of Seafarer Training Department of Shanghai Seafarer Training Centre, Shanghai Maritime University, Shanghai, China.
[12] Zhenhong Yun, Lunyuan Tao, Maritime Security -the key issue of the world, Journal of China Shipping, page 45-46, Vol.8, 2004.

# Maritime security: training, drills and exercises (*inherent value*)

L. V. Wade
*Training Ship "State of Maine", Maine Maritime Academy, USA*

## Abstract

ISPS and MTSA mandates changed the operational structure of all Maritime assets. The Maritime world is forging ahead with the first requirements in place, instituted and implemented. Now we are at the critical juncture of applying the edicts in our Security Plans, aboard ships, at shore facilities, in regions and in countries. These edicts require specific training and certifications. Drills and exercises are required. I intend to show how these have been promulgated on a Maritime Training Vessel. In a teaching/learning environment we are always striving to find innovative ways to reinforce by actual practice the concepts we introduce in the classroom. I intend to show that this is a valid methodology for insuring the greatest possible retention of the precepts introduced. Varied and unique as it is, the training insures better retention in the minds of the students. Choosing unique partners to train with, using their assets, which are at times very high tech, beyond the cost capability of most maritime training institutions, has proven effective for Maine Maritime Academy and the Training Ship "State of Maine". The value is spread to and from students to all participants in the drills and exercises and the resultant training each receives is value added to all. There is "Inherent Value" in this methodology from which we can all benefit
*Keywords: maritime security, vessel security plan, teaching, learning, drills and exercises, training partners, regional cooperation, USCG, National Guard, situational awareness.*

## 1 Introduction

01 July 2004, a date which delineated the point in time that the entire Maritime World would be tasked to implement the mandates of the International Maritime Organization's (IMO), International Ship and Port Facility Security Code

(ISPS) [1]. Details of the mandate were adopted and published in the International Convention for the Safety of Life at Sea Convention (SOLAS), 1974 as amended, Chapter XI-2.
The key to the mandates was the following relative to vessels:

- Established a Vessel (ship) Security Officer;
- Established a Vessel Security Plan;
  - Required Training;
  - Required Exercises;
  - Required tests and inspections;
- Established a Tracking Document;
- Established a Vessel Security Certificate;
- Established certain equipment requirements;
- Instituted means by which to promulgate the training and issue the documentation.

It is the intent of this paper to discuss the methods used at Maine Maritime Academy, aboard the training ship "State of Maine", to implement the mandates of ISPS, and in the United States the Federally mandated Maritime Transportation Security Act (MTSA) [2]. To clarify, MTSA, parallels the requirements of SOLAS, ISPS and applies to U.S. Vessels.

## 2 Chronology and implementation

### 2.1 The year 2003

IMO discussions relevant to the SOLAS amendments and ISPS were underway and material was being released as early as 2003. We were aware of some of the requirements being discussed and model courses being developed. However, we chose to implement some measures of training for our crew and students prior to the ship's deployment in May of that year.

Accordingly, we sent 3 staff officers to the Military Sealift Command for Chemical, Biological, and Radiological Training. We followed that training with two faculty members attending a Department of Defence sponsored training program designed to train instructors to teach Anti-Terrorism, Force Protection. At that point we required the entire ship's complement deploying for Cruise 2003 to take a training course (4 hours), which resulted in receipt of certification in Anti-terrorism, Force Protection. It should be noted that this course is not specifically intended for at sea deployments but rather it is intended for ALL members of an organization and or family. It is very much pertinent to a spouse shopping in a large market for daily sustenance as well as a student on shore leave in a big city. It teaches recognition of hazards and situational awareness.

During Cruise 2003 we refined our onboard security watches and awareness. Implementation of in port security measures was tested in Santa Cruz de Tenerife and Antwerp Belgium during that time. The in port implementation and subsequent adaptation was modelled on "lessons learned" [3].

During the fall and winter of 2003 into 2004 various personnel were trained in VSO, CSO and PFSO using the Model Courses developed by IMO. The

President of Maine Maritime Academy appointed CSO, VSO and FSO personnel.

### 2.2 The year 2004

The year 2004 found us deeply involved in assessing the vessel in preparation for writing and submitting our security plan; this was done by the vessel owner, The United States Department of Transportation, Maritime Administration. Maine Maritime Academy being in custody of the vessel and deemed its Operator was involved in the actual walkabout. Again in 2004 the previous year's pre-cruise instruction class and in port security was again offered and in fact required for all cruising personnel. During this cruise we also installed and implemented the mandated Automatic Information System (AIS) and Ship Silent Alarm System (SSAS). Returning from Cruise 2004 just prior to 1 July we found that MARAD had sent to us the required Ship Security Plan. Also following shortly was the Certificate of Security Compliance Certificate. A review of the received plan and a method to implement it was the subject of meetings between the VSO, CSO and other Security personnel along with Faculty and partnered experts in the field. During the winter of 2004 into spring 2005 the vessel security plan was amended and re-submitted for approval. A separate referenced section on SSAS was also submitted for approval.

### 2.3 The year 2005

Prior to Cruise 2005 in May, "State of Maine" received full approval of the amended plans and also received a new Certificate of Compliance based on an assessment by personnel of the U.S. Coast Guard from the Portland Maine Marine Safety Office. The Cruise 2005 found us implementing the training as we did prior to Cruises 2003 and 2004 and additionally implementing a system of access control and testing of our AIS and SSAS systems during the deployment. The simple but effective use of photo ID's and Bar Code Scanners played a dual role. It gave us instant knowledge of who was aboard and accurate control of those boarding, but also tended to significantly raise the entire security awareness situation in the minds of the students due to their continual use of this access control system; a benefit we had not envisioned prior to cruise.

## 3 Training (teaching)

### 3.1 Personnel (MMA population)

The MMA and Training Ship Population consists of the following types of personnel:

- Ship's Crew;
- Licensed Cruise Hires;
- Unlicensed Professional Cruise Hires;
- MMA Faculty and staff;
- Regimental staff;

- Dining Services Staff;
- Students.

### 3.2 Curriculum and training

Security Training is part of the curriculum in many academic courses at Maine Maritime Academy and because the ship is used as an alongside Lab for up to 10 months of the year the platform is always there requiring watches, maintenance and sometimes providing onboard berthing for students. Accordingly, it is integrated into the normal everyday life at MMA and plays an integral role in training our students, staff and faculty. Visitors to the ship also undergo security checks according to our vessel security plan and are therefore enlightened by the student watch-keepers as to what is required, while at the same time giving the students the opportunity to practise what they are learning.

In looking at the types of training and frequency of repeat training, we look carefully at the types of personnel listed above and endeavour to tailor the training to fit the group. In some instances individuals within a certain group may actually have security credentials in some fields. We try to match the individual, and his or her skills, to a segment of training if at all possible. The old adage of using the available resources certainly fits this instance and lends credibility to the teaching if it can be wound around a "sea story".

### 3.3 At sea (cruising)

While deployed, all students aboard are assigned Security watches at sea and in Port. The upper-class students (2/C) aboard are normally put in charge of the underclass (4/C) students and the 4/C report to the 2/C. Overall the Midshipman Officer of the Deck (MOOD) is parallel to a ship licensed Mate and is in charge of the security detail.

Prior to arrival in a port the Midshipman Cadet Officer (Rate) who is designated Security, Safety and Compliance Officer will issue a set of instructions for the security detail, having had approval from the VSO and Master. This sets out any particular issues at the port. The Rate will also take part in any security briefings and Declaration of Security with Port Officials should the need arise.

## 4 Drills and tests

### 4.1 AIS

AIS is an integral part of our training during bridge watch evolutions. Status change and its importance are stressed. Recognizing false information strings and improper operational techniques is important and is taught to the student population.

The early mandate for AIS equipment and the rush to define its role and operation actually worked to the advantage of those teaching its use as there are a few glitches that are seen pretty often in the information strings being sent out by ship's AIS.

EXAMPLE: A vessel entering St John Newfoundland with a Course Over Ground of about 270 degrees actually showed a ship's heading of 091 degrees; almost 180 degrees in error. The displayed icon in fact looked like it was backing into port and had the Speed Over Ground not been 17 knots that just might have been the case. Obviously the personnel on that ship's bridge had not checked the digital repeater that was sending heading information to the AIS.

Another opportunity arises when we find tankers "underway sailing". Unfortunately on most AIS units the scroll down menu for vessel status has "Underway, Sailing" at the top of the list and as most Mates "Sail" from every port, it is the logical first choice for them, when in fact, the correct choice "Underway using engines" is lower on the list and should have been the choice.

### 4.2 SSAS

SSAS is routinely tested; although the exact time and methods are not disclosed, the results are shared with the student population and they are aware that the shore side entities that are to respond to our alerts have, in fact, received the test message.

### 4.3 Bomb threat

Bomb threats, while deployed, may be easily tested as a drill by planting a "fake" box suitably labelled. This was actually done during cruise 2005 when two boxes were set out in locations about the ship. Bomb #1 was set in the path of the Security watchman making the rounds and we were fairly certain it would be readily discovered and the alert sounded. Bomb #2 was hidden so a search would have to be initiated and techniques for searching could be demonstrated and taught.

This is what actually happened, except that the officer in the space at the time it was discovered, instructed the watchman to take it up and toss it over the stern (it was planted in the steering gear room). Students do not always listen too closely and the student interpreted this to mean take it to the Engine Room Control Station and call the Bridge for permission to toss it overboard. Why he did not simply use the steering gear room phone is still a mystery to us, but this bomb, had it been real, would have been transported to perhaps the most vital area of the ship by one of OUR lads! Anyway, lessons are learned from that to be sure...the first of which is DON'T TOUCH IT!

## 5 Exercises

### 5.1 Cruise underway joint exercise

TS "State of Maine" conducted joint exercises with the U.S. Coast Guard and Maine Army National Guard Civil Support Team while underway in 2002. This exercise utilized the Air and Sea resources of the Coast Guard to accompany and deploy the National Guard team to the vessel via Helo. The team then used sophisticated air sampling and analysis gear to sweep an area of the ship, download the data collected to a laptop computer and uplink the data through a portable GAN Satellite feed. The team was then extricated by Helo. Several vital lessons learned resulted from this exercise not the least of which was the difficulty of moving about narrow ship passageways while suited in full gear including breathing devices, which left very little room for the backpack sampling unit. Student participation in this exercise resulted in valuable security liaison as well as communications and Helo operations training.

### 5.2 Alongside joint exercise

An exercise designed to train for boarding a ship from a small vessel was conducted in late 2002 while TS "State of Maine" was moored to her berth. A Mobile lab was set up capable of sampling and analyzing solid and/or liquid substances. The team first boarded a reconnaissance team via the pilot ladder and after reconnoitring hailed the balance of the search team to board. Meanwhile, their delivery vessel was taken out of the picture by a simulated casualty. Finding, analyzing and communicating the bio-hazardous material the team then had to exit the vessel.

Partners in this exercise, the USCG and Maine Army National Guard, enlisted the help of the Coast Guard Auxiliary to supply a boat to replace the Coast Guard vessel. To further complicate the mission we deemed a member of the strike team to have slipped on a ladder and broken his leg. This required an innovative way to transfer him to the waiting auxiliary vessel. After securing the casualty in a "stokes" litter a lifeboat was lowered to the main deck and the litter transferred to the lifeboat. It was then used as an elevator to lower the litter to the waters edge where the litter could be easily transferred to the Auxiliary vessel. Lessons learned from this exercise were that the teams had to be adaptable to contingencies and to utilize the ship's crew to assist in finding ways to help getting the tasks done in a safe and efficient manner. Backup plans and assets need to be in place and readily available.

### 5.3 State Police K-9

For several years prior to 9-11 the training ship had requested the use of Maine State Police Canine units to sweep the vessel for drugs prior to deploying for a cruise. We did this primarily as a deterrent and training exercise for the students. One thing that we found evident in our first sweep was that not all canines were happy or able to climb shipboard ladders. This forced the police handlers to sometimes carry their dogs up and down ladders. Of course, this was thought to be very funny and the handlers were the brunt of much joking from their fellow compatriots.

The State Police then asked if they could use the ship to train their units and we have been conducting such training ever since.

With 9-11, we immediately expanded this sweep of the ship to include bomb dogs as well as drug dogs. Training continues and the deterrent affect has been absolutely effective.

### 5.4 Area Maritime Security

Several opportunities have been available through our participation in Area Maritime Security initiatives. Vessels, personnel for casualties, planning and asset allocation have all been discussed, planned and at exercise time executed.

Additional exercise opportunities surface when an area exercise is close enough to warrant us elevating our MARSEC level because of the threat in the area. This is a real time "threat in the area" type drill that lasts for several hours and tests our ability to ramp up our security levels. Primarily involved are crew and students, however the entire community is impacted when our MARSEC level changes and certainly demonstrates to the community at large our readiness to react.

## 6 Summary (lessons learned)

Multiple opportunities arise in the real world of ship security within the ship's plan itself and in the liaison with shore entities and their facility plans. MMA has made it a point to participate in exercises, drills and area events whenever possible. The decision has been a good one and our students are well prepared to recognize and deal with different levels of security, both procedurally and operationally.

### 6.1 Building Block Principle of learning

One precept that we adopted in our security training is that of the Building Block Principle [4]. Our student population cannot have open access to our security plan as that is specifically forbidden, nor would it make sense. However, by introducing them to various aspects of the plan and early training during their first year at MMA, means that they will get to practice real, on board security watches on their first cruise. During their transition to the real merchant fleet in the $2^{nd}$ year they have a set of basic skills and training to take with them. They should be well prepared to participate in any shipboard security on any ship and at any facility.

The final two years at MMA, after cadet shipping, are spent participating in planning, executing and being in charge of a security detail. As upper class cadets they are in charge. They should be ready to react to any situation that may arise. Opportunities should arise for them to take part in a real ship security assessment. This task, and an audit which entails accompanying the U.S. Coast Guard inspector in the annual inspection, will mean the student, upon graduation and matriculation to the merchant fleet as Third Mate or Third Engineer, will have had four years of increasing involvement with Maritime Security.

Inherent value is built into the structure of the training program. It is an integral part of every step. Students learn best when they can relate to and see value in what they are doing. We have striven to make this program work and prosper. Results to date have been gratifying.

## 6.2 The next step

As we march on towards ISPS being integrated into STCW as a competency that must be assessed, we are positioning ourselves to restructure our training efforts to allow for periodic assessments. Because of our structure and the active participation of our students in all four years it will be an easy transition. Assessing the competency is the goal and we are developing the paperwork as this is being written.

Table 1: Student Security Training at MMA.

| When | What | Remarks |
|---|---|---|
| 1st year at MMA | Force Protection / Anti-Terrorism | Course and training |
| 1st Cruise aboard TS STATE OF MAINE (TSSOM) | Watches & Audits | Assigned to Security detail |
| 2nd Year at MMA | Various security segments imbedded in courses | Academic |
| Cadet Shipping | Merchant Ship | As Directed and as part of a Sea Project |
| 3rd Year at MMA | Various security segments imbedded in courses.<br>USCG Certificate of Inspection Self Inspection Program | Academic<br>Included audits, drills and procedures in the SIP program of Maintenance. |
| 2nd Cruise aboard TSSOM | Security Detail | In charge and direct liaison with Midshipman Officer of the Deck, Ship's Watch Officer and possible shore side involvement with facility plan |
| 4th year at MMA | Various security segments imbedded in courses | Academic |
| Upper Class Cruise | Ship Security Officer Model Course | Classroom, filed exercises and competency assessment |
| All 4 years | Access Control | Introduction to and use of security cards, electronic data logging and accountability |

### 6.3 Course certification

Maine Maritime Academy is proceeding to certify the Ship / Vessel Security Officer model course in two ways. First is to offer it as part of continuing education, and second is as incorporated in our curriculum as part of our normal STCW training. It is the intent that classroom and practical course work will take place aboard the training ship during cruises for all who are in the license officer program.

With the acceptance of a "Model Course" for Ship / Vessel Security Officer we are transitioning to provide the required course hours and involvement of all our students as shown in table 1.

### 6.4 Sample 2005 pre-cruise training

The pre-cruise training PowerPoint presentation in PDF format that was used in May of 2005 is attached as an addendum to this paper for those interested in seeing it.

## References


[1] Hesse, H. and Charalambous, N. New Security Measures for the International Shipping Community. WMU Journal of Marine Affairs, 2004, Vol 3, No 2, pp. 123–138.

[2] Congress, U.S. Subchapter H of Title 33, Code of Federal Regulations, Title 46 Automatic Identification System.

[3] Barth, Roland S., Lessons Learned: Shaping Relationships and the Culture of the Workplace. Corwin Press, Thousand Oaks. Pg 6.

[4] Building Block Principle of Learning Example: Learning to Read. http://ericec.org/princple.html

# Including ISPS requirements in the MET scheme of the Arab Academy for Science, Technology and Maritime Transport through its Regional Maritime Security Institute

M. E. D. M. El Ashmawy
*Arab Academy for Science, Technology and Maritime Transport, Egypt*

## Abstract

MET is generally defined as the process which provides education and training for seafarers at operational and management levels in the shipping industry. The continuous development of MET in AAST-MT depends on the ability to implement the requirements of international conventions and codes, such as the ISPS Code, and the capability of providing the necessary type of training to various cultures. The comprehensive new regulatory regime, adopted in a Diplomatic Conference on Maritime Security at the end of 2002, describes in detail what shipping companies, port authorities, ships' crews, and others should do in order to minimize any threat to the shipping industry. The Egyptian Government, represented by its Maritime Administration, has issued a national decree to establish the Regional Institute for Maritime Security. AAST-MT assumed responsibility to establish this institute in order to serve Egypt and regional countries in implementing the requirements of the ISPS code.
*Keywords: MET, enhance maritime security, AAST-MT, examination affairs, Regional Maritime Security Institute, implementation the requirements of ISPS Code.*

## 1 Introduction

MET is the process that covers matters relating to aspects of maritime and marine affairs such as nautical sciences, marine safety, environment protection, and maritime security. It is the wider aggregation of education and training systems in general. The questions raised are: how can a process be introduced which will meet the requirements of the new regulations in international conventions, in particular the new chapter XI-2 of SOLAS "Special Measures to Enhance Maritime Security, ISPS Code" on the developing of the skills of seafarers, and how to improve and intensify the ability of quickly adapting to diverse demands of the maritime industry.

Safety, security, efficiency of ships and clean environment of oceans require not only advanced technology of ships and equipment, but also an adequate level of manning and operational procedures.

AAST-MT with its Maritime sector is responsible for maritime education and training. All sectors are necessary to interface with the shipping industries and with IMO requirements in order to obtain the latest developments of International Conventions, Codes, and Resolutions as well as national requirements.

The present question is "what are the requirements necessary to achieve effective development of MET in the Academy and its maritime sector to meet the continuously increasing requirements in accordance with the amendments to International Conventions?"

AAST-MT has given high priority to the development of MET and to the development of human resources by aiming at the highest quality of MET on all levels. One of the subjects given a high priority has been the establishment of the Examination Affairs and its departments, because the most important factor affecting the improvement and standard of Maritime Security regimes is the human resources factor. The Egyptian Maritime Administration has issued a national decree to establish the Regional Institute for Maritime Security. AAST-MT assumed responsibility for establishing this Institute to implement the requirements of the ISPS Code.

## 2 Human resources

Since man first set sail accidents at sea have been increasing, but now we face a new type of incident: terrorist attacks. As the 21st century started, we expected to witness radical changes in the proficiency required by seafarers.

The influence of the human element is very high and is a very important factor in the process of carrying out the various functions of shipping companies. It plays the most crucial role in almost all operations at sea and ashore.

Education and professional training, as well as development of performance should be given due consideration. The proper implementation of the International Conventions will go a long way towards achieving these objectives, and a very significant point is the need for expedient crew training for tasks, which are very specialized and complicated. Emphasis should be placed on the important role played by those provide this training and we must ensure that they are highly qualified, well motivated and provided with a work environment that helps improve their skills and encourages them in carrying out their professional responsibilities.

# 3 SOLAS, 1974 Convention and ISPS Code

The SOLAS in its successive forms is generally regarded as the most important of all international conventions concerning the safety of merchant ships.

The end of 2002 saw the adoption at a Diplomatic Conference of a comprehensive new regulatory regime in the amendments to the SOLAS Convention and the related International Ship and Port Facility Security Code "ISPS". The ISPS Code became mandatory on July 1, 2004.

The amendments in SOLAS, 74 that aimed at enhancing maritime security on board ships and at ship/port interface area created a new SOLAS chapter dealing specifically with maritime security. This in turn, contains the mandatory requirement for ships to comply with the new International Ship and Port facility Security Code "ISPS Code".

# 4 Security culture

The ISPS code requires governments to collate and evaluate information regarding security threats and exchange such information with other contracting governments. Shipboard and port facility personnel need to be aware of security threats and report security concerns to the proper authorities for their evaluation. Governments need to provide security related guidelines for ships and port facilities. Therefore, we are actually talking about creating an entirely new culture amongst those involved in the day-to-day operation of shipping and port industries.

## 4.1 How to create maritime security culture

Maritime security culture is a new term, and it can become a reality although the implementation is not yet fully introduced. Two important factors can assist in cultural development within a community: time and the environment.

Maritime security culture is the way in which the maritime community behaves in different maritime sectors such as ships, ports, shipping companies as well as maritime institutes to prevent hazards to people, ships and cargo, ports, and shipping companies.

The concept of international maritime security comprises certain security standards which could be applied everywhere despite cultural differences. Uniform maritime education and training is the key to international maritime security culture. As the foundation of any culture is the human element, the provision of basic education and training is a prerequisite in preparing personnel.

The Regional Maritime Security Institute of AAST-MT is involved in this new system; the staff do all they can to ensure that the trainees acquire the concepts of security culture, and that the graduates return to key maritime positions where they are able to act as catalysts in promoting security culture. There is a need to promote security culture that requires the cooperation of security officers at sea and ashore.

Security culture must deal with the concept of the collaboration between management and workforce in the broader context. Safety and security of ships and ports as well as ship's personnel are surely the most important considerations. In 2002, IMO showed its changing priorities by adopting a new mission declaration, an evolution from the theme of "Safer Shipping, Cleaner Ocean" to "Safe, Secure, and Efficient Shipping on Clean Ocean". In essence, safety and security have the highest of priorities.

## 5 Arab Academy for Science and Technology and Maritime Transport "AAST-MT"

The AAST–MT was established in 1972 under the name of Arab Maritime Transport Academy (AMTA) in Alexandria, Egypt. Since that time, AMTA operated as a regional UNDP project, offering MET to qualify seafarers in the streams of navigation, marine engineering, radio officers, and commercial studies (UNCTAD) and seaman training.

Since its establishment, the Academy has had a visionary open-door policy approach, due to the international nature of the Maritime Transport industry as stipulated and enforced by the conventions and regulations issued by IMO. Because of the Academy's expansion in educational, training and research activities as well as engineering and management, the Economic and Social Council of the Arab league agreed to change the name to Arab Academy for Science and Technology and Maritime Transport.

### 5.1 AAST-MT from regional to global

The Academy is an active member in the Association of Arab universities, and has excellent relations with international specialized organizations, universities and research centres. After implementing and developing its Quality Assurance system covering programmes of studies in 1999, the Academy attained ISO 9001 from one of the highest certification bodies' world wide, DNV

The Academy won the Trophy of Sea Trade Awards in the Innovations category in 1999. The Academy places great expectations in its partnership with IMO to bridge the enormous gap that exists between developing and developed countries in the field of education training, quality of seafarers, technological aspects of ships and equipment implementation of International conventions and resolutions, port administrations and logistics. Let us all join forces to ensure safer seas and cleaner oceans as well as a secure environment and make this world a better place for the human race.

The Academy's excellent record in providing maritime education and training resulted in the signing of the "MOU" with IMO in October 2001, which was subsequently renewed for a further two years in October 2003. As a result, the scope of the MOU has extended thus ensuring the presence of the IMO in the region through the services provided by the Academy.

### 5.2 Examination affairs

#### 5.2.1 Introduction

In view of the importance of examinations and their role in ensuring quality of education and training, and based on the importance of the whole examination process, since its inception in 1972 the Academy has worked diligently towards improving examination regulations. There is collaboration with maritime education institutes worldwide and specialized reputable consultants in order to keep abreast of technological advances in the profession. The Examination sector, which includes eight departments, all of which are responsible, for supporting the process of MET, these departments are:

1. Maritime Transport Examination Centre for Management, Operational, and Support Levels.
2. Regional Examination Centre for Management, Operational, and Support Levels.
3. Port State Control Unit.
4. Regional Maritime Security Institute:
   In view of the importance of applying the ISPS Code as quickly as possible, the Academy acted at the international level in coordination with the Ministry of Transport of the Arab Republic of Egypt through supporting the Maritime Security Fund of the International Maritime Organization with a grant of US$ 15000. It merits mentioning that Egypt is the second country in the world after Germany to provide this support at the international level, which drove the Organization to support the Academy in the establishment of "The Regional Maritime Security Institute". The maritime teaching staff has excellent academic and industrial backgrounds and many have published papers on their specialization. The Academy is proud to have links with various industries on a national and international level, provide outstanding work experience opportunities.
5. Global Maritime Distress and Safety System (GMDSS).
6. Fisheries competency examination.
7. The activities of the International Maritime Organization "IMO":
   a. the Unit responsible for following up the meeting and Conventions of IMO;
   b. the Contact Office in Charge of the MOU signed with IMO.
8. Information centre.

## 6 The implementation of the ISPS Code in the Arab Republic of Egypt and other countries in the region

### 6.1 Introduction and the role of the Academy

After the 11$^{th}$ of September 2001 disaster in the United State of America, the IMO Secretary General emphasized the need to review the measures already adopted by IMO to combat acts of violence and crime at sea. The international community began confronting terrorism after those events.

Egypt has been one of the first countries, which accepted and signed the December 2002 amendments to the SOLAS Convention, and financially contributed in the enforcement of the implementation process. The Egyptian Maritime Authority has taken several steps to meet its international commitments, and to implement the provisions of the new chapter XI-2 amended to the SOLAS Convention. Within this context, and in view of the importance of applying the Code as quickly as possible, the Academy acted at the international level in coordination with the Ministry of Transport of the Arab Republic of Egypt through supporting the Maritime Security Fund of IMO with a grant of US $ 15000.

## 6.2 The implementation stage

The Egyptian Government has taken several steps to implement the ISPS Code, summarized as follows:

July 2003: Establishing the Regional Maritime Security Institute in "AAST-MT" Serve Egypt and all countries in the Region for assisting in the implementation process of the Code.

Conduct security assessments and setting up security plans, in addition to holding training sessions for personnel serving at sea, in shipping companies, and in port facilities in line with IMO Maritime Security Model Courses.

August 2003: The Minister of Transport issued decree No. 392 in 2003 pertaining to the establishment and concerning the formation of the Major Committee for Maritime Security, which set out the general framework of implementing the Code. The Major Maritime Security Committee headed by the Head of Maritime Transport Sector in order to effect coordination with concerned bodies, included but not limited to the following:

Port Authorities of Egypt: Alexandria Port Authority, Damietta Port Authority, Port Said Authority, and Red Sea Port Authority.

Ministry of Interior Sector in charge of port security: Port Police.

The Sector of shipping Companies operating ships hoisting the Egyptian Flag.

Education and Training Institutes exemplified by the Maritime Security Institute of AAST-MT, which is the only specialized and recognized maritime institute in Egypt.

Ships: Establishing a sub committee namely "The Sub Committee for Shipping Companies and Ships" to implement the provisions of the ISPS Code with respect to shipping companies and the ships hoisting the Egyptian flag.

Ports: Establishing a sub committee namely "The Sub Committee for Port Facilities" to implement the provisions of the ISPS Code with respect to port facilities.

The Major Committee approved the following in response to the recommendations of the follow-up committee in charge of the security of ships and companies:

1. Designating the Major Committee for the Security of ships and ports as the Recognized Security Organization (RSO) in Egypt.

2. Designating the Maritime Security Institute of AAST-MT Local Designated Organization in charge of conducting the preliminary security assessment of and setting up the security plan for shipping companies and ships.
3. Designating the recognized bodies in charge of auditing the security plan, checking its conformance with the requirements of the Code, and issuing the International Security Certificate for ships and companies only as follows:
   a. Lloyd's Germanischer (GL), Det Norske Veritas (D.N.V.), American
   b. Bureau of Shipping (ABS), Lloyd's Register (L.R), Bureau Veritas (B.V),
   c. Nippon Kaiji Kyokai (N.K.K), Greek Register, and Polish Register.
   d. Designating the Regional Maritime Security Institute of AAST-MT as the body in charge of conducting training as follows: ISPS Code familiarization course for all personnel serving in companies, ports and at sea, Ship Security Officer course, Company Security Officer course, and Port Security Officer course.

Determining the minimum governmental measures necessary for the implementation of the Code and the required documents for ports. In addition, entrusting the Regional Maritime Security Institute of AAST-MT with the task of implementing the requirements of the ISPS Code in cooperation with Ports Security Authority Egypt.

September 2003: The Maritime Security Committee has decided the following issues:

- The Maritime Security Committee has been nominated as the Recognized Security Institute.
- The Classification Societies to be entrusted with the task of auditing ships security plan and checking their conformance with international requirements have been determined through electing a number of IACS Group.
- Considering that Ports Police Administration has been playing an active role in implementing security measures in ports, it has been assigned the task of conducting security assessment and setting security plans in ports. The Ports Police Administration shall effect coordination with Regional Maritime Security Institute within the field of setting security plans and conducting security assessments in accordance with the documents and procedures stipulated in the ISPS Code.
- Port Facilities Assessment and Plans to be implemented in cooperation between Port Authorities, Internal Police, and the Regional Maritime Security Institute.
- Establishing and improving communication centres in each Port Authority connected to the Egyptian Maritime Sector Communication centre located at the Egyptian Maritime Administration.

- The Maritime Security Committee meets twice monthly to follow up the achievements and to facilitate the implementation process, which finalized on June 2004.

## 6.3 The Role of the Regional Maritime Security Institute

The Structure of the Institute:

1. Maritime Security, Ships. 2. Maritime Security, Port facilities.

The Institute provides the following:

*Training Session for Personnel Serving at Sea:*

1. Awareness of ISPS Code. 2. Company Security Officer.
3. Ship Security Officer.

*Training Sessions for Personnel of:*

1. Awareness of ISPS Code. 2. Port facility security Officer.

*Assessment and Plans:*

1. Security Assessment. 2. On-scene Survey.
3. Security Plane. 4. Follow-up implementation.

### 6.3.1 Quality assurance of maritime training

Implementing the requirements of the ISPS Code and applying it to ships, ports and companies, in addition to training personnel actually began in 2004. All port security plans have been ready since the end of May 2004. Training and testing the security plans began in June 2004, and the actual application was started in July 2004.

EGYPT: In the light of the foregoing account, AAST-MT played a major role in implementing the requirements of the Code in Egypt on the specified date through the Regional Maritime Security Institute.

*First*: Training Marine Personnel (started in October 2003): Training session for masters, deck officers, marine engineers, crewmembers and port personnel. The following numbers of trainees were trained:

Awareness of ISPS Code: 8000 trainees.

Ship Security Officer Session: 1500 trainees.

Company security Officers: 250 trainees.

Port facility Security Officer: 160 trainees.

*Second*: Ships Assessment and Planning: Within the context of setting security plans for shipping companies and ships hoisting the Egyptian flag, the Regional Maritime security Institute conducted contracts with shipping companies to conduct security assessment and setting up security plans.

Egyptian flagged vessels complying with ISPS Code: 100 %.

None conventions vessels operating in territorial water: 70 %.

*Third*: Port Facilities Assessment and Planning: The Institute and Port Police team was formed, the team conducted security assessments for major Egyptian ports and port facilities serving ships engaged in international voyages. All the requirements of the Code are in effect.

Government Ports: 100 %.

Specialized Ports (petroleum, minerals …etc): 60 %.

### 6.3.2 Regional recognition

The Regional Maritime Security Institute has been approved in Saudi Arabia, United Arab Emirates (UAE) and Lebanon as "Recognized Security Organization", and started cooperation with Saudi Ports Authority and Lebanon Maritime Administration in the implementation of the ISPS Code.

**6.3.2.1 Related regional activities** Due to the pioneering role of the Academy as one of the specialized institutions of the Arab League and as a centre of expertise in the maritime field, the Regional Maritime Security Institute contacted the Ministry of Transport and Communications of the UAE seeking approval for the purposes of implementing the requirements of the ISPS Code. The Ministry responded favourably and promptly issued two decrees for the year 2004 accrediting the Academy's Regional Maritime Security Institute as the body to implement the ISPS Code requirements in UAE, thus initiating cooperation with the Academy under this patronage.

UAE: The Institute organized a Regional Seminar and Workshop in Dubai, UAE at the end of February 2004 with the support and participation of IMO on the ISPS Code. The seminar was attended by official seniors from 15 Arab Countries and was successful in providing attendance with the urgency of complying with the requirement of ISPS Code before 1st July 2004.

### 6.3.3 The training courses in ISPS Code in the region

**6.3.3.1 The Republic of Lebanon "Scope of the Work"** The Institute has applied the ISPS Code and has implemented the security assessment and security plan for the 14 port facilities in Lebanon. This also includes measuring port facilities security officers' performances in accordance with IMO guidelines.
Awareness course: 50 persons.
Ship Security course: 150 persons.
Port Facilities Security courses: 80 persons.

**6.3.3.2 The Republic of Syria:**

- Ship security officers: 150 persons.

**6.3.3.3 The Hashemite Kingdom of Jordan**

- ISPS Code Familiarization (Awareness course): 28 persons.
- Ship Security course: 32 persons.

**6.3.3.4 UAE "Dubai"**

- Port facility security officer: 80 persons.

**6.3.3.5 Kingdom of Saudi Arabia "Scope of the Work"** The Institute participated in cooperation with the German Technical Cooperation Agency (GTZ) in the security assessment and development of security plans for 8 ports with 40 port facilities, all controlled by Saudi Port Authorities. Evaluation of ISPS Code was effected in each of the 40 port facilities as well as measuring the performance of security officers in port facilities.

- Port facility security officer: 92 persons.
- ISPS Code familiarization (Awareness course): 50 persons.

## 7 Conclusion

Due to full cooperation between Ministry of Transport, Port Police, Egyptian Navy and all security authorities in Egypt, the Regional Maritime security Institute was able to execute and fully implement the requirement of ISPS Code for all Egyptian flagged vessels and governmental ports before the dead line of 1st July 2004. Considering the experience gained by the Institute, the Academy completed the ISPS requirements and implementation in Kingdom of Saudi Arabia, Lebanon, Jordon and Syria. The mean objective in establishing "The regional maritime Security Institute" is to assess and help the regional countries and in particular African Nations to comply with ISPS Code requirements.

## References

[1] Lewarn, B., Maritime education and training- the future is now! *Proc. of 2nd Int. Conf. of IAMU,* Kobe, Japan, pp. 207-212, 2001.
[2] O'Neill, W., Safety and Security now inextricably Linked, IMO News, issue 4, pp. 4, London, UK, 2001.
[3] Heikki, V., The culture of safety at Sea, IMO news, issue 4, pp. 10-13, London, UK, 2001.
[4] IMO News, Assembly confirms security conference in December 2002, issue 4, pp. 18-21,London, UK, 2001.
[5] IMO News, IMO agrees raft of measures to bolster ship security, issue 1, pp. 6, London, UK, 2002.
[6] IMO News, IMO adopts comprehensive maritime security measures, issue 1, pp. 5, London, UK, 2003.
[7] IMO News, IMO urges early implementation of maritime security measures, issue 2, pp. 8-9, London, UK, 2003.
[8] IMO News, SOLAS security amendments and ISPS Code now in force, issue 3, pp. 7-8, London, UK, 2004.
[9] AAST-MT, www.aast.edu.
[10] IMO, www.imo.org.

# The fast track to ISPS Code and national security regulation implementation and the implications for marine educators

F. Anstey
*School of Maritime Studies,*
*Fisheries and Marine Institute of Memorial University, Canada*

## Abstract

A literature review of the national regulations of Canada, the United States, and the UK have revealed a number of factors which have affected the quality of instruction in the field of maritime security. The speed of development and implementation of the ISPS Code is the root cause of a plethora of problems affecting marine educators and trainers (MET). Port state security regulations have not completely matched the ISPS Code and the result has been a struggle to develop training that addresses both. Deviant national regulations have been often passed as "just-in-time" legislation. For training providers this problem is exacerbated as the seafarer's country of residence, the flag state of the vessel, and the port state visited, are frequently not the same. Many of the training topics listed in the ISPS Code are outside the purview of most maritime lecturers, and the IMO Train-the-Trainer Course has not been conducted in a timely enough manner. A number of administrations recognize the IMO model course outlines while others insist on guidelines and timelines that differ. The myriad of training providers that have surfaced, how such providers are scrutinized, and how the associated course offerings are approved, needs to be uniformly addressed. This may have significant impact on proposed amendments to the STCW Code for Ship Security Officer certification. Port State Control Officers have training, and expectations may vary from country to country or indeed from person to person.
*Keywords: ISPS, security training, train the trainer.*

## 1 Introduction

The events that unfolded in the United States on September 11, 2001 (9/11) have had enormous consequences, and the marine industry has not been immune from the resultant changes. These events lead the Commandant of the United States Coast Guard [1] to address the General Assembly of the International Maritime Organization (IMO), November 2001, and to urge it to implement measures, which addressed security within the maritime industry. The response of IMO [2] was to review, through Resolution A924 (22), the various security measures, and ultimately, through it's Maritime Safety Committee (MSC) and Maritime Security Working Group (MSWG), to develop the International Ship and Port Facility Security Code (ISPS) and the associated security measures. These were adopted by a Conference on Maritime Security, December 2002, and were arbitrarily scheduled to come into force on July 1, 2004, a scant one and a half years later.

## 2 Implementation

In order for Contracting Governments to implement the new security measures, they had to decide whether to apply the ISPS Code in total or to modify it to meet that country's specific objectives. Although 102 countries had agreed to the content of the ISPS Code, upon returning to their own jurisdiction, some determined that the Code did not address that country's concerns. The time taken to design, draft, and amend state legislation often meant that it was not finalized until close to the mandatory implementation date.

The United States had been working on security measures, as of October 2001. It had existing security regulations for passenger vessels, which it used to shape its submission for ISPS and to formulate its own Maritime Transportation Security Regulations (MTSR). It felt an urgency to implement such measures because of the direct attack of 9/11. It was therefore able to publish, for stakeholder feedback, on July 1, 2003, a draft of the national security regulations, and on October 22, 2003 the modified final version.

However, the United States, while formulating such legislation in a timely fashion, created problems for other jurisdictions. The US was concerned that the ISPS Code only identified Part A as compulsory. It was envisioned that without a mandatory use of part B, many vessels and port facilities might only pay lip service to the requirements of the ISPS Code. The US also had concerns with the limited number of ship types to which the Code applied. IMO [3] determined that the ISPS Code was applicable to certain categories of ships engaged on international voyages, namely passenger ships; cargo ships of 500 gross tonnage and upward; and mobile offshore drilling units. The United States expanded the list to included vessels of 100 gross tonnage and upward; certain towing vessels; and certain towed barges, amongst others.

It also had concern that "international voyage" as indicated by the ISPS Code, and defined by SOLAS, would not include voyages on the Great Lakes and St. Lawrence Seaway. The USCG [4] therefore required US flag and foreign flag vessels on those voyages to comply with the national regulations.

Other flag states that had vessels trading with the United States were impacted by the US regulations. If those countries applied only the requirements of the ISPS Code, then there would be many vessels not meeting the US threshold and thus, either having to submit security plans to the USCG or running afoul of port state control measures upon attempted entry into the United States.

Canada, which had a heavy reliance on trade with the United States, determined that it was advantageous to draft legislation, which closely followed the American model. On November 26, 2003, Transport Canada [5] issued draft legislation and undertook a cross-country public consultative process. This proposed legislation modified the list of applicable vessels, but not to the extent that the United States had. It included a section on offshore facilities; a section outlining a restricted area security clearance program; and it defined applicable voyages to include those between countries on the Great Lakes and St. Lawrence Seaway. Heavy lobbying by stakeholders resulted in a number of changes including the deletion of sections on offshore facilities, and the restricted area security clearance program. The final version was completed on June 15, 2004, just days prior to the July 1 effective date. As of July 2005 Canada is still in the process of drafting amendments to the Canadian Maritime Transportation Security Regulations (MTSR).

The European Parliament [6] published *Regulation (EC) no 725/2004* on March 31, 2004. This regulation instructed member states to, along with Part A of the ISPS Code, take fully into account the guidance of Part B, but it also identified sections of Part B which were to be treated as mandatory. It defined applicable ships as per the ISPS model but expanded the list to include domestic Class-A passenger ships effective July 1, 2005, and other domestic ships effective July 1, 2007.

This evolving process had obvious implications for marine educators. There were mandatory training requirements for security officers outlined within the ISPS Code and national regulations. As indicated by this representative sampling of regulations, some countries were drafting legislation, which was "just-in-time" and had variances to the ISPS Code and that differed from country to country. Ship and port facility owners, and training participants wanted relevant training in both the Code and pertinent national regulations. Classroom time was often used, not just reviewing the requirements of the ISPS Code, but also discussing how the various regulations would apply to individual vessels and port facilities. The relevancy of information given to students, particularly regarding national legislation, often depended on the timeliness of enrolment. Proactive companies intent on the early establishment of security plans and the early enrolment of crew or personnel into training courses were, by July 1, 2004, often operating with outdated and inaccurate information. It continues to be a challenging task for educators to deliver up-to-date information, particularly in terms of national legislation and guidance.

## 3 Participants and clientele

The maritime industry is a global one with seafarers from a multitude of countries, working on vessels flagged by an ever-increasing number of Contracting Governments. These ships visit a countless number of ports worldwide. The mariner may sometimes work on a vessel that requires security certification and at other times on one that does not. Subsequent employment may be found on a vessel of another flag state, with other security requirements. In addition to vessels there are thousands of designated port facilities covered by the new security code and security regulations.

These factors have also created challenges for marine educators. Participants are often trained, during time-off, at their country of residence. However, due to their vessel's flag or due to the port states that the ship is to visit, participants have little interest in the security regulations of their own country. The designated Ship Security Officer wants information that is relevant for their vessel. This will include national regulations for the flag state of their vessel and information regarding port state control measures for applicable port visits. The class composition, in terms of participants, of many courses may cover a number of permutations in terms of the country of residence, flag state, and port state control measures encountered. This has required of the trainer a body of knowledge that is varied, comprehensive, and as indicated previously, ever-changing.

The ISPS Code specifies training requirements for the Ship Security Officer (SSO); the Company Security Officer (CSO); the Port Facility Security Officer (PFSO); those, at both port facilities and onboard ships with security duties and those, at both port facilities and onboard ships without security duties. Each course requires its own learning objectives, and course material. Each may address the educational needs of a different category of learner. These factors have meant increased demands on both institutions and facilitators as they endeavoured to provide relevant training to all, particularly in the months before the mandatory implementation of the Code.

## 4 Training topics

On July 1, 2004, all applicable ships and port facilities were required to have implemented an approved security plan and to designate the appropriate security officers, and security personnel. Those persons, and in particular the CSO and appropriate shore-based personnel, the SSO, the PFSO and appropriate port facility security personnel, were to have received identified and appropriate training.

The IMO [7] ISPS Code identifies 25 areas of training that may be appropriate, for the position of SSO alone. Some of the listed topics include, relevant government legislation and regulations; methodology of ship security surveys; ship and port operations and conditions; knowledge of current security threats and patterns; recognition and detection of weapons and dangerous devices; methods of physical searches; and crowd management.

Port state control officers have recognized the Ship Security Officer training certificate as proof that the SSO has had the appropriate training. Therefore, as indicated by the IMO Model Course outline, the course is required to cover all of the topics as listed in the ISPS Code. Admittedly, the onus is on the appropriate security officer to include supplemental training where required. However, it would appear incumbent on the educator to have more than a passing knowledge of all the listed topics.

These topics can be divided into marine related topics and security related topics. Institutions have used trainers who have either a marine background or a military/security background and then provided supplemental training in the other general area, or have used a team approach, with a number of trainers with different backgrounds and experiences conducting the same course. In some cases the emphasis has been on life experiences or vocations of the facilitator, and with little emphasis on teaching qualifications.

Cost recovery requirements may necessitate increased course fees to cover the hiring of additional personnel. The ebb and flow of demand for security training may constrain the ability to have staff employed permanently, particularly security specialists, and thus require the availability of a number of contractual employees, which may in turn affect the continuity or quality of the course.

There was recognition by IMO that the mandated topics were not within the purview of most marine educators. Therefore, IMO [7] designed a six-day train-the-trainer security program, with a goal to provide eighteen offerings worldwide, to a target audience of security instructors of national training centres. Unfortunately, the IMO was also affected by the fast pace of implementation of the ISPS Code. According to an IMO [8] press release of August 6, 2004, 89.5 per cent of port facilities had approved security plans in place, and the compliance rate for ships was heralded at 90 percent. However, the train-the-trainer course was not scheduled to start until September of that year. This would imply that these port facilities and vessels had security officers that had not been trained by attendees of the train-the-trainer program.

## 5 Recognition and certification of training courses

IMO had foreseen that the area of training was to be problematic. In late 2003 the IMO, with the help of the Governments of the United States of America and India, provided model course outlines for courses for the Company Security Officer, the Ship Security Officer, and the Port Facility Security Officer.

Each included the course aims; the objectives; a list of suggested teaching aids; the course outline; a timetable; the learning objectives; and the instructor manual. IMO [9] indicated that the course outline was not intended as a tool to be rigidly followed but rather, "to identify the basic entry requirements and trainee target group for each course in universally applicable terms, and to specify clearly the technical content and levels of knowledge and skill necessary to meet the technical intent" of the ISPS Code. Training institutions were now provided with tools to more quickly formulate the required courses.

Canada decided that the IMO model courses were to be the basis for the required training. Due to time constraints, it was decided that it would not certify training institutions, but that Transport Canada would require those entities that were offering courses in Canada to submit their training packages for review. The agency provided feedback, which was followed with an audit of the course delivery. Those institutions that met the training requirements were listed on the Transport Canada web site, as being "recognized" training providers.

This approval model focused on the audit of training in Canada versus the audit of training providers that were training Ship Security Officers for Canadian flag vessels. This process left the onus on Contracting Governments to determine which training providers, within their national boundaries were recognized or certified. For port state control purposes it accepted at face value the training certificates of other Contracting Government unless there was "clear grounds" that there was an identified problem.

In the United Kingdom (UK) the Department for Transport [11] assigned the responsibility for ports and passenger ships to TRANSEC and the responsibility for cargo ships to the Maritime and Coastguard Agency (MCA). TRANSEC was responsible for accrediting and approving training organizations for Port Facility Security Officer training, while the MCA was responsible for SSO and CSO training. The MCA [12] procedure for accreditation of the training organization required the receipt of a letter of application along with an abundance of information, including the course program; lecture notes; visual aids; handouts; assessment forms; and instructor qualifications. The MCA then conducted an on-site audit, and subsequent to a successful evaluation, listed that organization as being certified by MCA.

This model, as applied to ships, focused not on where training had taken place, but rather the registry of the vessel. The SSO of a UK registered vessel would be required to undertake training at an MCA approved training facility. For some ship owners and training facilities, this created certain obstacles. For example, the SSO of a UK registered fishery patrol vessel trading in international waters but only visiting Canadian ports would be required to undergo training at an MCA approved training facility. If the facility were in the UK, training provided little exposure to the Canadian regulations. If the facility were in Canada, that institution would have to follow an approval process that only resulted in certification from the MCA.

If all countries followed this model, it would require training providers to undertake numerous, costly, time consuming, and repetitive auditing procedures. Normally training facilities would not know the flag state of the participant's vessel until the start date of training. If the training received were not recognized by the flag state it would necessitate that the participant receive redundant approved training. Training that is approved by the flag state of one vessel would not necessarily be approved for the SSO when working on a vessel of another flag state. This model leaves the onus on shipping companies and/or participants to determine if training providers are accredited by the appropriate flag state, with no common system in place for certification. Of course the other extreme would see Contracting Governments without an approval process or guidelines and therefore a limited assurance of quality control of training programs.

The required length of the security courses has caused some confusion. The IMO model courses provided an itemized time tabling, with a course length of three days for each of the CSO and PFSO courses, and two days for the SSO course. Contracting Governments have required course durations, which may vary from this model. The MCA [13] required the SSO course to be of a three-day duration; the CSO course to be of a four-day duration; and a combined course to be of a five-day duration.

This illustrates some of the challenges for training providers in the area of certification. The problem was exacerbated prior to July 1, 2004 as ship and port facility owners, administrations, front-line personnel, and training providers, with significant time constraint, struggled to determine the varying requirements.

## 6 Seafarers' training, certification and watch-keeping (STCW)

A Sub-Committee, of IMO [14] in a report to the MSC, January 2005, proposed amendments to the STCW Code. In Annex 6, it outlined new requirements for the certificate of proficiency for the Ship Security Officer. It specified the standards of competence, and detailed transitional provisions through to 2009.

These standards dictated that the candidate provide evidence of demonstrated competence, of appropriate level of knowledge, and of training and experience. The method for demonstrating competence would be through the assessment of evidence obtained from approved training or through examination. The Contracting Government would determine the agency responsible, and the method used for the oversight of approved training.

The transitional provisions determined that competence for existing SSO's would be established through either the approved seagoing service as an SSO; the performance of equivalent security functions; the passing of an approved test; or the completion of approved training.

There was a heavy emphasis on "approval" in these proposed amendments. Contracting Governments, and training institutions will be required to determine the approval process for each of these identified topics. In some cases this may necessitate another series of review procedures. For example, in Canada, after 9/11, the newly formulated branch of Transport Canada-Security & Emergency Preparedness-was responsible for all matters related to maritime security. It was the body, which reviewed all security training. Previously all courses governed by STWC were under the domain of Transport Canada-Marine Safety. Subsequent to the amendments to the STCW Code these two agencies will have to establish guidelines for the new approval process, and determine which department will be responsible.

To complicate matters the Sub-Committee, in Annex 10 of the report, determined that for Company Security Officer training there would be guidelines instead of mandatory requirements. The MSC also determined that there would be no mandatory requirements or guidelines for Port Facility Security Officer training, because the position was shore-based.

Most training institutions have offered training courses for the three identified security positions. In the months before July 1, 2004, they made use of the model courses to organize training and used the outlined procedures, to receive approval for those course offerings. With the adoption of the recommendations of the MSC there may now be a range of standards, and a number of regulatory bodies.

The speed in which the ISPS Code was to be implemented has contributed significantly to these evolving problems. The initial focus was to have approved security plans in place for the identified class of ships, and port facilities by the designated implementation date. It was recognized that training was required but the process appears to have unfolded in a reactive rather than proactive way. The recommended STCW Code changes will necessitate a review of course approvals and may lead to other modifications, which in the extreme, may force companies to spend more time and money on "approved" training.

## 7 Port state control measures

Ship owners, CSO's, and SSO's were concerned with port state control measures that could be encountered. This topic was the focal point of discussion in many security course offerings.

The IMO [15] issued guidance in a circular entitled Interim Guidance on Control and Compliance Measures to Enhance Maritime Security. It gave basic guidance for security training and qualifications of port state control officers (PSCO); for ships entering waters of another Contracting Government; for control of ships in port; and for inspections. This information, while of value, was dated June 10, 2004. A high percentage of SSO's, and PSCO's had already undergone training by this date, and therefore did not have this information provided to them during training. In any case, this guidance did not always reflect the type of inspection to be anticipated while visiting various port states.

Some port states were more proactive in identifying port state control measures. The USCG [16] issued guidance on such measures through Navigation & Vessel Inspection Circular (NVIC) 06-03, on December 15, 2003. It introduced guidelines for the port state control targeting and boarding program. It gave the ship owner and Ship Security Officer comprehensive guidance for demonstrating compliance during such an inspection.

Other countries did not have formalized procedures in place. Canada did not fashion the Security & Emergency Preparedness branch of Transport Canada, for marine security, until after 9/11. It previously had an aviation division and subsequently seconded most of the personnel for the marine division from it. As of July 1, 2004, it had not issued formal guidelines for security boarding and inspection, and indeed had to retrain personnel for PSCO duty.

Port State Control Officers reviewed certain documentation in order to determine a vessel's security compliance. One such document is the Declaration of Security (DoS). The ISPS Code gave guidance on the usage of the DoS but stated that the Contracting Government should determine when the use of this instrument is required.

The Canadian MTSR of June 15, 2004 stipulated four scenarios for such use, namely when entities were operating at different MARSEC Levels; when one party did not have a security plan; during an interface with a specific vessel such as a cruise ship; or if the security officer of either had specific concerns.

The USCG issued guidance, May 2004, for DoS usage. It consisted of two tables, which included various permutations of different types of ships and barges, both manned and unmanned, carrying or not carrying certain dangerous cargos; and of different types of port facilities. Ships and port facilities were to use this "DoS Applicability Decision Tool" to determine if the DoS were required.

The UK, through MCA, also issued guidance as to when a DoS was required. It identified nine specific situations for vessels to request use of a DoS and six situations for port facilities to initiate the DoS.

The fact that port state control guidance was often late in coming or that there were different state requirements for the use of the DoS indicates the challenge for marine educators to provide meaningful information to course participants. Personal experience has shown that reference calls to government representatives often resulted in changing or conflicting advice. It was not uncommon to find PSCO's, custom and immigration personnel, or local authorities in attendance at security courses, attempting to gain relevant information.

## 8 Conclusions

The events of 9/11 required a drastic and varied response. The drafting of the ISPS Code was the primary one by the maritime industry. As evidenced by examples discussed throughout this paper the speed of implementation created challenges for stakeholders, including marine educators and trainers.

A different approach to the implementation of the ISPS Code, whether by a phased-in approach, or by having an effective date which was further into the future would have allowed training institutions to conduct a proper needs/capability analysis, and to put more emphasis on the appropriate training of personnel. Greater effort, while drafting the ISPS Code, towards ensuring various state requirements were met, would have minimized the current variations in national legislation.

A certification process for security courses, which required only one audit procedure, and that was uniformly accepted by all Contracting Governments, would ensure more cost effective, timely, and uniform course offerings. It would have provided more standard guidelines, which were more conducive to the eventual STCW certification. The IMO Train-the-Trainer Program, while a worthwhile one, would have been more beneficial if offered in a timely fashion. These challenges, notwithstanding, marine educators and trainers will continue to play their part in the implementation of international security measures.

## References

[1] USCG, *Federal Register*, United States Coast Guard: USA, Vol. 68, No. 204, p. 60448, 2003.

[2] IMO, What led to the development of the ISPS Code? IMO Newsroom. http://www.imo.org/Newsroom/mainframe.asp?topic_id=897.

[3] IMO, *International Ship and Port Facility Code,* International Maritime Organization: UK, p. 8, 2003.
[4] USCG, *Federal Register*, United States Coast Guard: USA, Vol. 68, No. 204, pp. 60512, & 60485, 2003.
[5] Transport Canada, Security & Emergency Preparedness, *Marine Transportation Security Regulations,* Government of Canada: Canada, November 26, 2003.
[6] European Parliament. Regulation (EC) No. 725/2004, http://europa.eu.int/eur-lex/pri/en/oj/dat/2004/l_129/l_12920040429en00010005.pdf.
[7] IMO, *International Ship and Port Facility Code,* International Maritime Organization: UK, p. 73-74, 2003.
[8] IMO, IMO Train-the-Trainer courses to be launched in Egypt. IMO Newsroom.http://www.imo.org/Newsroom/mainframe.asp?topic_id=848&doc_id=3826.
[9] IMO, Security compliance shows continued improvement. IMO Newsroom. http://www.imo.org/Newsroom/mainframe.asp?topic_id=892&doc_id=3760.
[10] IMO, *Model Course- Company Security Officer (Draft),* IMO: UK, p.1, May 29, 2003.
[11] Department for Transport, UK Maritime Security-FAQ's. http://www.dft.gov.uk/stellent/groups/dft_transsec/documents/page/dft_transsec_030409.hcsp.
[12] MCA, Approval of Security Training Courses, MCA website. http://www.mcga.gov.uk/c4mca/mcga-guidance-regulation/mcga-ops-ms-home/dops-ms-training/dops_securitybranch-trainingcourses.htm.
[13] Turkentine, B. Personal communication, November 8, 2004, Maritime Security Inspector, MCA, UK.
[14] IMO, Sub-Committee on Standards of Training and Watchkeeping, *Report to the Maritime Safety Committee-36th Session,* IMO: UK, pp. 21-25, Annex 6 & 10, 2005.
[15] IMO, Marine Safety Committee, Circular 1111-Annex 2, http://www.imo.org/includes/blastDataOnly.asp/data_id%3D9381/1111.pdf
[16] USCG, NAVIC 06-03, http://www.uscg.mil/hq/g-m/nvic/03/NVIC%2006-03%20Ch-1%20Part1.pdf.
[17] MCA, Declaration of Security, http://www.mcga.gov.uk/c4mca/mcga-dops_ms_declaration_of_security.pdf.

# An analysis of port state control inspections related to the ISPS Code

M. Yilmazel & E. Asyali
*Dokuz Eylül University, School of Maritime Business and Management, Turkey*

## Abstract

The ISPS Code came into effect on the 1st of July 2004. The overall objectives of the Code are to establish an international framework involving co-operation between contracting governments, government agencies, local administrations and the shipping industry to detect maritime security threats and take pro-active measures against potential terrorist attacks against ships and/or port facilities which are the vital instruments of the international trade.

The Code aims to reduce the vulnerability of port facilities and merchant ships to terrorist attacks and to increase the security awareness of the industry. The ISPS Code is the first ever internationally and widely agreed proactive regulatory framework to safeguard the maritime industry, seaborne trade, and the world economy from terrorism. In this study the success level of implementation of the ISPS Code already achieved by the ship managers is analysed through the port state control databases of the major regional maritime administrations and MOUs such as the Paris MOU, the Tokyo MOU, the Black Sea MOU and the United States Coast Guard (USCG). The monthly statistics of ISPS non-compliant ships have been compiled based on the variables such as the ships' flag, type, gross tonnage (gt), and the nature of deficiencies between the 1st July 2004, when the ISPS Code came into force, until the end of those months with available statistics currently released on the websites of the respective MOUs. Common awareness of errors and lapses, best practices, sharing of information, and industry-wide co-operation will play a vital role in developing a security culture in the shipping industry.

*Keywords: ISPS Code, port state control, security culture, detention.*

# 1 Introduction

Within the maritime community, fraudulent documents and certificates; piracy and armed robbery against ships; phantom ships; illegal migrants and stowaways have far long been the security issues, but terrorism has not been seen as a significant maritime threat until the attacks on the passenger vessels *Achille Lauro* in 1985 and *City of Poros* in 1989 [1, 2, 3]. In 1986, the International Maritime Organization (IMO) had adopted a Convention on the Suppression of Unlawful Acts that contained some advice on security for cruise ships. The 11$^{th}$ September 2001 events changed dramatically the perspective, as ships with their cargo are suddenly perceived that they could be used as a weapon and ports could be either targets or locations of attacks to cause havoc in international trade and the international economy. As the ships, ports and cargoes are the key points for security at maritime transportation system, the ship/shore interface emerged as a main weak point. Thereby, the ISPS Code mainly aimed to focus on the cooperation and coordination between ports and ships about security matters.

Briefly, the IMO, through adding the issue of maritime security to its constitutional mandates, took the necessary initiatives to establish a legal framework on maritime security resulting in the adoption of a new chapter in SOLAS on maritime security (Chapter XI-2) and a totally new international Code on ship and port facility security (ISPS) [4, 5]. Both of these documents entered into force on the 1st of July 2004. Remarkably, for the first time the remit of the SOLAS Convention was extended to shore facilities when the Solas Convention Amendments were adopted in December 2002. The ISPS Code not only applies to ships but also to the ship/port interface areas.

As world trade is highly dependent on maritime transport, effective and practicable security measures are needed to ensure that the international transportation system is protected from the acts of terrorism. The global nature of maritime transport requires that appropriate security regulations and standards be achieved through international consultation and consensus [1].

Maritime security covers four major inter-related areas. These are the ship; the crew, the cargo; and the port facilities. As a weak link in one of these areas will affect the overall transport security, a continuous assessment of risks by all participants in a "chain of responsibility" approach is a requirement. The maritime community must develop and maintain her "security culture" similar to her "safety culture". Compared to the level of implementation of the ISM Code and its associated level of safety culture which took the maritime industry more than a decade to achieve, the maritime industry has been constraint by a very limited transitional period to adapt to the requirements of the ISPS Code and develop an associated security culture.

Although there were many doubts about the haste in implementation, effects, practicability and effectiveness of the ISPS Code among the shipping practitioners, an intensive effort was performed globally to ensure the highest possible level of compliance by the governments, shipping and port industries. However, the increased number of crews in order to cope with the new requirements under the ISPS Code; the potential "wave of lawsuits" over charter contracts when problems such as off-hire situations arise from the Code; difficulty in motivating crews about code and of course security-related surcharges imposed by some port facilities, are some of the drawbacks of this new era [6].

## 2 Control mechanism

For an effective and efficient management of security in maritime transportation, control function plays an important role. Control is the process of monitoring activities to ensure that they are being accomplished as planned, and correcting any significant deviations. There are three different approaches to designing control systems. These are market, bureaucratic and clan control [7]. Maritime community provides a good example of bureaucratic control which is defined as an approach that emphasizes organizational authority and relies on administrative rules, regulations, procedures, policies, standardization of activities, well-defined job descriptions, and other administrative mechanisms to ensure that employees exhibit appropriate behaviours and meet performance standards. Parties in maritime industry are expected to adhere closely to the international conventions and stay within the guidelines. Establishing a safety and security culture is a way to apply clan control in which the shared values, norms, traditions, rituals, beliefs, and other aspects of the organization's culture regulate employee behaviours.

Port State Control is a widely used control mechanism among the shipping industry where generally bureaucratic control is applied. Port State Control (PSC) is a ship inspection process of foreign vessels in national ports to verify compliance with various major international maritime conventions, The driving force behind the PSC is to identify and eliminate sub-standard ships jumping flag state control, promoted and supported as a second line of defence.

## 3 Control process related to maritime security measures

In order to ensure the effective implementation of the ISPS Code, the control function plays an important role because; control is not only the process of monitoring activities to ensure that they are being accomplished as planned, but also a way to correct any significant deviations.

Ships, the shipping companies, port facilities and contracting governments have detailed responsibilities under the ISPS Code. One of the main responsibilities of Contracting Governments among others as per the ISPS Code/A-4.3 is; exercising control and monitoring compliance measures where contracting governments may not discharge and delegate their responsibility to a recognized security organization.

The legal references enabling the port states to exercise control on maritime security matters is set by the SOLAS Convention and the ISPS Code. SOLAS Reg. I-19 regulates "Control and Compliance Measures" in general. SOLAS Reg. XI-2/9 regulates the security related control function and the ISPS Code

Part B-4 sets the security related responsibilities of contracting governments in details, under the title of "control and compliance measures" from paragraph 4.29 to 4.46.

Regulation XI-2/9 of SOLAS describes the control and compliance measures applicable to ships. It is divided into three distinct sections; control of ships already in a port, control of ships intending to enter a port of another Contracting Government, and additional provisions applicable to both situations.

Regulation XI-2/9.1, control of ships in port, implements a system for the control of ships while in the port of a foreign country where duly authorized officers of the Contracting Government have the right to go on board the ship to verify that the "International Ship Security Certificate" or "Interim International Ships Security Certificate" issued under the provisions of Part A of the ISPS Code are in proper order. Then, if there are clear grounds to believe that the ship does not comply, control measures such as additional inspections or detention may be taken. This reflects the customary control mechanism under the port state control regime. Regulation XI-2/9.3 describes the safeguards that promote fair and proportionate implementation of these additional measures (ISPS-B/4.30).

Regulation XI-2/9.2 applies the control measures to ensure compliance to ships intending to enter a port of another Contracting Government and introduces an entirely different concept of control within chapter XI-2, applying to security only. Under this regulation measures may be implemented prior to the ship entering port -not in port- to better ensure security. If officers have clear grounds for believing that the ship is in non-compliance with the requirements of Regulation XI-2 or Part A of the ISPS Code, such officers may take steps in relation to that ship including denial of entry into port.

Both control mechanisms, in or out of the port, are based on the concept of clear grounds which means evidence or reliable information that the ship does not correspond with the requirements of Chapter XI-2 or Part A of this Code, taking into account the guidance given in Part B of the Code. Examples of possible clear grounds under regulations XI-2/9.1 and XI-2/9.2 are listed in ISPS-B/4.33.

In exercising control and compliance measures, as per ISPS-B/4.43, the duly authorized officers should ensure that any measures or steps imposed are proportionate. Such measures or steps should be reasonable and of the minimum severity and duration necessary to rectify or mitigate the non-compliance. No more favourable treatment principle is applied to the ships flying the flag of a State, which is not a Contracting Party to the Convention and not a Party to the 1988, SOLAS Protocol, and the ships below the Convention size as well.

## 4 Methodology

This paper presents the statistical analysis of the security related ship non-compliance data obtained from the monthly detention statistics released via the websites of the various MOUs on port state control and the USCG [8, 9, 10, 11]. The above mentioned data of the Black Sea MOU, from the 1st of July 2004 to the 1st April 2005; Paris MOU, from the 1st of July 2004 to the 1st of June 2005;

Tokyo MOU, from the 1st of July 2004 to the 1st of June 2005, and the USCG, from the 1st of July 2004 to the 1st May 2005, was duly scanned and processed into relevant statistical information.

The statistical information achieved for the ISPS non-compliant ships detained within these regional PSC regimes through the inspections conducted between the above stated periods were based on the variables such as the ship's age, flag, gross tonnage (gt), type, and the nature of the security related deficiencies.

## 5 Findings

It is seen that the overall number of ships detained within the above-specified PSC regions within the specified periods is 2511, of which 259 ships (10.3%) were detained on security grounds. The detention rates (Total Detentions on Security Grounds over Total Ships Detained) for each individual region are: the Black Sea MOU 6.6%, the Paris MOU 8.7%, the Tokyo MOU 4.4%, and the USCG 45.7%. The highest detention rate by USCG is highly remarkable among the others. It is also found that 46% of the detentions were due to only security grounds (see Table 1).

Table 1: Detention rates on security grounds.

| | **Black Sea MOU** (1.7. 04/ 1.4.05) | **Paris MOU** (1.7. 04/ 1.6. 05) | **Tokyo MOU** (1. 7. 04 / 1 .6 .05) | **USCG** (1.7.04 / 1.5.05) | **TOTAL** |
|---|---|---|---|---|---|
| **Total Detentions on Security Grounds** | 17 | 84 | 46 | 112 | 259 |
| A* | *13* | 57 | *31* | *19* | *120* |
| B** | *4* | 27 | *15* | *93* | *139* |
| **Total Ships Detained** | 258 | 964 | 1044 | 245 | 2511 |
| **Detention Rate (%)** | 6.6 | 8.7 | 4.4 | 45.7 | 10.3 |

* A: detentions with only security grounds.
**B: detentions with security grounds plus other non-compliances.

The overall detention figures on the grounds of security reveals that 4.6% of the ships detained are under 5 years old, 18.1% are between 5 to 14 years old and 77.3% are 15 years old and over. Therefore, we can undoubtedly confess that older ships are reflecting non-compliance with the requirements of the ISPS Code more significantly. This finding is also valid for each individual PSC areas (see Table 2).

It is worth noting that 45% of the overall detentions on the security grounds are attributed to 5 flags only where Panama has the highest score with 52 detentions. Table 3 lists the five flags with the numbers of detentions, with the exception of the Russian Federation, all of them Flags of Convenience (FOCs).

Table 2: ISPS non-compliant ships classified by ship's age.

| Age | Black Sea MOU | | Paris MOU | | Tokyo MOU | | USCG | | TOTAL | |
|---|---|---|---|---|---|---|---|---|---|---|
| | Det. No | Rate (%) | Det. No | Rate (%) | Det. No | Rate (%) | Det. No | Rate (%) | Det. No | Rate (%) |
| **Under 5 years** | 0 | 0,0 | 1 | 1.2 | 3 | 6.5 | 8 | 7.1 | 12 | 4.6 |
| **5 to 14 years** | 1 | 5.9 | 6 | 7.1 | 4 | 8.7 | 36 | 32.1 | 47 | 18.1 |
| **15 years or over** | 16 | 94.1 | 77 | 91.7 | 39 | 84.8 | 68 | 60.8 | 200 | 77.3 |

Table 3: ISPS non-compliant ships classified by ship's flag (Top 5).

| Flag | Black Sea MOU | | Paris MOU | | Tokyo MOU | | USCG | | TOTAL | |
|---|---|---|---|---|---|---|---|---|---|---|
| | **Det. No** | Rate (%) | Det. No | Rate (%) | Det. No | Rate (%) | Det. No | Rate (%) | Det. No | Rate (%) |
| **Panama** | **0** | 0,0 | 11 | 13.1 | 9 | 19.6 | 32 | 28.6 | 52 | 20.1 |
| **Russian Federation** | **3** | 17.6 | 13 | 15.5 | 11 | 23.9 | 3 | 2.7 | 30 | 11.6 |
| **Cambodia** | **3** | 17.6 | 0 | 0.0 | 12 | 26.1 | 0 | 0.0 | 15 | 5.8 |
| **DPR Korea** | **3** | 17.6 | 7 | 8.3 | 2 | 4.3 | 0 | 0.0 | 12 | 4.6 |
| **Georgia** | **5** | 29.4 | 6 | 7.1 | 0 | 0.0 | 0 | 0.0 | 11 | 4.2 |

Considering the type of ships, the detention rate on account of ISPS Code non-compliance is the highest for general cargo ships (45.2 %), followed by bulk carriers (23.2%), and refrigerated cargo carriers (8.1%) respectively. The figures are inconsistent in the different MoU PSC areas due to the trade patterns prevailing through them. Low detention rates of containers ships, tankers and passenger ships, where the security risks are perceived to be relatively higher, are worth noting as an optimistic record for the already achieved goals of the Code for maritime security (see Table 4).

By the gross tonnage (gt), the percentage of the detentions of the ISPS non-compliant ships is the highest for 1001-2500 gt (29 %), followed by 10001-25000 gt (21%), 2501-5000 gt (17 %). Summing up, this means that the ships up to 5000 gt makes up 46% of the overall detentions on security grounds. The inconsistency with the figures could be a reason of the different trade patterns prevailing in ach individual PSC regions similar with the findings by the ship's type. For instance, within the Black Sea MOU region 94.1% of the detentions on security grounds are the ships between 1001 and 5000 gt, while 75% of the detentions are the ships bigger than 5000 gt (see Table 5).

Table 4: ISPS non-compliant ships classified by type of ship.

| Ship's Type | Black Sea MOU | | Paris MOU | | Tokyo MOU | | USCG | | TOTAL | |
|---|---|---|---|---|---|---|---|---|---|---|
| | Det. No | Rate (%) | Det. No | Rate (%) | Det. No | Rate (%) | Det. No | Rate (%) | Det. No | Rate (%) |
| **General Dry Cargo Ship** | 15 | 88.2 | 57 | 67.9 | 26 | 56.5 | 19 | 17.0 | 117 | 45.2 |
| **Bulk Carrier** | 0 | 0.0 | 2 | 2.4 | 5 | 10.9 | 53 | 47.3 | 60 | 23.2 |
| **Refrigerated Cargo Carrier** | 0 | 0.0 | 6 | 7.1 | 9 | 19.6 | 6 | 5.4 | 21 | 8.1 |
| **Passenger Ship** | 1 | 5.9 | 1 | 1.2 | 0 | 0.0 | 9 | 8.0 | 11 | 4.2 |
| **Ro-Ro** | 0 | 0.0 | 8 | 9.5 | 1 | 2.2 | 2 | 1.8 | 11 | 4.2 |
| **Oil Tanker** | 0 | 0.0 | 3 | 3.6 | 0 | 0.0 | 6 | 5.4 | 9 | 3.5 |
| **Containership** | 0 | 0.0 | 1 | 1.2 | 0 | 0,0 | 7 | 6.2 | 8 | 3.1 |
| **Chemical Tanker** | 0 | 0.0 | 0 | 0.0 | 1 | 2.2 | 7 | 6.2 | 8 | 3.1 |
| **Other** | 1 | 5.9 | 6 | 7.1 | 4 | 8.7 | 3 | 2.7 | 14 | 5.4 |

Table 5: ISPS non-compliant ships classified by gross tonnage (gt).

| Gross Tonnage (gt) | Black Sea MOU | | Paris MOU | | Tokyo MOU | | USCG | | TOTAL | |
|---|---|---|---|---|---|---|---|---|---|---|
| | Det. No | Rate (%) | Det. No | Rate (%) | Det. No | Rate (%) | Det. No | Rate (%) | Det. No | Rate (%) |
| **500-1000 gt** | 0 | 0.0 | 12 | 14.3 | 8 | 17.4 | 6 | 5.4 | 26 | 10.0 |
| **1001-2500 gt** | 9 | 52.9 | 36 | 42.9 | 19 | 41.3 | 11 | 9.8 | 75 | 29.0 |
| **2501-5000 gt** | 7 | 41.2 | 19 | 22.6 | 7 | 15.2 | 11 | 9.8 | 44 | 17.0 |
| **5001-10000 gt** | 0 | 0.0 | 9 | 10.7 | 4 | 8.7 | 10 | 8.9 | 23 | 8.8 |
| **10001-25000 gt** | 1 | 5.9 | 7 | 8.3 | 7 | 15.2 | 41 | 36.6 | 56 | 21.6 |
| **25001 gt or more** | 0 | 0.0 | 1 | 1.2 | 1 | 2.2 | 33 | 29.5 | 35 | 13.5 |

# 6 Feedback on the current situation

The early implementation phase had its own difficulties mainly originated from the lack of understanding the philosophy, rapid transition, resistance to new codes that seemed not to be related with the work activities, and the lack of internalisation. Maritime community had experienced a new era and fuelled with its old and strong cultural heritages achieved a satisfactory level of implementation of this Code in a relatively short period.

However, all over the world an intensive process was applied to ensure the highest possible level of compliance by the governments, shipping and port industries. Main problems faced with the early implementation of the ISPS Code seems to be related to ISSC, access control procedures, inadequate Master/SSO familiarity with overall SSP, inadequate crew familiarity with own ISPS roles and responsibilities, restricted area marking and control, inadequate security record-keeping, inadequate monitoring of ship's security integrity, ship-port interface (declaration of security-DOS), SSAS performance characteristics, sub-standard attitude and awareness, and lack of enough experience of ships' crew about the ISPS Code [12].

Feedback by ship management companies, masters and security officers on ISPS Code-related incidents affecting ships is promoted by MARISEC for the purpose of identifying and addressing problems. Potential incidents related to port state actions or requirements in respect of security related matters which impact on the operations of ships were determined as follows: ISSC acceptance; additional information demands from port state inspector; port state control attitude; MARSEC level incompatibility between ship and port facility; degree of liaison with/co-operation from Port Security; problems over agreement on a Declaration of Security; excessive information demands before entering port, current and historical information; problems caused by trading history; access control issues; restricted areas; monitoring; storing of any delivered spares and provisions; and cargo operations [13].

According to survey by the European Sea Ports Organisation to assess the status of implementation of the ISPS Code in the EU, 8 months after 1st July deadline; the general impression is that the implementation of the ISPS Code has been smoother than feared. No ship has ever refused to enter a EU port facility due to its non-compliance, and concluded that some adaptations have been necessary and difficulties might have been overcome through additional personnel, equipment and resources [14].

## 7 Conclusions

As a conclusion of the statistical analysis of the security related ship non-compliance data obtained from the monthly detention statistics released via the websites of the various MOUs on port state control and the USCG, it is found that; the overall detention rate (10.3%) on security grounds is relatively low which seems as an evidence for the success of the ship managers on reaching the desired level of compliance with the Code, where remarkable higher detention rate (45.7%) by the USCG is found to be an exception to this fact. Older ships, especially 15 years old and over reflects the highest rate of non-compliance (77.3%) with the requirements of the ISPS Code. It is also seen that four of the five low-compliant flags are Flags of Convenience (FOCs). According to overall detentions the rate of ISPS non-compliant ships is the highest for general dry cargo ships (45.2%), followed by bulk carriers (23.2%). Low detention rate of container ships, tankers and passenger ships, with perceivable high risks, have low detention rates. The smaller ships with lower gross tonnages (gt) are having higher detention rates, whereby ships up to 5000 gt makes up 46% of the overall detentions on security grounds. According to statistics, the most common areas of non-compliance are failure of keeping continuous synopsis records (CSR), and improper ISPS related certificates, i.e. the ISS Certificate and the SSO Certificate.

Finally, in the light of the above findings, we believe that; in this relatively short transition period, common awareness of errors and lapses, best practices, sharing of information, and industry wise close co-operation has played and will be playing a vital role to develop a security culture in the shipping industry.

## References


[1] Maitland, C., *Maritime Security and the IMO, Where Does It Fit In? What Is It Doing*, The Marine Log Conference on Maritime Security, Washington, DC January 30, 2002.

[2] ABS, *Guide For Ship Security*, American Bureau of Shipping, Houston, pp.7 2003.

[3] Signals, *Ship Security, ISPS Code Briefing*, The Loss Prevention Newsletter For North of England Members, Special Issue, January, Tyne, pp.1 2003.

[4] SOLAS Convention, Consolidated Edition, International Maritime Organization, London. 2001.

[5] *International Ship and Port Facility Security Code*, International Maritime Organization (IMO) Publications, Northampton. 2003.

[6] Lloyd's List, *ISPS Benefits Doubtful, Says German Tramp Owner*, Berkenkopf, K., October 28, 2004.

[7] Robbins, S.P. and Coulter, M. *Management*, Eight Edition, Pearson Prentice Hall, pp. 458-460, 2005.

[8] Black Sea Memorandum of Understanding On Port State Control http://www.bsmou.org/.

[9] Paris Memorandum of Understanding on Port State Control http://www.parismou.org/ParisMOU/Detention+Lists/default.aspx.

[10] Tokyo Memorandum of Understanding on Port State Control http://www.tokyo-mou.org/.

[11] USCG, http://www.uscg.mil/hq/g-m/pscweb/MonthlySummary.htm.

[12] Ship Security and Port State Control http://www.shipgaz.com/english/ses/documents/shipsecurityandportstatecontrol.pdf (17.5.2005).

[13] ISPS Code Implementation Joint Industry Feedback Report, http://www.marisec.org/isps/isps-feedbackreport.pdf (1.6.2005).

[14] Survey on Implementation ISPS Code / EU Regulation in EU Ports, European Sea Ports Organisation, http://www.espo.be/policy/position%202005/FINAL%20summary%208%20March%202005.pdf (6.5.2005).

# Towards effective implementation of the ISPS Code onboard ships

E. Othman & A. Halawa
*Maritime Safety Institute, Arab Academy for Science, Technology and Maritime Transport (AAST&MT), Egypt*

## Abstract

The International Maritime Organization (IMO) adopted a new set of security measures in December 2002, introducing the International Ship and Port Facility Security Code (ISPS Code), which imposes responsibilities on governments, shipping companies and port authorities to enhance the security of ships and port facilities.

Both the ISPS Code and the IMO Model Course 3.19 require that the Ship Security Officer (SSO) and shipboard personnel who have specific security duties, have specific security knowledge and receive training in a number of security tasks. This paper discusses some of the vital factors which may restrain the effective implementation of the ISPS Code onboard ships.

The instructors of Maritime Education and Training (MET) may find difficulty in performing a number of training requirements. As well, using a non-maritime instructor may not be practical. MET instructors may possibly require additional security training in security organization, so as to be able to deliver valid, reliable and practical ship security training, in order to meet the preset training objectives.

Important questions that raise themselves now are: how the additional security duties could be performed efficiently, in the same time using the same number of crew. Moreover, are member states willing to amend their manning legislations, considering other commercial and economical factors?

Recognizing, the similarity between the ISPS Code and the International Safety Management (ISM) Code in many areas, security and safety managements must integrate, in order to reduce the workload on the ship's crew, considering that the consequences of security breaches and accidents could be the same.

*Keywords: maritime security, safe manning, ISPS Code, ISM Code, MET instructors, security training, security implementation, maritime administrations.*

# 1 Introduction

IMO has adopted the International Convention on Standards of Training, Certification and Watchkeeping for Seafarers (STCW 78/95) in order to enhance the maritime safety and environmental protection through improving the performance of the human element. The Convention had created roles for the administration, MET institutions and shipping companies in the implementation process of the convention, in order to establish global minimum standards for seafarer's competency according to the provisions of the convention.

Following the devastating September 11, 2001 attacks on USA, IMO has adopted comprehensive security regime for the international shipping industry. Security measures include amendments to SOLAS convention and the introduction of the ISPS Code.

The Code consists of two parts. Part A is mandatory. It contains detailed security related requirements for governments, port authorities and shipping companies. Part B contains a serious of guidelines about how to meet these requirements. Furthermore, the conference adopted a number of resolutions, in order to facilitate the implementation and the application of those security measures to ships and port facilities.

The ISPS Code requires a number of functional security requirements for ships and port facilities; in addition, ships will be subject to the processes of survey, verification, certification and control measures, in order to ensure their compliance with the provisions of the Code. Moreover, shipping companies will be required to designate Company Security Officer (CSO).

The training requirements of ISPS Code are included in section 13; however, the Code embodies a number of training requirements in other sections [1].

# 2 MET systems and the security training requirements

The IMO sub-Committee on Standards of Training and Watchkeeping (STW) has endorsed draft amendment to STCW convention. They require the introduction of new STCW regulation VI/5, new STCW Code section A-VI/5 and section B-VI/5. The proposed amendments were introduced to set the standards for the minimum mandatory training and certification of SSO.

The STCW Convention Article 1(2) [2] provides that, "The parties undertake to promulgate all law, decrees, orders, and regulations and to take all other steps which may be necessary to give the convention full and complete effect." In other words, the maritime administrations of the member States are responsible for the implementation of the security training requirements as required by the ISPS Code and STCW convention. The convention also requires the administrations to ensure the qualifications of the instructors, supervisors and assessors for the type and level of training or assessment involved [3].

The trend in the MET systems has been for MET institutions to provide all required training for seafarers after been approved by the administration. However, barely any administration applies any check or confirms the ability of an MET institution of providing newly introduced training programme; possibly, one of the reasons is the lack of the sufficient technical expertise to perform such control in some administrations.

In addition to the four columns of STCW Code, which specify the minimum standards of a competence, IMO model courses and IMO instruments, such as the Conventions, Codes, Guidelines, are usually the main foundations for developing a curriculum.

Generally, MET instructors are ex-seafarers; however, many of them are holders of academic degrees. Nevertheless, most of MET institutions have implemented many programmes to enhance the pedagogical skills of their instructors to fulfil the requirements of the STCW convention. In addition, the MET course at the World Maritime University (WMU) was established to assist the maritime instructors to better understand the skills of effective teaching.

Based on our knowledge of the field of experience and qualifications of the MET instructors, the question raises itself now, are the MET instructors capable of providing valid, reliable as well as practical training for all the security training requirements, as specified in the ISPS Code and the IMO model course?

However, using non maritime instructors with security backgrounds may not be practical, bearing in mind that, they may not be able to provide realistic training, due to their lack of knowledge about ships layouts, designs and tasks related to the ships operational matters. Moreover, the SSO is a seafarer as considered by STW in its 35$^{th}$ session and not security personnel.

Conceivably, MET instructors may require additional security training in a specialized security organization, such as coastguard academies, police academies or naval academies to be able to deliver valid, reliable and practical ship security training, in order to meet a number of the security training objectives.

## 3 Maritime security and safe manning of ships

IMO resolution A.890 (21) defines the principles of safe manning of ships to ensure the safe operations and pollution prevention from ships, which SOLAS Convention applies. The resolution specifies the factors that shall be taken into account in determining the minimum safe manning level of ships, and in providing guidelines for applying the principles of safe manning. Moreover the resolution lays down the responsibilities of both the administrations and shipping companies in manning their ships.

Resolution A.955 (23) adds the shipboard security duties to the factors to be considered in determining minimum safe manning level of ships. Flag States are required to take into account such requirements and issue the required documents of minimum safe manning to the ships entitle to fly their flags; in the same way, ISM Code requires companies to ensure that each ship is manned according to national and international requirements.

On the other hand, in order to ensure efficient and practical security measures applied onboard ships, shipping companies should embody the required shipboard security duties, as required by ISPS Code, in the routine shipboard operations.

Conceivably, Ship Security Assessment (SSA) is the best event to discover the necessary security measures required for the ship, as SSA is the cornerstone in preparing the Ship Security Plan (SSP) Mahoney [4].

However, ships are required to act against different security levels, for example security level one requires certain activates such as, “Controlling access to the ship”, “Monitoring of deck areas and areas surrounding the ship”, “Controlling the embarkation of persons and their effects”. Such activities could be achievable with the same number of crew, as it could be integrated with the requirements of other regulations and the routine shipboard operations.

Nevertheless, additional protective measures shall be implemented if the security level is raised to level two, part (B) of the ISPS Code provide guidance in implementing a range of security measures required by the SSP at every security level.

For instance, a number of security measures could be carried out to protect the access to the ship, when security level two is declared such as, “Assigning additional personnel to patrol deck areas during silent hours to deter unauthorized access”, “Increasing the frequency and detail of searches of persons, personal effects, and vehicles being embarked or loaded onto the ship”, “Establishing a restricted area on the shore-side of the ship, in close co-operation with the port facility”, Deterring waterside access to the ship, including, for example, in liaison with the port facility, provision of boat patrols”.

The questions that raise themselves now, are whether those additional security duties could be achieved by using the same number of crew onboard? Are most of the flag States willing to increase their minimum manning level taking into account those additional security duties? Recognizing that, the criteria in obtaining the minimum safe manning of ships differs from one State to another and not harmonized, considering many factors include national, social, economical and commercial factors, in addition to the IMO principles of safe manning.

Taking into consideration that, ISPS Code is just beginning its implementation onboard ships, and many of its pros and cons will reveal only after certain period of time. However, the international maritime community, represented in the IMO must begin to establish more effective instruments to ensure that the minimum manning levels onboard ships complies with the newly introduced maritime security requirements, in addition to other safety and operational requirements.

## 4 Incorporating maritime security into the Safety Management System

IMO resolution A.741 (18) has adopted the ISM Code for the purpose of safe operations of ships and for pollution prevention by providing systematic approach to control safety and quality management for shipping companies and onboard ships, in the form of developing, implementing and maintaining a Safety Management System (SMS).

Both ISM and ISPS Codes aim to establish systems for safe management and secure operations onboard ships. However, there is a similarity in the implementation process of both of them including, the designation of CSO in ISPS Code verses the Designated Person Ashore (DPA) in ISM Code, the requirements of defining and emphasizing the authority of the master, as well as, the requirements of training and familiarization of the personnel of the related tasks and duties to be performed under the requirements of the Codes.

Furthermore, establishing Safety Management Manual (SMM) to describe how to implement the safety management system including the procedures and plans for the safety of critical ship operations are required in the ISM Code versus SSP in the ISPS Code.

Moreover, both Codes are similar in many other areas such as, each Code covers designated ship and shore staff, emergency preparedness, drills and training, documented procedures, checklists, exercises, record-keeping, internal and external audits, maintenance, and others. In addition, both Codes implement a similar system of verification, control and certification, including the duration and validity of the certificates.

ISM and ISPS Codes, among other regulations, have increased the administrative workloads on ship's officers. This has created excessive workload, which resulted in early retirement of many seafarers. It has created a global shortage in ship officers; as, the cost of training new officers is high and time consuming. Moreover, ship officers spend more time in doing paper work than supervising the routine shipboard operations, such as cargo, maintenance and navigation.

The consequences of security breaches and accidents could be the same, security and safety managements have to incorporate to provide practical implementations for the security requirements onboard ships. Harmonizing ISM and ISPS procedures makes practical and economic sense, as the two Codes have a great deal in common. However, the confidentiality issue of the security information has to be considered in performing such harmonization.

The researchers believe that, there should be harmonization between the procedures of the two codes. This has been applied in the Liberian administration [5] by harmonizing both the ISPS and ISM audits. The shipping companies are allowed to incorporate the shipboard security requirements into the Company's Safety Management System (SMS). Moreover, the Cayman Islands administration [6] has harmonized the verifications of both the Safety Management Certificate (SMC) and the International Ship Security Certificate (ISSC).

Certainly, more maritime administrations as well as shipping companies will realize the benefits of incorporating the maritime security requirements into a broad management system including both safety and security issues.

# 5 Conclusions

In order to improve the implementation of the requirements of the ISPS code onboard ships and to avoid some of the difficulties, which may hold back its effectiveness, the researchers recommend the following conclusions:

In order to ensure the validity, reliability as well as practicability of the security training provided by MET institutions, keeping into consideration that, MET instructors are not specialized in maritime security matters. Maritime administrations should ensure that MET institutions provide practical and valid security training.

The present manning levels onboard many ships will impede the possibility of performing the required security measures effectively. Flag States are required to review and amend their manning legislation to ensure the effective and practical performance of the security measures among other shipboard operations. IMO is required to establish more effective minimum safe manning instrument to assist Flag States in doing so.

Incorporating the maritime security requirements into the safety management system is necessary; in order to ensure the effective implementation of the security measures and to reduce the work load onboard ships.

## References


[1] Ketchum, J., Training requirements of the International Ship and Port Facility Security (ISPS) Code. Unpublished lecture handout, World Maritime University: Malmö, 2004.

[2] International Maritime Organization. International Convention on Standards of Training, Certification and Watchkeeping for seafarers, 1978, as amended in 1995 and 1997 (STCW Convention), Author: London, 2001.

[3] Morrison, W.S.G., Competent crews = safer shipping, World Maritime University: Malmö, 1997.

[4] Mahoney, W., Effective ISPS implementation with existing manning. Proc. of the marinelog maritime and port security conference, Marinelog: Washington, 2004.

[5] Republic of Liberia. Bureau of maritime affairs, marine notice ISP-00, Web Site, http://www.liscr.com.

[6] Cayman Islands shipping registry, Shipping notice CISN 18/04 ISPS, Web Site, http://www.caymarad.org.

# International Ship and Port Facility Security (ISPS) Code: the perceptions and reality of shore-based and sea-going staff

C. Burmester
*Southampton Institute of Higher Education, UK*

## Abstract

This paper investigates the implementation of the ISPS Code and the related perceptions of shore-based and sea-going staff. The literature review identified issues of practical importance and shortcomings from which research questions and objectives were derived. These were then triangulated with observations made during an internship in the Quality Department of a ship management company. Consequently, inductive research methods were used for answering the research questions and a questionnaire-based survey was developed. The initial contact with ship management companies located in the UK, Cyprus, Germany, Norway and the Netherlands was made by post, using an introductory letter, with a shore-based and a sea-going questionnaire attached. The primary research survey took place between July and September 2004. The number of questionnaires sent to individuals was 218, which produced a total number of 111 completed sea-going questionnaires and 40 completed shore-based questionnaires. The survey's aim was two-fold. It examined the implementation issues and a perception comparison between sea-going and shore-based staff. The obtained data from 32 questions was analysed and discussed in detail, listing the findings from both survey groups. The survey showed the ISPS Code shortcomings and identified areas that require amendment, which were in the main congruent with warnings and criticism identified in the literature review. In addition, the survey gave evidence and examples that the ISPS Code does not provide uniform standards and clear guidelines, which led to recommendations being made.

*Keywords: ISPS Code, implementation, perceptions, survey, PSC attitude, training, flag state, workload.*

# 1 Introduction

The aim of the research was to investigate the implementation of the International Ship and Port Facility Security (ISPS) Code (2002) and to examine if there was a difference in the perception of shore-based compared to sea-going staff. The following introduction provides a brief explanation of events and influences leading up to the implementation of the ISPS Code.

The attack on the French tanker "Limburg" off the coast of Yemen in October 2002, the ramming of "USS Cole" by a small boat laden with explosives in 2000 and the terrorist attacks of September 11$^{th}$ 2001 led to a review of the International Maritime Organisation's (IMO) "measures and procedures to prevent acts of terrorism, which threaten the security of passengers and crews and the safety of ships" [1].

This led to the ISPS Code being developed and which was adopted on the 12 December 2002 in the amendments to the International Convention for the Safety of Life at Sea (SOLAS), 1974, chapter XI-2. Compliance with the Code became mandatory on 1 July 2004 and was implemented and enforced by contracting Governments. Around 120 Governments worldwide have signed up to this convention by the 1 July 2004.

The ISPS Code applies to all passenger ships, high-speed craft and all cargo ships of 500 gross tonnes and more, on international voyages, and mobile offshore drilling units. Port facilities affected by the ISPS Code are those visited by these ships engaged on international voyages [1].

The objectives of the ISPS Code are to "establish an international framework involving co-operation between contracting Governments, Government agencies, local administrations and the shipping and port industries to detect/assess security threats and take preventative measures against security incidents affecting ships or port facilities used in international trade" [1].

The ISPS Code differs from previous regulations and conventions, as it is not self-contained within the shipping industry. The ISPS Code aims to prevent acts of terrorism. It consequently is an issue of state security and "as such the Code is driven by political impetus that does not recognise the commercial pressure of international trade" [2]. Therefore governmental intelligence agencies that ensure safety and security might get directly or indirectly involved with the ISPS Code; these are far less tolerant stakeholders. Overall, as Wall [3] stated "the consequences when things go wrong are quite serious".

# 2 Result of the literature review

This literature review has examined and defined the reasons, scope and considerable range of the ISPS Code. The rationale for the ISPS Code being introduced is a safety and security issue, driven by political impetus and reaching into the sphere of state security. The scale of the ISPS Code is extensive. The commercial ramifications, which may affect the viability of merchant shipping operations, are far reaching but as yet are unknown due to the relatively short time the ISPS Code has been in operation. However, the ISPS Code entry-into-force date passed with little noticeable disruption to merchant shipping. The question arises as to who will carry the burden of ISPS Code related costs? Will it ultimately be the end consumer as freight rates will rise and taxes might be imposed?

Various authors voiced concern regarding the proper implementation within the deadline which proved well founded and were confirmed by the IMO openly admitting that the deadline had not been met. Like any other global statutory Code the ISPS Code aims at providing uniform global standards and clear guidelines. The literature review identified various shortcomings in this area and gave examples. Furthermore, this review led to a focus on the identification and evaluation of ISPS issues of practical importance. The fundamental questions arising were:

- Has standardisation been achieved?
- Is the ISPS Code working satisfactorily and what are the possible shortcomings, if any?
- Are effective ship/shore relations supporting the implementation of the ISPS Code?
- Do shore and sea-going staffs have the same perception of the implementation and is it workable?

The answers will only be found by evaluating how people and entities that are directly affected by the ISPS Code such as, for example, ship managers and their shore-based personnel and seafarers, perceive the ISPS Code. There is no doubt that the interesting legal implications will not be known for some time and these have therefore not been the topic of this research, however the unknown practical quantity of the ISPS Code, has been the topic of this paper. This led to the definition of the following aims.

## 3 Methodology of questionnaire

Inductive research methods were found to be appropriate for the survey as most commonly used for social contexts and in social science research. The following methods were used:

- observations during an 8 week summer internship in June and July 2004;
- informal interviews;
- primary research:
    - introductory letter;
    - shore based staff questionnaire ;
    - sea going staff questionnaire;
- comparison, cross-referencing and analysing of the material collated.

## 4 Selection and justification of methods

It was decided that ship management companies were likely to be the best access point to shore-based and sea-going International Ship and Port Facility Security

(ISPS) Code related information. A fundamental willingness of ship managers to co-operate with this project was established. An introductory letter accompanied by two questionnaires and a self-addressed envelope was sent to all identified ship management companies located in the United Kingdom, Cyprus, Germany, Norway and the Netherlands. The necessary address data was obtained from the World Shipping Directory [4]. An introductory letter together with the shore-based and the sea-going questionnaire were addressed and sent to a total of 233 Managers, or Company Directors, within ship management companies. Fifteen addresses turned out to be either incorrect, or the individual did not fall into the intended survey category. Therefore a total number of 218 potential participants received the questionnaires.

The letter asked for Managing Directors, Managers, Company Security Officers and Company Internal Auditors to complete the shore-based staff questionnaire and for Masters, Chief Officers and Ship Security Officers to complete the sea-going staff questionnaire. Out of courtesy, all the before-mentioned potential participant categories were invited to take part in the survey. However, it was expected that most likely only the Company Security Officer (CSO) and Master would complete the questionnaires, which was shown in the results. This outcome was welcomed as these "key informants" have the necessary knowledge to respond and are likely to be a more reliable source of information than other sources. It has to be noted that some CSOs fulfil multiple roles within their organizations.

Table 1: Number of questionnaires sent and returned.

| Number of questionnaires sent and returned in the survey of July – September 2004 | | | | | |
|---|---|---|---|---|---|
| Total number of questionnaires sent to individuals | Total number of companies addressed | Total number of sea going questionnaires returned | Percentage of sea going replies | Total number of shore based questionnaires returned | Percentage of shore based replies |
| 218 | 197 | 111 | 50.9% | 40 | 18.4% |

The survey contained thirty-two questions. Of these four were aimed at establishing the profile of the respondents. The remaining twenty-eight questions were designed to investigate into ISPS Code implementation issues and the perceptions of sea-going compared to shore based respondents. At the end of the survey the respondents were given the opportunity to give comments in an open format. The number of questionnaires returned was 40 for shore-based questionnaires, which equates to 18.4% of the total, and 111 for sea-going staff questionnaires, which equates to 50.9%. However it has to be said that each ship manager manages more than one ship so the figure of 50.9% does not relate to the total number of ships that could have been reached, if each ship manager's ship had participated. On the other hand, it can be assumed that 111 replies constitute a good sample of European ship managers' sea-going responses.

The interviewees' location was widely dispersed; therefore it seemed advisable to conduct the questionnaire survey by mail and/or by e-mail.

A rapport was established with those who granted cooperation, using e-mail for communication. In these communications great care was taken not to be considered intrusive and to reassure that the information obtained from the questionnaires would only be used for the purpose of this dissertation. Reassurance was given to participants that confidentiality was guaranteed and no company information would be distributed as a result of this research. The e-mail version of the questionnaires facilitated communication with the vessels with quick response times.

Presenting and analysing collected data truthfully and cross-referencing was important in order to achieve undistorted conclusions and accurate recommendations.

# 5 Results and discussion

The survey showed 97% to 99% issuing of International Ship Security Certificates (ISSC) as reported by shore-based and sea-going respondents, indicating almost complete compliance with ISPS Code's requirements by 1st July 2004. A new global standard such as the International Ship and Port Facility Security (ISPS) Code is worthless without proper implementation and compliance. It is ultimately the initiative and co-operation of seafarers' that is relied upon to prevent breaches in maritime security. It was acknowledged by Wall [3] and others that the ISPS Code was "forced" through in an unprecedented short time frame and was far from perfect. This lead to appeals by Grool [5] and others to apply the Code with a sense of pragmatism and common sense, confirming that it contained shortcomings and with the need for details to be amended later [6,3]. The compliance on entry-into-force date of the ISPS Code showed that the maritime industry could adopt such complex measures within a much tighter time frame than previously believed possible; which might encourage bodies such as the International Maritime Organisation (IMO) to make progress on other conventions in a shorter time in the future.

The need for ISPS Code amendments, foreseen in the literature review, was confirmed by results of a survey conducted by the author of this paper. The survey showed ISPS Code shortcomings and identified areas that require amendments, as explained in more detail later. Additions and amendments to the ISPS Code are being debated currently in the International Maritime Organisation (IMO) working group [7]. Whether this will be accomplished as speedily as the introduction of the ISPS Code remains to be seen. Amendments are usually proposed to the Facilitation Committee (FAL) of the IMO. A proposal for example made during the 31st session (19-23 July 2004) will be adopted in the July 2005 Committee session, to enter into force on 1 January 2007.

The survey's aim was two-fold; to examine implementation issues and obtain a perception comparison between sea-going and shore-based staff. The questionnaires themselves were sub-categorised into two areas of investigation. The introductory part was aimed at building a profile of the participants and which confirmed that participants were those who hold most responsibility with regards to ISPS Code duties. The main body related to how and when ISPS Code compliance was obtained on the one side, and established what needs to be done to further improve the ISPS Code on the other side.

The survey results regarding ISPS Code implementation issues are in the main congruent with warnings and criticism identified in the literature review and observations made during an internship, which allowed for findings to be triangulated; examples being non-uniform standards with regards to geographical areas of operation, training, varying international standards in compliance of ships and ports and the exclusion of ships under 500gt, as raised by [8, 9, 10]. Pre arrival notifications were identified by [10] as an area of non-standardisation. This is of particular interest as a report for the European Commission in 1998 addressed the issue of uniform arrival and departure documents and procedures [11] and recommended a common set of ship arrival and departure forms based on IMO FAL forms 1, 3, 4 & 5. It is therefore surprising why such common procedures have not been implemented into the ISPS Code from the start. The survey found, that sea-going and shore-based respondents are in agreement that all these issues need to be addressed.

The issue of training was also raised in the literature review and comments made in the survey suggest that according to the respondents, ISPS Code related training needs to be reviewed. It was the view of the respondents that training would benefit from being more clearly defined and incorporated into STCW 95, as this would avoid duplication of training and eliminate variances in training requirements between flag states. An added complication is that at present one flag state does not necessarily approve training undergone in fulfilment of another flag state's requirement. Furthermore, findings from an OECD survey should be incorporated that highlighted the importance of providing practically orientated training, rather than emphasising theoretical knowledge [12].

The findings of the survey further identified arguments regarding the security issue of the Automated Identification System (AIS) and pilotage. The area of AIS (which falls under SOLAS Chapter 5, Safety of Navigation) was intentionally not touched upon in the literature review and the survey, as it would merit a dissertation topic on its own. The same applied to the Continuous Synopsis Record (CSR) and Ships Security Alert System (SSAS). The security aspect of pilotage, raised in the survey by respondents, is recommended to be addressed by the working committee of the IMO.

A detailed analysis of the responses showed, that for some of the questions a different ISPS Code implementation perception by the two survey groups might be of relatively little or no relevance and/or consequences regarding an effective ship-shore relationship. For example, one question examined the co-operation and support provided by the flag state in implementing the ISPS Code. The survey findings confirmed the literature findings, namely considerable performance differences amongst flags, and the poor performance of the Panama Flag. The perception of sea-going and shore-based respondents differed for this question, but a possible explanation was given as this could be explained by the fact that the ship managers were dealing directly and repeatedly with the flag to fulfil ISPS requirements and obtain certification whilst the sea-going staff had little direct dealings with the flag administration. It is believed that this difference did not affect the ship-shore relationship.

The survey further revealed that there are specific areas of the ISPS Code implementation that were in need of improvement. This also identified differences in the perception of respondents. For example, 35% of the sea-going respondents regarded additional training as the most pertinent area, while only 18% of the shore respondents rated this as a priority in their response. In contrast, the highest rated area of concern to shore-based respondents, with 29%, was a review of procedures, whereas the sea-going respondents rated this area at only 19%. On the one hand it might be argued that this indicates that both areas need addressing. On the other hand one could argue that this identified areas of conflict between shore and sea, where one side demands more training whilst the other wants to provide a review of procedures. Differences in perception are acceptable as long as they have no underlying root causes that make the cooperation between sea and shore counter-productive.

The results of the survey showed that effective ship/shore relations were supporting the implementation of the ISPS Code. Without these, the task of ISPS Code implementation would not have been accomplished. Especially the open comments made by respondents showed similar attitudes, values and an overall perception of the ISPS Code implementation issues.

The analysis of the data showed both common perceptions and differing perceptions in various areas between the sea-going and shore-based respondents and further resulted in the identification of ISPS Code related issues that require addressing in the future, of which the main ones are:

- Uniform standards:
    - Procedures;
    - pre-arrival notifications;
    - compliance of port facilities;
    - emergence of a global "two-tier" compliancy regime (certain countries and geographical areas failing to be compliant and/or to meet standards);
    - training.
- Workload (paperwork distracts from other duties, especially in Short Sea Shipping).
- Port State Control (PSC) attitude; especially the alleged heavy handedness of the United States Coast Guard (USCG).
- Human element related aspects (denial/delay of shore leave, crew security checks).
- Pilotage (conflict of time available versus security checks; necessary equipment of pilots that might be an infringement on security, example "ladder" knife).
- Automated Identification System (AIS) (accessibility to possible terrorists).
- ISPS Code requirements infringe International Safety Management (ISM) Code and Standard Training Certification and Watchkeeping Convention (STCW95) requirements.

This survey provided qualitative and quantitative ISPS Code implementation related data, which could form the basis of further research. The survey also confirmed points identified in secondary literature. Furthermore, the positive response rate to the survey would suggest that the survey topic is of interest to those directly affected by the ISPS Code and the shipping industry. Notwithstanding the limitation of the survey (size of sample, snapshot nature of the research and restriction to a geographical area), given the broad scope of the questions, the cross section of respondents and the higher than expected number of responses obtained, this indicates to the author that the results and data obtained are substantive and therefore of value in assessing the implementation and perceptions of sea-going and shore-based staff.

# 6 Summary and conclusion

The research investigated the implementation of the ISPS Code by examining secondary data, in the main literature and observations made during an internship, and primary data obtained from a survey. The survey investigated the implementation of the ISPS Code and perceptions of shore-based and sea-going staff. Many of the findings of the survey underpinned results identified in secondary material. Examples of these were an increased ISPS Code related workload especially for sea-going, but also for shore-based staff; human element related aspects, such as denial and/or refusal of shore leave and/or joining of vessels; and non-uniform standards such as training, Port State Control attitude, port ISPS Code compliance. However, the analysis of all data collated from the survey has also brought to light issues that should be addressed and can provide the basis for further research. Examples were non-uniform pre-arrival notifications and that ISPS Code security checks reduce the working time available for pilots during sensitive passages when the focus should be first and foremost on navigational matters.

The survey confirmed almost complete compliance with the ISPS Code. Ship's ISPS Code compliance was made possible due to an immense effort and close cooperation between ship and shore personnel. However, the survey showed that there seemed to be a division between those who believed the ISPS Code to be a "curse and burden inflicted on the shipping industry", as quoted by one respondent, and those who perceived benefits from the ISPS Code. Effective ship/shore relations supported the implementation of the ISPS Code. Overall there were areas of different perception between sea-going and shore-based staff which was, upon closer inspection, not impeding the overall success of implementation.

The ISPS Code is identical on paper for every ship operator, ship and seafarer around the world. Despite this, regional variance in implementation success was identified to the extent of the danger of an emerging two-tier shipping system. The harmonious cooperation between all the stakeholders involved in the ISPS Code process was identified as a problem. Shipping is only one of the stakeholders affected by the ISPS Code but it had to bear the brunt of the ISPS Code implementation and endure the hardest scrutiny. Ports, which are closely linked to governments that ratified the ISPS Code, should have been the forerunners in ISPS Code implementation, but instead ports were the weakest link and fell behind with compliance. A certain amount of disillusion from seafarers and shore-based staff was detected with regard to the strictness of implementation for ships on one side and the slackness to apply the same rigueur on ports on the other side. As respondents commented, "if the security measures in ports would work then hardly any unauthorised person should be able to reach a vessel whilst in port in the first place" and "without good port security there is little a ship can really do against organised crime or terrorism". Furthermore, certain geographical areas were identified as unable or unwilling to meet ISPS Code requirements and so globally different standards have emerged.

Evidence was given that the ISPS Code was announced on introduction as being an unfinished product that needed amending. The data from the survey showed numerous ISPS Code shortcomings. It was demonstrated by an example that, lessons from the past of how to harmonise and facilitate procedures were not incorporated into the ISPS Code. This left mainly the shipside of the ship/port interface to struggle with inadequacies that put burdens on the sea-going and shore-based staff. However, by implementing the ISPS Code in a timely manner, the shipping industry demonstrated that it was, despite all odds, capable of complying with the ISPS Code in practice. Demands to apply the Code with a sense of pragmatism and common sense were voiced within the industry, which reflected that implementing such a far reaching international convention is both complex and maybe cumbersome, leaving refinements and changes to be made later.

It was shown that the ISPS Code does not provide uniform global standards and clear guidelines, which might be partially due to different governmental interpretations of ISPS Code requirements. The way forward could be summarised by learning from those countries and companies where the ISPS Code has been successfully implemented. The main point would be to make the ISPS Code more user-friendly, consistently applied and workable. It should be examined whether the ISPS Code indeed infringes on other conventions such as the ISM Code and STCW 95, by security measures impinging on safety matters, and the workload of the ISPS Code contravening standards for manning, working hours and rest periods. Clearly a Code that is detrimental to other conventions must be remedied as quickly as possible before accidents and incidents result from it. The main task should not be to work harder or burden especially the seafarer with ever increasing paperwork, manuals and directives, but to let common sense and practicality prevail and work smarter. An international Code should be streamlined and workable from the outset. From the above it is also recommended to address and rectify the identified shortcomings with regards to global uniform standards in a speedy and un-bureaucratic manner so that there is a consistent application of agreed practices. The ISPS Code procedures have to be streamlined, pre-arrival notifications standardised, port facilities have to be critically and impartially evaluated with regard to their ISPS Code compliance, and the emergence of a global "two-tier" compliance regime has to be counter-acted by knowledge transfer and financial support. However, some of these issues might prove difficult to achieve due to global culture differences, the resources available and the willingness of governments to be adaptable and to co-operate. Sea-going respondents to the survey asked for more ISPS Code related training, which is in accordance with known research, recommended to be more practical orientated rather than theoretical. International agreed standards and working guidelines are recommended to be introduced to eliminate the heavy-handedness of Port State Control officers.

To finally conclude, the objectives of the ISPS Code are to "establish an international framework involving co-operation between contracting Governments, Government agencies, local administrations and the shipping and port industries to detect/assess security threats and take preventative measures against security incidents affecting ships or port facilities used in international trade" (IMO, 2003, p. iii). As indicated in the research and results from the survey, much has been achieved by the implementation of the ISPS Code, however, there appears the need for a lot of work still to be done in the area of uniformity of standards and human related aspects to make the ISPS Code a successful security tool.

## References

[1] IMO *ISPS Code*, 2003 Edition. London: IMO ISBN 92-801-5149-5, 20.

[2] Moloney, E. (2003) "The International Code for the Security of Ships and of Port Facilities". *Port Technology International*, Autumn 2003, London: Henley Publishing Ltd.

[3] Wall F. *personal communication* at the *IMarEST conference 20 /21 November 2003*, London: Institute of Marine Engineering, Science and Technology.

[4] World Shipping Directory. 14th ed [2 volume set] Lloyds Register-Fairplay, 2003, ISBN 1901290409, 2003-2004.

[5] Grool, R. "Ships and cargoes: terrorist tools?" *Seaways* February 2004.

[6] Norton Rose. "Improving Maritime Security: the ISPS Code". Available from www.nortonrose.com/publications, accessed 06 Dec. 2003.

[7] Cooper, N "ISPS after implementation". *Seaways*, February 2005.

[8] McKay, R. "Australia to allow non-ISPS ships to berth". *Lloyds List,* 30 June 2004.

[9] Sagen, A. "Where are the ISPS standards?". *Know How Publishing, Norway,* No 3-2003.

[10] Bell, D. "After the hiccups, a workable Code please". *Lloyd's List*, 22 July 2004.

[11] Maritime Research Centre, Southampton Institute (UK) and Partners. "Comparison of Documentation in Short Sea Shipping and Road Transport". For The Directorate-General for Transport (DG VII), The European Commission. Nov 1998.

[12] OECD. "*Availability and Training of Seafarers*". Maritime Transport Committee, Jan. 2003.

# Seaborne trade effects of international terrorism and effectiveness of the anti-terrorist policy

D. Kanev
*Nikola Vaptsarov Naval Academy, Varna, Bulgaria*

## Abstract

This paper investigates the effects of international terrorism on seaborne trade and the effectiveness of the different anti-terrorist policies. First, in order to evaluate the level and severity in which terrorism and the threat of terrorism can disrupt international seaborne trade flows, it gives some estimates of the effects on trade flows and transportation costs. They prove the necessity of implementation of a new, effective and global anti-terrorist policy. After that two possible kinds of policies are analysed; supply-side policy, which raises the cost of terrorism, and demand-side policy, which is based on reducing its expected benefits. Analysis reveals that the second type of anti-terrorist policy is much more effective. It discourages terrorism by further political democratisation, support for market competition and economic decentralization, and international coordination and cooperation in reducing the risk of terrorism.
*Keywords: economics of terrorism, cost-benefit analysis, anti-terrorist policy.*

## 1 Introduction

Terrorism, or the forceful pursuit of political goals by individuals, not affiliated with any formal national institution, is not a new phenomenon and has always served those, who believe violence against innocent civilians presents the most expedient path towards power. In many modern societies terrorism has set deep roots and its manifestations in Spain, Northern Ireland, Israel, India and many other states have been in the centre of public interest for decades. Nevertheless until several years ago no one in the world has considered the possibility of waging a worldwide war on terrorism. Quite the contrary – terrorism was viewed as an isolated problem, which does not greatly harm the international community and therefore should be dealt with at the local level. In consonance with this the economic theory has not paid great attention to the problem. The pioneering researches of Garry Becker concerning crime [1] and William Landes regarding highjacking of airplanes in the 60s and the 70s [2] are among the small number of examples of the opposite.

September 11th 2001 changed fundamentally the way we treat terrorism and placed it as one of the top issues on the social agenda. The terrorist threat to the marine sector was also quickly spotted and today an increasing number of governments, international institutions, business organizations and authors take account of both how terrorism in other spheres affects international sea trade and the increasing interest of terrorists towards the marine sector as an ultimate goal as well as an important part of the logistics chain of their attacks. Many arguments support this observation.

Shipping already became a subject of attacks in the 80s when the two cruise ships *Achille Lauro* and *City of Poros* were attacked in the Mediterranean. Over the last five years there have been other symptomatic examples that demonstrated terrorists' maritime attack capability and the direct threat that terrorism poses to seagoing vessels - the attacks on the USS Cole in 2000 and the French oil tanker Limburg in 2002. Today the threat to the marine industry is so realistic that England's First Sea Lord and Chief of the Naval Staff, Admiral Sir Alan West, has officially warned that Al Qaeda and other terrorist groups are plotting to launch further attacks on merchant shipping [3].

There is also a risk that terrorists can use seagoing vessels as weapons in their attacks. To illustrate this danger, in 1998 an Al-Qaeda cargo vessel carried explosives to Mombassa in Kenya that later were used in the bomb attacks on the US embassies in Kenya and Tanzania that killed over 220 people and injured more than 5,000. The terrorists' potential for such operations is sufficient and U.S. intelligence has reported that Al Qaeda owns and operates at least 15 cargo freighters worldwide [4]. These vessels, carrying a flammable cargo, such as liquid natural gas, could be exploded or sunk in a port, damaging the facility and blocking commercial traffic [5]. For example, the destruction that can be caused by such floating bombs is severe, as the detonation of a tanker carrying 600 tonnes of liquefied petroleum gas would cause a fireball of 1,200 metres in diameter destroying almost everything within this range. Beyond this range, a large number of fatalities and casualties would occur [6].

The use of marine transport as a conduit for weapons of mass destruction would have even more dangerous consequences. Examining this danger the consulting firm Booz Allen Hamilton ran a strategic simulation in which "dirty bombs" - devices that use conventional explosives to disperse radioactive material - were discovered in cargo containers at three US ports. The cost to the economy from the resulting disruption of trade was estimated $58 billion [7]. Of course, in the worst scenario these ships could be used for importing a weapon of mass destruction into the country. Even a relatively small nuclear weapon detonated in a major seaport might kill between 500,000 and 1 million people; directly destroy up to $500 billion worth of property; cause losses due to trade disruption of $100 to $200 billion; and impose further indirect costs of up to $1.2 trillion [8].

The possibility of using the marine industry as a back door through border and immigration controls should also not be overlooked. Terrorists can enter as illegal passengers or crewmembers. There are around 1.2 million officers and crewmen manning the world's merchant fleets, ships can be abducted, crew certificates falsified, and control of professional access cannot be guaranteed at reasonable costs. Another channel for infiltrating terrorists is through hiding them inside cargo containers and shipping them. A real attempt for such a channel was discovered in October 2001 when Italian authorities found a suspected Al Qaeda terrorist inside a shipping container bound for Canada. The container originated in Port Said, Egypt, and inside the container were airport maps and a phoney airplane mechanic's certificate. Much more recently, two suicide bombers entered the port of Ashdod, Israel, by hiding inside a cargo container. They ended up killing dozens of people [9].

The conclusion from all these facts is that today, terrorism poses a real threat to the global marine sector and takes advantage of the capabilities that shipping offers for achieving the terrorists' goals. The perils that follow make it imperative for us to look at this problem seriously from a scientific point of view. This is the main goal of the present paper. In it the point of view would be that of the economic approach through which we will first analyse the genesis of terrorism, the behaviour of terrorists and why they would use shipping for fulfilling their goals, and second we will assess the efficacy of the alternative mechanisms for neutralizing terrorism. Doing this we will demonstrate the capabilities of the economic approach in the fight against terrorism. With a similar approach we will be seeking two more results: to increase the attention of the economic community to this problem, and to stimulate decision makers to take into account economic arguments.

## 2 The terrorist threat from the economic point of view

The fundamental characteristic of the economic approach is the assumption of rational behaviour and the search for effective alternatives of people's actions. This distinctive point stays also in the basis of the economic approach towards terrorism. It means that economics considers the latter not as a pathological deviation, but as behaviour of rational individuals, who have no better means for achieving their political goals.

The rationality assumption allows us to consider terrorism as a specific form for participation in the political process and to find in terrorist attacks both clearly defined political goals – redistribution of political and economic power, and effective methods for their achievement – imposing additional economical and political costs on those who are in power under the condition that they follow the policy that does not correspond with the goals of the terrorists. Although their actions take innocent victims, these victims are just an instrument for achieving the political goals and cannot be considered a direct measurement of the created effect [10]. Quite the contrary, in most cases terrorists are not concerned with the number of victims and the size of destruction, but are more interested in the political consequences on the state policy. The rationality of terrorists is confirmed not only by their organized and well aimed actions but also by the way in which they react to the counteractions to terrorism. Thus for example the placement of metal detectors at airports in 1973 redirected the terrorist activities from high-jacking to kidnapping people; the tightened security around politicians leads to an increase in attacks against other famous representatives of the attacked nation; to the increased security measures on airports and the national boundaries after September $11^{th}$ terrorism replied with attacks against underground and railway transport, maritime industry and seaports.

The behavioural assumption of rationality allows for the explanation of terrorists' decisions on the number and size of terrorist acts as dependent on marginal benefits and costs of terrorism.

Marginal benefits from terrorism are a function of the degree to which terrorists are able to achieve their goals. They depend on a number of factors: (1) the media and public interest; (2) the extent to which terrorist attacks can increase the number of supporters of terrorists' causes and destabilize the political system; and (3) the level of negative economic consequences following from the direct material and human losses, formation of negative economic expectations, decrease in the trade flows, losses on stock exchanges, limitations of immigration and educational exchange, diminishing tourism and investments. Although the potential of attacks on maritime trade to cause political instability is lower in comparison to attacks on land, this is not the same if terrorists decide to attack large and important national and international seaports. That is why at a recent conference in London, maritime security experts predicted a "spectacular" attack of this sort sometime in the near future [11].

In order to determine the level of terrorism we should also consider the terrorists' costs for human and material resources, information and training of participants. The first determinant of costs and therefore of terrorists' decisions whether to attack or not, is the amount of resources available and the difficulties associated with conducting the attacks. In this connection in comparison to attacks on most land-based facilities maritime targets are difficult, requiring a very sophisticated planning, training, and coordination. This is another reason why maritime terrorism is still rather rare, and why terrorists are less likely to attack more secure major ports. At the same time it is inevitable that all current measures that emphasise on land security will make attacks on maritime transport and ports cost effective and more attractive in the future.

This analysis can be furthered in order to define the optimal ways for limiting terrorism. There are two alternatives here – to decrease the number and intensity of terrorist attacks by increasing costs, or by decreasing the benefits from terror. Costs can be increased through negative or positive stimuli.

Among negative stimulus there are many active measures, limiting the threat against all potential goals through capturing the leaders and destroying the infrastructure, logistics chains, training centres and other material resources of terrorists. Recent examples of such measures are the economic sanctions and military operations against the Taliban regime in Afghanistan and Saddam Hussein in Iraq. Another kind of negative stimulus follows from tightening up global security measures and investments in infrastructure that prevent terrorist acts by making them more difficult to undertake. Examples of this are installation of metal detectors on airports, increasing the level of security at international embassies, tightening visa controls and security in public buildings, and increasing punishment for captured terrorists. In the area of international maritime transportation, examples of reactions with the same goals are the measures of the International Maritime Organization (IMO) set out in a new chapter XI-2 of the amendments to the Convention on the Safety of Life at Sea 1974 (SOLAS) and a new International Ship and Port Facility Security Code (ISPS Code). Among the national efforts complementing these international measures are the US Container Security Initiative (CSI) and Radiation Detection Initiative (RDI), as well as Regulation (EC) No 725/2004 of the EU that extends the scope of the IMO requirements to domestic ships and associated port facilities.

Positive stimuli have the goal to increase the alternative cost for participation in terrorist operations by creating incentives for giving up terrorist activities [12]. Some examples for such positive stimuli come from the Republic of South Africa, Spain, Northern Ireland, Israel, India and recently Iraq. They include payments for voluntarily returned weapons, amnesty for previous terrorist actions, witness defence programs, including the political wings of terrorist organizations in the socio-political life of the country, granting limited autonomy to certain territories and allowing the former terrorist organizations to govern them. Such measures and policies are able to limit terrorism because they deprive terrorist organizations of valuable human resources, decrease their level of internal organization and destroy their social capital as well as the trust among their members and supporters.

Although all these supply side measures for limiting terrorism are wide spread, their efficiency is low. One reason is the weak reaction of marginal costs. First, this is due to the lack of methods for influencing the intrinsically motivated terrorists, who do not react to external stimuli, created by punishments and rewards. In their cases the attempts to influence them are absolutely inefficient or can even create negative effects – persecuting terrorism can further strengthen the motivation of terrorists, to turn them into martyrs and to be interpreted as a signal that terrorism is considered as a serious threat by the enemy and that the sacrifices it requires are worth it [13].

Second, the reaction of marginal costs is weak because of the terrorists' reaction to measures for obstructing their acts. When certain actions are undertaken for increasing security in one direction, terrorist attacks there decrease, but at the same time attacks in other directions increase; non-efficient forms and technologies of attack are interchanged with others; attacks are postponed in time; the number of attacks decrease but their cruelty increases; attacks are aimed against targets and countries that are not as well-protected [14]. In the specific conditions of maritime transport, for example, the efficiency of the ISPS Code measures which cover ships of 500 gt or more and port facilities that serve international ship traffic can easily be neutralized by terrorist attacks on smaller vessels. Other examples are the US CSI and RDI. Their specific focus on the security of major transhipment ports leaves significant space for terrorist attacks. Shie gives three arguments for that [15]: First, the emphasis on upgrading the security of major ports neglects the fact that these represent only a single link in the transportation chain, in which other branches cannot be secured within reasonable expenses. Second, the CSI conducts security checks only on *US- bound* containers. Therefore even if a tampered container arrives at a major port, if it is destined for a port other than the US, it is more likely to escape notice. Third, as major ports increase security, terrorists will look for other maritime targets or other means to target those ports.

Even if the measures for increasing the costs of terrorists were efficient, there is another reason that makes this policy inefficient in the long run: supply-side measures influence not only marginal costs but also marginal benefits from terrorism. When one country spends billions for "war on terror" this not only harms the terrorists but can also give them additional benefits that exceed their losses. Thus reaction against terrorism increases the benefits from it, makes terrorism even more attractive and returns as a boomerang to those who have initiated it.

There are several reasons for such a development.

First, limiting terrorism through a policy of deterrence has a negative effect on the economy. On the one hand it centralizes the economic relations, concentrates economic power in the hands of a small number of economic actors and decreases the competitive character of economies. The latter makes the economic basis of a society more vulnerable to terrorist attacks. It can be easily destabilized by terrorists and thus, the attacks are able to achieve their goals in an easier manner [16].

On the other hand, if supply-side measures are to be efficient they have to be exceptionally expensive and would cause a considerable burden on the society. For example in the case of maritime business the global ocean-liner shipping industry owns approximately $155 billion in vessels, containers, marine terminals and other direct operating assets [17]. There are hired 1.2 million people employed and only in the US almost 16 million people work in port-related jobs, producing $210 billion in federal, state and local taxes annually [18]. Each year 15 million containers make over 230 million journeys through the world's ports. They account for about 90% of the world's traded cargo by value and the economic effect of the latter is significant. As the Economist points out "all that would change if as a reaction of the increasing terrorist threat containers were screened, as airline passengers are. At the moment (2002), inspectors examine only 2% of containers, and often only after the containers have already travelled hundreds of miles from a port to a big city like Chicago or Detroit.

The potential damage that routine screening might cause was clear from the two-day wait at the American-Canadian border after September 11$^{th}$ : it nearly caused chaos at Detroit's car factories, which rely on flows of parts from Canada. The burden and disruption of extra security would weigh heavily on a shipping industry that is already suffering from the economic slowdown" [19]. It is not a coincidence that among the main obstacles to the previously mentioned programmes CSI and RDI are their expenses and the danger for disruption of operations and trade. That is why the predominant evaluations are that they are a useful start in addressing cargo security, but it is simply not feasible to scan every single container that goes through a port, as this would have grave ramifications on the efficiency of the global trading system [15].

Second, when additional measures are undertaken on the supply side, they cause media interest and create more terrorists than they deter. One of the reasons is that the deterrence policies are an asymmetric answer, which limits the democratic rights not only of terrorists but also of the greater part of society. This increases frustration and spreads it among broader social groups, changes their preferences and beliefs, radicalises the atmosphere, proves the basis for extremist behaviour and attracts more supporters, financial, material and human resources for the terrorists' cause [20]. Another reason is that a strong reaction against terrorism weakens the political system of democratic societies and leads to political centralization, under the conditions of which terrorist attacks can more easily destabilize the system. The measures for limiting terrorism through encouraging giving up terrorist actions lead in the same direction – by offering a free exit from terrorist activities they reduce the barriers for entering it and thus increase the numbers of individuals willing to undertake it.

All these problems lead to the conclusion that supply-side measures are an inefficient reaction against terrorism. To a large degree this gives a reason to agree with Lake's opinion [21] that, in fact, these measures work in favour of terrorists and are a part of their provocative strategy. The marginal groups with high political ambitions and little influence in society can realize their goals only if they can force their opponents to behave in an extremist manner. When terrorists attack, their objective is not to cause immediate material and human losses, as they cannot destabilize the societies under attack and thus achieve their political ambitions. But the reaction of these societies to the attacks can lead to the achievement of these ambitions, as September 11$^{th}$ proved. The terrorist attacks on the Twin Towers caused a disproportionally strong and massive emotional reaction. It took enormous social resources – much more than the terrorists from Al Qaeda could destroy, many innocent people were killed wounded or humiliated, historical and religious monuments were destroyed. Although the actions against Afghanistan and Iraq led to the capturing of many terrorists, today it is absolutely clear that supporters of terror and terrorism as a method are more numerous and stronger and the world has become a less secure place than before.

All this dictated that influencing the marginal costs of terrorism should be moderate and should not be used as a main method of fighting against terror. The economic reasoning then offers only one alternative – to decrease the marginal benefits from terrorism. Taking under consideration the already mentioned four factors that determine the size of marginal benefits from terrorism – influence upon the media, the economy, the political stability and the number of supporters we can point out measures that work in that direction. They are political, economic, media and propaganda.

The political reaction includes as a first step political decentralization and forming a network of multiple decision-making centres [16]. Unlike the hierarchic structure, the network structure cannot be destabilized easily and if one of its elements is attacked, the rest easily take its functions. A number of political principles allow applying this – separation of powers, political pluralism and forming multiple-level governance with a high degree of autonomy. Another political reaction to terrorism is democratisation. On the one hand it offers non-violent methods of representation and defence of individual political positions. On the other hand it increases political activity of the population and gives an impetus for political competition. Under conditions of democracy there is no need to attract public attention through inhumane acts of violence and there is no need for marginal groups to turn to terrorism, as a form for expressing their political positions and gaining more support. Quite the opposite, in the democratic conditions those who resort to terror have a lot more to lose and the extremist strategy is inefficient.

Economic measures for limiting the benefits from terrorism are also related to decentralization. When a strong level of concentration characterizes a business the attack against it will paralyse the entire society, because other economic subjects can hardly take up its functions. If the economy has a highly competitive structure, taking out a particular economic player will not be a problem, because competitors will quickly substitute for this particular player. The economic effects of the September 11$^{th}$ attack confirmed the relationship between the level of competition and the resilience against terrorist actions. Despite the enormous material and human losses, the attacks against the WTC had only temporary influence and the after-effects were quickly neutralized. The conclusion is that developing competition and market mechanisms are one of the strongest means of fighting against terrorism. It makes its successes only temporary and deprives it of strategic advantages in the costs-benefits ratio.

More measures that limit the benefits derived from terrorism and thus decrease its level can be introduced into this analysis. In order to prevent from turning the media into a propagandist of terrorists' ideas, the government should have an active media policy. In the world of Internet and many information sources the attempts for control over the media and information are absolutely inefficient and can have a negative result. In this area, democracy and informational pluralism have no alternative and the information war on terrorism demands that governments are present and dominate with the persuasiveness of their position.

Last but not least, an important way of limiting the benefits of terrorism is not to allow the deterrence policy to use exaggerated force and thus to create more terrorism. Terrorism is a provocative strategy and wins, not through causing direct damage with its strikes, but with the costs of the reaction caused by it in the attacked societies. Therefore this reaction should be moderate and controlled not by emotions and desire for revenge but by sound judgment and strategic vision of the future. Of course, it is hard to respond in a rational manner to terrorist acts, which in their cruelty go beyond the scope of the human mind, but this is where the great challenge of the war on terror lies. The way to achieve this is through forming broad coalitions, in which participants are necessary, not for their resources or with formally approving declarations, but for the sound reason of nations not affected emotionally. Thus, the allies can signal through their willingness to participate or not in the coalition when power used to combat terrorism goes out of control and actually starts serving the purposes of terror.

As a conclusion of this paper we have to note that all its ideas should be taken cautiously and after thorough national and international discussions. We did not have as a goal to answer and even less to solve all the questions and problems, posed by terrorism on modern societies and in particular on the maritime sector. If we were able, though, to initiate a discussion on these topics we will be very glad. The questions raised require quick and adequate answers. In answering them the economic approach has numerous advantages and our civil and professional duty is to offer it to the decision makers.

## References


[1] Becker, G. Crime and Punishment: An Economic Approach. Journal of Political Economy, 1968, 76, 169-217.

[2] Landes, W. An Economic Study of US Aircraft Hijackings, 1961-1976. Journal of Law and Economics, 1978, 21, 1-31.

[3] Lloyd's List. First Sea Lord warns of al-Qa'eda plot to target merchant ships. 5 August 2004.

[4] Mintz, J. U.S. Fears Terrorists at Sea. Washington Post, December 31, 2002.

[5] Richardson, M. Terror at Sea: The World's Lifelines are at Risk. The Straits Times Interactive, 17 November 2003.

[6] Sheppard, B. Maritime Security Measures. Jane's Intelligence Review, 1 March 2003.

[7] Richardson, M. A Time Bomb for Global Trade: Maritime Related Terrorism in an Age of Weapons of Mass Destruction. Singapore: Institute of Southeast Asian Studies, 2004, 112-114.

[8] Lukas, A. Protection without Protectionism Reconciling Trade and Homeland Security. Center for Trade Policy Studies, April 8, 2004 No. 27.

[9] Sandler, T., Scott, J. Terrorist Success in Hostage Taking Incidents: An Empirical Study. Journal of Conflict Resolution, 1987, 31, 35-53.

[10] Addison, T., Murshed, S. Transnational Terrorism as a Spillover of Domestic Disputes in Other Countries. Discussion Paper No. 2002/120, UNU/WIDER, Helsinki, 2002.

[11] Ambrogi, S. Experts: Al Qaeda Maritime Threat Growing. Reuters, February 18, 2004.

[12] Frey, B., Luechinger, S. How to Fight Terrorism: Alternatives to Deterrence. Defense and Peace Economics, 2003, 14:4, 237-249.

[13] Muller, E., Opp, K. Rational Choice and Rebellious Collective Action. American Political Science Review, 1986, 80, 471 - 488.
[14] Enders, W., Sandler, T. The Effectiveness of Antiterrorism Policies: A Vector-Autoregression-Intervention Analysis. American Political Science Review, 1993, 87, 829-844.
[15] Shie, T. Ships and Terrorists – Thinking Beyond Port Security. Pacific Forum CSIS Honolulu, Hawaii. October 15, 2004.
[16] Frey, B., Luechinger, S. Decentralisation as a Disincentive to Terror. European Journal of Political Economy, 2002, 20:2, 595.
[17] World Shipping Council, http://www.worldshipping.org.
[18] American Association of Port Authorities, http://www.aapa-ports.org.
[19] The Economist. When trade and security clash. Apr 4th 2002
[20] Laqueur, W. The Age of Terrorism. Boston: Little, Brown, 1987, p. 87.
[21] Lake, D. Rational Extremism: Understanding Terrorism in the Twenty-first Century. Dialog-IO, 2002, Spring, 15–29.

# A ship monitoring system using a communication satellite for maritime safety

K. Inoue, H. Usui, K. Hirono & W. Sera
*Faculty of Maritime Sciences, Kobe University, Japan*

## Abstract

Any subsequent action to ensure safety can be made only when the current safety level is shown quantitatively, and safety cannot be attained if there is any discrepancy in safety recognition between the controlling party and the controlled party. That is, the significance of Assessment Technology, which is an important technology for safety management, cannot be overlooked. Furthermore, it is nonetheless important to ensure shared common safety recognition between operators of the base station on shore and the navigators on board.

The primary target of this study is to establish a ship-shore communication network using satellite communication technology between the Fukae Maru and the base station in the Fukae campus. The secondary target is to develop assessment technology that is capable of quantitatively assessing safety in various ship operating modes required for assisting safe ship operation from the shore side. And, the ultimate goal of this study is to promote research and development on safety management technology to assist the safe operation of ships from shore, by incorporating assessment technology into the prototype experiment system for the ship-shore communication network.
*Keywords: safety management system, information technology, assessment technology, safe ship operation.*

## 1 Introduction

The approach to safety management of ship operations has recently been shifting from the ship-based safety management to shore-based safety management, which relies upon two-way ship-shore communication techniques.

In this study, the concept of shore-based safety management is defined as a system to achieve the safe operation of ships by having base station on shore constantly monitor the operating conditions of ships in all navigating modes, and analytically assessing data transmitted from each ship, processing such data into the safety information, and feeding back timely safety instructions together with safety guidelines for the navigator.

The important tasks to realize shore-based safety management using two-way ship-shore communication techniques are: (1) how to realize two-way ship-shore communication, (2) what ship operating information needs to be monitored, how such information is to be processed, and how the processed information should be transmitted from shore to ships as safety-assisting information, and (3) how to eliminate safety recognition gaps between ships and shore.

As is shown in Figure 1, in this study, a ship-shore communication network using the satellite communication is established between the Fukae Maru (450 GT training ship owned by Kobe University, Faculty of Maritime Sciences) and the base station within the Fuka campus, whereby studies are conducted for the purposes of developing safety management techniques to assist safe ship operations from shore.

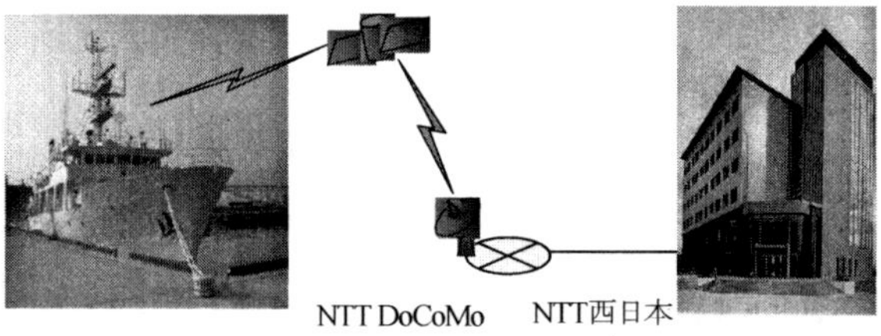


Figure 1: Concept of two-way ship-shore communication using the satellite communication.

In this study, in addition, on the basis of the concept that safe ship operation cannot be achieved if there is any disparity in the recognition of safety between the controlling side and the controlled side, which has been lacking in conventional studies, the practical usefulness of the newly developed safety management system will be verified through experiments with actual ships.

The safety management system developed in accordance with such a concept is based on the safety management that matches the recognition of the navigator. As a result, it is expected that the system would be widely accepted by mariners on board, who do not welcome control from others.

Furthermore, this system is not only useful for managing the safety of individual ships but it is also possible to develop a Vessel Traffic System; i.e., safety management of traffic flows in a specific sea area.

A benefit is that it might be feasible to enhance the Vessel Traffic System, from the conventional information system to a new system for a shore-based control system.

### 1.1 Forming a ship-shore communication network

Before conducting this study, Japan Marine Science Inc. introduced the Web Pilot, a ship-shore communication system using satellite communication, onboard the Kibou, a techno-superliner owned by Shizuoka Prefecture, whereby the usefulness of the system was verified on an international voyage to Shanghai.

Later, the company and this research laboratory conducted a joint research project to form an improved system between the Fukae Maru and the base station within the Fukae campus, taking over from the basic concept of the Web Pilot system.

The processes thereafter include: agreement to participate in the NTT DoCoMo Packet Network concluded in 2001; test operation commenced of ship-shore communication using the satellite communication by combining the data collection system through the shipboard LAN of the Fukae Maru and the communication management system within the base station of the Fukae campus; and in 2002, a high-performance computer capable of handling data transmission/reception control on the side of the Fukae Maru, and a high-speed, large-capacity computer for high-speed data processing and graphic data transmission at the base station within the Fukae campus were introduced.

Furthermore, additional efforts for enhancing utility have been made to improve the software for communication management, thus the foundation for the hardware and the software necessary for this study has been completed.

In 2003, research and development on safety management technology was started to support the safe operation of ships using the prototype system of the ship-shore communication connecting the Fukae Maru and the base station within the Fukae campus through the satellite communication. Figure 2 shows a view of the base station within the Fukae campus.

Figure 2: Base station within the premises of the university (Academic Exchange Building, 4th Floor).

# 2 Development of quantitative assessment technology of ship-handling risk, which is hidden behind various ship-handling modes

## 2.1 Monitoring ship operating information

In parallel with work to complete the ship-shore two-way communication network, safety studies were conducted on various modes of ship-handling related to information that is required to be monitored, how such information is processed, and how such safety-assisting information should be transmitted from shore to ships.

Concerning monitoring, ship operating information on position, course, speed, and ship motions of the Fukae Maru, natural environmental information on wind direction, wind speed, wave heights, wave direction, and period, and, in addition, traffic environmental information by Radar PPI image, engine operating information represented by all information displayed on the engine console comprise the basic monitoring information, and these items of information are made available in real-time at the base station on shore.

Besides the above, all data and information collected and imported into the shipboard LAN through ship-borne equipment and various sensors are made available for monitoring by requesting from shore as necessary.

## 2.2 Assessment technology for safety evaluation

On the assessment technology that quantitatively assesses safety in various ship-handling modes, which are required for assisting the safe operation of ships from shore, our Research Laboratory has successfully developed models for quantitatively assessing risk levels in terms of objective numerical indexes for a variety of risks such as dragging anchor, breaking failure of mooring rope, destruction of a pier, overrun, collision with shore installations, ship-to-ship collision, grounding, and capsizing, which are associated with anchoring, berthing/unberthing operations, in-harbour ship-handling, navigation in narrow channel, ocean navigation under heavy weather, and accumulated technical expertise.

For example, risk assessment models were proposed for assessing anchoring operations, using the probability of dragging anchor, and risk index of dragging anchor [1, 2], and for assessing mooring alongside a quay using rope breaking probability [3].

For ship-handling when berthing to a quay, a model capable of assessing latent risk of overrun and latent risk of destruction of a quay was proposed by introducing the concept of safety allowance [4, 5].

Furthermore, for ship-handling difficulties in harbour and in a narrow channel, where water area is restricted, and in waters where traffic is congested, Environmental Stress model (ES model) were proposed, while for grounding risk and collision risk, Unsafe Ship-handling model (US model) were proposed that reflected the risk-assessment technique from the viewpoint of probabilities of accident occurrence [6-13].

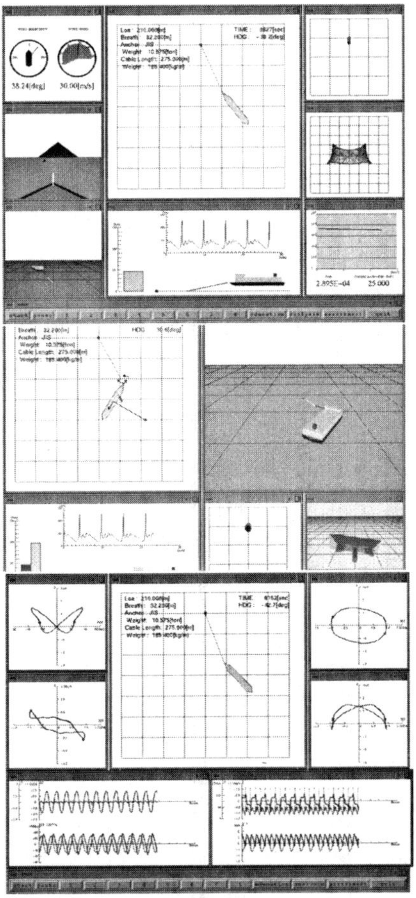

Figure 3: Assessment information images of anchoring and dragging anchor at the shore base station.

In waters with heavy traffic congestion, in particular, judging collision risks and selecting measures for collision avoidance constitute a major point of consideration. Concepts of Collision Danger Line (CDL) and Cone-shaped Collision Danger Line (CDL triangle) have been developed and proposed as practical methods for navigators to readily assess risk under a specific safety standard [14, 15].

The significance of quantitatively assessing latent risks in all ship-handling situations is to obtain basic information that enables the navigator to take the next step with confidence on the basis of the current verified safety level. When viewed from the standpoint of managing safe ship operation, these constitute indispensable factors for developing an alert system and a safety advice system for a variety of ship-handling nodes. Figures 4 and 5 show examples of assessment information images at the shore base station.

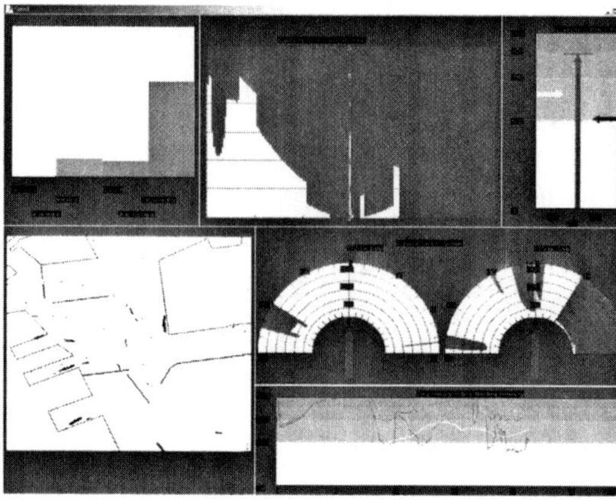

Figure 4: Assessment information images of ship-handling difficulties at the shore base station.

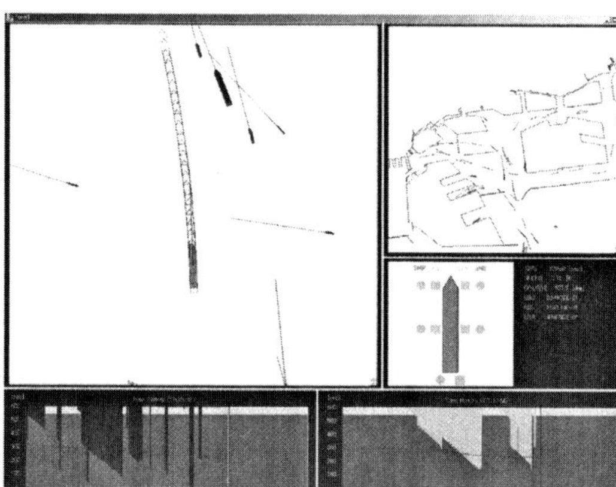

Figure 5: Assessment information images of collision and grounding risks at the shore base station.

## 3 Problems of human conflicts between the controlling party and the controlled party

For the preferred embodiment of an alert system and a safety advice system in the safety management of ship operation, it is necessary to compare the risk levels that can be outputted by these assessment models and the permissible risk levels.

The shore-based safety management of ship operation is prone to descend into mere inorganic information exchanges. In reality, however, there are human beings at both ends of the communication system, and the occurrence of human errors arising from conflicts between man and information, man and machine, and between men must be carefully assessed.

Prototype experiments operating an actual ship were carried out from the end of 2003 to 2004. In an experiment carried out as a part of this project, the results of the ship-handling option on shore created on the basis of data transmitted from the Fukae Maru, while passing through Tomogashima Strait and Osaka Bay, received and analysed by the shore base station, were transmitted back to the ship as instructive information.

The results of this experiment show frequent disparities between local judgments onboard the ship based on practical visual information and the base station's data-dependent judgment, thus suggesting the need for confirming mutual intent.

To help reduce such human conflicts between the controlling party and the controlled party, system-wise efforts were made through graphic processing techniques to provide the base station with the same three-dimensional visual information that is actually seen by navigators onboard the ship.

The effectiveness of this system improvement has been validated by the prototype experiment connecting the Fukae Maru with the base station through satellite communication; i.e., it is confirmed that the system is useful for transmitting appropriate real-time alerts/safety advice for the navigator [16].

Figure 6 is a photo of an experiment carried out to reproduce in real-time scenes of the Fukae Maru going astern in the pond of the university, making a turn and departing there from.

Figure 7 shows an example of the assessment information image for assisting collision avoiding manoeuvres using the results mentioned above.

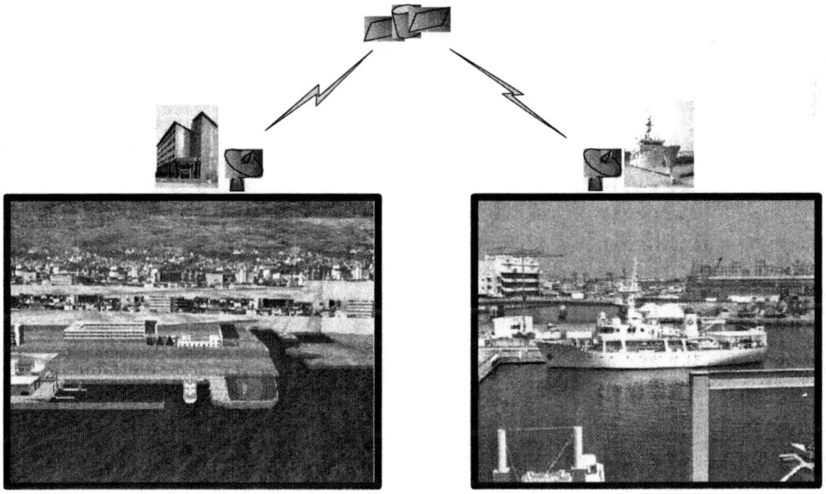

Figure 6: Reproduced three-dimensional vision information at the base station (Left: Reproduced base station image, Right: Site view).

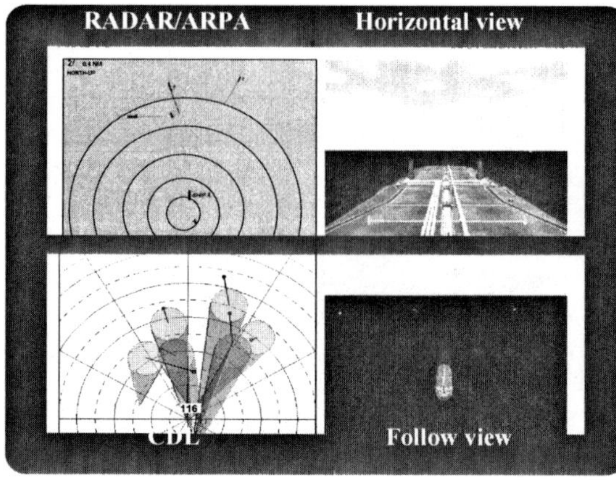


Figure 7: Collision-avoiding judgment assisting assessment information image at the shore base station.

## 4 Concluding remarks

Research and development on the safety management technology for shore-based assistance of safe ship operations has been steadily promoted by operating the prototype system of the ship-shore communication network between the Fukae Maru (450 GT) owned by Kobe University, Faculty of Maritime Sciences and the base station within the premises of the Fukae campus, using satellite communication.

This paper introduces the current state of the development of safety management technology for shore-based assistance of safe ship operation being undertaken by the Ship-Handling and Marine Traffic System Research Laboratory of the Maritime Sciences Faculty, Kobe University.

The project has just been started, and much is still to be completed in the future through our renewed efforts.

## Acknowledgements

This study has been implemented with FY2001/2002 subsidy from Ministry of Education, Science and Culture, joint research with Japan Marine Science Inc., and project research aid from Kobe University.

The author of this paper wishes to acknowledge his deep indebtedness to all of the joint researchers and the crew of the Fukae Maru.

## References

[1] Inoue, K. et al., Safety Assessment of Mooring at Anchor under Stormy Weather, The Journal of Japan Institute of Navigation, Vol.74, pp19-28, March 1986 (in Japanese).

[2] Inoue, K. & Usui, H., Guideline for Safe Anchoring Based on a Risk-Index of Dragging Anchor –Wind Force, Wind Depth and Anchor Cable to be Paid Out, The Journal of Japan Institute of Navigation, Vol.90, pp233-241, March 1994 (in Japanese).

[3] Inoue, K. et al., Reliability Analysis of Mooring System under Stormy Weather, The Journal of Japan Institute of Navigation, Vol.71, pp103-114, September 1984 (in Japanese).

[4] Inoue, K., Seta, H. & Masuda, K., Guideline for Speed Reduction in Berthing Manoeuvre, The Journal of Japan Institute of Navigation, Vol.107, pp169-176, September 2002 (in Japanese).

[5] Inoue, K., Guideline for Desirable Berthing Operation, The Journal of Japan Institute of Navigation, Vol.82, pp43-52, September 2002 (in Japanese).

[6] Inoue, K., Evaluation Method of Ship Handling Difficulty for Navigation in Restricted and Congested Waterways, The Journal of Navigation, The Royal Institute of Navigation, Vol.53, No.1, pp167-180, January 2000.

[7] Inoue, K., Rating the Quality of Ports and Harbours from the Viewpoint of Ship-Handling Difficulty, Proceedings of 12th International Harbour Congress, pp.203-214, September 1999.

[8] Inoue, K., Masuda, K. & Sera, W., Guideline to Assess the Safety of Marine Traffic–I. –Evaluation of Shiphandling Difficulty based on the Environmental Stress Model, The Journal of Japan Institute of Navigation, Vol.107, pp169-176, September 2002 (in Japanese).

[9] Fukuchi, N., Shinoda, T., & Ono, T, A Stochastic State-transition and Safety Assessment for Marine Accidents Based on Human Factors (Part 1; Tensional Stress by Measuring Fractal Nature of Heart Rate Variability), Journal of the Society of Naval Architects of Japan, Vol. 188, pp465-478, December 2000.

[10] Inoue, K. et al., Assessment Model of Ship Handling Safety by Noting Unsafe Situation as an Index, Journal of the Kansai Society of Naval Architects, Japan, Vol.241, pp205-210, March 2004 (in Japanese).

[11] Inoue K., Concept of Potential Area of Water as an Index of Risk Assessment of Ship Handling, The Journal of Navigation, The Royal Institute of Navigation, Vol.43, No1, pp1-7, January 1990.

[12] Inoue, K., Sera, W. & Masuda, K., Evaluation of Shiphandling Safety based on the Concept of PAW, The Journal of Japan Institute of Navigation, Vol.99, pp163-171, September 1998 (in Japanese).

[13] Inoue, K., et al., Guideline to Assess the Safety of Marine Traffic–IV. – Estimation of Potential Danger of Near Miss, The Journal of Japan Institute of Navigation, Vol.102, pp203-209, March 2000 (in Japanese).

[14] Pedersen, E., Inoue, K. & Tsugane, M., Evaluation of a Radar Plot and Display Technique for Anti-collision Assessment of Multiple Targets in True Vector Representation by Application of the Environmental Stress Model, The Journal of Japan Institute of Navigation, Vol.106, pp1-12, March 2002.

[15] Pedersen, E., Inoue, K. & Tsugane, M., On Decision Making in Connection with Optional Anti-collision Manoeuvres by High Speed Craft in Waters Congested by Conventional Speed Vessels, The Journal of Japan Institute of Navigation, Vol.107, pp177-183, March 2002.
[16] Tsugane, M., Inoue, K., Hirono, K & Sera, W., A Study of Effectiveness of Collision Danger Line Information for Actual Ship Handling, The Journal of Japan Institute of Navigation, Vol.109 pp125-131, September 2003 (in Japanese).

# The ISPS Code as a component of onboard resources in Bayesian analysis

V. A. Loginovsky, A. P. Gorobtsov & V. E. Kuzmin
*Navigation Department, Admiral Makarov State Maritime Academy, St Petersburg, the Russian Federation*

## Abstract

Nowadays, the influence of resources on safety and security at sea is one of the most critical elements of the existing management system. The already enormous regulatory workload on crew under ISM Code, STCW, SOLAS and MARPOL has now increased due to ISPS Code requirements. This again puts more stress on human and organisational factors in general, and deck officers' attention and performance in particular. The importance of human resources can be well reflected in a model, but is difficult to reveal through statistics. Since Bayesian networks naturally represent causal chains, that is, cause-effect relationships between parent and child nodes, we can supply evidence of past events, and then run the Bayesian network to see what the most likely future outcomes will be. Their strength is that they are robust if missing some part of the information, and will make the best possible prediction with whatever information is present. Therefore they were used for modelling crew resources. The modelling proves an overload on crew members, and shows the limited resources on board ship. To ensure efficiency of ISPS Code procedures, extra training is required which should be incorporated into the general curriculum of MET institutions. More attention to security issues should be paid on the part of Port Facilities. ISPS Code related inspections should consider the availability of manpower on board to ensure efficient performance.
*Keywords: ISM Code, ISPS Code, crew resources, Bayesian networks.*

## 1 Introduction

Nowadays, the influence of resources on safety and security at sea is one of the most critical elements of the existing management system. Ship officers are responsible for planning, communication, navigation, ship handling and many other routines, including procedures under the ISPS Code. To enhance safety and security at sea we must ensure that the right people are in the right place at the right time to counteract a possible intrusion. With the introduction of the ISPS Code, the "Principles of Safe Manning" were challenged to consider how additional shipboard security duties may contribute to crew member fatigue and thus might create a hazard to the continuous safe navigation of the world's merchant fleet.

The shipping industry already constrained by SOLAS, STCW, MARPOL, ISM Code and ISPS Code requirements, is also constantly exposed to extremely tight commercial pressure to minimize the operational costs. Additional security measures under the ISPS Code resulted in a so-called "ISPS Code charge" which varies from 5 to 9 € per cargo unit.

To cope with competitors, shipping companies have to resort to measures aimed at cost reduction. Very often this leads to lower wages for crew, resulting in lower competence and reduced numbers of crew, or longer contracts. The number of seafarers trained in developed countries is constantly decreasing. Unpopularity of seafaring as a profession may lead to a lack of professionally qualified staff. On the other hand a lack of clarity in expectations for each position may confuse the post holder and might lead to under-preparedness. This situation might be aggravated by faster promotions. It is often claimed that the new generation of seafarers is less experienced. Sometimes it takes only 2 years for a junior officer to become Chief Mate. Navigation and ship handling are no longer an art, it is an occupation associated with long periods of isolation from shore.

Multinational crews are common nowadays. Anecdotal evidence shows that cases where the Chief Officer was of Polish nationality, the 2nd and 3d Officers were of Russian nationality, ratings were of PR Chinese nationality are not at all exceptional. This loosens the ties between the Shipping Company and the crew member on board the company ships. Different languages, different cultures, as well as different wages and contract duration do not encourage cooperation, safety or security. In addition we would argue, that often crews are being recruited from developing countries which have no tradition of a "safety culture".

At the same time ship traffic is increasing every year, becoming more and more intensive. To ensure fast turn-around, the time a ship is staying in the port is decreasing mostly due to the introduction of modern cargo handling technology. In some countries crew members experience to have shore leave because of ISPS Code requirements.

All this leads to a violation of STCW 95 and ILO Convention No. 180 requirements, resulting in excessive fatigue, decreasing level of safety and security. The impact of manning levels on the implementation of ISPS Code as well as on the implementation of many other regulations is a legitimate matter of concern of the IMO, National Maritime Administrations and ship managers. Attempts to rectify these deficiencies lead to tightening of inspections, increased bureaucracy and resulted in a so-called "paper-safety" culture. This term denotes safety on paper but not in reality due to lack of resources. The ISM Code was initially introduced to solve some of these problems. Unfortunately it does not seem to be effective in many companies. Numerous and tedious inspections will again put more stress on already exhausted crews in general, and deck officers in particular.

It is obvious that the "Principles of Safe Manning" should require a security component and that this regulation – if it is to achieve its desired result – may be asking too much of many of the already overloaded shipboard personnel.

An already enormous regulatory workload of crew under ISM Code, STCW, SOLAS and MARPOL was increased due to ISPS Code requirements. Together with reduced numbers of crew, this situation might endanger safety and security at sea. It begs the question: Do we have enough resources to provide for additional security measures according to level 2 or 3?

The main challenge of this research is to develop a model showing the impact of the ISPS Code on workload and crew performance. Such an impact on crew workload should not be considered separately from all of the other duties of the ship's crew. A limited number of crew members, often only the barest necessity to meet the requirements for rest hours specified by the above mentioned conventions (STCW and ILO 180) demands a systematic approach to an analysis of the impact the ISPS Code has had on shipboard organization. Such an analysis is especially necessary in the case of ships employed in short -sea navigation and at Maritime Security Level 2 and 3. One of the mathematic tools, which could be used for solving this problem, is Bayesian Network (BN).

### 1.1 Bayesian network

As all work onboard is performed by the crew with no additional support available, it is inexpedient to address issues of ISPS Code compliance, ISM Code compliance or watch keeping at sea and in port separately. The resource model must take into account both individual duties and the whole task. Risk modelling is an essential part of the Formal Safety Assessment (FSA) methodology. There are two ways to quantify risk, through a priori statistics and through models.

The disadvantage of using traditional statistics is that statistics only represent the past, and cannot take into account recent developments or new requirements. Risk modelling is the proactive approach, whereby risks are assessed before the accident takes place.

This is at variance with maritime history, where regulations are often adopted only after catastrophic accidents have been analysed. The importance of human resources can be well reflected in a model, however, difficult to reveal through statistics. Since Bayesian nets naturally represent causal chains, that is, cause-effect relationships between parent and child nodes, we can supply evidence of past events, and then run the Bayesian network to see what the most likely future outcomes will be. Their strength is that they are robust if missing some part of information, and will make the best possible prediction with whatever information is present; therefore they were used for crew resources modelling. HUGIN is the Bayesian network tool used in the research reported in this paper.

# 2 Main part

## 2.1 ISPS Code history

In essence, the ISPS Code takes the approach that ensuring the security of ships and port facilities is basically a risk management activity and that to determine what security measures are appropriate, an assessment of the risks must be made in each particular case. Hazard identification (HAZID) is a method used to systematically go through a system or an operation with the aim to identify and discuss hazardous elements/conditions. One of the objectives of this paper was to identify all-important hazards regarding lack of available resources on board ships influencing both security and safety. This hazard identification forms the basis for a formal safety assessment (FSA), consisting of the following steps:

hazard identification, risk analysis, Risk Control Options (RCO), recommendations for decision-making.

The purpose of the ISPS Code is to provide a standardized, consistent framework for evaluating risk, enabling governments to offset changes in threat with changes in vulnerability for ships and port facilities. Because each ship (or class of ship) and each port facility present different risks, the method in which they meet the specific requirements of this Code should be determined and eventually approved by the Administration or Contracting Government, as the case may be. In order to communicate the threat at a port facility or for a ship, the Contracting Government sets the appropriate security level. Security levels 1, 2, and 3 correspond to normal, medium, and high threat situations, respectively. The security level creates a link between the ship and the port facility, since it triggers the implementation of appropriate security measures for the ship and for the port facility.

## 2.2 Model description

Figure 1 gives a brief overview of the risk model developed by Bayesian network for resources. Resources in this study were defined as available human manpower on board the vessel. Various experts and data sources were used to ensure a solid foundation for the dependencies and figures entered into the model. An extensive survey among seafarers was held to serve as a base for modelling. A questionnaire "Sufficiency of resources for performing conventional duties" with more than 86 questions was developed within the framework of this research. More than 150 people took part in this survey, all of them were Masters, Chief Officers or OOW.

An Object-Oriented Bayesian network (OOBN) is a network that, in addition to the usual nodes, contains instance nodes. An instance node is a node representing an instance of another network. In other words, an instance node represents a subnet. Of course, the network of which instances exist in other networks can itself contain instance nodes, whereby an object-oriented network can be viewed as a hierarchical description (or model) of a problem domain.

In this model we took into account only ship resources as the crew component is the most fragile and exposed in the security scheme. All other components of the model were fixed. It consists of the following instance nodes (subnets) (Figure 1) shown as rectangles as opposed to original nodes shown as ellipses.

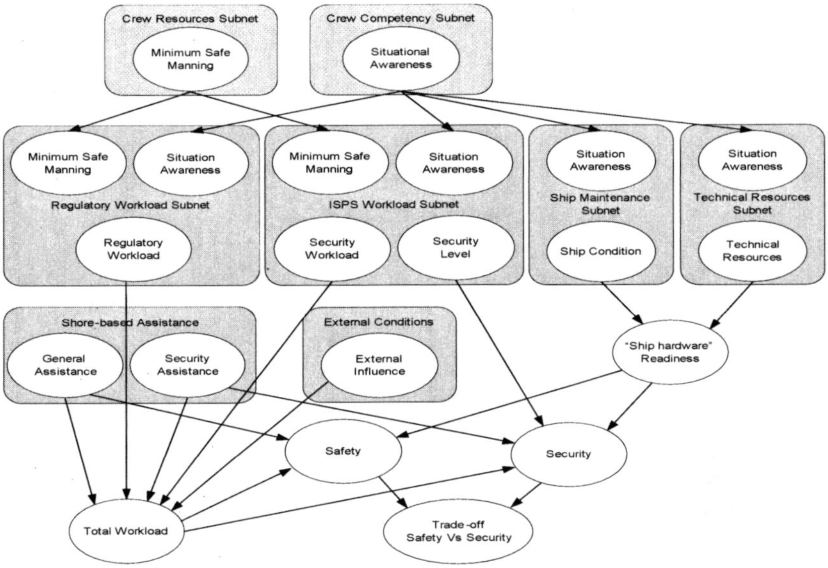


Figure 1: Bayesian crew resource model.

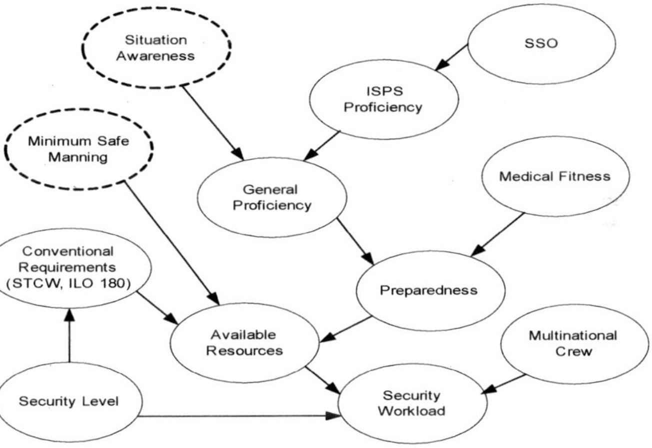


Figure 2: ISPS Code workload subnet.

The most valuable output from a model is not the overall risk level that is predicted by the model, but the structure itself and all the contributing factors that enable an understanding of the failure mechanisms. It thus gives a quantified result whenever one of the input parameters is altered. In other words, each node could be identified as a Risk Control Measure (RCM), and their influence on safety and security could be monitored.

The ISPS Code workload subnet consists of the following nodes:

• **SSO**

The node indicates the experience of the Ship Security Officer, his proficiency in security training and other security procedures. Every node is a vector with several states, e.g. $\text{vector} = \begin{pmatrix} \text{State 1} \\ \text{State 2} \end{pmatrix}$, here it is a vector with two states: - Experienced, - Non-experienced.

It could be written as $\text{SSO} = \begin{pmatrix} \text{Experienced} \\ \text{Non} - \text{experienced} \end{pmatrix}$

The probabilities in this node are based on statistics/expert data, derived from SSO training courses.

• **ISPS Code proficiency**

The node describes the crew proficiency in ISPS Code procedures. States: - Standard, - Low. The probability for this node is derived from expert data, based on results of security training programs held at Makarov Training Centre.

• **Situation awareness**

This node is an output node of Crew Competency subnet. This node shows results for professional crew competency based on the following factors:
sea experience, ship and trading area familiarization, professional competency, additional training, company's policy for non-compulsory training, tendency to hire cheaper (less qualified) crew, company's training budget.
States: - Aware, - Not aware. The probability input is derived from Crew Competency subnet.

• **General proficiency**

This node joins the nodes "ISPS Code proficiency" and "Situation awareness" and describes whether the crew member has a standard or a low (sub-standard) level of general skills. States: - Standard, - Low

• **Medical Fitness**

This node describes the physical and mental condition of the crew member, and indicates whether the crew member is fit to perform assigned duties and has 3 states:
- Fit, - Impaired, - Unfit

• **Preparedness**

This node is dependent on the nodes "General Proficiency" and "Medical Fitness". States: - Prepared, - Not Prepared. It is assumed that if the crew member is unfit, it is 100% not prepared for ISPS Code procedures; but if the crew member is impaired its preparedness is reduced by 20%. It is stated that crew member with standard level of skills are often less tolerant to minor health problems.

• **Minimum Safe Manning**

This node is an output node of Human Resources subnet.

• **Security Level**

This node describes crew workload depending on Maritime Security Level as compared to normal operation of the ship. States: - Level 1, - Level 2, - Level 3. It is supposed that within Level 1 additional workload because of ISPS Code procedures amounts to 5-10%, within level 2 -30% and within level 3 – up to 45-50% as compared to normal ship operation.

• **Conventional requirements (STCW, ILO-180)**

The node denotes standards described in STCW and ILO-180 conventions regarding rest and working hours. States: - Conventional, i.e. meeting the above mentioned requirements, - Insufficient, i.e. compromising the above mentioned requirements.

• **Available resources**

This node is made in order to gather the nodes for "Conventional requirements", "Minimum safe manning" and "Preparedness" into one. This approach is a software trick to reduce the amount of probability input. If the number of arrows onto the subsequent node is reduced, the size and the complexity of the conditional probability tables (CPTs) is also reduced. It describes whether we have available resources depending on the above nodes. States: - Available, - Not available.

• **Multinational crews**

The node shows dependence of crew cooperation in case of security threat or other emergency. States: - Multi-national crew, - Mono national crew.

• **Security workload**

This node is the output node for this subnet. It means that data from this subnet will be summarized in this node and sent to other Bayesian networks for further processing. It shows whether we have normal or high security workload. This node is dependent on maritime security level node, available resources node and crew nationality node. States: - Normal, - High. The probability input is derived from questionnaire and expert data.

The results obtained with the model are not contradictory to common sense. This proves that the model is adequate to the process researched. Basically, the model was developed for an analysis of tendency (conceptual model) and not with the aim of getting accurate figures. Therefore the model may have some limitations including those inherent in Bayesian networks:

1. An imperfect model due to an imperfect understanding of the domain, an incomplete knowledge of the state of the domain at the time where a given task is to be performed, a randomness in the mechanisms governing the behaviour of the domain, or a combination of these. We hope this imperfectness is minimized because the research team consists of professionals.
2. An incompleteness of the model due to some missing nodes (auxiliary nodes, which are not important in our opinion or nodes with insufficient data record tracking). For example, the node of education level was not taken into account simply because there was no data available on dependency of education grade.
3. The great redundancy of the model leads to low a sensitivity of the output results. This is a signal to introduce "weighting" of nodes.
4. A priori data were used for modelling. This data was based on experts' opinions derived from a questionnaire survey held among 150 deck officers of different qualifications. A frequency interpretation assessment was used

instead of probabilistic approach due to an insufficiency of data available. This approach is acceptable for practical analysis.

## 2.3 Model analysis

Figure 3A shows the trade-off between safety and security depending on maritime security level.

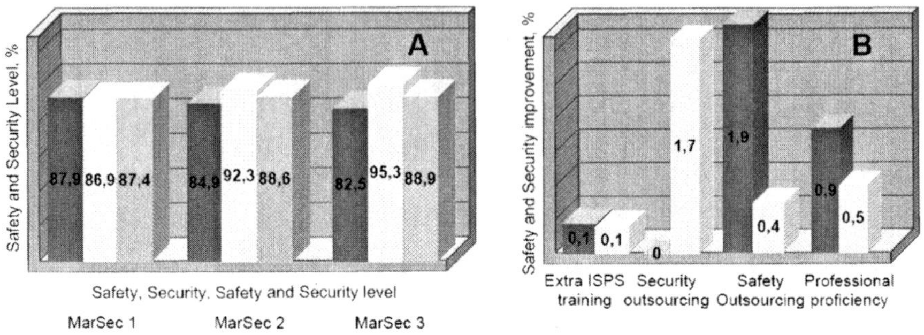


Figure 3: A. Trade-off: Safety vs. Security. B. RCO Rating.

The results show that when changing security level from 1 to 2 we still have some small gap because the total level of safety and security changes positively by 1% (from 87% to 88%). But that gap is not as great as required by level 2 where as we can see the safety level reduces to 86, and at level 3 where the summary level is practically the same as at level 2. This means that we have insufficient resources; to increase security we have to compromise safety which is absolutely unacceptable.

Figure 3B shows the safety and security level changes depending on selected RCO, so-called RCO rating based on modelling results. As can be seen from the graph, a delegation of some duties ashore yields positive results. Also, a distinct connection between safety and security is seen. With a decrease in total workload we obtain an improvement both in safety and security, as the crew member has more time to deal with shipboard routines.

Apart from technical RCO there could be RCM aimed at Human Element. The main element of this group, which is called Crew Resources RCO (CR RCO), is to enhance crew performance via additional training and additional personnel. Crew Resources RCO includes the following RCM (nodes):

**Safety culture** - The introduction of a safety culture on board ships should be a long term goal for any shipping company, as this not only enhances safety and security but also reduces the risk of overall negligence and poor maintenance at rather low cost. Moreover it gives a good motivation for crew members to take an active part in the SMS on board ship.

**Simulator training** - The training as required by the STCW Convention is the minimum, and it is further argued that improved navigator training would have a positive effect on the safety and security level of the vessel. An example of an improved navigator training is advanced ship manoeuvring, including training of crisis situations which can only be done safely in simulators.

The second RCO group deals with shore-based activities. The main idea of this group is to facilitate ship board routines either remotely via special services such as chart updating service ashore or directly, by the port facility to take the main part of the security workload during the ship's stay in port.

Figure 4 shows changes in security level depending on the implementation the level of selected RCM connected with shore-based activities.

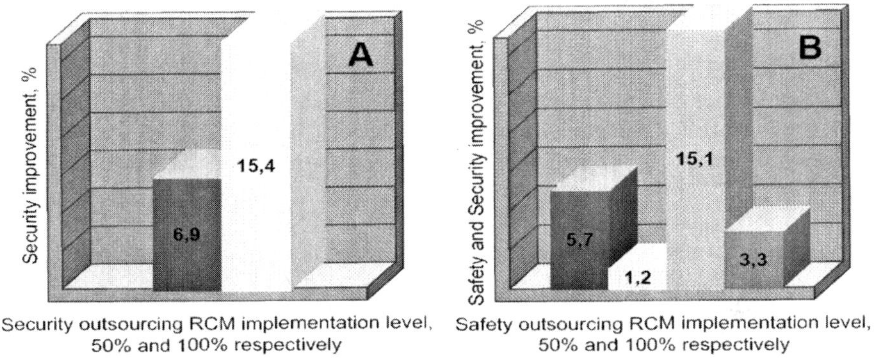


Figure 4: Security and safety outsourcing RCM.

It can be seen that outsourcing of security duties to port facilities (Figure 4A) greatly enhances security on board as port facilities are less limited in their resources. It could be that outsourcing of some ship routines to shore management (Figure 4B) enhances both safety and security as it makes more time available for performing other duties.

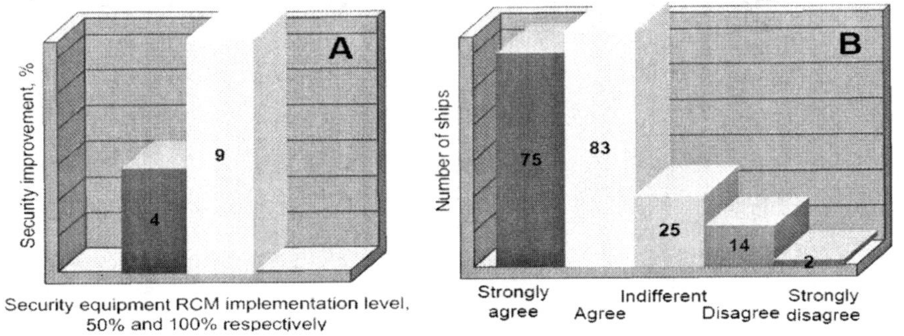


Figure 5: A. Security equipment B. ISPS Code does overload.

The third RCO group deals with technical measures aimed at reducing workload through an automation of shipboard operations, for example the installation of certified security equipment such as gangway alarm or intruder alarm. Figure 5A shows changes in security level depending on the implementation of such security equipment.

## 3 Conclusions

Nowadays it is hardly possible, that we could find one or two new effective measures which allow us to considerably raise the level of safety and security, therefore only a complex system of such measures could produce tangible results. The ship's crew is limited in number as well as in resources. To cope with their numerous duties, officers should be more competent to be able to do more things within allocated time. For example, to keep ship's charts folios updated an experienced Navigation Officer needs less time than his less experienced colleague. With an unchanged crew size any increase in workload implies the need for a higher competency of crew members to be able to complete their duties in time. The better the education of an individual, the better is the situation awareness. In other words here we have direct link between ISPS Code and MET.

Crew competency is the measure of ship safety and security. The number of crew depends on its qualification within reasonable limits. It is common to duplicate equipment to increase its redundancy but the same principle should be employed for crew resources too. To enable a level playing field for shipping companies, the number of less competent crew should be increased on board as compared to well-educated and trained crew.

When comparing our results with other reports we could note consistency in results shown on Figure 5B taken from "Questionnaire findings on experience on ISPS Code implementation from crew/vessel point of view" by Tim Charalambous.

Another finding of this research is the necessity to build a single unified ISM-ISPS Code System, Security and Safety Management System (SSMS), as all of security and safety aspects of ship's operation should be checked and monitored simultaneously, not separately as it is currently done. Presently too much stress is put on the ship's crew, to address security issues. Having much more resources available, undoubtedly, port facilities should be more involved.

Outsourcing of security duties to port facilities is one of the ways out to reduce crew workload without compromising safety and security.

## References


[1] NAV 49/inf.2 Large passenger ship safety: effective voyage planning for large passenger ships, report submitted by Norway, IMO, 2003.

[2] MSC/Circ.1023, MEPC/Circ.392 Guidelines for formal security assessment (FSA) for use in the IMO rule-making process, IMO, 2002.

[3] HUGIN manual and software, HUGIN Expert A/S, Denmark, 1995-2005.

[4] Charalambous T., Questionnaire findings on experience of ISPS Code implementation from crew/vessel point of view, DFM Presentation, www.thedigitalship.com.

# The impact of stowaways and illegal migrants by sea: a case study in Taiwan

Y.-H. Chen[1], S.-L. Chen[2] & C.-H. Wu[1]
[1]*Department of Merchant Marine, National Taiwan Ocean University, Taiwan*
[2]*Department of Maritime Business, Australian Maritime College, Australia*

## Abstract

The development of stowaway and illegal migrant problems worldwide is believed to induce public resentments because of its negative impact on social order and the financial burden it imposes on the public and private sectors. In addition, stowaways and illegal migration have become part of an organised crime because organised criminal trans-national groups are involved in the smuggling and trafficking of migrants by sea. Taiwan has been confronting a rising number of stowaways and illegal migrants coming from Mainland China by sea since 1987, when the interactions between both sides (Taiwan and Mainland China) of the Taiwan Strait at a social level was allowed. Such phenomenon has induced significant impacts on Taiwan's society. In the context of the worldwide phenomenon of stowaways and illegal migrants, this paper aims to investigate the economic and social impacts concretely and practically. It especially focuses on investigating the current phenomenon and major impacts of stowaways and illegal migration by sea to Taiwan and aims to suggest appropriate measures for tackling this problem.
*Keywords: stowaways, illegal migrant, smuggling of migrants, human trafficking, maritime security.*

## 1 Introduction

The International Maritime Organisation (IMO) [1] defines a stowaway as "A person who is secreted on a ship, or in cargo which is subsequently loaded on the ship, without the consent of the ship-owner or the master or any other responsible person and who is detected on board the ship after it has departed from a port, or in the cargo while unloading it in the port of arrival, and is reported as a stowaway by the master to the appropriate authorities." An alternative definition for attempted stowaway as "A person who is secreted on a ship, or in cargo which is subsequently loaded on the ship, without the consent of the ship-owner or the master or any other responsible person, and who is detected on board the ship before it has departed from the port."

However, the IMO's definition of "stowaway" does not cover all aspects of illegal entry to a country by sea, because migrants may be transported by a known responsible person. For example, the practice of Chinese people migrating illegally by sea to Taiwan, which will be discussed later, do not entirely follow the given definition of "stowaway" since, instead of being secreted on a ship, migrants presence is always known to those Taiwanese or Chinese fishing vessels transporting them, which are usually bought or hired by snakeheads. In practice, stowaways entering a country without the required documents are illegal migrants. Therefore, this study will use the term "stowaways and illegal migrants" to discuss the issue of illegal entry to a country by sea.

For the past decade, many countries have encountered a serious problem with respect to the entry of stowaways and illegal migrants, caused mainly by external factors and mainly due to political, social and economic changes that occurred worldwide, especially in Asian and African countries. NEP&I [2] categorised types of stowaways as refugees, economic migrants, asylum seekers, illegal migrants and criminals. According to United Nations High Commissioner for Refugees (UNHCR) figures [3], the number of people giving "cause for concern" worldwide had risen from about 15million in 1990 to 19.8 million in 1997 and keeping at this range though in 2004 stood at 19.2million, causing a corresponding rise in the number of stowaways.

In addition, security incidents recorded at the gateway to maritime security by Class NK [4] categorised maritime security into attack, drugs, hi-jacking, sabotage, smuggling and stowaway (Table 1). These records show a total of 23 stowaway cases involving 279 stowaways, 34 resulting deaths, 4 murders and 3 cases of drowning.

Table 1: Maritime security incidents.

| | Africa | Asia | Europe | South America | North America | Near East | Oceania |
|---|---|---|---|---|---|---|---|
| Attack | | 2 | | | | | |
| Drugs | | 4 | 13 | 29 | 11 | 1 | 10 |
| Hi-Jacking | 6 | 14 | | 3 | | | |
| Sabotage | | 3 | | 1 | | | |
| Smuggling | | 5 | 3 | | 1 | 1 | |
| Stowaway | 1 | 5 | 5 | 2 | 10 | | |

While IMO [5] annual statistical data on stowaways suggested an annual decline in the number of stowaway incidents as well as in the number of persons during the 1999-2004 period (Figures 1 and 2), the IMO Maritime Safety

Committee (MSC) [6] reported a trend of increased number of incidents of trafficking or transportation of illegal migrants between 2000 and 2004 (Figures 3 and 4). These data were obtained on the basis of a reporting procedure since December 2000 on a biannual basis, to keep track of incidents related to unsafe practices associated with the trafficking or transport of illegal migrants by sea.

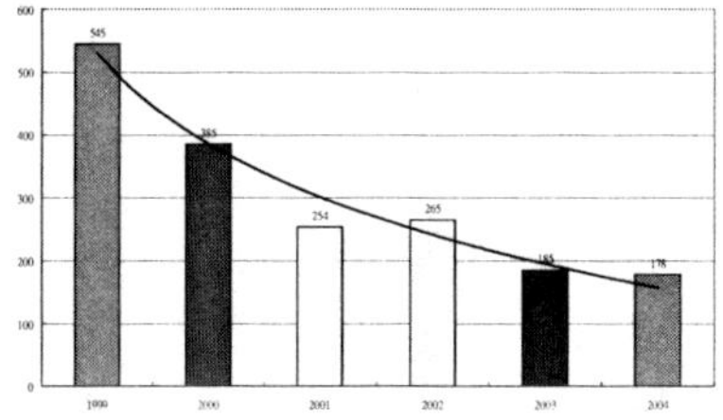

Figure 1: IMO Statistics of stowaway incidents: no. of incidents.

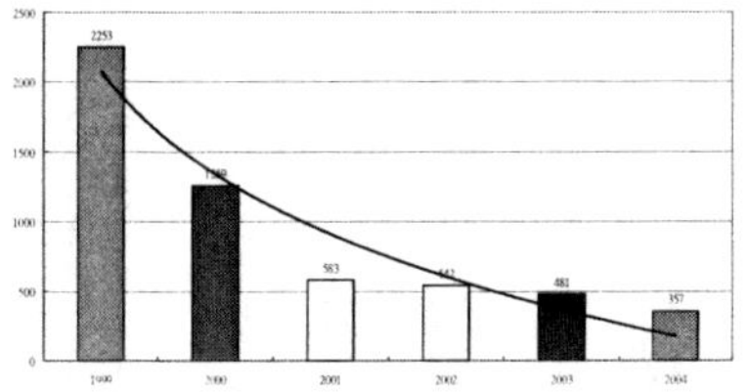

Figure 2: IMO statistics of stowaway incidents: no. of persons.

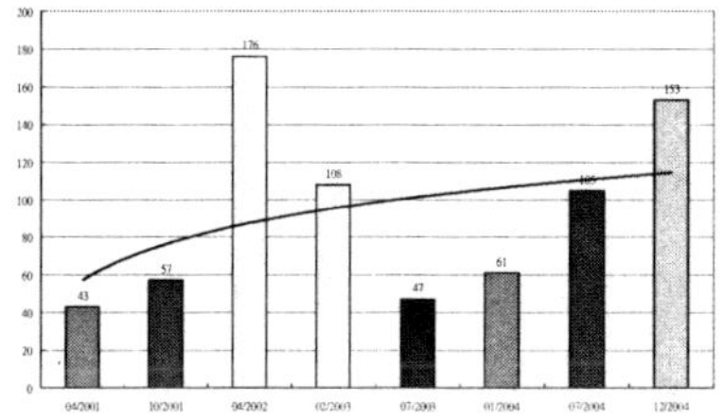

Figure 3: IMO statistics of illegal migrants by sea: no. of incidents

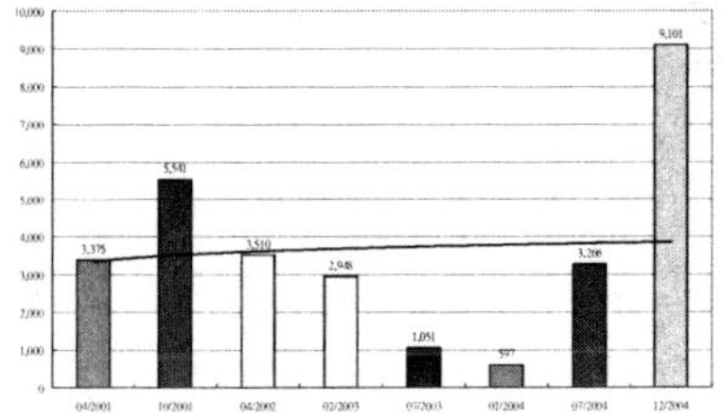

Figure 4: IMO statistics of illegal migrants by sea: no. of persons.

Stowaways and illegal migrants not only impact on the society of the receiving countries but also become a major burden, resulting in huge financial losses to both the public and private sectors. In the context of worldwide phenomenon in respect of stowaways and illegal migrant, this paper will aim to investigate its economic and social impacts concretely and practically.

Taiwan has been confronting a rising number of stowaways and illegal migrants coming from Mainland China by sea since 1987, the year in which interactions at social level between both sides of the Taiwan Strait (Taiwan and Mainland China) were allowed. Such a phenomenon has induced significant impacts on Taiwan's society. Therefore, this paper will focus on Taiwan area and investigate the current situation concerning the problem of stowaways and illegal migration and its major impacts, including economic and social impacts and will to suggest appropriate measures for tackling this problem.

## 2 Some facts from Taiwan

On 26 August 2003, the crew of two Taiwan-registered fast-moving boats, discovered to be involved in smuggling Chinese women to Taiwan. They tossed 26 women overboard in an effort to escape a Taiwanese Coast Guard's interdiction. Six women drowned and twelve were rescued, while eight others who swam ashore were arrested. The incident indeed shook Taiwan's public and attracted much attention in the media.

In Taiwan, almost all stowaways and illegal migrants come from Mainland China. Such stowaways and illegal migrants increased after the government allowed the interactions between both sides of the Strait at social level in 1987. The number of stowaways reached 5,944 in 1993. Statistical data reported by the Mainland Affairs Council, the Immigration Office National Police Agency and Taiwan's Coast Guard [7, 8, 9] show an average of 2,053 Chinese stowaways or illegal migrants were detained between 2000 and 2004, however, only 1,651 were repatriated (Table 2). The average detention time of 188 days for every illegal migrant was more than the 20 days specified by the Kimmen Agreement reached by Red Cross Chapters of both Taiwan and China in 1990 to serve as a benchmark for the repatriation of illegal Chinese migrants. In fact, it seems many stowaways and illegal migrants had successfully evaded arrest or detention and remained hidden in the community for some time. The total number of illegal migrants arrested by Taiwan's Coast Guard between 2000 and 2004 was 1,394, which only accounted for 31.50% of the number of illegal migrants reported by the Mainland Affairs Council over the same period.

Table 2: Number of illegal migrants from Mainland China.

| | Number of Illegal Migrants from the Mainland China | | Illegal Migrants arrested by Taiwan's Coast Guard | |
|---|---|---|---|---|
| Year | Number of illegal migrants | Number of repatriations | No. of Incidents | No. of Persons |
| 2000 | 1,527 | 1,230 | 74 | 74 |
| 2001 | 1,469 | 1,948 | 124 | 124 |
| 2002 | 2,032 | 1,402 | 244 | 876 |
| 2003 | 3,458 | 2,237 | 526 | 1,385 |
| 2004 | 1,783 | 1,440 | 426 | 776 |
| Total | 10,269 | 8,257 | 1,394 | 3,235 |
| Average | 2053.8 | 1651.4 | 278.8 | 647 |

Initially, stowaways or illegal migrants to Taiwan could be categorised as economic migrants looking for a better life as Taiwan was considered a prosperous country with a well-developed and growing economy. The majority of Chinese stowaways or illegal migrants were therefore male, seeking work opportunity in Taiwan to improve the living standard of their families in China. But such motivation had changed due to the economic recession from 2000 and the number of persons who stow away for such motivation has therefore decreased in recent years. Instead, because of the lure of Taiwan's lucrative sex trade, many Chinese women are attracted to migrate to Taiwan for prostitution purpose, and thus the number of illegal Chinese female migrants has increased (Chiang and Lin [10]0. In 2003, Taiwan's police and Coast Guard Administration had arrested 1,299 illegal Chinese migrants, of which 1,031 were women. As a consequence, Mainland women have emerged as the main source of Taiwan's thriving but illegal sex industry. However, it is worth noting that the profitable sex industry has also attracted the attention of organised crime groups and encouraged them to engage in the criminal activities of smuggling or trafficking of Chinese women. Although the majority of Chinese female migrants, smuggled or trafficked to Taiwan by snakeheads, are unaware of the real reason for their illegal trafficking, not all the Chinese women smuggled into Taiwan for prostitution purposes are deceived by their smugglers. Many of them were prostitutes in China and get smuggled voluntarily for the hope of earning more money in Taiwan than they could at home. In addition, the deterioration of fishermen's livelihood as a result of decreased resources derived from the fishing grounds in Taiwan's sea area, difficulty of finding alternative jobs and the attraction of substantial profits to be gained from human smuggling have contributed to their involvement in transporting illegal Chinese migrants to Taiwan as and when requested by snakeheads. This has further promoted the development of human smuggling across the Taiwan Strait.

## 3 Impacts

Stowaways and illegal migrants not only impact on the society of the receiving countries but also become a major burden, resulting in huge financial losses to both the public and private sectors. In fact, the costs in time and manpower spent on sorting out the practical and administrative consequences of a stowaway or an illegal migrant incident, as well as the delays to ships can be out of all proportion to the initial problem. Increased stowaways and illegal migrants have induced public resentment, which will continue to act as a stimulus for governments to enact more and more preventative legislation. As a result, this legislation will impose further burdens on ship owners and masters and subject them to greater public accountability. In addition, there are expenses arising from the presence of stowaways on board a vessel, which are normally the responsibility of the owners/operators of that vessel. The UK P&I Club estimates that the stowaways cost the shipping industry in excess of USD 20 million per annum [11]. Subject to the vessel's terms of entry, these costs will normally be covered by the P&I Club. For the 1995-2000 policy years, the number of reported cases reached 2,091 and costs incurred by the Club to USD 11.6 million in detention, repatriation, deportation etc. By 1999 the costs had doubled in four years. A stowaway case reported by the club that occurred in the US showed that total expenses of around USD 45,000 were incurred for each stowaway by the Charter P&I Club [12]. For example, according to the data obtained through interview from the largest Taiwanese shipping company [13] 14 stowaway cases were reported with a total of 28 stowaways during the period of 1997-2003. Exact costs incurred by the company were not known but if the amount of USD 45,000 were used for estimation, it would induce additional costs of USD 1.26 million for the company. While relevant costs for managing stowaways can be covered by the P&I Club, all costs may not be covered and could be reduced or rejected if the Club's Directors consider that the member did not take adequate steps to prevent the stowaways from boarding.

In addition to the increased costs to owners, recently there has also been an increasingly worrying trend, that is, a threat to the security of ships' crews by hostile or large groups of stowaways or illegal migrants. The likelihood of violent behaviour arising amongst the stowaways themselves or being directed against the crew should be considered. The number of stowaways on board is also a consideration, especially if that number is high in proportion to the number of crew. In all cases, the ship's crew should try to take appropriate security precautions. The concern of maritime security associated with stowaway is also contained in the International Ship and Port Facility Security (ISPS) Code, which has come into effect on 1 July 2004. Shipping companies have to comply with the new rules to improve maritime security by installing security equipment, which is estimated to cost at least US$1.3 billion a year although such expenditure is not for preventing stowaways only DFAT 2004 [14].

Illegal migrants can have negative effects on a country's community. Morganelli [15] indicated that the majority of illegal migrants in the U.S. are engaged in criminal activities. Another concern has arisen because of increase in stowaway and illegal migrant activities. As a great deal of money can be made from smuggling people, there is growing evidence that international organised criminal groups are involved in smuggling people by sea. Stowaways and illegal migration has become part of organised crime, which consequently brings great harm to the migrants themselves. For example, since the late 1980s Chinese smugglers known as "snakeheads" have smuggled tens of thousands of illegal migrants into the US. Migrants looking for an escape from their economic and sometimes political hardship at home are willing to pay an increasingly high price for a one-way ticket out, causing the trade in human cargo to flourish. For instance, Friebel and Guriev [16] pointed out that China-US smuggling fees that reached USD 35,000 in mid 1990s continued to rise up to USD 40-50 thousand since then. The fee for passage from China to Europe, or from India to the US are lower but still above USD 20,000. China-Taiwan smuggling fees are about USD 9,000. Many of the illegal migrants debt-financed these fees and because of repayment burden they have been controlled and deprived of their rights by snakeheads or intermediaries ever since they arrived at the destination. This has caused severe human rights problem.

The illegal migration in Taiwan also has had several negative impacts as those stated above. Firstly, human smuggling activity has hampered public security both in Taiwan and Mainland China because traffickers or snakeheads are usually organised criminal groups, which often commit criminal activities, such as defrauding and abduction. In particular, the increasing number of illegal Chinese female migrants forced to become prostitutes in brothels in Taiwan has decreased public security and proved a very tough problem for Taiwanese law enforcement agencies to cope with. Secondly, illegal migrants pose a threat to Taiwan's disease control system. The tragedy of the Serious Acute Respiratory

Syndrome (SARS), outbreak in China, is an example. Thirdly, the growing number of detained Chinese migrants is a drain on Taiwanese taxpayers since money has to be spent to provide them with board and accommodation, health care and other essentials. Taipei Times [17] reported that with an average detention time of 188 days for every illegal migrant and considering more than 2,500 Chinese detainees are always awaiting repatriation, the cost of repatriating these migrants amounts to more than USD 4million a year. Besides, additional costs are incurred by the government as a result of purchasing advanced electronic equipment on patrol vessels and ashore for the detection of suspicious boats.

## 4 Prevention and solutions

Smuggling by sea brings harm to migrants and since crime at sea falls under international law a highly complex legal area for the country authorities. Hence from legal aspects pertaining to prevention and handling procedures, measures for combating and related recommendations the UN, UNHCR and IMO [18] have carefully adopted provisions in the UN and IMO treaties and resolutions such as IMO's FAL and SOLAS Conventions, ISPS Code, Circulars and reports from MSC, FAL and COMSAR committees. In addition to above measures for preventing and dealing with smuggling of migrants, many other international organisations, different states, many public and private sector organisations have also been devoting themselves to dealing with problems of stowaways and illegal migrants. Concerning the Taiwan's maritime security, the Taiwanese government and all maritime stakeholders shall be taking up these matters concerning stowaways and illegal migrant by complying with all international requirements and establishing an inter-state cooperative scheme.

The problem of human trafficking in and through Taiwan has also raised international concern. In the third annual Trafficking in Persons Report [19], Taiwan was listed as a source, transit, and destination region for persons trafficked for sexual exploitation and forced labour. Victims of trafficking are brought to Taiwan from Mainland China, Thailand, Cambodia, Vietnam, Indonesia and the Philippines. Accordingly, the Taiwanese Government should make substantial efforts to prevent and eliminate these illegal activities. At present the Government has adopted some measures for dealing with such problems, including enforcement of laws that criminalise general trafficking activity and financial support to non-governmental organizations for promoting public awareness for in this area. These measures in fact comply with the requirement under international legislation relating to stowaways and human-smuggling issues.

The relevant regulations for criminalising snakeheads and dealing with illegal migrants are specified in the Act Governing Relations between the Peoples of the Taiwan Area and the Mainland Area. In order to eliminate smuggling and human trafficking activities, the government in October 2003, revised some clauses of the legislation and increased penalties against smugglers and snakeheads. Additional penalty clauses have also been amended, for example, the ship owner, operator, or master of any vessel will be severely penalised for involvement in transporting illegal migrants to Taiwan. These could lead to cancelling or revoking pertinent licenses or certificates; suspending or revoking the professional license or eligibility of the said master or seafarers; expropriation of the vessel by competent authority will if the owner uses it for transporting illegal Chinese migrants.

In addition to legislative measures, several other measures against the migrant smuggling activities by sea should be taken by the Government. Firstly, it is important for the Taiwanese government to reinforce cooperation and strengthen communication network among relevant domestic law enforcement agencies so that the movement of illegal migrants can be effectively detected and controlled and the smugglers and organised crime groups behind these activities may be traced. Secondly, as the tide of illegal Chinese migrants can possibly not be stemmed without cooperation between Taiwan and China, cooperation between law enforcement agencies across the Taiwan Strait should be promoted by establishing a two-way communication scheme so that effective combating of illegal migration activities can be achieved. However, because of the fact that political conflict has impeded bilateral cooperation for solving the illegal migrant problem, the measures of seeking cooperation with the Mainland are somewhat difficult to implement. Nevertheless, the Taiwan Government could attempt to seek international assistance to find solutions to the communication problem with the Mainland.

Thirdly, illegal migration can also be prevented through constant air and sea surveillance. Thus additional modern sea patrol vessels with capabilities to sail under difficult weather conditions are needed to meet the increasing duty demands of the Coast Guard to conduct patrols effectively. Also, advanced electronic equipment on patrol vessels and ashore is needed for detection of suspicious boats for possibility of faster and effective intervention. Adequate air patrol along the coastline and maritime area in conjunction with sea patrol should be planned to safeguard the sea border. Finally, with regards to involvement of Taiwan's fishermen in smuggling of illegal migrants, in addition to imposing serve penalties, the Taiwanese Government must make a serious effort to educate fishermen about the risks and costs of engaging in smuggling and transporting illegal migrants. Government should also provide assistance to improve their livelihood

## 5 Conclusions

The stowaway and illegal immigration problem will not be completely solved as long as worldwide political, economic and social inequalities exist. Nevertheless, efforts must still be made by countries to prevent and tackle the problem. Smuggling and trafficking illegal migrants by sea is of high international concern as it results in criminal, immigration, human rights and national security threats. Necessary measures, which have been taken worldwide to combat illegal migration by sea, include criminalisation of smugglers and snakeheads, compliance with international laws and guidelines and cooperation among States.

The different political and economic situations between Taiwan and China, the unique geographic position featuring an extensive and long coastline have contributed to the phenomenon of illegal Chinese migrants by sea into Taiwan. In particular, the lure of the profitable sex trade in Taiwan has contributed to more and more illegal migration incidents, which are usually organised and operated by smugglers and snakeheads. As a consequence, the influx of illegal Chinese migrants has induced public resentment because it has had negative effects on Taiwan's society. For example, it has led to an increase in criminal offences and loss of work opportunities for Taiwanese citizens. Human smuggling has also diminished public security in Taiwan as well as in Mainland China because traffickers or snakeheads usually have connection with organised criminal groups.

The illegal migration across Taiwan Strait is expected to continue unless China takes steps to improve its political situation, economic stability and equality among its citizens. Nevertheless, measures should still be taken by the Taiwanese Government in order to tackle the problem of illegal migration and human smuggling to secure stability of Taiwan's society. Defining migrant smuggling as a felony is expected to contribute substantially to such measures. More efforts should be made to promote cooperation and exchange information between law enforcement agencies across the Taiwan Strait by establishing a communication link. It is necessary to reinforce cooperation and strengthen communication networks among relevant domestic law enforcement agencies so as to detect and effectively control the movement of illegal migrants and for halting organised crime groups behind them. To safeguard the sea border, the Coast Guard's continuous sea patrolling, supplemented by air patrolling, should be conducted. Additionally, the Taiwanese Government should be deeply concerned about fishermen's livelihood. It should provide them moral advices to prevent them from being the middlemen for snakeheads in transportation of illegal migrants to Taiwan.

## References

[1] IMO, Convention on Facilitation of International Maritime Traffic, FAL 28/10 Annex 1, International Maritime Organisation, London, 2000.

[2] NEP&I, Stowaways, Signals Special Edition, No.6, North of England P&I Association, Newcastle, England, 2001.

[3] UNHCR, Global Refuge Trends, http://www.unhcr.ch/cgi-bin/texis/vtx/statistics.

[4] Security Incident, Maritime Security Information, NIPPON KAIJI KYOKAI Safety Management Systems Department, http://sms.classnk.or.jp/ispshp/html/English/incident_e.htm.

[5] IMO, FAL.2 Quarterly Reports and Annual Statistics on Stowaways Incidents (FAL.2/Circ.58-88, 26/4/2001-25/5/2005).

[6] IMO, MSC.3 Biannual Reports on Illegal Migrants – unsafe practices associated with the trafficking or transport of migrants by sea (MSC.3/Circ.1-8, 30/4/2001-16/3/2005).

[7] MAC, Statistics of illegal migrants and repatriations Mainland Affair Council, http://www.mac.gov.tw/big5/statistic/ass_lp/d5/9404.pdf.

[8] Immigration Office, National Police Agency, http://www.npa.gov.tw /stats.php.

[9] Coast Guard Administration, http://www.cga.gov.tw/Statistics/Year /list07 .xls.

[10] Chiang, S.K. and Lin, B.C., An investigation of illegal migration across the Taiwan Strait, *Proc. of the Central Police University Conference*, Central Police University, Touyen, Taiwan, 2003 (in Chinese).

[11] UK P&I Club, *Stowaways Cost More than $20 Million a Year*, http://www.ukpandi.com/ukpandi/infopool.nsf/HTML/87B808F09D8E9C 2480256DA9003EEDC4?Open&Highlight=2,stowaway.

[12] Charter P&I Club, Charters Club Claims Examples Web Site, http://www.else.co.uk/charterers/Claims%20Examples/Claims_Index.htm

[13] Manager, Department of Risk Management, Personal communication, 15 June 2005, Evergreen Marine Corporation, Taiwan.

[14] DFAT, *Combating Terrorism in the Transport Sector, Economic Costs and Benefits*, Economic Analytical Unit, Department of Foreign Affairs and Trade Australian Government, Canberra, p.23, 2004.

[15] Morganelli, J. M., *The Subcommittee on Immigration, Border, Security and Claims*, Testimony of Northampton County, Pennsylvania, Wednesday, October, 2003, http://usinfo.state.gov/regional/ea/chinaaliens/ morganelli.htm,

[16] Friebel G., Guriev, S.: *Smuggling Humans: A theory of Debt-Financed Migration*, Institute for the Study of Labour, IZA DP No.1025, 2004.

[17] Taipei Times, *Risking death for a better life*, 29 August 2003, Taipei (in Chinese).

[18] IMO, Information resources on stowaways/migrants/treatment of persons rescued at sea, *IMO Library Services*, IS No.33, IMO, 2005.

[19] The Associated Press State & Local Wire, *Taiwan Praised for Trafficking Efforts*, 14 June 2003, http://www.protectionproject.org/daily_news /2003/ne614.htm.

# Definitions of human factor analysis for the maritime safety management process

Z. Er & M. Celik
*Department of Marine Transportation and Management, Maritime Faculty of Istanbul Technical University, Turkey*

## Abstract

There has been a growing recognition that human errors, rather than equipment problems, have been responsible for approximately 62% of pollution and marine accidents over the past 15 years. Human factors in the following categories are resulting in 15% rating error, 30% deck officer error, 2% engine officer error, 8% pilot error and 7% shore-based personnel error. In the maritime domain the root causes of accidents and the casualties can be sub-classified as mechanical failure or in general terms reliability failure (non-human) and the human error that has direct effect on the accident occurrence. At this stage human error can be classified in three major categories with the same approximation of the STCW Code 1995 amendments. The first category is operational based human errors, the second category is the management based human errors and the third category is the combination of the first and second category that might cause a considerable accident or disaster by triggering chain events. In this respect the terminology of an incident might be described as a triggering event, such as a human error or a mechanical failure that creates an unsafe condition and might result in an accident. Hence the root cause, the immediate cause, the incident, accident, consequence and its impact can be defined as the casual chain. Accidents that occur in complex systems are determined by internal and external factors and the term triggering event has a great significance, rather than causal event, to describe the final stage of the accident chain. The aim of this paper is to categorize a quick and easy method for the collection of knowledge about human error in the maritime safety management process and the description of the human factor using accident reports as empirical material.
*Keywords: human factor, safety management, shipping, IMO requirements, human error, taxonomy in ergonomics.*

# 1 Introduction

The design and operation of ships has evolved and continues to develop, driven by structural change in the industry, new technologies, new regulations and changes in manning. When considering maritime safety, it is necessary to address both the human factor and the technical solutions in the broadest sense, not just the immediate causes of actual or potential failures. Whilst this combined approach is taken in some incident analysis, whether after the event or as part of a proactive safety assessment, there is still a tendency to treat the human and the technical elements independently of each other. An integrated approach is required if full understanding is to be achieved. A simplistic technical approach tends to recommend local reactive solutions, such as the addition of more alarms, which may assist but will add complexity so the underlying cause may not be resolved. A purely human factor approach tends to promote administrative solutions, which may not be fully effective on their own. Of course, there are many aspects of ship design that have a direct impact on human performance, such as ship motions, accessibility, lighting and noise levels and basic habitability. Classification Rules provide some cover for these aspects but the maritime industry needs to grasp human factor issues at a higher, more integrated level to make a real difference to safety. There are many lessons to be learned from the experience of other sectors, to prevent the maritime industry learning the same lessons the hard way.

# 2 Definitions of basic terms

Human Factor is the body of scientific knowledge about people and how they interact with their environment, especially when working. Human Factors, or the Human Factor, are terms which are often misinterpreted and are used as covers for the Human Element or even Human Error. A simple way to view human factors is to consider three main aspects: the person, the job (task, environment and equipment), and the organization and management, and how they together with the environment in which the organization and person are operating and the impact on the behaviour of people.

The term "the human element", or "the human factor" is often heard in conversations of persons having little or no true knowledge of "human factors" or "human factors engineering". It is often used by persons to express their personal bias or prejudice concerning the behaviour of certain people related to a specific event being examined. When something goes wrong, the term "the human element" is typically used. In this sense, it is an attempt to blindly judge or blame people as being "idiots", or worse. As such, it is a term that should not be used by human factors professionals.

Applying human factors to the design and operation of a ship or its systems means taking into account human capabilities, skills, limitations and needs. Human Factors should not be confused with the term Human Resources which is a closely related activity that addresses the supply of suitably qualified and experienced staff. When considering the operation or design of any ship and its systems both of these domains should be considered as Human Resources for the selection and preparation of staff able to do the required work and Human Factors to account for the use of people as a component of the system. Both domains contain a number of sub-domains:

Human Factors (Fitting the job to the person):

- Human Factors Engineering – The comprehensive integration of human characteristics into the definition, design development, and evaluation of a system to optimize Human-Machine performance under specified conditions.
- Health Hazards - The identification, assessment and the removal or reduction of short or long-term hazards to health occurring as a result of normal operation of a system.
- System Safety - The human contribution to risk when the system is functioning in a normal or abnormal manner.

Human Resources (Fitting the person to the job):

- Manpower - the number of personnel required, and potentially available, to operate, maintain, sustain and provide training for a system.
- Personnel - The cognitive (trainability and mental aptitude) and physical (fitness levels, physical size, gender) capabilities required to be able to train for, operate, maintain and sustain a system and provide optimum quality and quantity of the crews to man the ship.
- Training - The instruction or the education, and on-the-job or part-task or full-mission training required to provide personnel with their essential job skills, knowledge, values and attitudes.

On the other hand human engineering has been defined (similar to the term "human factors engineering") as a discipline concerned with designing man-made systems so that people can use them effectively and safely, and the creation of environments suitable for human living and work [1].

## 2.1 Human factors viewed as human characteristics

The phrase "human factors" is often used to mean "human characteristics". Various human factors in this sense generally fall into one of three groups of human characteristics: (1). physical characteristics, (2). physiological characteristics, and (3). psychological or behavioural characteristics. These groups of human factors are not necessarily mutually exclusive. Here human factors are defined the nature of our "humanness", that is, the characteristics of "being human".

Physical human factors include physical attributes of the human body, such as height, weight, arm reach, and centre of gravity. Physiological human factors include such things as muscle strength and endurance in different body positions, visual acuity, tolerance to extremes of temperature, and frequency range of human hearing. Psychological or behavioural human factors include things such as mental reaction time to various stimuli, various acquired meanings associated with certain colours (red often means "danger"), the capabilities and limitations of short term memory, and “expectancy” as an element of perception. In addition, there are cultural norms that must also be taken into account. For example, in the standard international cultural environments, electrical switches go “up” to turn on and “down” to turn off; hot water valves are on the left of the faucet outlet and cold water valves are on the right; electrical dials turn clockwise to increase flow, but a fluid valve turned clockwise will decrease flow.

As a competent person, the human factors specialist or engineer does not attempt to judge human factors as right or wrong, correct or incorrect. Rather, the human factors specialist merely attempts to understand and define these factors, or human characteristics, so that their strengths and weaknesses, and their capabilities and limitations might be taken into account when designing systems where persons are to be an essential component.

### 2.2 Human factors engineering

Human factors engineering is the discipline dedicated to optimizing the relationship between technology (system hardware and software) and the human operator of various systems. Any man-machine system can and should be the target of human factors engineering [2]. Human factors engineer designs things to provide the “best match” between system user capabilities and limitations and the relevant system hardware components that impose physical, physiological, and/or psychological demands on such users.

### 2.3 Ergonomics

The terms ergonomics and human factors are often used synonymously. Both describe the interaction between the operator and task demands, and both are concerned with trying to reduce unnecessary stress and resulting injury to persons engaged in a certain activity or operating certain equipment. The term ergonomics originated as a European term while the term human factors is more often used in the United States [3].

## 3 Human error

Errors occur both as random events and in situations where the design of a system, a procedure, or of the intended interaction between a human and a system is faulty in that such interaction makes human actions prone to error. Thus it is not sufficient just to make a generalized statement about human error, such as to error is human, without knowing the mechanisms which are at work and which may provide some explanation concerning errors that are committed. Knowing this information will help in the understanding of errors and in supporting the detection, diagnosis and correction of errors.

Sanders and McCormick [4] defined human error as an inappropriate or undesirable human decision or behaviour that reduces or has the potential for reducing effectiveness, safety, or system performance. Two things should be noted about this definition. First, an error is defined in terms of its undesirable effect or potential effect on human performance and systems operations. Second, an action does not have to result in degraded system performance or an undesirable effect on people to be considered an error. As a result the decision or action has the potential for adversely affecting the system operations or human performance for it to be considered an error.

In the analysis of human error in industrial plants, 80 to 85% of the errors that occur are attributable not to human characteristics, but to error-likely conditions [5]. In these situations, people are "set up" for error by the system design. These error-inducing situations include deficient procedures, poor communication, inadequate training, misleading information, and poor equipment design. Many of these errors are entirely preventable. Identifying error likely situations is a first step toward minimizing or eliminating errors.

In addressing human error reduction, Wiener [6] states that the first step in error reduction is to identify the errors. Identifying human errors is not always a straightforward task. Errors can be obvious but are more often subtle. There are six methods of identifying potential errors that have been used successfully in other industries. They include brainstorming using representatives of the area of interest; critical incident techniques; structured walkthroughs or reviews of standards, procedures, or systems; surveys and questionnaires; observation; and analysis of confidential reporting systems [6]. Once potential errors are identified, a risk assessment should be done to weigh the potential errors according to their severity. The next steps in effective error management are to identify the current defences, evaluate the effectiveness of the current defences, and identify additional defences needed. Finally, an effective mechanism should be established for reporting potential errors and addressing them once they are identified.

### 3.1 Human error viewed as human nature

Humans are bound by specific innate characteristics, which are not subject to significant change, but dictate specific behaviour under particular circumstances. Such behaviour must be considered as part of human nature and not mislabelled as human error. Human error may result from a combination of human nature, random error, design induced human error, and true human error.

### 3.2 Human error viewed as random error

True human error must be distinguished from random error. Random errors committed by system operators are non-predictable by both system designers and operators. An example of a random error would be the reflex action that causes a wrong control to be activated as a result of an unexpected mosquito bite. Random errors can also involve improbable but normal extremes of human variation. For example, even persons who are well trained and have repeatedly used a well-designed system will occasionally make inadvertent errors related to rare and unintended (and uncontrollable) variations in required hand-eye coordination.

### 3.3 Human error viewed as design induced human error

An axiom of human factors engineering states that, "How a system is designed will dictate how it can and will be used". True human error must be distinguished from design induced human error where some (engineering or administrative) aspect of the system design (such as a lack of safety features, the presence of reasonably anticipated operator distraction or overload, or the presence of excessive or contradictory system demands) predisposes such error; that is, where the system operator is set up to make the error by some design aspect of the system. Such errors, if they can rightfully be called errors at all, are predictable and therefore preventable through re-design.

### 3.4 True human error

True human error is most properly defined as an action that would not have been committed (or an action that would not have been omitted) by ordinary, reasonably prudent persons under the same or similar circumstances, while taking common human factor limitations into account, and after eliminating other forms of human error from consideration.

True human error can only be said to occur when the system in which it takes place has been well engineered (according to the basic principles and reasonable application of safety engineering and human factors engineering) and the demands imposed on adequately trained system operators are realistic in relation to human factor (human nature) capabilities and limitations of such persons. Only under such circumstances is the system operator truly free to choose his or her actions.

One method that can be useful to distinguish between true human error and other forms of alleged human error is to ask this question: If a thousand reasonably prudent persons were placed in the same or similar circumstances, would a significant number make the same or similar error? If so, one's search for causation must go beyond the apparent identification of simple human error.

### 3.5 Primary human error and incidental human error

Primary human error can be thought of as error made by those who have a primary assigned or special responsibility and the special expertise to focus on the subject matter of the error. An incidental human error, in contrast, is error made by those who have a secondary or oversight responsibility or lack the special expertise to focus on the same issue.

### 3.6 Slips, lapses and mistakes

The most common types of error in everyday life are slips and lapses. They are usually treated together, as they are psychologically related and occur in the same mental modes and for similar reasons. They occur mainly in skilled behaviour, and examples include a misplaced action, the wrong thing moved or simply forgetting an intended action [7].

The difference between slips and lapses is that slips relate to observable actions, associated with attention or perceptual failures, whereas lapses are more internal and generally involve failure of memory [8]. Slips have nothing to do with the validity of the goals set up for the particular action, they are simply errors committed when trying to reach that goal, right or wrong. But when the goal is in itself inappropriately chosen, the error is classified as a mistake. Mistakes occur at higher mental levels (i.e. errors of thought), and examples include misjudging a situation or making poor decisions [7]. Reason [9] puts it this way: mistakes are linked to the planning stage, lapses to storage stage and slips to the execution stage.

## 4 IMO requirements relating to human factor analysis

In 1997, the IMO Assembly adopted a Resolution that indicated a step change in its approach to maritime safety by moving from a regulatory regime to that of a safety culture with a strong emphasis on the human element. Among its goals the requirements are indicating to promote and communicate, through human element principles, a maritime safety culture and heightened marine environment awareness and to provide a framework to encourage the development of non-regulatory solutions and their assessment, based upon human element principles. Thus today, all IMO Committees are instructed to consider the human element when developing new or amending existing performance standards.

Much of this change has been brought about by the Joint MSC/MEPC Working Group on the Human Element. The Group has also been directly involved in the development of the ISM Code, the guidelines on fatigue, and of the Human Element Analysing Process (HEAP). HEAP is a practical and non-scientific checklist to assist regulators in ensuring that all the human element aspects related to the ship and its equipment, and the master and his crew, have been taken into consideration when introducing or amending IMO instruments.

Two recent updates to SOLAS clearly demonstrate IMO's change in direction from a regulatory regime to that of a safety culture with a strong emphasis on the human element. Chapter II-2 (Construction - Fire protection, fire detection and fire extinction); part E deals exclusively with human element matters such as training, drills and maintenance issues, and part F sets out a methodology for approving alternative designs and arrangements. Chapter V-15 features the decisions that affect bridge design, the design and arrangement of navigational systems and equipment on the bridge and bridge procedures. Bridge Resource Management, information processing and decision-making, workload, human error, fatigue and distraction, together with clarity of controls, alarms, displays and status indication are all addressed. Indeed in the light of the development of Chapter V-15, there is a feeling that the scope of the regulations should be widened, to encompass everything that could influence the watchkeeper's function on the bridge.

The requirements of the relevant IMO performance standards for the Electronic Chart Display and Information System (ECDIS), radar, plotting aids, Automatic Identification System (AIS), Integrated Bridge System (IBS) and

Integrated Navigation System (INS) have caused serious human-system interface problems, in terms of the integration and presentation of navigation related information on the bridge. These problems are, however, being addressed by the International Electro-technical Commission (IEC) on behalf of the IMO.

## 5 Conclusions

The importance of knowledge should not be underestimated, but it must be applied to the real world at some point, and it would be beneficial to give the authorities and mariners some guidelines on how this knowledge can be used, instead of providing theoretical models.

According to the UK P&I Club, human error costs the maritime industry \$541m a year [10]. From their own analysis of 6091 major claims (over \$100,000) spanning a period of 15 years, the Club has established that these claims have cost their members \$2.6bn, 62% of which is attributable to human error. In its loss prevention work, the Club is placing a much greater emphasis on pinpointing root causes in respect of personal injury and other incidents. It recognises that investigators often identify the persons most responsible for incidents (active failures) without uncovering the underlying factors (latent failures).

While the human factor issues are discussed among the stakeholders of the maritime industry, several definitions are used to define the aspects of human interacting with a ship and her equipment. In this respect, it might be useful to analyze the true meaning of definitions and this study proposes the literature survey for the true meaning of definitions that can easily be applied by ship management companies while establishing their ship performance analysis based on human factors engineering. On the other hand, this paper proposes a taxonomy for Administrations and ship management companies to sort their obtained data and evaluate the right classification of errors to take relevant pro-active measures in order to prevent re-occurrences of nonconformities and deficiencies.

## References


[1] Huchingson, R. D., *New Horizons for Human Factors in Design*, McGraw-Hill, 1981.

[2] Kantowitz, B. H., *Human Factors: Understanding People-System Relationships*, John Wiley & Sons, 1983.

[3] Dekker, S., *Investigating Human Error.* Linköping: Swedish Centre for Human Factors in Aviation, 2002.

[4] Sanders, M. S., McCormick, E. J., *Human factors in engineering and design,* McGraw-Hill 1987.

[5] Steinbrink, J., *Human error plagues maintenance activities*, Industrial Maintenance & Plant Operation, March 1997. www.impomag.com.

[6] Wiener, E. L., Human factors in aviation. San Diego, CA: Academic Press, Inc, 1988.

[7] Norman, D., *The Design of Everyday Things.* New York, USA: Doubleday 1988.
[8] Christensen, P., *Human Performance and Limitations.* NAR & TFHS 2002.
[9] Reason, J., *Human Error*. Cambridge, England: Cambridge University Press, 1990.
[10] UK P&I Club, *Just waiting to happen, The work of the UK P&I Club.*
[11] The International Maritime Human Element Bulletin, Issue No.1, p.3 October 2003.

# Protecting seafarer's rights – the need to review the implementation of the ISPS code

A. Balbaa
*Nautical Department, College of Maritime Transport and Technology, Arab Academy for Science, Technology and Maritime Transport, Alexandria, Egypt*

## Abstract

The International Ship and Port facility Security Code (ISPS) has many measures for maintaining the security of a ship and port. In addition, a required port security plan facilitates the access of visitors, land-based labourers and workers, and seafarers' welfare to ships in ports. Certainly the code will enhance maritime security on board and in ports, but extra work has fallen on an already overburdened crew and master. Although the seafarers' support has increased maritime security, they are most likely considered to be victims of terrorist attacks, pirates and armed robbers. Piracy procedures are incorporated into the ship security plan; also stowaways should be prevented through the ship's own security system. Therefore, extra work will be necessary to maintain the required level of security and to detect the threat. On the other hand, the security measures implemented in some countries is creating problems for seafarers wanting to go ashore, and apply for individual visas. In addition, seafarers should maintain ship safety and protect the marine environment. Certainly the code will enhance maritime security and keep the sea and seafarers secure, but there is a need for proportionate measures that protect seafarers' fundamental rights and freedom.
*Keywords: seafarers' rights, shore leave, ISPS code, piracy, extra workload, seafarers' identity document.*

## 1 Introduction

Ship-borne trade is an indispensable pillar of the global economy. The global economy relies on a productive and efficient maritime sector. Seafarers play a vital role in maintaining stability and promoting sustainable growth in the maritime sector [4]. The rights and welfare of seafarers constituting the human element of the shipping industry must be respected and given priority by all the parties involved (flag states and port states).

The ISPS code is designed to improve security and better protect people and cargo, as well as ports and international shipping, against terrorism through its identity and transparency. The code deadline passed without any difficulties. There are many positive aspects of the code, but its implementation has revealed some negative points, especially for the seafarers on board the ship as well as in some countries. Difficulties that face the seafarers are the refusal of shore leave, extra loads, piracy procedures and stowaway prevention. Certainly it is very important to look forward to keeping the seafarers' rights to encourage them to join such a field at a time when the industry is already short of quality officers worldwide.

## 2 Historical background

The hijacking of the Italian cruise liner Achille Lauro, in October 1985, marked one of the first actual terrorist acts recorded in modern maritime history. Following this incident, the International Maritime Organisation adopted resolution A.584 (14) on measures to prevent unlawful acts that threaten the safety of ships and security of their passengers and crews. The International Maritime Organisation did not stop working towards the development and, adoption of conventions and security regulations, IMO adopted, in March 1988, the Convention for Suppression of Unlawful Acts against the Safety of Maritime Navigation [1]. The Organisation had adopted some other security instruments such as: MSC\Circs.622 and 623, as revised, on the guidelines for administrations and industry on combating acts of piracy and armed robbery against ships; MSC\Circ.754 on passenger ferry security, providing recommendations on security measures for passenger ferries on international voyages shorter than 24 hours, and ports; Assembly resolution A.871 (21) on guidelines on the allocation of responsibilities to seek the successful resolution of stowaways cases;

Since the tragic events of September, 11, 2001 in the United States, Assembly resolution A.924 (22) (November 2001) called for a review of the existing international legal and technical measures to prevent and suppress terrorist acts against ships at sea and in port, and to improve security on board and ashore, aiming to reduce risks to passengers, crews, and personnel on board ships and in port areas.

IMO responded swiftly and firmly by developing new requirements under the International Convention for the Safety of Life at Sea (SOLAS), 1974, as amended, namely the new chapter XI-2 on the special measures to enhance maritime security and the International Ship and Port Facility (ISPS) Code which was adopted by the SOLAS conference in December 2002. The new provisions entered into force on 1 July 2004, only 18 months after their adoption.

# 3 ISPS code and parties' responsibilities

The purpose of the ISPS code is to improve a standardised framework for evaluating risks, enabling governments to offset changes in the threat levels with changes in vulnerability for ships and port facilities. Through a number of minimum security requirements for ships and port facilities, the ISPS code will enhance security.

## 3.1 Contracting governments' responsibilities

Under SOLAS chapter XI and part A of the Code, Contracting Governments can establish Designated Authorities within Government to undertake their security responsibilities under the Code.

The setting of the security level is the responsibility of Contracting Governments and should apply to their ships and port facilities.
The code defines three levels for international use:

- Security level 1, normal
- Security level 2, lasting for a period of time when there is a heightened risk of a security incident; and
- Security level 3, lasting for the period of time when there is a probable or imminent risk of a security incident.

As mentioned in SOLAS chapter XI-2 and the ISPS Code, certain information should be provided to IMO, effective communication between company, ship security officers and the port facility security officers responsible for the Port Facility their ships serve should be made available.

## 3.2 The company and the ship responsibilities

The Company Security Officer should be appointed by any shipping company operating ships to which the Code applies. IMO recommends that ship operators appoint an officer (who could be the master) to be responsible for the security of the individual vessel (the ship security officer).

The responsibilities of the ship security officer are:

- Advising the master on the threat assessment for the voyage and agreeing the ship's response.
- Regular security inspections of the ship.
- Implementing and maintaining the ship's security plan
- Proposing modifications.
- Encouraging security awareness and vigilance on board the ship.
- Liaising with port security officers during the ship's visit and with the ship's operator.
- Reporting, as appropriate, all occurrences and suspected occurrences of unlawful acts.
- Co-ordinating the implementation of the ship security plan with the appropriate port security [2].

The responsibilities of the Company Security Officer are ensuring that a Ship Security Assessment (SSA) is undertaken and that a Ship Security Plan (SSP) is prepared to which the code applies. The Company and Ship Security Officer are required to monitor the continuing effectiveness of the plan, including undertaking independent internal audits.

### 3.2.1 Master as Ship Security Officer

The master will bear the majority of administration and communication burdens. The SSO (if not the master) will still have to clear any decisions taken with CSOs and PFSOs on any security related issues with the master, and although he has overriding authority, this could lead to delay, confusion and duplication of efforts at critical times.

### 3.3 The port facility

Contracting Governments should undertake a Port Facility Security Assessment (PFSA) of their Port Facilities. The responsibilities of the Port Facility Security Officers are defined in the ISPS Code, as are the requirements for training they require and the drills they will be responsible for undertaking. The Port Facility Security Officer is responsible for the preparation of the Port Facility Security Plan (PFSP).

## 4 Current realities

July first came and went without significant problems: a few detained ships only. The United States Coast Guard reported that only 19 vessels out of 1378 inspected were denied entry during the first week, and only 30 were detained in port. The cost to the world shipping industry of the ISPS code so far has been $2.6 billion and there will be about $1.5 billion to pay each year. On the plus side, the efficiency gains and reduction in theft and fraud will far outweigh the costs.

On 28 July 2004, IMO confirmed that 89.5% of more than 9000 declared port facilities had had their port security plans approved and that more than 90% of ships had been issued with IMO approved security certificates [3]. Also information suggests that almost 94% of the contracting governments to the SOLAS convention have approved security plans for 97% of the declared port facilities, which in total number in excess of 9600 worldwide.

## 5 ISPS code and seafarers' rights

It is known that seafarers work in a truly global industry, often falling between the gaps in national and international laws. The ISPS code came into being to enhance the maritime security and protect the passengers and crew on board. To take such measures, it was required from seafarers to do some tasks to keep the standards, but these tasks have added extra loads onto the seafarers in addition to the other tasks they perform: maintaining safety and protecting the marine environment. The improper implementation of the ISPS code in some countries created some difficulties to the seafarers such as shore leave, identity cards, piracy and stowaways. These difficulties are discussed in the following sections.

## 5.1 Shore leave, visa and seafarers

The need to afford special protection to seafarers is a major task. The seafarer's welfare is the most important issue, and shore leave is the most important element to keep seafarers welfare in the best condition. Nowadays, in some ports the seafarers face refusal to go on shore leave even for medical care; they might feel somehow rejected or their services not sufficiently recognized. As known, the maritime industry is short of quality officers worldwide and is also short of numbers in both officers and ratings as shown in Table 1. On the other hand, as known to all of us, a ship's stay in port has became very short and the seafarers' free time has become very limited, so, it will be worthy if the port authorities treat seafarers as partners in the fight against terrorism, and facilitate their access to ports and shore facilities. This treatment by the port authorities will provide every opportunity to relax and recover before seafarers again have to take their ships out to sea in pursuit of their peaceful objectives in the service of world trade.

Table 1: The estimation of supply and demand of world seafarers. (Source: BIMCO\ISF 2000.)

| District | Year 2005 | | | | Year 2010 | | | |
|---|---|---|---|---|---|---|---|---|
| | Senior officers | | Ratings | | Senior officers | | Ratings | |
| | Demand | | Supply | | Demand | | Supply | |
| OECD | 162000 | 231000 | 129000 | 169000 | 166000 | 233000 | 113000 | 150000 |
| East Europe | 36000 | 40000 | 62000 | 122000 | 37000 | 40000 | 62000 | 138000 |
| Africa\ Latin America | 131000 | 157000 | 39000 | 95000 | 134000 | 156000 | 44000 | 102000 |
| Far East | 89000 | 148000 | 134000 | 332000 | 91000 | 147000 | 140000 | 342000 |
| Indian Sub-continent | 15000 | 26000 | 35000 | 115000 | 15000 | 26000 | 39000 | 127000 |
| Total | 432000 | 602000 | 399000 | 832000 | 443000 | 603000 | 397000 | 858000 |

In one recent example the chief officer of a tanker was deported from the USA and band for ten years for going down the gangplank to take a draft reading. In another, a Russian officer, whose visa was in order but had not been checked by port officials, spent a night in jail before being deported for going ashore to make a call from a public phone only meters from his ship [8]. In some countries, they ask for individual visas; seafarers have to pay more costs to apply for visas and other related costs, although many seafarers do not know whether they will visit such countries asking for that kind of visa during their period of service on board.

## 5.2 Identity cards and seafarers

Seafarers need access to port facilities for welfare purposes, in order to enable them to carry out their international moves; these facilities could be shore leave, joining or transferring to a ship and repatriation. The Seafarer's Identity Document Convention, 1958 (No.108) [5] requires a government to issue a seafarer's identity document to each of its nationals who is a seafarer This entitles the seafarer to go on land for shore leave in another state which has ratified the convention, and may also enable the seafarer to transit without a visa to join his ship or for repatriation purposes. The function of the identity card is very important and could solve many problems met by the 1.2 million seafarers who will then be given the freedom of movement necessary for their well-being and for their professional activities if it is implemented in the right manner. The ILO Convention No. 185 Seafarers' Identity Document Convention (Revised), 2003 came into force on 09.02.2005 [6]. It contains many facilities for seafarers including the upholding the principle that seafarers should not be required to hold a visa for the purposes of shore leave. On the other hand there are some statements in some articles that should be more accurate, defined and specified to avoid personal misunderstandings (Clear ground "1-Article 6, national security).

## 5.3 Piracy, stowaways and seafarers

Seafarers and the maritime industry have been threatened by a growing piracy problem in many parts of the world; the total number of piracy and armed robberies against ships so far reported to IMO is 3.674, an increase of 21 since 30 September 2004 [7]. The piracy procedures are incorporated into the ship security plan where it is required for the ship's crew to fight such piracy through the piracy procedures.

The ISPS code contains procedures to prevent stowaways reaching ships via ports, which means that a ship's own security system will have to try and prevent stowaways from boarding the vessel. Fighting piracy and preventing stowaways are tasks of a ship's crew; the owners seem to cover themselves and apply the international and national measures by issuing copious instructions for crew on extra watches, extra lookouts, extra pre-planning and post-incident response, but no word about extra crew to carry out all this extra work is added to seafarers, beside the other main tasks relating to safety and marine pollution prevention. At the same time the code will do little to address the piracy problem because piracy is directed against ships and not sovereign states. We must ensure that we do not increase the workload of already overburdened seafarers and that their fundamental rights, freedoms and basic dignity are protected.

## 5.4 Psychological aspects and seafarers

Nowadays, it is clear that the shipping industry (ports, coastal states, nations...etc.) treat seafarers as potential terrorists, the placing of armed guards at the foot of the gangway is rightly offensive to seafarers. A Russian officer, whose visa was in order but had not been checked by port officials, spent a night in jail before being deported for going ashore to make a call from a public telephone only meters from his ship; OECD workshop [9].

### 5.5 Ship owners and seafarers

Some ship-owning companies have even been required to pay for armed guards to prevent foreign seafarers from leaving their ships. In some countries the owners have to apply for a crew list visa and pay its cost; many ship operators try to reduce crew levels to a minimum and are reluctant to provide extra security staff or install new technology [10].

## 6 IMO and seafarers

IMO has asked for a proper balance between enhancing security and protecting human rights. On June 7, 2004, IMO adopted an international circular (MSC/ Circular 1112) that provides guidance to countries on shore leave and access to ships under the ISPS code. IMO has asked the International Christian Maritime organisation, governments and other non-governmental organisations to report to IMO any instances where the implementation of the ISPS code has adversely affected seafarers. The positive side of the ISPS code is that it will do for security what the ISM Code did for safety and ship management, which is to put the whole subject under one standard set of rules and procedures.

### 6.1 Security measures raising fatigue concerns

Seafaring is an isolating job. Separation from family and relatives for long periods of time, the working and social environment are unnatural and no training can prepare crew for the vagaries of life at sea, dislocation and increased isolation, since unreasonable implementation of the ISPS code will significantly impact upon the seafarer's health and well being and the safe operation of the ship. It is widely accepted that subjective perceptions, performance and psychological change are core symptoms of stress and this is a major contributor to fatigue [11].

## 7 Conclusions

Differences in interpretation of the Code in some countries:

1. The need for consistent interpretation of the ISPS Code is a major demand.
2. Denying shore leave to ship staff worsens their fatigue and loneliness.
3. A reasonable number of crew on board is a major concern to avoid extra loads.
4. The correct implementation of the Code should be observed and controlled by IMO, avoiding the restrictions of the national security rules.

5. Problems concerning piracy and stowaways should be given more international importance, especially with the national states.
6. The ISPS code will do for security what the ISM Code did for safety and ship management.
7. Intervention papers from seafarers and ship-owners are required at maritime safety committees.
8. Convention 185 should be fully corrected and implemented with the observation and control from IMO and ILO.

## References


[1] Hesse, H., Charalambous, N., New security measures for the international shipping community. WMU Journal, vol.3, No.2, p 124, 2004.

[2] Frequently Asked Questions – part 3, International Ship and Port Facility Security (ISPS) Code, Germanischer Lloyd Version 02\2003.

[3] JTIC Briefing: maritime security clampdown forces compliance, Jane's. http://www.janes.com\secuirty\internationalsecurity\news\jtic040811

[4] Programme of Action to promote the Welfare and protect the Rights and Interests of Filipino Seafarer in the 21st Century, www.philsolnl \A02h\PSAP-Conf2002-inn02htm

[5] C108 Seafarers' Identity Documents Convention, 1958, www.ilo.org\ ilolex\cgi-lex\convde.p1?C108

[6] C185 Seafarers' Identity Document Convention (Revised), 2003, www. ilo.org\ilolex\cgi-lex\convde.p1?C 185

[7] IMO, MSC.4\Cir.60, 19 November 2004, www.imo.org

[8] Royal, Seafarers' right to shore leave defended, The Sea, issue 171, 2004.

[9] OECD Workshop on maritime transport, Seafarers' Comments on Relevant Regulatory and Political developments, Paris, 4-5 November 2004.

[10] Flags of Convenience Campaign Update www.itf.org.uk\english\ flagconvenience\reports\2002

[11] ISMA concerns for seafarers' welfare, www.isma-london.org

[12] IMO, SOLAS 1974, Chapter XI. London. 2002

[13] IMO, ISPS Code part A, London 2002.

# Section 3
# Current issues in maritime education and training

# The doctrine of seaworthiness in the context of the ISPS Code and the relevant amendments to SOLAS 1974

N. Anwari
*World Maritime University, Malmö, Sweden*

## Abstract

This paper considers the potential impact of the ISPS Code and the relevant amendments to SOLAS 1974 on the doctrine of seaworthiness. The substance of the discussion is based on case law from both common and civil law jurisdictions.

At the outset, the absolute obligation of seaworthiness under English common law is discussed. The duty of a company, as defined in the ISPS Code with regard to maritime security matters is illustrated using a hypothetical scenario.

Since most of the charter parties and the bills of lading incorporate the provisions of the international conventions such as the Hague Rule or the Hague-Visby Rules, the company is required to exercise due diligence in providing a seaworthy ship. In this context, the ship should also comply with all ISPS Code provisions. This duty will be analysed in terms of the development of the Ship Security Plan and also with respect to a necessary co-ordination with the port facility.

In addition, a part of the paper will be devoted to the concept of Limitation of Liability in the light of the new maritime security regulations.
*Keywords: seaworthiness, due diligence, security, SSO, CSO, PFSO, privity, SSA, SSP, limitation of liability.*

*Paper not available at time of going to press.*

# Beyond rules, knowledge and skill

M. E. Manuel
*World Maritime University, Sweden*

## Abstract

This paper refers to a study, conducted in the context of a dissertation at the World Maritime University, about the place of the affective domain in maritime education. The study found, through a survey, case studies and a review of the literature, that this domain is considered very important in the industry. Very different methods and standards are currently employed in attempts to achieve educational objectives in this domain. Conclusions drawn include recognition that maritime education and training institutions (METI) need to specify these objectives and create a climate in which seafarers are trained beyond compliance for a culture of excellence and possession of desirable attitudes and values. It is recommended that associations such as the International Association of Maritime Universities (IAMU) lead the way in seeking to benchmark best practices in this context and stimulate the global Maritime Education and Training (MET) community to commit to this as a basis for any future legislation or setting of global standards in this domain.
*Keywords: affective education, safety culture, educational objectives, attitudes, values, ethics.*

## 1 Introduction

It is indisputable that good education and training in any industry is critical to the success of that industry. Like all other industries, the maritime industry has to educate and train human resource to accepted levels of the industry; and with changing times, knowledge and innovations, people already in the field ought to have their knowledge updated regularly.

By nature of its business, the maritime industry has the added dimension of being a truly global enterprise. In spite of this, however, global harmonization of maritime education and training standards have long been a challenge. The industry, to a greater degree than most, has to base its success on people with very varied national, cultural and other backgrounds, cooperating efficiently in excellent teamwork. Again, unlike most other industries, repercussions of a deviation from the "learned" principles often have major and disastrous consequences, which tend to gain negative global attention to the detriment of the industry.

With respect to the training and education of seafarers, an emphasis has been placed on knowledge and skill acquisition over the years. Ideally, however, three domains should form the objectives of an educational system: cognitive, psychomotor and affective, Bloom [1]. STCW 78 lays emphasis on what seafarers have to know to be deemed competent. STCW 95 focuses on what seafarers should be able to do [2]. Beyond this is another level – the kind of people seafarers should be, or a focus on knowledge, ability and willingness to behave appropriately under all conditions.

There is a perception that the affective domain is largely ignored in current global MET practices. At best it is done, but is not specifically acknowledged – certainly not at the level of a global standard. Proponents of this view, suggest that attitudes/values/ethics do matter and that there is a need for the maritime industry to address the affective domain of education specifically – emphasise on it as much as it has emphasized on the cognitive and psychomotor domains.

A brief study was carried out at the WMU (in the context of a dissertation) to find out to what extent the affective domain is considered relevant to the industry, and whether current training methodologies cover this domain. A valid question raised is whether the evolution of the industry vis-à-vis current status and trends require education beyond cognitive and psychomotor skills. If this is indeed required, what is being done in the industry to meet this need?

## 2 The safety culture

Attitude, a concept covered by the affective domain underlies culture. It is not easy to define exactly what culture is.

"Although 'culture' is a notoriously complex concept, it can be broadly defined in terms of the shared practices, mental habits and norms which shape people's identities and influence their attitudes and behaviours. These practices, habits and norms are generated and assimilated by people in a variety of settings including, in the context of particular national or ethnically-based cultures (i.e. in terms of traditional practices and language), but also in particular institutional/organisational settings and professional contexts. All cultures are generally seen by academic commentators [3] as being subject to change, contestation and re-formulation over time, rather than being fixed and static."

Culture affects perception of risk, safety and appropriate behaviour. The importance of culture in the maritime industry is accentuated by the increase in the global supply base of manpower. Few ships today are manned by crew from one country. Arguably nationality is one of the more superficial of cultural identifiers. Even where the crew are from one country, culture in a wider sense separates people in attitudes based on other factors such as gender, experience, age, or education.

It would be therefore necessary to truly identify what attitudes are desired and then to strive to achieve them at all levels of the industry; essentially starting with education and training of all the industry's human resource. The executor of this education and training need not be only the Maritime Education and Training Institutions (METI), but they certainly would have a prominent role.

The result in any attempt to streamline the activities of an industry would vary from individual to individual and organisation to organisation. Kelman [4], in regard to attitudes and how they motivate actions, sees three levels of compliance, identification and internalisation. This has some similarity to Mathiesen's conception of the three cultures that characterise the maritime industry [5,6] – evasion, compliance and safety cultures. To these three Sudhakar [7] adds the "uninformed culture".

## 2.1 Uninformed culture

In this culture there are gaps in knowledge about the requirements of a safe operation. There is possibly a perception that increased focus on safety actually increases accident risk.

## 2.2 Evasion culture

Those in industry who have this attitude seek to circumvent rules for economic gain. Quality is sacrificed based on the belief that it costs too much. All means are employed to maximise profits by minimum compliance with existing regulations, be they national, regional or international. This kind of culture thrives on a perception of an adversarial relationship between the regulators/enforcers and the organisation. The "them versus us" attitude means that all means are used to "win" at the expense of regulations.

## 2.3 Compliance culture

Those of this culture tend to actively comply with the existing regulatory demands. Every effort is made to meet such standards albeit probably grudgingly. Motivation to comply is often limited to a desire to avoid the unpleasant or restrictive consequences of non-compliance. Behaviour is adopted not because of a belief in content, but for the avoidance of specific punishment. In a revealing study, Kelman [4] found that "when an individual adopts an induced response through compliance, he tends to perform it only under conditions of surveillance by the influencing agent". It is obvious that if a global industry is characterised by this kind of culture there will be enormous demand on the resources for enforcement and surveillance. Unfortunately, the bulk of industry actors are in this category, an observation confirmed by a detailed and broad survey by Anderson [8]. He states with reference to the IMO's International Safety Management (ISM) code that:

"One thing that the survey confirmed is the very wide spectrum of compliance that exists across the industry. It would appear that most companies and ships which require documents of compliance and safety management certificates do have their pieces of paper but few would actually seem to have a functioning safety management system from which all tangible benefits were being derived."

In an environment characterised by evasive and compliance cultures, it is not surprising (but regrettable) that unilateralism of legislation/enforcement as well as criminalisation of seafarers will increase. Like the evasion culture, the basic compliance culture may be characterised by an adversarial relationship with regulators and enforcers. Although trying to comply at all costs, rules and regulations are seen as burdens which are not welcome especially when the motivation for compliance is avoidance of punishment and not desire for rewards.

### 2.4 Safety culture

This is the culture exhibited by quality conscious industry members. This goes over and above the existing legal requirements, subsuming the compliance culture and going beyond it. Behaviour is congruent with a basic value system. This corresponds to the higher levels of Bloom's taxonomy in the affective domain – valuing, organisation and characterisation. The pursuit of excellence and quality is done for its own sake in the belief that it is the ethical thing to do and is the best way to achieve long-term economic sustainability. Industry standards, which sooner or later became law, are set by proponents of this culture – setting benchmarks ahead of legislation. This mindset is by far the most progressive and what the industry needs. Those who practise this kind of culture have identified with and internalised values that make them act consistently in an appropriately safe and ethical manner. It will necessarily mean compliance with the existing regulations, but from a motivation of genuine respect for the underlying values and not necessarily by fear of the consequences of non-compliance.

All the definitions and comments regarding culture in the literature stress attitude. Ultimately it is the attitude of individuals at all levels that shape the organisational culture. The challenge is to determine how these individuals get these attitudes and whether such attitudes and the behaviours they lead to, can be influenced in any way by the system of education they go through. As shown in Figure 1, if METI operate in, and seek to inculcate, a culture that influences the values and attitudes of their students with respect to global maritime goals, these will in turn (dependant on "attitude conviction") lead to observable behaviours that help to achieve and reinforce the desired safety culture.

An analogy can be drawn between the industrial cultures described and those prevailing in the MET setting.

- An MET system that falls short of STCW will lead to the "production" of officers, and by extension, key personnel in industry who lack the basic knowledge and skills. Such personnel are the building blocks of an "uninformed culture" in shipping.
- A system that meets the minimum standards as required by STCW, may produce personnel who have a compliance mentality and perfunctorily work to get by with minimum standards, seizing on every opportunity to

evade the regulations when motivated by other factors e.g. financial gain. This results in an evasion culture. Where the individual is so inclined and the organisational culture facilitates this, this can be evidenced by a compliance culture. Evasion may then be avoided, but no effort is made to work beyond the requirements.

- The best systems seek to train beyond knowledge and skill and ingrain into seafarers, a culture of values and commitment to ideals that see such seafarers identify fundamentally with the global goals. Such systems produce personnel who are driven by excellence and are only satisfied with continuous efforts to improve, no matter the status quo of global regulation. These form the building blocks of a safety culture.

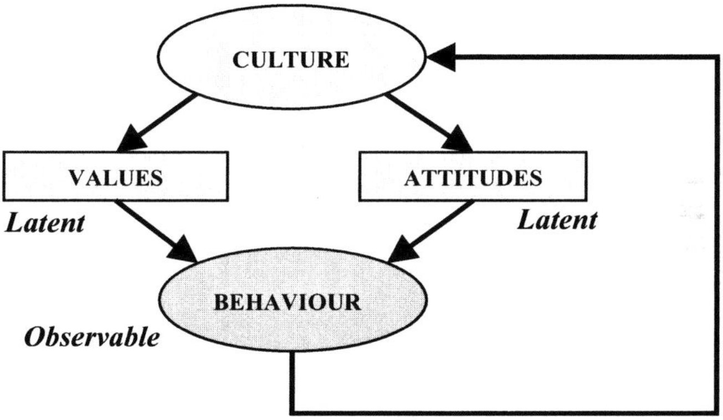


Figure 1: Relationship between the elements of culture.

It is appreciated by many that the need for this latter kind of seafarer is real and that attitudes are as necessary as knowledge and skill in achieving and maintaining the needed safety culture and efficiency. Ho [9], puts it succinctly: "Speaking English is no longer enough. Knowing maritime technology is no longer sufficient. Reading the manuals is not adequate. Applying traditional management techniques is no longer applicable. The unforgiving demands for excellence and compliance will require training and education beyond skills. What we need is to develop the Seafarer of the Future who is mature, responsible, well-rounded, has a fundamental strength of character, is empowered and aware of how his actions affect the whole".

The situation is analogous to how prior to the ISM Code, shipping companies were guided by numerous rules and regulations. As important as these were and still are, the industry recognised that they were not enough and that, (in the words of the ISM Code preamble) "in matters of safety and pollution prevention it is the commitment, competence, attitudes and motivation of individuals at <u>all levels</u> that determines the end result" [10]. Similarly it would appear that beyond knowledge, skill acquisition and "simple" compliance with the regulatory requirements of STCW, education and training needs to "grow" the kind of officer who is suitable for a diverse, dynamic and challenging industry.

Knowledge and skills alone can never guarantee performance. When MET at a global level is characterised by the "safety culture" mentality, it will complement the ISM's "top-down" approach to achieve a safety culture with the needed "bottom – up" approach.

## 3 The affective domain

In the dissertation study, the affective domain (of attitudes, values and ethics) was broadly defined as covering those issues that relate to, arise from or influence feelings or emotions [11] or an individual's inclination to act or refrain from acting in a certain manner due to personal convictions, quality of character and conscience. In this context, the domain is deemed to include such values as honour, rule keeping, responsibility, loyalty, truth, integrity, security, environmental and safety consciousness, respect for social order, respect for the dignity and right of others, social interaction and similar values. Educational objectives in this domain are defined by Bloom *et al* as "objectives which emphasise a feeling tone, an emotion or a degree of acceptance or rejection. Affective objectives vary from simple attention to selected phenomenon to complex but internally consistent qualities of character and conscience" [12].
There are varied definitions for and a wide range of words used to describe affective education. In 1994, a conference in Europe to discuss this domain, as it was evidenced in different educational systems in Europe, came up with the following definition:
"By affective education is meant that part of the educational process that concerns itself with attitudes, feelings, beliefs and emotions of students. This involves a concern for the personal and social development of students and their self-esteem ... A further important dimension goes beyond the individual students and concerns the effectiveness of their relationships with others, thus interpersonal relationships and social skills are recognised as central to affective education" [13].

## 4 Research questions and methodology

Questions addressed in the study were:

1. Of what relevance is training in the affective domain in the maritime industry?
2. Do current training and educational systems address training in this domain?
3. How can existing methodologies of teaching, assessing and certifying education in the affective domain be optimised (or incorporated if non-existent)?

Questionnaires were designed to solicit information regarding the first two research questions.

The questionnaires were targeted at specific MET institutions and other identifiable and relevant bodies. The criteria for choosing the institutions were:

- perceived leadership and input in industry;
- regional representation;
- role of nation or region in manpower provision and/or training.

In developing the final questionnaires, pilot questionnaires were sent to 13 MET students of the World Maritime University, 10 other students of the same institution with varied backgrounds and countries of origin and 2 professors. Amendments were made to the final questionnaires based on comments from the pilot.

In addressing the third research question a critical analysis was made (using library and web based resource as well as interviews) of existing views and ideas expressed by different writers and the industry as a whole. Some case studies were used to further examine the relevance of attitude training in the maritime industry. Conclusions were drawn based on all of the above and recommendations made in the light of the findings.

This paper does not seek to imply that the current training emphasis on competence is misplaced. The author is of the firm view that there are many positive attainments in the STCW with its emphasis on cognition, skills and demonstrated ability. What the study seeks to do is to discuss the inclusion of the affective domain (in a more specific way) in the consideration of competence. The basis of this is the argument that all the knowledge and ability is irrelevant and practically limited in use if individuals, for one reason or the other, will not or are unable to use them.

## 5 Study findings

Below are sample responses from the questionnaire (limited due to the necessary brevity of this article). The full dissertation – "Beyond rules, skills and knowledge: maritime education and training for optimised behaviour" – with more detailed survey results and case studies, is available in the WMU library.

- *A lack of attitudinal and ethics training is detrimental to the maritime industry*
- *Are there standards (international or national) used specifically for affective objectives in the institution? If yes, what is this standard?*

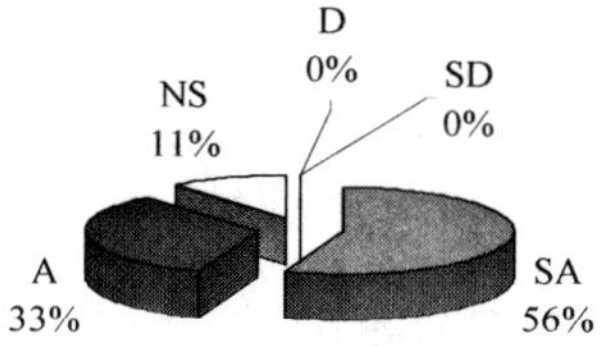


Figure 2: Value of training in attitudes. SA – Strongly agree; A – Agree; NS – Not sure; D – Disagree; SD – Strongly disagree.

50% of respondents answered "NO"
50% answered "YES"

22% of all respondents mentioned STCW as the relevant standard
17% of all respondents mentioned ISO (some together with STCW)
39% mentioned national standards. Of these almost 71% (28% of total) mentioned national standards as being the only relevant standard.

## 6 Conclusions drawn from study

With regard to the first two research questions, both the survey results and the analysis of the literature (including a number of case studies) indicate an emphatic agreement that affective objectives are important and relevant to the needs of the maritime industry and that METI have a significant role in fostering these objectives in prospective and practising seafarers. The survey and literature show that a wide variety of methods are used to try to achieve these objectives. These range from classroom lectures/seminars to paramilitary training and other extra-curricula activities. Standards mentioned include STCW 95, ISO and various national standards. The use of the STCW is debatable since this convention is not considered by others to address the domain with the specificity being researched. The same applies to the ISO. What emerges clearly is that there is no uniform global standard for the affective domain. Considering the importance of the domain, as revealed by the study, and the resources put into this by some institutions and companies, it is obvious that the possibility of having such a global standard (possibly in the context of STCW) must be explored.

## 7 Role of the International Association of Maritime Universities (IAMU)

With the introduction of STCW 95, the IMO is, to a large extent, meeting the challenge of education and training. However, in this diverse world, there is a limit to what can be legislated at an international level. Issues of sovereignty and national preferences are hurdles that the organisation has to contend with. In that context, the STCW 95 can only be the minimum standards to which all agree. As has been said, "it is a skeleton to which national administrations should add flesh" [14]. In the absence of such global educational and training standards, METI should add to the skeleton and thereby stimulate the global industry's demand for quality, with respect to right attitudes, till the point where STCW 95 can be legislated as a standard.

Associations and groupings of educational institutions (IAMU is one such prominent grouping) are often not as limited in their decision making by governmental pressure as the IMO probably is. They remain ideal fora within which these issues can be discussed, clear conclusions reached, practices benchmarked and standards set on a voluntary basis. It is often the case, that when practice becomes the norm in such associations, such practices are more easily transferred as a legal standard to the global industry. There is certainly no denying the strength and influence of associations such as IAMU.

## 8 New trends

New products such as Affective Computing and Affective Learning Technology that are designed for the affective learning domain are appearing. An example is the work of a research group in the Massachusetts Institute of Technology [16]. Most of these products are well beyond the research phase and are being used in many industries. Other examples are products by companies such as SimuLearn, WILL Interactive and Insight Experience, which are marketing products relating to the affective domain, including ethics, teamwork, innovation, leadership, conflict management and motivation [15]. These kinds of products help to meet one of the major challenges in affective education – that of assessment. With such products, assessment can be made more valid and reliable.

## 9 Recommendations

- Further research into the affective domain and the specific objectives that should be sought.
- Benchmarking of best practices and the dissemination of these to help global MET.
- Industry to build on the foundation of such benchmarking to achieve uniform and global standards.
- Research into the use of computer based testing to allow for more valid and reliable assessment in this domain.

## References

[1] Bloom, B.S., *Taxonomy of educational objectives: The classification of educational goals*, Longmans: New York, 1956.

[2] Lewarn, B., *Seafarer training – Does the system defeat competence?* Paper submitted to the 3rd General Assembly of the International Association of Maritime Universities, September 23-26, 2002, Maine, 2002.

[3] Vickers, I., Baldock, R., Smallbone, D., James, P., & Ekanem, I., *Cultural influences on health and safety attitudes and behaviour in small businesses,* HSE Books: Norwich, p. 3, 2003.

[4] Kelman, H.C., Compliance, identification and internalization; three processes of attitude change. *The Journal of Conflict Resolution*, **2**, pp. 51-60, 1958.

[5] Mathiesen, T.-C., Safety in shipping: An investment in competitiveness. *BIMCO Review 1994*, Stroudgate Plc. for BIMCO: London, pp. 56-58, 1994.

[6] Mathiesen, T.-C., Safety management and loss control. *BIMCO Review 1996*, Stroudgate Plc. for BIMCO: London, pp. 133-134, 1996.

[7] Sudhakar, U. R. P., *Promoting safety culture in shipping: Issues and strategies.* Paper presented to Institute of Marine Engineers (India) - Visakhapatnam Branch, April 15, 2005, Visakhapatnam, India, 2005.

[8] Anderson, P., *Cracking the code: The relevance of the ISM Code and its impact on shipping practices,* The Nautical Institute: London, pp. 202 – 210, 2003.

[9] Ho, D. M., *IT... all begins with people.* Digital Ship Plus, **23**, pp. 14-16, 2004.

[10] International Maritime Organisation [IMO], *International Safety Management (ISM) code,* IMO: London, 2002.

[11] Merriam-Webster collegiate dictionary. [Electronic resource]. 1996.

[12] Bloom, B.S., Krathwohl, D.R. & Masia, B.B., *Taxonomy of educational objectives: The affective domain*, Longman Group: London, 1973.

[13] Lang, P., Towards an understanding of affective education in a European context (Chapter 1). *Affective education: A comparative view,* eds. P. Lang, Y. Katz & I. Menezes, Cassell: London, pp. 3-15, 1998.

[14] Chowdhury, F. R., Personal communication, 21st February, 2005, Delegate to IMO.

[15] Adkins, S. S., Beneath the tip of the iceberg, *T+D,* **58 (2)**, pp. 28-33, 2004.

[16] http://affect.media.mit.edu/index.php.

# What is quality in a maritime education?

B. Paine-Clemes
*California Maritime Academy, California State University System, USA*

## Abstract

How do we know that we are delivering quality in a maritime education?

If we are measuring a product, do we count the number of students who secure jobs upon graduation, or do we look for stellar career achievements? How do we describe our ideal graduate? Do we care about character education? Do we measure knowledge? If so, do we define it as technical expertise or as a more general cultivation of the intellect? Or do we determine the qualities that employers say they want?

If we are measuring a process, do we address student growth in measures defined by Perry, Chickering, or Astin? Do we measure institutional systems by the criteria of Baldridge or Total Quality Management (TQM)? Do we apply the Seven Principles of Good Practice in Higher Education? Do we define quality as "community" by Boyer's six principles?

In a world made uncertain by terrorism and change, when split-second decisions about security must be made by highly trained mariners, those of us in maritime education must ask ourselves: How do we define quality in our education, and how do we know we have it?
*Keywords: quality, cognitive or affective growth, I-E-O model, Baldridge, Total Quality Management (TQM), National Survey of Student Engagement (NSSE), Seven Principles of Good Practice in Undergraduate Education.*

## 1 Can quality in higher education be defined?

Van Damme [1] argues that despite "twenty years of expertise and operational experience in quality assurance in higher education," there is no "growing consensus on how the concept of quality should be defined." There are too many systems of quality assurance and too many possible criteria.

However, we can still raise some questions that might help to define quality in a maritime education. Keeping in mind that, as Van Damme [1] says, any definition must entail "a concept of academic quality that recognizes variety and diversity," we will establish a few commonalities that might lead us to an answer, whether we are defining quality as a product or as a process.

## 2 Do we define quality as a product?

If so, how do we characterize the ideal output, and how do we measure it?

### 2.1 Is quality determined by the achievement of our graduates?

If we decide that it is, we must be clear about how we define achievement. Are we counting the number of students who secure jobs upon graduation, or are we looking for impressive careers? We must first define what we want to measure before we determine how.

At Cal Maritime over 90% of graduating seniors have jobs, with an average starting salary of about $60,000 [2]. On the other hand, we have little information about the long-range careers of our graduates. We do know that one of them became president of the college in 1996 and that others have successful careers in venues as diverse as Disneyland and Hanjin. We know, according to a survey, that employers are fairly satisfied with our graduates. However, if we wish to measure their achievement in earnest, we would need to design a long-term longitudinal study following graduates 5, 10, 15, and even 25 years after they graduated. We would need to ask them, at each stage, how happy they were, whether they were meeting their career goals, and whether they considered themselves successful. We would also need to interview their supervisors and co-workers to check for triangulation of results, ascertaining whether those working with them agreed with their self-evaluations. It is doubtful that most colleges would have the resources or patience to pursue such a long-term study.

Of course, we can interview graduating seniors to determine their level of satisfaction. But will a twenty-two-year-old graduate have the same perspective as a forty-year-old chief engineer? It's questionable.

### 2.2 Is quality determined by the character of our graduates?

If so, we must decide what traits define our ideal. Will we recommend "The Qualifications of a Naval Officer" attributed to Jones [3]? If so, we will agree that "It is by no means enough that an officer of the Navy should be a capable mariner.[…] He should be as well a gentleman of liberal education, refined manners, punctilious courtesy, and the nicest sense of personal honor." If we prefer such criteria, how shall we assess whether our graduates have internalized them? At Cal Maritime [4]—where we stress the "core values" of dedication, honor, integrity, responsibility, and trust—we have a certificated leadership program assessed by a system of portfolios and mentors. However, as the program is in its infancy, we have not yet assessed its effectiveness.

### 2.3 Is quality determined by the knowledge of our graduates?

If so, what sort of knowledge do we claim, and how do we measure it? Do we cite the large percentage of students passing their licensing exams? Do we ask outside experts to accompany our training cruises or watch our simulation exercises, to comment on the skill with which our students can manage a ship or master STCW competencies?

Or do we aim to produce well-rounded, educated citizens of the world? Mass Maritime [5] has a rich core of electives demanding that a student be a well-rounded graduate, with many courses in humanities and the social sciences. If we are aiming at this output, how do we measure it?

### 2.4 Is quality determined when our graduates meet the needs of industry? If so, what traits do employers say they want?

The Cal Maritime Industry Review Board, a committee of executives, meets regularly with the Academic Dean to advise him on the needs of employers. During a session in January 2001 the board, in a response echoing the remarks attributed to John Paul Jones, said that technical expertise is assumed in a graduate; what employers want—and sometimes fail to find—are skills in critical thinking, oral and written communication, problem solving, and multi-tasking. At Cal Maritime we have examined our curriculum and instituted more assignments and exercises requiring these skills, but we have no surveys or interviews to measure whether employers have determined a significant difference in our graduates. We also have no institutional pre- and post-tests to measure the skills of students upon entry and graduation.

## 3 How can we measure quality as a product?

Do we use surveys, interviews, focus groups, observations of tasks? How do we know that they are working?

Clearly, the method must be determined by the purpose, the resources, and the methodologies of a well-constructed experiment in the social sciences. Triangulation of results is important: if a focus group, a series of interviews, and a survey all yield the same data, it is more likely to be valid than if an interview yields one set of information and a survey, another. Methods should be varied; interviews can enrich the bare numbers of surveys, and surveys can be used to suggest the questions in later interviews.

Another point to keep in mind is Pascarella's rule that "input is the best predictor of output" [6]. A top college may boast that it produces government leaders and Nobel Prize winners, but can it take all the credit for their achievements, or do the advantages of social class, background knowledge, or genetics play a contribution?

This point brings us to the next major question.

## 4 Do we define quality as a process?

The Accountability movement in the U.S.A. measures quality by the achievement of outcomes. However, Chaffee and Sherr [7] question this assumption: "You cannot inspect quality into a product or service at the end of the line. Quality requires not just the detection of defects, but also their prevention. . . . All work is a process. The details of organizational processes are important because they are the substance of organizational work that ultimately produces the results." If we look at process in a maritime institution, what are some factors to consider?

### 4.1 Is quality defined by the cognitive growth of our students?

In the 1960's William Perry achieved fame by defining a theoretical framework for cognitive growth during the college years. Though some details of his framework have been disputed, and there is some evidence that it is slightly different for most women [8], the broad outlines are still accepted.

By interviewing Harvard students in the 1960's, Perry [9] defined nine stages of intellectual growth, usually delineated into four broad stages. In stage 1 the thinker is a dualist, believing that there is a right and wrong answer to every question and that Authorities have the answers. The function of the student is to listen to Authorities, soak up their knowledge, take notes, and reproduce the correct answers on tests. Eventually, however, the student discovers that Authorities can disagree, and cognitive dissonance sets in. At first the student may wish to discriminate between False and True Authorities, but eventually he or she decides that truth must be relative and that different people can rightfully hold different opinions. At this point the thinker enters Stage 2, Multiplicity. Everyone's opinion appears to be equal, everyone has a right to his or her own opinion, and the instructor is sometimes scorned for "grading me on my opinion." Research following Perry's study [10] has revealed that during this stage, young men tend to argue their own opinions and young women tend to listen carefully to the opinions of others, empathizing with them and trying to understand them. The emphasis, however, is on the belief that one opinion is as good as another. Eventually, however, some thinkers realize that not all opinions are equal. Some problem-solving methods yield better results. Some reasoning is more logical and free of bias. Experts have a better grip than novices. At this point the thinker enters the stage of Relativism, understanding that opinions are only as good as the knowledge and reasoning upon which they are based. The thinker learns to discriminate among so-called opinions and realize that some are flimsy constructs based on prejudice and irrationality whereas others are sound hypotheses based on reasoned judgment and experience. The thinker learns to apply the better models of reasoning to arrive at conclusions.

The final stage is called Commitment. The thinker becomes dedicated to a chosen set of values and achieves a strong sense of identity and responsibility—perhaps even an identification with Authorities.

If we wish to produce graduates who are committed to the search for truth and who can examine their own reasoning impartially, we may wish to employ such a framework and assess students as they enter, begin the third year of study, and exit. We might assess them, as Perry and Baxter Magolda did, with interviews; or as Alverno College did [11], with essays later evaluated for level of reasoning. This method can be expensive and time-consuming but can yield rich data about the impact of the college experience on the thinking processes of young adults. In this way we can measure both product and process.

### 4.2 Is quality defined by the affective or personal growth of our students?

Rather than addressing cognitive development, Chickering [12] delineates the personal challenges that young adults face: Developing Competence, Managing Emotions, Moving Through Autonomy Toward Interdependence, Developing Mature Interpersonal Relationships, Establishing Identity, Developing Purpose, and Developing Integrity. He believes that higher education has a responsibility to help young adults navigate these emotional crosscurrents. He also defines environmental factors contributing to this purpose: Clear and Consistent Institutional Objectives, Institutional Size, Student-Faculty Relationships, Curriculum, Teaching, Friendships and Student Communities, and Student Development Programs and Services. A quality education, as Chickering describes it, should not address the intellect alone but should actively assist young people with their personal growth. The goal of higher education is a successful citizen.

### 4.3 Is quality defined by the overall influence of our environment on our students' growth?

Like Chickering, Astin is concerned about the college experience as a whole. In his famous I-E-O model [13], he recommends measuring the impact of college by defining Inputs, Environment, and Outputs. The Input is the student upon matriculation: the intellectual ability, background, knowledge, personality, predispositions, motivation, and skills. The Environment consists of the entire college experience: the courses, the co-curricular activities, the relationships with students and faculty, the knowledge, the intellectual breakthroughs. The Output is the graduate: "the student's characteristics *after* exposure to the environment." According to Pascarell and Terenzini [14], though, it can be difficult to define what variables caused the Output. Because students take different classes, experience diverse teaching styles, and join different clubs, they belong to a number of distinctive different "subcultures". Hence the difference *within* an institution may be greater than that *between* institutions.

Another element is the quality of the student's engagement with the learning process. The National Survey of Student Engagement (NSSE) [15], based upon the work of Astin and Chickering, measures variables such as time spent out of class studying or contacting faculty. The assumption is that the more engaged the student is with the learning process, the more impact the environment has on his or her development.

## 5 How do we measure quality as an institutional process?

Which system is optimal? Or do we need, instead, objectives that will help us create our own systems?

### 5.1 Do we use the Baldridge criteria?

The well-known Baldridge criteria have been adapted to higher education in a 52-page report [16] suggesting seven global measures of quality: Challenges; Leadership; Strategic Planning; Student, Stakeholder, and Market Focus; Measurement, Analysis, and Knowledge Management; Faculty and Staff Focus; Process Management; and Organizational Performance Results. If we want a thorough inventory of institutional quality, these criteria would be enough.

### 5.2 Do we use TQM?

Total Quality Management (TQM) assumes that most employees want to perform well but are hampered by flaws in the system. A vivid example is "the bead game" [17]:

> A large bowl contains 1,600 white beads and 400 colored beads. Colored beads are defects. Employees are equipped with a paddle containing 50 bead-sized indentations. They scoop the paddle into the bowl, and it comes out containing 50 beads. The beads are hot, so workers cannot touch the beads or container.

The goal is to have no more than five defects for each immersion of the paddle. The flaw in the process soon becomes evident: the beads are scooped out randomly, and nothing the players do can make a difference. By sheer chance, some workers scoop out more than five flawed beads.

> People who play the Bead Game soon recognize both its parallels with actual work situations—setting goals, trying hard, motivating, warning—and its hopelessness. Ultimately, the best and perhaps the only way to obtain lower defect rates is lowering the proportion of colored beads in the bowl. But the workers cannot lower the proportion, for they are dippers, not process designers, purchasers, or managers.

Hence, for TQM [7], "The primary job of administration is to remove the barriers that prevent people from achieving quality work processes."

### 5.3 How do we determine a quality process?

Let us say that the administration of a maritime college decides to buy a simulator. However, the president of the college is concerned about the budget. He tells the Director of Simulators to choose the best machine possible for the lowest possible cost. The director asks to visit maritime institutions in other countries to investigate their equipment. No, he is told, that will be expensive. Then the director asks to interview the faculty, to ascertain their future needs. No, he is told, the faculty might want too expensive a simulator, with unnecessary frills. The Director of Simulators should use his judgment simply to buy the "best" equipment for the needs now.

The Director has been invited to play the "bead game". Without appropriate data or funding, he will choose equipment that will be obsolete within ten years. He may even be blamed when dollars are spent later for replacements or upgrades.

In a personal interview, Green [18] said that it is "crucial" to scour the world investigating state-of-the-art equipment "to know enough to buy what you really need." It is also important to allocate funds for software with sophisticated "modelling." The best equipment, he says, "uses black magic to recreate" situations "in the real world." For instance, the Haven simulator pump "doesn't go from zero to fifty. . . . The needle fluctuates and pressure gradually builds," replicating "diagnostic tools that an engineer in practice would really use."

Even more, says Green, "Faculty must be involved" in the choice of equipment. What lessons can they envision today, 5 years from now, 10 years from now? What can they imagine that they would like a simulator to do? A quality process, he believes, emerges when there is quality equipment used by well-trained instructors who know how to employ it for optimum effects in class.

### 5.4 Do we apply the Seven Principles of Good Practice in Undergraduate Education?

According to these principles [19], good practice in undergraduate education "encourages contact between students and faculty, develops reciprocity and cooperation among students, encourages active learning, gives prompt feedback, emphasizes time on task, communicates high expectations, and respects diverse talents and ways of learning." If we wish to apply these criteria, Chickering and Reisser [12] recommend that we investigate six areas: Institutional Climate, Academic Practices, Curriculum, Faculty, Academic and Student Support Services, and Facilities. Other resources [20] have been developed to apply these criteria in diverse ways.

### 5.5 Do we define quality as "community" by Boyer's six principles?

Boyer [22] defined six traits by which the quality of an educational institution should be judged: "an educationally purposeful place where learning is the focus, an open place where civility is affirmed, a just place where persons are honored and civility is affirmed, a disciplined place where group obligations guide behavior, a caring place where individuals are supported/service is encouraged, a celebrative place where traditions are shared".

These principles, though not a coherent system in the manner of Baldridge and TQM, have inspired initiatives in the Cal Maritime strategic plan.

## 6 What is the answer to this question, then?

In a world made uncertain by terrorism and change, when split-second decisions about security must be made by highly trained mariners, how do we define quality in our education, and how do we know we have it?

### 6.1 There is a three-part, tentative answer

First, we must entertain campus conversations about quality. We must agree on what we are trying to achieve: technical proficiency, cognitive growth, character development, intellectual breadth and depth, or a particular combination thereof. Second, we must devise a series of measures to assess whether we are achieving our goals. Are we doing what we say we're doing? How do we know? At Cal Maritime the Mechanical Engineering and Engineering Technology Departments have defined specific objectives, traced them through the curriculum, and evaluated them in course portfolios, student portfolios, student exit interviews, and cruise evaluations. The ABET 2000 criteria have furnished the standards, and the faculty have meticulously implanted and measured them in multiple ways. Pronchick [23], adds, "The results of assessment must be used to re-examine and improve the processes that are in place." We must ask not only "How are we doing?"" but "How can we do better?" "In TQM," says Pronchick, "this is the Shewart cycle: PLAN (Define quality, develop ways to improve quality); DO (Implement the improvements); ASSESS (Did quality improve?); ACT (Keep what works, discard what doesn't). We must know what we're doing, why, and how we can do it better. This point brings us to the third factor.

The mission and objectives of the institution must be clear, and they must be aligned throughout the curricular and co-curricular experience. At Dickinson College, according to Kirp [24], "The key goals are printed on a laminated wallet card, widely distributed so that everyone, from the trustees to the ground keepers, can know at a glance where Dickinson is heading." At Alverno College [25] students are trained to progress from beginning to advanced levels in eight core abilities, with sophisticated forms of feedback and self-assessment to ensure the progress of all. In brief, these colleges follow the advice of Smith [26]: "Everyone, drawn from all parts of the institution, must share a common vision and a consistent set of assumptions if the university is going to be effective."

### 6.2 Where do we go from here?

"Continuous improvement" is the mantra of quality control, from the process-oriented system of TQM to the product-oriented emphasis of Accountability in the U.S.A. With the plethora of available measurements, we have difficult choices to make in establishing a quality system. But we must all try to hit this ever-moving target.

The time for change is now, and our students must be ready to meet an uncertain future.

## References

[1] Van Damme, D., "Quality Assurance in an International Environment: National and International Interests and Tensions." International Quality Review: Values, Opportunities, and Issues: Major Papers Presented to the CHEA 2002 International Seminar, CHEA Occasional Paper, CHEA

Institute for Research and Study of Accreditation and Quality Assurance, Council for Higher Education Accreditation: Washington, D.C., p. 3, 2002.
[2] Bunk, M., "Shipping Out: The Pacific Ocean is the Classroom for California Maritime Academy Students," 29 May 2005, Daily Republic, Online. http://www.dailyrepublic.com/articles/2005/05/29/top_stories/news01.txt.
[3] Bogle, L.L., and Howitt, J.I., Ensign, U.S. Navy, U.S. Naval Institute, Naval History, **18 (2)** "The Best Quote Jones Never Wrote," April, 2004. Online. http://www.usni.org/navalhistory/Articles04/NHBogleApr.htm.
[4] California Maritime Academy. "Cadet Leadership Development." Online. http://www.csum.edu/StudentDevelopment/CadetLeadership.asp.
[5] Massachusetts Maritime Academy, "College Catalog: Academic Programs," pp. 29-32. Online. http://www.maritime.edu/pdf/catalog/h-academic_programs.pdf.
[6] Pascarella, E.T., "Identifying Excellence in undergraduate education: Are We Even Close?" Change: the Magazine of Higher Learning, **33 (3)**, p. 21 of pp. 18-23, May-June 2001.
[7] Chaffee, E.E., & Sherr, A.A., (eds). Quality: Transforming Secondary Education, Report Three, 1992 ASHE-ERIC Higher Education Series, ERIC Clearinghouse on Higher Education: Washington, D.C., p. vii, 1992.
[8] Baxter Magolda, M.B., Knowing and Reasoning in College: Gender-Related Patterns in Students' Intellectual Development, Jossey-Bass: San Francisco, 1993; also Belenky, M.F., Clinch, B.M., Goldberger, N.R. and Tarule, J.M., Women's Ways of Knowing: The Development of Self, Voice, and Mind, Basic Books, HarperCollins: U.S.A., 1986.
[9] Perry, W.G., Forms of Intellectual and Ethical Development in the College Years: A Scheme, (Chapter 5). 1968; rpt. Jossey-Bass: San Francisco, pp. 64-197, 1999.
[10] Baxter Magolda, M.B., Knowing and Reasoning in College: Gender-Related Patterns in Students' Intellectual Development, Jossey-Bass: San Francisco, p. 48, 1993.
[11] Mentkowski, M., Moeser, M., and Strait, M., Using the Perry Scheme of Intellectual and Ethical Development as a College Outcomes Measure: A Process and Criteria for Judging Student Performance (Vols. 1 and 2), Office of Research and Evaluation, Alverno College: Milwaukee, Wisconsin, revised edition, 1984.
[12] Chickering, A.W., & Reisser, R., Education and Identity, second ed., Jossey-Bass: San Francisco, 1994.
[13] Astin, A., What Matters in College? Four Critical Years Revisited, Jossey-Bass: San Francisco, p. 7, 2001.
[14] Pascarella, E.T., and Terenzini, P.T., How College Affects Students, Jossey-Bass: San Francisco, pp. 80-105, 1991.
[15] Kuh, G.H., "Assessing What Really Matters to Student Learning: Inside the National Survey of Student Engagement," Change, **33 (3)**, pp. 10-17,

66, May-June 2001; also Kuh, G.H., Laird, T.F.N., & Umbach, P.D., "Aligning Faculty Activities and Student Behavior: Realizing the Promise of Greater Expectations, Liberal Education, **90 (4)**, pp. 24-31, Fall 2004; the NSSE website at Indiana University, Bloomington, www.iub.edu/~nsse.

[16] Baldridge National Quality Program: Education Criteria for Performance Excellence; National Institute for Standards and Technology. Online. http://www.quality.nist.gov/Education_Criteria.htm

[17] Chaffee, E.E., & Sherr, A.A., (eds). Quality: Transforming Secondary Education, Report Three, 1992 ASHE-ERIC Higher Education Series, ERIC Clearinghouse on Higher Education: Washington, D.C., 1992. pp. 59-61

[18] Green, S., Technical Manager of Engineering Simulators, California

[19] Maritime Academy, Personal interview, 16 May 2005.

[20] Chickering, A. W., & Gamson, E.F., "Seven Principles for Good Practice in Undergraduate Education," Carnegie Foundation for Higher Education & American Association of Higher Education, AAHE Bulletin, **39 (7)**, pp. 3-7, 1987,. Online. Original article at possibly inactive link, http://aahebulletin.com/public/archive/sevenprinciples1987.asp; also at http://honolulu.hawaii.edu/intranet/committees/FacDevCom/guidebk/teachtip/7princip.htm.

[21] Some applications appear online at Michigan State University, http://www.msu.edu/user/coddejos/seven.htm; Panitz, T., "Implementation Ideas," http://home.capecod.net/~tpanitz/7ideas.htm; and Chickering, A., & Ehrmann, S., "Implementing the Seven Principles: Technology as Lever," Teaching, Learning, and Technology Group, http://www.tltgroup.org/programs/seven.html.

[22] Boyer, E., 1990, as quoted in: McDonald, W.M., and Associates, Creating Campus Community: In Search of Ernest Boyer's Legacy, Jossey-Bass: San Francisco, p. xviii, 2002.

[23] Pronchick, S., Chair, Mechanical Engineering Department, California Maritime Academy. Personal communication, 16 June 2005.

[24] Kirp, D.L., Shakespeare, Einstein, and the Bottom Line: The Marketing of Higher Education, Harvard University Press: Cambridge, MA, U.S.A., and London, U.K., p. 57, 2003.

[25] "About Averno." Alverno College. Online. http://www.alverno.edu/about_alverno/ability_curriculum.html

[26] Smith, P., "Curricular Transformation: Why We Need It, How to Support It," Change, **36 (1)**, p. 31 of pp. 28-35 (January-February 2004).

# Sustainable development model for maritime training and education using the Six Sigma approach

I. D. Er[1] & O. Gurel[2]
[1]*Department of Marine Engineering, I.T.U. Maritime Faculty, Turkey*
[2]*Department of Maritime Transportation and Management Engineering, I.T.U. Maritime Faculty, Turkey*

## Abstract

The existing international shipping regulations require effectiveness measures that are carried out at all levels within training institutions. The Six Sigma approach could thus be utilized by IAMU member institutions for performance improvement and approaching excellence in training and education services. The core commitment to institutional capacity enables the MET institution to consider resource issues from a holistic perspective, and to consider capacity as an institutional attribute beyond the minimum compliance and a review of assets. Looking at itself through a "lens" of institutional capacity enables the MET institution to re-examine what it is in terms of its capacity to fulfil its aspirations, and to integrate and synthesize findings and recommendations for improvements gained through its self review. This paper illustrates the advantages and techniques of the Six Sigma approach that could be directly applied for quality improvement at IAMU member institutions while simultaneously integrating those requirements of the international conventions adopted by the International Maritime Organization.
*Keywords: Six Sigma, training quality, MET institutions, safety management, effectiveness improvement.*

## 1 Introduction

For the assurance of maritime safety and environmental pollution prevention objectives, the STCW 95 Code requires quality standards for all training institutions in accordance with regulation I/8 IMO [1]. The existing regulation requires that effective measures should be carried out at all levels in the training institutions. The main objective of the quality standard is to train and certify the crew members in an efficient, continual improvement approach complying with the requirements of IMO Conventions such as SOLAS, MARPOL, STCW, COLREG, LOADLINE and ILO amendments.

It is obviously seen that the quality assurance of a MET institution becomes much more complicated when safety, environment and quality management criteria need to be integrated into the existing dynamic processes of a training institution while defining the knowledge, understanding, skills and competence. The assessment activities of all MET institutions' management and operational levels on a worldwide basis result in another crucial constraint caused by different national backgrounds. In the competitive atmosphere of MET institutions' processes, the Six Sigma approach is proposed in this paper for IAMU member institutions that are seeking excellence in maritime training and education.

## 2 Six Sigma

Six Sigma is a concept that was originated by Motorola Inc. in the USA around 1985. At that time, they were facing the threat of Japanese competition in the electronics industry and needed to make drastic improvements in their quality levels [2]. Six Sigma was a way for Motorola to express its quality goal of 3.4 defects per million opportunities (DPMO) where a defect opportunity is a process failure that is critical to the customer. Motorola set this goal so that process variability is ±6 standard deviation from the mean [3]. They further assumed that the process was subject to disturbances that could cause the process mean to shift by as much as 1.5 standard deviation off the target; Montgomery [4]. Factoring a shift of 1.5 standard deviation in the process meant then results in a 3.4 DPMO [3,4]. This goal was far beyond normal quality levels and required very aggressive improvement efforts. For example, 3 sigma results in a 66,810 DPMO or 93.3% process yield, while Six Sigma is only 3.4 DPMO and 99.99966% process yield (these computations assume a 1.5 standard deviation shift in the process mean). It should be noted that there is no need to operate all the processes at the Six Sigma level. The appropriate level will depend on the strategic importance of the process and the cost of the improvement relative to the benefit.

If a process is at the two or three sigma level, it will be relatively easy and cost effective to reach the four sigma level. However, to reach five or Six Sigma will require much more effort and more sophisticated statistical tools.

The effort and difficulty increases exponentially as the Process Sigma increases. Ultimately, the return on investment for the improvement effort and the strategic importance of the process will determine whether the process should be improved and the appropriate target sigma level as a goal.

Six Sigma can be defined as an organized and systematic method for strategic process improvement and new product and service development that relies on statistical methods and the scientific method to make dramatic reductions in customer defined defect rates. This definition highlights the importance of improvements based on the customer's definition of a defect.

A key step in any Six Sigma improvement effort is determining exactly what the customer requires and then defining defects in terms of their "critical to quality" parameters. From a goal setting perspective, Six Sigma advocates establishing goals based on customer requirements, not on internal considerations. Using customer requirements is certainly not something that is unique to Six Sigma, but it is important from a goal theory perspective. Six Sigma also uses unique metrics including Process Sigma measurements, critical-to-quality metrics, defect measures and improvement measures [5,6]. One of the first steps in the improvement process is to measure the current Process Sigma.

Six Sigma uses a structured method, whether the task is process improvement or new product design. In the case of process improvement, the method is patterned after the plan, do, check, act (PDCA) cycle [7]. One popular method uses define, measure, analyze, improve and control (DMAIC) as the five steps in process improvement. A somewhat different set of steps called Design for Six Sigma is used for radical or incremental product design (define, measure, analyze, design and verify). Whatever method is chosen, however, it is important that the method be carefully followed and a solution not offered until the problem is clearly defined. Data and objective measurement is critical at each step of the method. The standard statistical quality tools are incorporated into the structured method as needed. Finally, Project Champions who identify strategically important projects for the improvement teams and provide resources, typically receive an orientation to Six Sigma rather than detailed training.

# 3 Application model for MET institutions

## 3.1 Identification of principle boundary conditions

The training and education concept can be analyzed in four categories for determining the general expectations and reaching the customer satisfaction philosophy.

a. Knowledge, which enables people to understand what they learn in relation to what they already know [8]. Knowledge is both practical and theoretical. Theoretical knowledge provides people with the ability to generalize from unique instances. With theoretical knowledge, people can accumulate many years of experience; such as twenty years. Otherwise, with only practical knowledge, people will have only one year repeated twenty times.
b. Know-how, which enables people to do. Know-how takes people past merely understanding. Know-how enables people to put knowledge to work [8]. Know-how differs significantly from knowledge. Knowledge can be organized into intellectually tight compartments, and these compartments may be taught as a subject unto themselves. Know-how, on the other hand, requires the purposeful organization of knowledge

from many different areas of learning. As know-how is extended to higher and higher levels of accomplishment, it requires extension to more and more areas of knowledge. When teaching know-how, it is impossible to put bounds on the areas of knowledge that will be encompassed.

c. Wisdom is the ability to distinguish what is important from what is not; [8,9]. Wisdom enables people to set priorities on how to use the resources of time, energy, and emotion.

d. Character, as Covey has said, is a combination of knowledge, know-how, and wisdom coupled with motivation [8]. People often recognize the development of character by certain character traits, among which might be listed: honesty, initiative, curiosity, truthfulness, integrity, cooperativeness, ability to work alone, ability to work in groups, self-esteem. It is up each MET institution to identify what to include in each of these four categories. It appears that in maritime education and training, attention is given only to the first of the four categories, with the last two not even given lip service. In maritime education the lecturers often believe that at the university level their sole duty is to develop knowledge and pass it on to the next generation. The development of a student's character is none of their business.

Coupling concept with Six Sigma

In this study the utilization of the Six Sigma model is proposed consisting on the institutional objectives, core functions, and organizational structures for ensuring sustainability and the evaluation method for effectiveness.

This study offers various levels of competency categories on a worldwide basis for maritime training institutions, as it is also required by the STCW Convention. The various competency categories will be as follows:

- For maritime training institutions, that seafarer's competency below 500 GRT and 750 kW in accordance with the STCW 95 regulation II/3, III and the additional administration's requirements.
- For maritime training institutions, that seafarer's competency between 500 and 3000 GRT, 750 and 3000 kW in accordance with the STCW 95 regulation II/2, regulation III/1 and III/3.
- For maritime training institutions, that seafarer's competency above 3000 GRT and 3000 kW in accordance with the STCW 95 regulation II/1 and II/2, regulation III/1, III/2.
- For training institutions that their graduates are employed on board the ship as support or assistant staff and officers like radio operator/officer, radio-electronic officer, electrician, electric/electronic officer, medical officer, steward, cook, amateur seaman etc.
- For training institutions, that their graduates are employed in shore based organizations.
- Ship Management Companies (superintendents, operation, technical, crewing and fleet managers).
- Docking and Ship Repair Companies.
- Ports and Terminals.

- Chartering and Brokerage Companies, agencies and other miscellaneous fields of industry that serve the shipping business.

Hence, as the Six Sigma approach focuses on customer requirements, it is better to define who is the customer of the MET institution and what are the expectations of the customer. In this consideration the relationship between supplier and customer, and in addition the product that is provided by the MET institution, could be defined as follows.

Actually the maritime student is not a product. The product is the education of the student. In the manufacture of this product, as with any other product, it is essential that the worker (student) be an active participant in the design and creation of the product. The student, who is the person who stays with the learning process longest, should learn to become the co-manager of his or her education. This means, according to the tenets of quality management, that the student should be involved, consciously and with skill, in the continuous improvement of the processes that create the product.

The customers for the education of the maritime student are several. These are, in order of importance:

1. The maritime student, who must live with the product for the rest of his or her life. The student must become the co-manager of the production of the education and, having such a personal stake, must be considered first when attempting to define what it means to have quality in education.
2. The maritime student's parents and immediate family who, in many instances, are paying for the product and might also live with the results for the rest of their lives.
3. Potential employers who will rely on the education of the student after graduation to achieve the purposes of their enterprises.
4. Society at large, which pays a substantial proportion of the cost of the education and requires the future participation of the student as a citizen in the operation of government, as a contributor to the general welfare of society, and as a taxpayer who will support the education of future generations of students.

After defining the basic interrelationship between product and customer, it is necessary to define the special boundary conditions of MET. In the shipping business the management of training and education can be considered as the technical and the commercial management of maritime activities. The new regulations or rules that will be established by IMO have to be taken into account as research work and the requirements of new rules have to be amended in relevant department curriculums in an efficient manner. As well as the Port State Control parameters, the effects of these parameters in the shipping environment cause rapid, positive changes in the improvement of ship management. As a result a lecturer's academic research has to point out port state control inspection results and the classification society's survey requirements that complies with the statuary certification of vessels. From the Commercial side of ship management, the charterers' complaints and the condition of clauses in the charter party directly affect the claim handling process. The marine casualties or cargo damages that have a direct significant impact in training needs must be considered.

In order to overcome the above constraints the utilization principles of Six Sigma into the management system of a MET institution is summarized in Table 1.

Table 1: Utilization principles of Six Sigma for MET institutions.

| What Six Sigma will provide MET Institutions? |
| --- |
| Confidence to :<br>- the students, maritime industry, government and society<br>- the faculty management<br>that the requirements for quality are continuously met |
| An effective marketing tool |
| Unambiguous definition of the responsibility and authority of all persons involved in teaching, learning, research including: professors, teaching assistants, students, administrative staff, technicians and support staff |
| For the adequate determination of the customer requirements for quality |
| For the continuous information monitoring and feedback system |
| Adequate documentation of the program, course design activities and output |
| Adequate documentation of the student entrance requirements, hiring/ employment of new staff and material |
| Identification and traceability of all records, students, courses, research progress |
| Ensure that there are procedures available for control of the teaching, learning, research processes, including: reliability of laboratory, computer, library equipment, simulators, student counselling as well as continuous feedback to the student |
| For the adequate documenting procedures for conducting and reporting the results of all tests, assessments, exams, quizzes including graduation |
| Adequate documentation of academic advancements, merit awards and/or non-conformance |
| Adequate control of student, staff and research failure |
| Internal quality audits, management reviews |
| Adequate use of statistical techniques |

When we focus on Safety Management courses in MET institutions, it is necessary to identify the Safety Management System of shipboard operations and the significance of the ISM Code appears only slightly [10]. While the ISM Code consists of safety and environmental pollution prevention procedures [11] the STCW Convention covers the competence of shipboard personnel, and the Six Sigma covers the DMAIC approach requirements that enable a MET institution to design core Safety Management System courses in an appropriate manner. For this reason the integrated requirements' application for the Safety Management System course concept is defined below to enable a baseline for the design process.

There are many links between the ISM Code and Six Sigma as a project management tool. Defining the elements in the Six Sigma approach constitutes structures and responsibility and course program layout and curriculum establishment procedures. In the active learning approach, the ISM Code found it more practical to define such responsibilities in separate sections such as the safety and environmental protection policy (clause 2), company responsibility and authority (clause 3), designated person(s) (clause 4), master's responsibility and authority (clause 5), resources and personnel (clause 6), verification review and evaluation (clause 12). Clause 7 of the ISM Code corresponds to the following elements of the Six Sigma approach such as the elements of "measuring" and "analysis". Clause 8 of the ISM Code corresponds directly to emergency preparedness and response matters that need to be involved in the "define", "analyze" and "improvement" elements of the Six Sigma approach. Clause 9 of the ISM Code, although it covers a wider field of shipboard operations, matches the "measurement", "improvement" and "control" elements of the Six Sigma approach. The concerns of clause 10 of the ISM Code are divided into the monitoring and measurement, and operational control elements of the Six Sigma approach. Similarly the concerns of clause 11 of the ISM Code could be interpreted under the element of "define" for the safety management system documentation, document control and records traceability in the Six Sigma approach. Clause 12 of the ISM Code corresponds to the "improvement" and "control" elements of the Six Sigma approach.

More detailed links between the ISM Code, and the elements of the Six Sigma approach are given in Table 2; Er and Furusho [12].

Table 2: Links between ISM Code and Six Sigma considerations.

| **Active links between the ISM Code & Six Sigma** | **Define** | **Measure** | **Analyze** | **Improve** | **Control** |
|---|---|---|---|---|---|
| 2. Safety & Environmental Protection Policy | ■ | | ■ | ■ | |
| 3. Company Responsibility & Authority | ■ | | ■ | | ■ |
| 4. Designated Person(s) | ■ | | | | |
| 5. Master's Responsibility and Authority | ■ | | | | |
| 6. Resources and Personnel | | ■ | ■ | ■ | ■ |
| 7. Development of Plans for Shipboard Operations | | ■ | | | |
| 8. Emergency Preparedness | ■ | | ■ | ■ | |
| 9. Reports & Analysis of Non conformities, Accidents | | ■ | | ■ | ■ |
| 10. Maintenance of Ships & Equipment | | ■ | ■ | | ■ |
| 11. Documentation | ■ | | | | |
| 12. Company Verification, Review and Control | | | | ■ | ■ |

Similarly the comparisons between the ISM Code, STCW Convention, MARPOL Convention and Six Sigma approach as a project management tool are given in Table 3. The STCW Convention stipulates in some detail that MET institutions must be able to demonstrate that the relevant STCW provisions have been implemented to ensure that the aims of the convention are met, i.e. that seafarers employed on board are competent, qualified and can indeed perform their duties safely and effectively.

Table 3: Comparison of ISM Code, STCW, MARPOL and Six Sigma.

| | **ISM Code** | **STCW Convention** | **MARPOL Convention** | **6σ for MET Institution** |
|---|---|---|---|---|
| **Field of Application** | Management of safety at sea and pollution prevention | Training, certification and watchkeeping | Prevention of pollution from ships | Improvement of existing management system performance, minimizing defects |
| **Applicable to** | Ship Management | Administration, training services, MET institutions, ship management companies and shipboard operations | Shipboard operations for all types of ships | All MET institutions that wish to implement realistic based quality improvement |
| **Purpose: Demonstrate compliance with** | Managing safety and pollution prevention | Training, certification and watchkeeping requirements | Reducing the risk of pollution form ships | Self declaration of conformance |
| **Means: Implemen-tation of** | Safety Management System | Training Management System | Pollution prevention regulations and rules | Integrated System approach for project management |
| **Scheme of certification** | Shore based audit and shipboard audit | Organization's Audit | Flag State survey program | NIL |
| **Validity** | 5 years subject to audit | 5 years subject to assessment | 5 years subject to surveys | NIL |
| **Compliance** | Mandatory | Mandatory | Mandatory | Voluntary |

# 4 Conclusion

Appropriate implementation of the Six Sigma project management approach elements within the parallel view of international shipping rules and regulations can enable MET institutions to undertake planning and evaluation appropriate to their needs to accomplish and improve the achievement of their missions and purposes. In this respect MET institutions shall undertake both short-term and long-term planning including the candid and realistic analyses of internal and external opportunities and constraints. It shall respond to financial and other contingencies, establishing feasible priorities, and developing a realistic course of action to achieve the identified objectives that are defined in IMO Conventions. Institutional decision-making, particularly the allocation of resources, shall be consistent with planning priorities. The MET institution shall systematically collect and use the data necessary to support its planning efforts and to enhance institutional effectiveness.

Thus, through its organizational design and governance structure, the MET institution can create and sustain an environment that encourages teaching, learning, scholarship, and where appropriate research, and it shall assure provision of support adequate for the appropriate functioning of each organizational component or department. In this consideration the MET institution can periodically evaluate the effectiveness of its system of governance using the results of statistical data that are obtained due to the strategic planning phase in the means of self-assessment. The advantage of the Six Sigma tool can enable the MET institution's activities by controlling the process as a backward and forward data-driven process. This means the actions will be taken step by step. The steps will define the aspects, analyze the impacts, measure the significant impacts, and then tailor a solution that could be named as the target.

While focusing on educational effectiveness, articulating a collective vision of educational attainment, organizing for learning and becoming a learning organization milestone can easily be incorporated within Six Sigma.

Articulating a collective vision of educational attainment centres on the degree to which the MET institution sets goals and obtains results for student learning at both the academic and program levels; these are:

- clearly stated and widely understood;
- appropriate for the type and level of the degree or credential offered; and adequately assessed to ascertain mastery of these levels.

Organizing for learning centres on the alignment of appropriate MET institutional assets and characteristics with the goal of producing high levels of student learning, consistent with the mission of the MET institution; these include:

- curriculum, pedagogy, and method of delivery;
- faculty recruitment, development, scholarship in support of improved teaching and learning, rewards, and incentives;
- organizational structures and processes;
- information resources and planning capacity;
- student services and co-curricular activities; and
- resources and facilities.

Consequently becoming a learning organization centres on the degree to which the MET institution has developed systems to assess its own performance and to use information to improve student learning over time that:

- are systematic and regular;
- reinforce a climate of inquiry throughout the institution;
- reflect the input of stake-holders and an awareness of the distinctive characteristics of its students;
- identify key dimensions of performance that include student learning and
- are based on standards of evidence that prominently feature in the educational results.

## References

[1] International Convention on Standards of Training, Certification and Watchkeeping for Seafarers 1978 as amended in 1995 (STCW Convention), International Maritime Organization press, London.
[2] Harry, M.J. and Schroeder, R. (2000). Six Sigma: The Breakthrough Management Strategy Revolutionizing the World's Top Corporations, Doubleday, NY.
[3] Breyfogle, F.W., Cupello, J.M., Meadows, B. (2001). Managing Six Sigma: A Practical Guide to Understanding, Assessing, and Implementing the Strategy That Yields Bottom-Line Success, Wiley, NY.
[4] Montgomery, D.C. (2001). Introduction to Statistical Quality Control, 4th Edition, Wiley, NY.
[5] Hahn, G., Hill, W., Hoerl, R., Zinkgraf, S. (1999). The impact of Six Sigma improvement - a Glimpse into the Future of Statistics. The American Statistician 53 (3), 208–215.
[6] Harry, M.J. (1998). Six Sigma: A Breakthrough Strategy for Profitability, Quality Progress 31 (5), 60–64.
[7] Shewhart, W.A. (1939). Statistical Method from the Viewpoint of Quality Control, Graduate School of the Department of Agriculture, Washington, DC.
[8] Bloom, B.S. (1996). Taxonomy of Educational Objectives - The classification of education goals, McKay press, NY.
[9] Spanbauer, S.J. (1987). Quality first in Education, Fox Valley Technical College Foundation press, Wisconsin.
[10] Er, I.D. and Sogut, O.S. (1999). An Overview of Management Standards for Ship Management Companies: Journal of Naval Architecture and Shipbuilding Industry, 47, 153-156 p.
[11] Interpretation of the International Management Code for the safe operations of ships and for pollution prevention (ISM Code) adopted by IMO Resolution A 741.(18), International Association of Classification Societies press, London, 1996.
[12] Er, I.D. and Furusho, M. (2003). Enhancement of Environmental Care with Six Sigma Approach, Sixth International Conference on the Mediterranean Coastal Environment, 7-11 October, Ravenna Italy, Vol. 2 pp. 1145-1156, 2003.

# Use a good "TOP-DOWN" design to train students' abilities

J. Wu, K. Zhou, J. Jin, X. Zhao & L. Yao
*School of Transportation, Tianjin University of Technology, P.R. China*

## Abstract

In this paper, the authors introduce the "TOP-DOWN" approach to the design of courses in higher maritime education. In an effort to improve the students' abilities to meet the requirements of the global maritime transport development, we propose to change the education plan from teaching the students the knowledge requirements to an approach which trains their abilities. In that way students will be better able to comply with the human resource requirements for officers and engineers in the area of global maritime transport.
*Keywords: TOP-DOWN design, training, abilities.*

## 1 Introduction

Over the last two or three decades, global maritime transportation has rapidly developed and up-dated the technology used on board ships. With ships becoming more and more advanced, it is now an issue for the nautical and engineering academies to consider, in particular the issue of how to educate senior seafarers who will have to master modern navigation technology available on board ships.

## 2 Making a good "TOP-DOWN" design

Most maritime universities are institutions where students are not only taught knowledge, but where they are also trained, e.g. in the use of technology to navigate a ship. In the traditional course design, the emphasis lay on teaching the necessary knowledge, but with today's rapid development of technology, it was found that when more and more knowledge is taught, the teaching program has to be adjusted continuously, leaving the educators no other choice but to increase the teaching hours. Year by year, we found ourselves busy in adjusting the education plan. Finally we found that we had entered a monstrous circle. But, how could we stop this monstrous circle?

### 2.1 A possible solution

After studying all related factors affecting course design, we reached a joint key point, which is that the academy should adjust its teaching direction from mainly focusing on training students using the technology to focusing on improving their abilities to continuously up-date their knowledge after having completed their college period. In this adjustment period, the Tianjin University of Technology carried out a teaching reform, which focused on the so-called "TOP-DOWN" design [1]. By adopting this new international concept of an education method, many complex problems will be simplified. Instead of relying on the sub-systems having developed their own advanced teaching techniques, the "TOP-DOWN" design emphasizes the whole system's capability of training. The "TOP-DOWN" is a design method, which aims to satisfy the top requirement what should be done at the lower sections, from the top layer to the foundational layer, step by step.

As a starting point and in order to improve the basic knowledge of the students', we have to carry out a "technical orientation" for the students. Then we re-arranged the contents of the courses and adjusted the teaching hours. Furthermore, we selected sub-systems related to the courses, such as competent teachers, suitable teaching materials, experiments, practical training sessions and other miscellaneous related training courses of professional skills.

Every sub-system is based on the following key points:

- firstly, it should be designed to meet the respective requirements;
- secondly, it should be optimized as far as possible;
- thirdly, enough space should be left to the students for self-study and self-development.

To set up courses and train the students only according to the skills or competence of the teacher will only lead to an "accumulation" of skills in how to use high technology. The proportion of their knowledge systems will not be satisfied even though great efforts have been made and long teaching hours have been used. In the concept of "TOP-DOWN", teaching is considered as an integrated system, and great importance is placed on the design of this system. In order to achieve a good result it is only necessary to develop an excellent "TOP-DOWN" design for the respective courses. If this is not kept in mind, some difficulties will be encountered, such as a lack of teaching quality, talent knowledge system, ability structure, and most importantly the management of the university's teaching resources. One way to achieve this is to prepare the training scheme and the guidance of a teaching plan separately in order to guarantee a good "TOP-DOWN" design.

### 2.2 Targets set

The students, or should we rather say the officers and engineers in the not too far away future, should acquire three different kinds of abilities within their college period:

- strong ability to work independently;
- excellent language and communication skills;
- general management skills, based on law consciousness.

In order to increase the ability to work independently, we should mainly teach the students how to analyze and solve real-life problems by themselves, using the knowledge they have been taught in class as well as new knowledge which they may have acquired by self-study. We recognise that the speed of development of modern ship-handling technology as well as other ship devices is much faster than that of our teaching materials. In addition, due to the limitation of teaching hours, the level of knowledge of individual teachers and also the technical limitations of university experiments, it is impossible for the students to learn and master all the necessary knowledge about ships during their university period. Therefore, it is very important that students should be capable to carry out self-study and solve problems by using the knowledge they have learned [2].

In order to increase the language and communication skills, the main task is to train the students' ability of collecting all kinds of information and also to exchange ideas with other persons. As a characteristic of the maritime industry, officers and engineers should master a foreign language fluently. The language skills are not only essential for them to collect information more effectively in order to ensure the safe navigation of the ship, but also to exchange and communicate conveniently with other officers and engineers who are on board the same ship to form a team to accomplish shipping tasks together, or with personnel ashore or onboard other vessels to ensure the safety of navigation. General management skills are based on law consciousness that refers to do things legally, to operate the ship according to operational rules and regulations and to increase the ability of cooperating with others. As different countries have different cultures, ideas and consciousness, the laws of different countries often are also different from each other. It is therefore necessary for the students to learn and master local laws and regulations. At the same time, they should also learn how to protect their legal rights and interests by using the weapon of law. The university has to frame its own scientific and logical programme development and to set up a scientifically based and sensible "TOP-DOWN" design, which can express modern advanced educational concepts. These are just some of the basic steps when setting up a "TOP-DOWN" design for courses teaching the specialty of maritime transportation.

## 3 Paying attention to training students' abilities

In order to train students' abilities as mentioned before, we have mainly adjusted our course design and added some education contents as follows:

### 3.1 STCW related courses for officers and engineers

In order to comply with the requirements of the International Convention on Standards of Training, Certification and Watchkeeping for Seafarers (STCW78/95) and the regulations promulgated out by the Ministry of

Communication and Maritime Safety Administration of the PRC, we have selected officers and engineers eligible for training courses. The key point is to ensure that the students complete the compulsory theoretical training in maritime functions, such as: cargo handling, cargo stowage, marine operation management and human resources management. The main emphasis of the training regime lies on students to acquire the theory, using the knowledge they have learned at the university and through their self-studies as well as relevant practical sessions. They also need to practice other teaching items which include cargo plan, route planning, and ships in-port and out-port operations, all-weather navigation, fault diagnoses, and prevention of accident, either on board a real ship or in the ship handling simulator [3].

### 3.2 Improving students' language and communication skills

Adding to the training of students the improvement of their language and communication skills will greatly enhance their ability to collect and exchange information [4]. The method is: students should finish two essays in English in order demonstrate their language skills in exchanging information. The students themselves can select the subject of the first essay. The topic could be their daily study and life or popular science knowledge. The second report should cover a professional topic in the maritime field, which would introduce new technology and new developments in some detail. The duration of each task is 30 minutes. In addition to these two tasks, the students should answer some related questions. In order to complete the two essays, students need to collect, select, review and summarize all the materials available e.g. in the library or through some own research. The students can then finish the preparation of their essays and also the oral defence.

Such tasks will improve the research skills of finding and reviewing available material. Furthermore the student's abilities of proper expression can be trained, and at last the aim of language ability can be reached.

### 3.3 Training students' ability to work independently

In order to improve the students' ability to work independently, we have added after class science and technology activities, which we believe should also cover closely the subject of navigation. For example, recently our after class science and technology activities included: researching and manufacturing solar powered lifeboat, or the network of maritime safety education which students are studying. Through these after class activities, students have learned some new knowledge. In particular, through the development of solar powered life boat, the students have not only had a better understanding of the potential use of solar energy, but have also learned a great deal of professional knowledge relating to shipboard lifesaving devices.

Another example is the maritime safety educational network, where students have to analyze the underlying reasons of a maritime accident, repeat the accident scenario on the computer screen and analyze the wrong operation that led to the accident by using a ship-handling simulator. Students can put their discussion and research results on the network. We found that the students showed a more safety conscious attitude, and, after long discussions they prepared a safety warning to navigators. It would seem that the after class science and technology activities have aroused the learning interests of the students, fostered better studying habits, and most importantly, changed the attitude of students from passive ("made me study") to active ("I want to learn").

## 4 Teaching results

We are quite confident that the ability of self-study and practical problem solving of students have been improved. The ability to collect relevant material, to gather and summarize information, and the ability to communicate in English has been enhanced remarkably. The students are much more aware of laws and regulations governing the safe operation of ships. As a consequence, our university's examination pass rate of national officers and engineers has reached the top level in recent years.

When summarizing our experience, we would say that the fundamental goal for us is to improve our maritime transportation education, recognise and adapt to recent development in science and technology, so that qualified students are entering the shipping industry. To achieve this, the most successful method has been found to the "TOP-DOWN" course design concept, which improved the whole course design. Theoretical and practical examples have been used and demonstrate the success in this approach.

## References

[1] Jin Jianguo, Wu Jianhua, et al. Application of Modern Teaching Methods to study of Navigation and Marine Engineering Technology. The 5th Annual General Assembly of IAMU, 2004.

[2] Wu Jianhua, Cao Zuoliang, et al. Imitation Platform for Robot Based on Virtual Reality Technology. 4th International Conference on Virtual Reality and Its Applications in Industry, Proceedings of SPIE, 2003.

[3] Wu Jianhua, Wang Ting et al. Combination Case Study with Theory Teaching, Proceedings of the 7th CMIT 2004.

[4] Wu Jianhua, et al. Bilingual Teaching Practice, Journal of Tianjin University of Technology Vol.18, 2002.

# Strategic curriculum in the Faculty of Maritime Sciences, Kobe University, aiming at fostering and enhancing motivation toward Maritime Science

T. Fukuoka
*Faculty of Maritime Sciences, Kobe University, Japan*

## Abstract

In Japan, maritime related educational organizations are currently facing a difficult situation in acquiring potential young people who will shoulder the responsibility for the maritime society in the near future. The Faculty of Maritime Sciences, Kobe University, has started using a new curriculum since the first semester of 2004. A number of subjects provided in the first one and half years after enrolment are intended to give motivation towards maritime science to the students who entered the faculty without sufficient knowledge of maritime science to meet the educational objectives of the Faculty. That is mainly due to the university admission system in Japan, i.e., high school students tend to select his or her university based on the score of the common test conducted annually by the Government. In this paper, a strategic curriculum provided by our faculty is presented to show how the motivation and knowledge of maritime science could be fostered and enhanced in conjunction with a strategic admission system. Our curriculum in the first semester after enrolment aims to entertain students with the sea and ships using a high performance cruiser, cutters, etc., followed by teaching fundamentals and common sense in the field of maritime science. Students learn those introductory subjects in the first one and half years. Then, they are given an opportunity to select their preferred department from the three departments of *Maritime Technology Management*, *Marine Transportation Systems* and *Marine Engineering*. As far as the Department of *Maritime Technology Management* is concerned, which has the primary role of fostering seafarers, almost thirty percent of the students are enrolled through a recommendation based admission system in order to welcome students who have enough enthusiasm towards maritime science at the time of the entrance examination. The strategies introduced here would be a great help for other maritime education organizations where the number of applicants tends to decrease.
*Keywords: strategic curriculum, decrease of young people, Package Admission System, Common Entrance Examination, Seafarer's Certificate.*

# 1 Introduction

## 1.1 Growing difficulty in acquiring potential students

The population of 18 year old young people reached a peak at the beginning of the 1990s. It is continuously decreasing. By 2007, the number of applicants is predicted to be equal to the total admission capacity of universities and other higher education institutes in Japan. Some universities have already been forced to close, and others are confronted with serious financial problems. Figure 1 illustrates the transition of the situation for Japanese universities over these thirty years.

According to a recent report, only 14% of high school students study physics. As a result, the number of students who want to learn at the faculties related to science and technology is decreasing. These situations also put Kobe University, Faculty of Maritime Sciences (KUFMS) into a difficult situation in acquiring potential students.

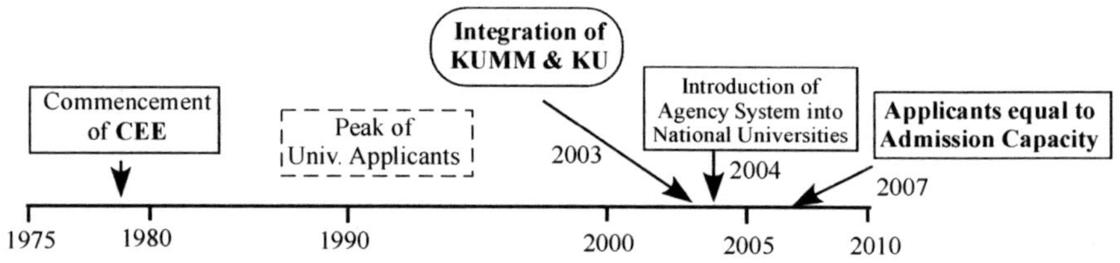


Figure 1: Transition of the situation of Japanese universities.

## 1.2 Situation of KUFMS

Kobe University, Faculty of Maritime Sciences (KUFMS), originated from Kobe University of Mercantile Marine (KUMM). KUMM was unified with Kobe University (KU) two years ago. KU is one of the largest universities in Japan and has a high reputation from educational and research points of view.

In the past, when the occupation of a seafarer was regarded as superior to others in many respects such as income and working conditions, maritime universities in Japan could have easily acquired potential students without any specific strategy. Such a situation was the same in the case of fishery high schools. However, the number of young people who want to be seafarers started to decrease in accordance with the rapid economic growth in Japan. This is mainly because they regarded the daily life of a seafarer as a severe one, which also creates a serious situation to KUFMS. The primary mission of KUFMS is to foster young people working for maritime and related societies as well as seafarers. Therefore, it is significantly important to acquire competent students with a sufficient scholarship at the time of enrolment.

# 2 Admission system in Japan and how students select universities

## 2.1 Admission system in Japan

Ordinarily, university applicants take the entrance examination in the following manner. Following the *Common Entrance Examination* (CEE) conducted by the Ministry of Education, they take the entrance examination imposed by the target university. Although a number of universities, especially private universities, select students only based on the CEE score, most national universities adopt the aforementioned procedure.

Another popular admission system is *Admission by Recommendation* (ABR). A considerable number of universities introduced the ABR system more than twenty years ago. The ABR applicants are not allowed to take the examination of other universities once they pass the examination. The ABR system has brought a great advantage namely that universities can acquire students with enthusiasm and interest towards the education and research fields provided by each university. On the contrary, the CEE scores of the applicants tend to be lower compared with those of the students following the ordinary entrance examination system.

## 2.2 How students select universities

In Japan, universities are roughly divided into two categories according to their specialized fields, i.e., the fields of science and technology and the fields of human and social science. University applicants ordinarily select their target university from either field. Needless to say, the applicant's interest and enthusiasm toward the education and research fields are the most decisive factor when selecting universities. At the same time, the CEE score has become a crucial factor as well.

## 2.3 Merits and demerits of CEE

The *Common Entrance Examination* (CEE) was introduced into the admission system in Japan about twenty-five years ago. The CEE has continuously been conducted all the time up to now while being subjected to various modifications. It is worth noting that the introduction of the CEE has changed the Japanese education system in many respects. The original intention of the CEE was to guarantee the fundamental scholarship of university applicants. Undoubtedly, the CEE has brought a great merit to the applicants. Based on the CEE score, they can choose the target university with a high possibility for success.

At the same time, the CEE has created a new university ranking system. That is, every university has come to be ranked according to the CEE scores of their applicants. In other words, through twenty-five years of execution, the CEE might have become a kind of governor of the entrance examination system in Japan. This situation has significantly changed the standard of how an applicant selects the target university. One can say that the selection of a university not only depends on the interests toward the education and research fields but also the CEE score of each applicant. Frankly speaking, some applicants tend to take the examination of the university with which they have the highest likelihood of passing. In addition, high schools and preparatory schools also follow the stream stated above. In order to obtain as many successful applicants as possible, they sometimes guide the students according to the CEE score when deciding the target university.

### 2.4 Enthusiasm and interests toward maritime science

It is defined by KUFMS that the scientific principles of *maritime science* are fundamentally supported by science and technology and closely related to social science. Our applicants seem to consider KUFMS as one of the faculties relating to science and technology fields. Meanwhile, KUFMS is sometimes regarded as a faculty aimed at fostering seafarers from its history. Although bringing up seafarers is it's most important mission as an educational organization, the real situation is that only twenty-five percent or less of the faculty graduates become seafarers nowadays. Most of the other graduates contribute to the maritime society or its related fields. Considering the serious situation explained so far, therefore, it is significantly important for KUFMS to acquire competent students by means of an effective admission strategy and to offer an attractive curriculum enhancing the motivation of the freshmen.

## 3 Strategies for acquiring potential students and offering effective curriculum

### 3.1 Outline of KUFMS's strategy

Taking account of the current situation explained in Sections 1 and 2, KUFMS has introduced the following admission policy and introductory education system. Figure 2 schematically shows the outline of KUFMS's strategy.

#### 3.1.1 Admission

In addition to young people having a natural interest in maritime science, KUFMS is making efforts to acquire potential students with sufficient scholarship, who are attracted to science and technology and also have some interest in the sea and ships. The strategy is to welcome applicants from a larger population.

#### 3.1.2 Introductory education

By providing an attractive introductory curriculum on maritime science, KUFMS intends to stimulate the interest of freshmen towards maritime science.

The strategy is that the motivation towards maritime science could be enhanced through an effective and attractive curriculum, while the improvement of the students' scholarship on fundamental subjects, such as mathematics, physics, etc., is fairly difficult after the enrolment.

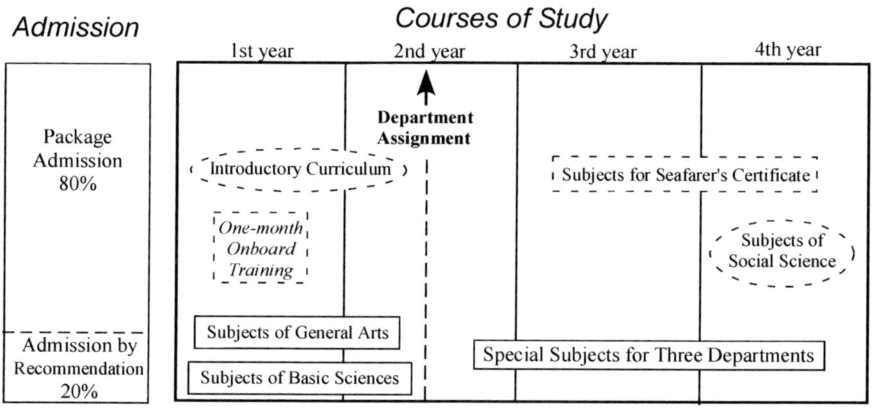


Figure 2: Outline of KUFMS's strategy.

## 3.2 Concrete plans

### 3.2.1 Package admission system

Students are admitted through the *Package Admission System* (PAS), which means that they enter KUFMS without their department being assigned at the enrolment. One and half years later, each student chooses his or her department. If the number of students exceeds the capacity of each department, the determination is made on the basis of the number of credits that the students have received in the first year. This admission system provides several advantages to both KUFMS and the students. KUFMS can acquire competent students with a high scholarship from a larger population. Besides, this system urges the students to study hard in order to be assigned to their target department.

For students, they can choose their department after they have learned the fundamentals of maritime science through introductory subjects in the first year. Accordingly, students can continue learning in the department in which they really want to learn.

### 3.2.2 Attractive subjects for enhancing the motivation toward maritime science

Three subjects aimed at enhancing the students' motivation are prepared in the first year. *Marine Sports* and *Boat Handling*, *Learn from the Sea*, and *Swimming* have two objectives, i.e., for students to enjoy and learn about the sea and ships. Another subject, *General Study I*, is also important, in which students can learn the outline and the objectives of the three departments of KUFMS through a series of lectures provided by twelve teachers specializing in different research fields. These four subjects intend to offer sufficient information for the students when selecting his or her department in the second year.

### 3.2.3 One-month onboard training in the first summer

Experience of onboard ship training enables the students to learn what maritime science is. For students having any difficulty in the onboard ship training from physical or mental points of view, alternative short-term ship training called the *Onboard Seminar for Maritime Science* is prepared by using KUFMS's training ship, FUKAE-MARU. The period is usually less than one week. Additionally, those students who took the credit of the onboard seminar and hope to get a seafarers' certificate are urged to take the *Onboard Seminar for Maritime Science* in the next summer.

### 3.2.4 Opportunity to learn Social Science

A special subject group, which is commonly open for three departments, gives an opportunity for any student to learn several subjects provided by Faculties of Law, Economics and Business Administration. This unique curriculum is in line with KUFMS's education policy.

### 3.2.5 Equal opportunity to be a seafarer

The *Department of Maritime Technology Management* has the priority in fostering seafarers. The students assigned to the other departments are also given an opportunity to take credits required to be seafarers. This system increases the probability for the Maritime Society to acquire capable seafarers.

### 3.2.6 Class teacher system

Two or three teachers are assigned as a *Class Teacher* to each department in order to guide students in their study, campus life and so on. Class Teachers also help students to find jobs at graduation. This thoughtful system follows KUMM's tradition.

# 4 Analysis and estimation of current status

## 4.1 Entrance examination

The average CEE score of the applicants distinctively increases after integration, which means the success of the integration program and the introduction of the *Package Admission System.*

## 4.2 Students' records in the new curriculum

Records of the first students of KUFMS after the integration are slightly better than those of the former KUMM's students.

## 4.3 Assignment of students to three departments

KUFMS consists of three departments, *Maritime Technology Management, Maritime Transportation Systems* and *Marine Engineering*. Each department has the prescribed student numbers of ninety, fifty and sixty. In the case of *Maritime Technology Management*, the number of applicants was a bit smaller than the prescribed one. Just after enrolment, almost half the freshmen hoped to be *Marine Engineering* students. It is considered, therefore, that the situation has been improved due to our introductory curriculum. However, further efforts should be made to provide a better education system for freshmen. Incidentally, *Maritime Technology Management* students can select either the *Navigation* course or the *Ship Engineering* course at the time of department assignment.

## 5 Concluding remarks

Evaluation of KUFMS's strategy is to be done at the graduation of the first students. KUFMS is determined to take any possible countermeasure to improve the education quality even in the progress of the current curriculum.

Finally, KUFMS has the confidence that the strategies proposed here make it possible to complete the mission of fostering competent graduates working for domestic and international maritime societies.

## References

[1] Fukuoka, T., Innovation of Education System Toward 21st Century at Kobe University of Mercantile Marine, IAMU Proceedings of Inaugural General Assembly (2000), pp. 1-5.

[2] A New educational System of Maritime Science 1n 21st Century proposed by Kobe University of Mercantile Marine, IAMU Proceeding of Third General Assembly (2002), pp. 1-5.

# Mainstreaming health in maritime education and training

D. E. Lucero-Prisno III[1], S. Muramatsu[2], S. Hisamune[3] & M. Ehara[2]
[1]*International Maritime Health Association, Philippines*
[2]*Tokyo University of Marine Science and Technology, Japan*
[3]*Hachinohe University, Japan*

## Abstract

Death, injuries and diseases remain a major problem among the world's seafarers. A few reasons are: lack of knowledge on health problems related to maritime work, occupational risks, vulnerability due to mobility, exposure to diseases in other places, behaviour and practices, and access to medical and health service information. Despite the mandatory training as stipulated in the STCW Convention, health knowledge is not translated to actions while on board ships. In fact, the practice of self-medication aggravates the problem.

The radio-medical service is not popularly used and tends only to be used in situations of extreme necessity on board. The consequence of this ill health, accidents and deaths may result in loss of productivity, loss of income for the family and the national economy and a high cost to the insurance industry, in particular the P&I Clubs.

Increasingly, pre-medical examination is being requested in an effort to limit health claims, which may amount to millions of dollars every year.

One approach to contain the problem is mainstreaming health in maritime education and training. Methodologies and approaches on mainstreaming will be discussed in this paper.

*Paper not available at time of going to press.*

# Advanced education and research on marine propulsion – new method for analyzing propulsion performance in service

M. Uchida[1] & E. Nishikawa[2]
[1]*Faculty of Maritime Sciences, Kobe University, Japan*
[2]*Emeritus Professor, Kobe University of Mercantile Marine, Japan*

## Abstract

The most important subject of logistics is to make an effective transportation of cargo and people. Seafarers who are involved in sea-transportation take responsibility not only for safety of operations but also for economical and environmentally friendly operations. It is very important to grasp the knowledge of real-time ship propulsion performance on board in order to optimize operation and maintenance planning. Ship propulsion performance deteriorates in service because of increase in the hull resistance and deterioration of the propeller performance caused by the adhesion of sessile organisms on its surface. However, only the relationship between the ship velocity and the shaft power can be directly detected on board. It is impossible to divide the propulsion performance into the influence of hull resistance and propeller performance by the conventional analysis method. The authors, by carrying out model experiments in ship model basin and actual ship experiments on the Fukae-maru which is installed with a shaft torque meter and a shaft thrust meter, have developed and proposed a new analyzing method, which by numerical calculations can estimate, in service, the hull resistance and the propeller performance individually.

According to this proposed method of analyzing ship propulsion performance in service, the hull resistance performance and the propeller performance can be grasped individually; therefore, the prevailing surface condition of hull and propeller can be estimated correctly. The proposed method can be useful in making an effective maintenance plan, and to achieving an economical and an environmentally friendly operation.
*Keywords: propulsion performance, hull resistance, propeller performance, propeller thrust, shaft torque, aged deterioration.*

# 1 Introduction

Propeller and hull surface of actual ships are fouled and their roughness increase in service, due to various causes such as deterioration of painting, adhesion of sessile organism, cavitation erosion, etc. The increase of roughness induces increase of hull resistance and deterioration of propeller performance. Both of them lead to same result such as increase of power and decrease of ship speed. Therefore, the deterioration of propulsion performance cannot be divided conventionally into effects of hull and propeller from logbook data analysis.

A new analyzing method has been developed paying attention to the relation between propeller torque and thrust characteristics. The new method can divide the propulsion performance into the hull performance and the propeller performance by the analysis utilizing logbook data, sea-trial data, propeller open characteristics and self-propulsion factors.

# 2 Proposed analysis method

## 2.1 Typical conventional method

The propeller shaft torque can be usually measured through the torsional strain or can be estimated from the specific fuel consumption and the shaft revolution speed in actual ships at sea. On the other hand, the propeller shaft thrust is not measured in normal merchant ships because the compressive rigidity of propeller shaft is extremely larger than the torsional rigidity and it is difficult to measure the propeller shaft thrust.

The propulsion performance of actual ship at sea deteriorates due to various factors, such as weather, sea condition, hull fouling, propeller fouling and so on. The monitoring method of propulsion performance has basically been by the analysis of Log-data for relationship between the M/E power and the ship velocity, as shown in Figure 1. It is impossible to investigate the effects of the hull resistance and the propeller performance individually.

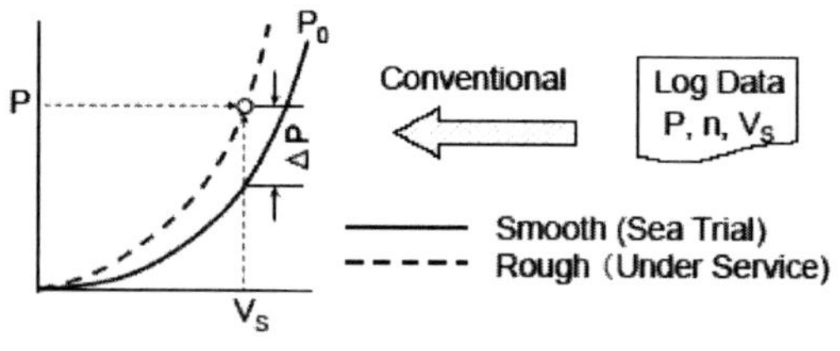


Figure 1: Typical conventional analysis.

## 2.2 Outline of proposed method

A certain relationship should exist between the deviation of the shaft torque and the shaft thrust of a fouled propeller from clean propeller performance. If the relation between them could be detected properly, the shaft thrust can be estimated from the measured shaft torque in service and the propeller performance in clean condition, and then the variation of propeller performance due to the surface fouling can be estimated. Therefore, the variation of hull resistance is also estimated from the propeller thrust by taking into account of the thrust deduction coefficient.

The estimation method for the change of torque and thrust through the change of drag caused by the propeller surface fouling was proposed by Kaizu [1]. The method was based on the evaluation method for the scale effect of propellers proposed by ITTC 1978 [2]. SR233 [3] also carried out development of an advanced monitoring method for ship performance by use of the ITTC 1978 method. The estimated results of propeller surface roughness by both methods agree qualitatively with actual measurements that the torque increases and the thrust decreases caused by the surface roughness, but there are large differences quantitatively between the actual and the estimation results.

The new analyzing method for propulsion performance of actual ship has been developed and proposed by the authors [4] by carrying out of model propeller experiments with various artificial roughness, numerical calculations based on hydrodynamic theory and actual ship experiments on a training ship equipped with thrust measuring device. The outline of the proposed method is as follows and as shown in Figure 2.

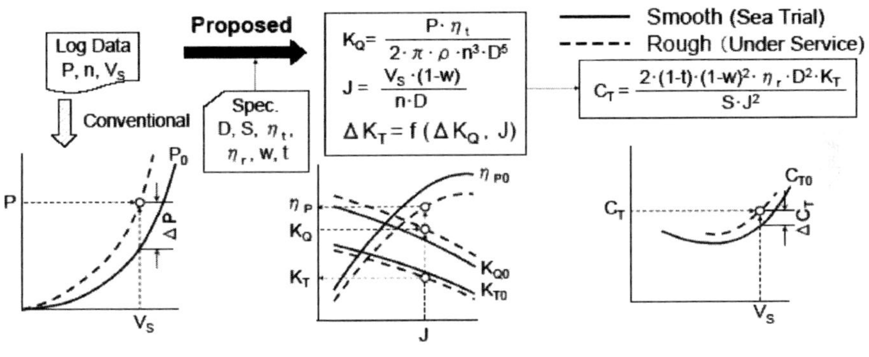


Figure 2: Concept of proposed analysis.

Step 1. To grasp certain relationship between the deviations of the torque and the thrust:
Propeller performance is estimated under clean and several fouled conditions by model experiments or numerical calculations and the relation between the deviation of the torque and the thrust is grasped in advance.

Step 2. To estimate the propeller performance in service:
The present torque coefficient is calculated from measured torque in service, and the present thrust coefficient is estimated by using of the

relation obtained in the step 1. The present propeller performance in service can be estimated.

Step 3. To estimate the hull resistance in service:
The present hull resistance can be estimated from the propeller thrust by taking into account of the thrust deduction coefficient.

### 2.3 Estimation of roughness effects on propeller performance

The procedure for estimation of roughness effects on propeller performance consists of two steps. In the first step, the boundary layer calculation is done for two dimensional blade section. The propeller blade section is regarded to be deformed due to the surface roughness, apparently by the growth of a thickness of the boundary layer. In the second step, the vortex lattice model, based on lifting surface theory, is adopted for the calculation of a three-dimensional propeller performance.

#### 2.3.1 Boundary layer calculation for two dimensional blade section

Yamaguchi [5] has developed a prediction model for the viscosity effects on hydrodynamic characteristics of 2D hydrofoil and the FORTRAN77 program package has been opened as a freeware. The boundary layer displacement thickness can be estimated by this model. The estimation of roughness effect on 2D blade section can also be carried out by the program with minor modification. The principles of modelling and calculation process are described in [5] and the author's paper [6].

#### 2.3.2 Three dimensional propeller performance calculation

The three dimensional vortex lattice model is used for the calculation of the propeller performance. Each blade section of propeller is considered to be deformed by the boundary layer displacement thickness due to the surface roughness. The effects of surface roughness are taken into account as the change of camber curve and blade thickness.

#### 2.3.3 The relation between deviations of propeller thrust and propeller torque

The relation between the deviations of the propeller thrust coefficient and the propeller torque coefficient can be grasped by several calculations described above at a certain number of surface roughness conditions.

The validity of the prediction method is confirmed by a comparison with model experiments in the author's previous paper [6]. The principle of calculation process is described in the paper.

## 3 Results and discussion

The calculation and experiment results of a propeller open performance under several fouled conditions are shown in Figure 3. The relation between deviations of fouled propeller performance from that of the clean propeller performance is shown in Figure 4 with results of simplified method by Nishikawa and Liu [7] and ITTC 1978 method. It can be said in general that the proposed estimation method for propeller roughness effect is pretty accurate.

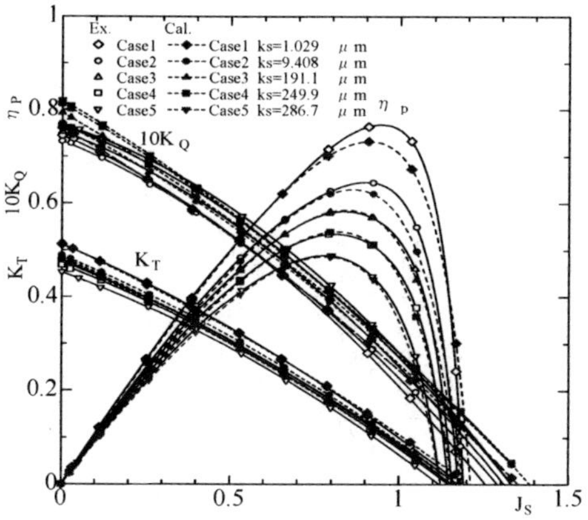


Figure 3: Experiment results of fouled propeller performance.

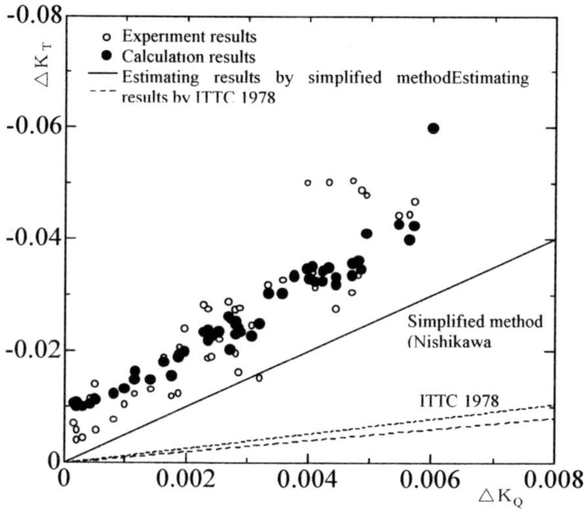


Figure 4: Relation between $\Delta K_T$ and $\Delta K_Q$.

The proposed method for analysis was applied to training ship "Fukaemaru" in actual service. She is equipped with torque meter as well as thrust meter. A series of speed tests were carried out in order to investigate the effects of hull and propeller surface fouling on propulsion performance. The experiment results and estimation results obtained by the proposed method are shown in Figures 5 and 6. As seen, it can be said that the estimation results explain very well the deterioration of propeller performance and hull resistance.

In order to investigate its application for general ships, an analysis of Ab-Log data of an ocean going vessel was carried out according to this proposed analysis method. The estimation results of propulsion performance are shown in Figures 7and 8. Figure 7 shows time history for 6 years, with two dry-dockings.

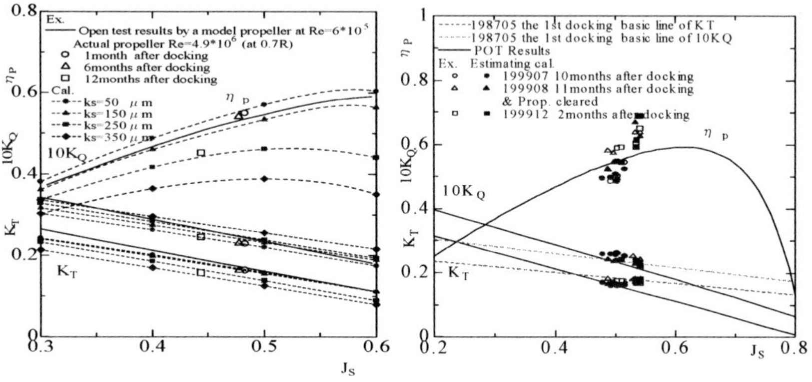


Figure 5: Propeller performance of "Fukaemaru" in service.

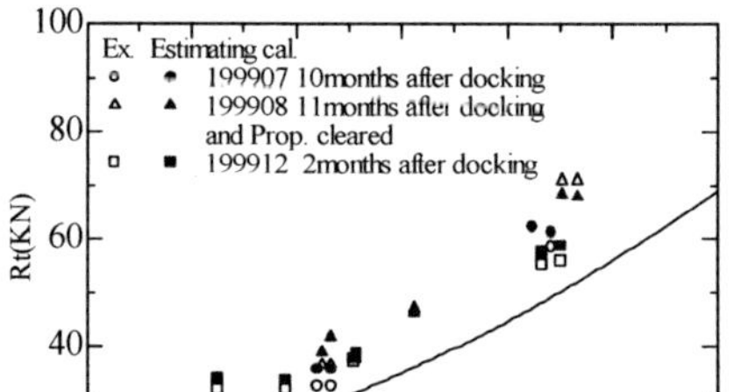


Figure 6: Hull resistance of "Fukaemaru" in service.

The propeller performance tends to deteriorate reasonably as the time passes from the previous docking and tends to recover due to cleaning works at dry-dock. But, it is difficult to see a certain trend of changes in the hull resistance performance. Figure 8 shows all the data of propeller open characteristics and the hull resistance coefficient respectively during first service term, i.e. in clean condition between the start of service and the first docking. The estimation results spread on both the figures. However, there is a specific distribution pattern, i.e. the advanced ratio especially extends to a wide value although the measured torque does not change widely. The value of the data of ship speed is wondered about the accuracy. If the ship speeds data would include a certain error, the analysis results are affected as shown in Figure 9. An error in ship speed data has a great influence on the estimation of results, especially of hull resistance, because the present thrust performance is estimated from the present torque coefficient and the performance of clean propeller, and the hull resistance is obtained from the propeller thrust. It should be stressed that a ship speed measurement device is not generally disputable, however it is pointed out that there is an ample scope for improvement of recording method of ship speed in a logbook. In an ordinary way average ship speed during a watch period is obtained from the running distance for 4 hours. Attention must be paid to the fact that a ship speed data of logbook includes a substantial error for propulsion performance analysis.

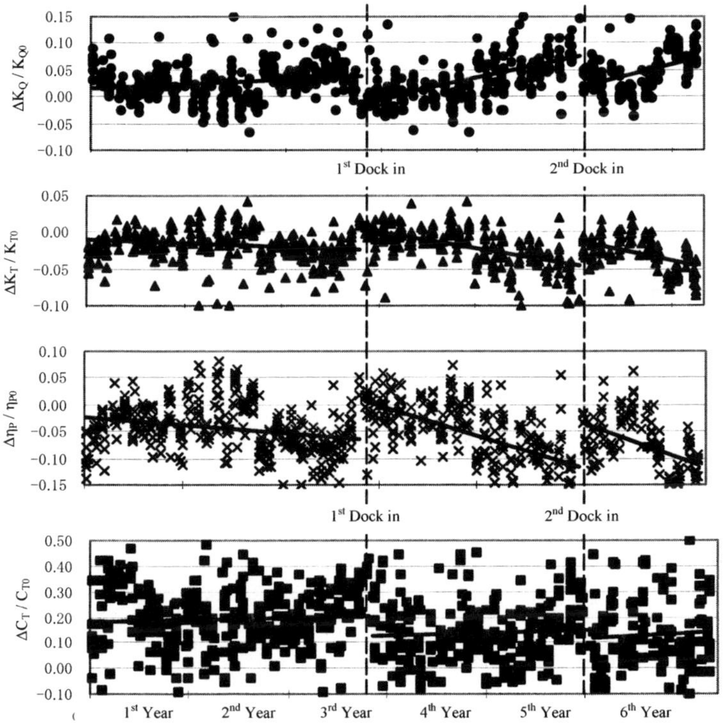


Figure 7: Time history of propulsion performance of an ocean going vessel.

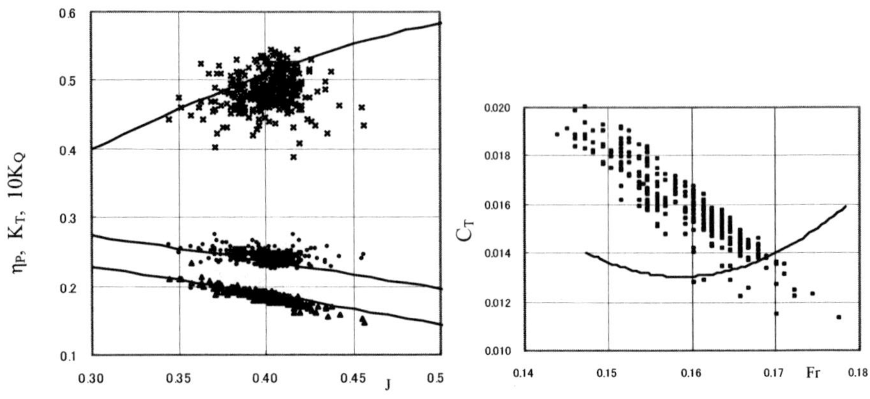


Figure 8: Propeller performance and hull resistance coefficient of an ocean going vessel.

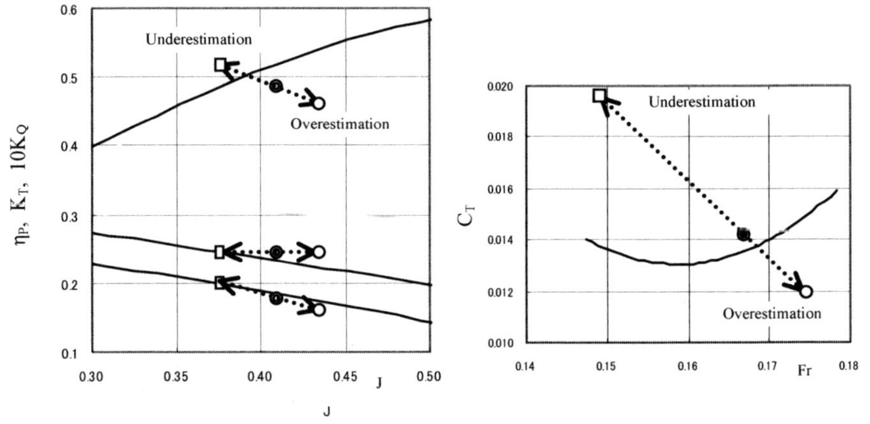


Figure 9: Influence of ship speed error on propeller performance and hull resistance coefficient.

## 4 Concluding remarks

The new method for analyzing propulsion performance, which in actual service can analyze the aged deterioration of propeller performance and hull resistance individually, has been described. The method is based on the relationship, grasped in advance, between the deviations of the torque and the thrust of fouled propeller from the clean propeller performance. It has been confirmed, through speed tests on "Fukaemaru" in actual service, that this method is able to estimate the roughness effects of propellers by comparison of experimental results of model propeller with artificial roughness, and to divide reasonably the propulsion performance into propeller performance and hull resistance. The method was also applied for Ab-Log data analysis of an ocean going vessel. The estimation results are influenced significantly by the error of ship speed data. In order to investigate the application of this method for ships in general, it is essential to collect actual data of various kinds of ship, such as Log-data, sea-trial data, specifications, self-propulsion factors, etc. Since it is confirmed that the proposed method is valid basically, authors would like to improve the method.

## References

[1] Kaizu, G., Propeller Surface Roughness and Efficiency I & II, Ship Science, Vol.35, No.11 & 12, pp. 52-61 & 61-66, 1982 (written in Japanese).

[2] Report of Performance Committee, Proceedings of 15$^{th}$ ITTC, pp 359-392, 1978.

[3] Report of Basic Investigation on Advanced Monitoring of Ship, SR233, 1998 (written in Japanese).

[4] Wan, B., Nishikawa, E. and Uchida, M., A Study of On-Board Monitoring and Analysis System of Ship Propulsion Performance – An Estimation Method of Propeller Performance with Surface Roughness Effect –, Journal of the Kansai Society of Naval Architects, Japan, No.239, pp. 55-60, 2003 (written in Japanese).

[5] Yamaguchi, H., Freeware "prblg.f", http://www.fluidlab.naoe.t.u-tokyo.ac.jp/~yama/prog/index-e.html, 1999.

[6] Wan, B., Nishikawa, E. and Uchida, The Experimental and Numerical Calculation of Propeller Performance with Surface Roughness Effect, Journal of the Kansai Society of Naval Architects, Japan, No.238, pp. 49-54, 2002.

[7] Nishikawa, E. and Liu, Q., Analysis of Actual Propulsion Performance of the Ship in Service by Examining the Voyage Data, Proceedings of International Marine Engineering Conference of CSNAME, Shanghai, 1987.

# Evaluating sea experience with an eye mark recorder in a ship handling simulator

O. Arslan[1], M. Furusho[2] & S. Kum[1]
[1]*Istanbul Technical University Maritime Faculty (ITUMF), Turkey*
[2]*Kobe University, Faculty of Maritime Sciences (KUMS), Japan*

## Abstract

This study analyses the navigator's eye movement on the navigation bridge simulator. The main objective of this study is to find the differences between the sea experience level and educational level to evaluate the navigator's sea experience; this by fixation points in the ship-handling simulator. A measurement device ("EMR-8") is used for recording eye movements. There are three kinds of examinee groups, each group has 4 examinees.

Group 1 is 2nd class, deck department students who have up to 2.5 months sea experience onboard training as a cadet. Group 2 is 4th class, deck department students who have up to 12 months. Group 3 is ocean-going masters who have different experiences as master or chief officer. The same scenario was used by each examinee. The visual field was divided into three parts inside, outside and others. Significant results, as shown below, were obtained by the comparison with differences among the groups.

In Group 1, the examinees paid less attention to sailing. They had a remarkable difference in fixation duration between the inside and the outside; their fixation duration for "other places" was much longer than the other groups, and they had very little experience in using the inside equipment. In Group 2, the examinees showed differences in capabilities as a navigation officer which could be based on their sea experience and educational program. In Group 3, the examinees were professional seafarers, so they were able to pay more attention to all kinds of navigational information such as target ships or navigational aids. The study shows that sea experience as a seafarer or a cadet could be evaluated by using the eye mark recorder utilizing the ship-handling simulator.
*Keywords: human factors, eye movements, sea experience, ship handling simulator.*

# 1 Introduction

Navigation technology has been rapidly developing in recent years. The fixing of position and the handling of ships are more easily done than before because of information technology [1,2]. This study analyses the navigator's eye movements and uses the same environmental conditions for carrying out the same simulator scenario. The main objective of this study is to find the differences between the sea experience level and educational level, and to evaluate the navigator's sea experience by viewing points when using the ship-handling simulator.

# 2 Experimental study

A measurement device "EMR-8" was used for recording the eye-movements of examinees at the Istanbul Technical University Maritime Faculty (ITUMF) Ship Handling Simulator. The examinees were divided into three groups according to their experience levels. Each group had four examinees at ITUMF [3].

Figure 1: EMR-8 Instrument [5].

Group 1 was 2nd class deck department students who had up to 2.5 months sea experience onboard training as cadets. Group 2 is 4th class, deck department students who had up to 12 months sea experience. Group 3 was ocean-going masters who had different sea time as either master or chief officer. All examinees were equipped with the EMR-8 instrument, and it was the same scenario of passing through the Istanbul Strait, Turkey. The EMR-8 had a recording unit, which could record all the areas looked at by the examinees and with eye-marks. 20,000 raw data was obtained for each examinee in 10 minutes.

Figure 1 shows how to use EMR-8 during experimental studies. The left side of the figure is the main part of EMR-8 used for calibration and synchronization with eye movements. The right part of the figure is human interface of EMR-8 which is used for recording both eye movements and looking area. The apparent screen, which records data by human interface, is on the lower side of Figure 1.

### 2.1 Analyzing method

The visual field was divided into three parts: inside, outside and others. The "inside" part had three components: instruments, indicators and engine telegraph. The "outside" part had three different components the sea condition, navigational aids around the navigable area and target ships. "Others" means all meaningless images and saccade of eye-movements. Their viewing points and durations were recorded by a continuous weaving sight line on the image picture. The raw data was tabled by using the "frame by frame method".

Table 1: Tabled by "Frame by frame" method [4].

| | nautical ins. | Indicators | eng. telegr. | nav. aids | Target | sea | other |
|---|---|---|---|---|---|---|---|
| 08:05:50 | | | | | | | |
| 08:05:52 | | | | | | | |
| 08:05:54 | | | | | | | |
| 08:05:56 | | | | | | | |
| 08:05:58 | | | | | | | |
| 08:06:00 | | | | | | | |
| 08:06:02 | | | | | | | |
| 08:06:04 | | | | | | | |

Every cell shows 1/30 per second, and coloured cells show the duration of looking period to fixation points in the experimental studies.

## 3 Results

Table 2, Figure 2 and Figure 3 show a remarkable difference in the using of nautical instruments between Group 1 and the others. Members of Group 1 used the nautical instruments less than others. There is also a big difference within Group 1 between the members use of nautical instruments. But conversely, there is more homogeneity within the other groups. Group 1 looked to "other" places more than the others.

Table 2: Percentage and duration of examinees to fixation points.

| | INSIDE PART | | | OUTSIDE PART | | | | | | |
|---|---|---|---|---|---|---|---|---|---|---|
| | nautic ins. | indicator | telegraph | nav. Aids | target | sea | other | | INSIDE | OUTSIDE |
| GROUP1-1 | 7181 | 449 | 0 | 523 | 123 | 1675 | 2102 | 12053 | 7630 | 2321 |
| | 59,58% | 3,73% | 0,00% | 4,34% | 1,02% | 13,90% | 17,44% | 100,00% | 76,68% | 23,32% |
| GROUP1-2 | 877 | 146 | 80 | 1971 | 988 | 5153 | 2440 | 11655 | 1103 | 8112 |
| | 7,52% | 1,25% | 0,69% | 16,91% | 8,48% | 44,21% | 20,94% | 100,00% | 11,97% | 88,03% |
| GROUP1-3 | 981 | 492 | 954 | 624 | 290 | 10402 | 688 | 14431 | 2427 | 11316 |
| | 6,80% | 3,41% | 6,61% | 4,32% | 2,01% | 72,08% | 4,77% | 100,00% | 17,66% | 82,34% |
| GROUP1-4 | 6281 | 648 | 354 | 654 | 355 | 1842 | 1835 | 11969,0 | 7283,00 | 2851,0 |
| | 52,48% | 5,41% | 2,96% | 5,46% | 2,97% | 15,39% | 15,33% | 100,00% | 71,87% | 28,13% |
| GROUP2-1 | 4795 | 206 | 0 | 1628 | 450 | 3892 | 298 | 11269 | 5001 | 5970 |
| | 42,55% | 1,83% | 0,00% | 14,45% | 3,99% | 34,54% | 2,64% | 100,00% | 45,58% | 54,42% |
| GROUP2-2 | 6320 | 631 | 0 | 980 | 378 | 2704 | 988 | 12001 | 6951 | 4062 |
| | 52,66% | 5,26% | 0,00% | 8,17% | 3,15% | 22,53% | 8,23% | 100,00% | 63,12% | 36,88% |
| GROUP2-3 | 6438 | 1272 | 0 | 654 | 124 | 3235 | 224 | 11947 | 7710 | 4013 |
| | 53,89% | 10,65% | 0,00% | 5,47% | 1,04% | 27,08% | 1,87% | 100,00% | 65,77% | 34,23% |
| GROUP2-4 | 7703 | 1071 | 0 | 71 | 0 | 2349 | 536 | 11730 | 8774 | 2420 |
| | 65,67% | 9,13% | 0,00% | 0,61% | 0,00% | 20,03% | 4,57% | 100,00% | 78,38% | 21,62% |
| GROUP3-1 | 4588 | 34 | 0 | 883 | 2587 | 3601 | 488 | 12181 | 4622 | 7071 |
| | 37,67% | 0,28% | 0,00% | 7,25% | 21,24% | 29,56% | 4,01% | 100,00% | 39,53% | 60,47% |
| GROUP3-2 | 4458 | 492 | 0 | 1329 | 714 | 4415 | 271 | 11679 | 4950 | 6458 |
| | 38,17% | 4,21% | 0,00% | 11,38% | 6,11% | 37,80% | 2,32% | 100,00% | 43,39% | 56,61% |
| GROUP3-3 | 6960 | 34 | 9 | 1574 | 655 | 894 | 2366 | 12492 | 7003 | 3123 |
| | 55,72% | 0,27% | 0,07% | 12,60% | 5,24% | 7,16% | 18,94% | 100,00% | 69,16% | 30,84% |
| GROUP3-4 | 4477 | 1306 | 0 | 2276 | 194 | 2778 | 1053 | 12084,0 | 5783 | 5248 |
| | 37,05% | 10,81% | 0,00% | 18,83% | 1,61% | 22,99% | 8,71% | 100,00% | 52,42% | 47,58% |
| GROUP1 | 31,59% | 3,45% | 2,56% | 7,76% | 3,62% | 36,40% | 14,62% | 100,00% | 37,66% | 62,34% |
| GROUP2 | 53,69% | 6,72% | 0,00% | 7,17% | 2,05% | 26,04% | 4,33% | 100,00% | 60,43% | 39,57% |
| GROUP3 | 42,15% | 3,89% | 0,02% | 12,52% | 8,55% | 24,38% | 8,50% | 100,00% | 46,10% | 53,90% |

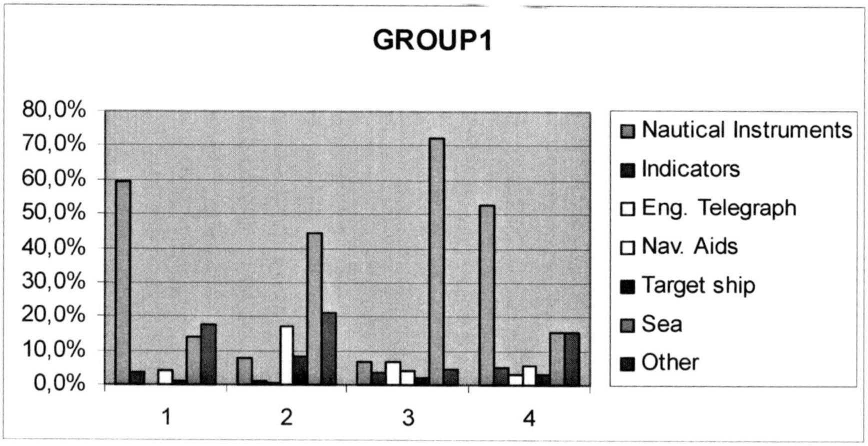


Figure 2: Percentage of Group 1 members' fixation duration of fixation points.

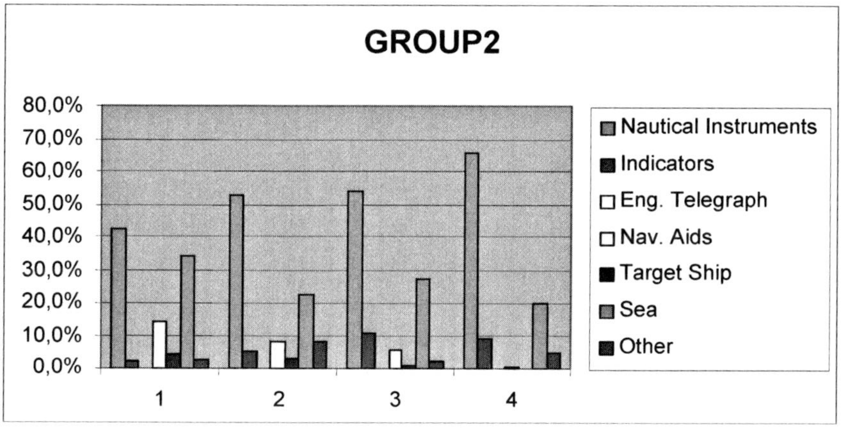


Figure 3: Percentage of Group 2 members' fixation duration of fixation points.

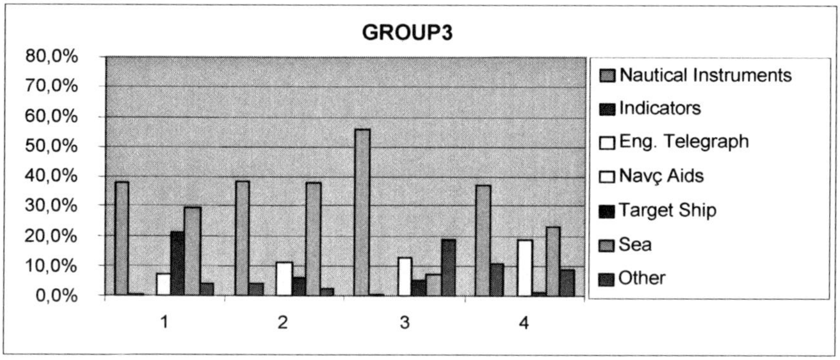


Figure 4: Percentage of Group 3 members' fixation duration of fixation points.

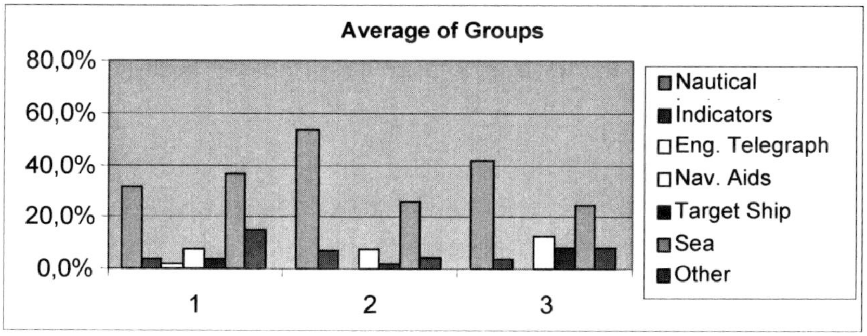


Figure 5: Percentage of group's average fixation duration of fixation points.

The fixation duration to one point in Group 2 is longer than Group 3, and Group 2's fixation duration to inside parts is longer than other groups.

The fixation duration to target ships and navigational aids in Group 3 is more than in other groups. The difference between inside and outside of fixation duration in Group 3 is less than in other groups.

## 4 Consideration

Significant results are shown in Figure 6. The authors obtained the comparisons between the groups.

As for Group 1, who were all beginners, the examinees paid less attention to sailing. They had a remarkable big difference of fixation duration between the "inside" and "outside". Their fixation duration of "other places" was also so much longer than in the other groups. Also they had little experience in using inside equipment.

As for Group 2, the examinees had intermediate characteristics as navigation officers between professionals and beginners. Their differences in capabilities as a navigation officer should be based on their sea experience and educational program. They had moderate knowledge of the use of instruments, and not enough experience, so their fixation duration to the instruments was longer than in the professional group. As for Group 3, examinees of this group were professional, so they paid more attention to all kinds of navigational information, target ships, and navigational aids and alike. Their fixation duration of instruments was the shortest of all because they had knowledge of and experience in using the instruments.

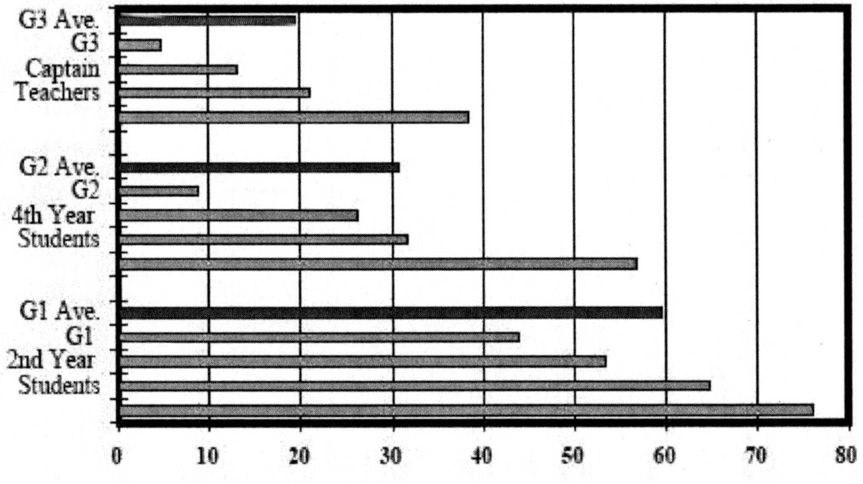


Figure 6: Percentage of examinee's fixation durations between "inside" and "outside" area.

In Figure 6, red depicts the average of the group's fixation duration between the "inside" and "outside" area. Blue depicts the difference between the duration of the inside and outside area examinee by examinee for each group. Remarkable differences can be seen between the different groups in this figure.

## 5 Conclusion

Experience and educational levels play an important role on eye mark fixation points and fixation duration. The more sea experience increases attention on the Navigation Bridge. Lower educational level and little sea experience decrease the use of nautical instruments. The more sea experience decreases the fixation duration of one fixation point. Finally, sea experience as a seafarer or a cadet obtained by actual onboard experience can be evaluated by using the eye mark recorder when using the ship-handling simulator.

## Acknowledgements

The authors gratefully acknowledge operational and technical support by Japan International Cooperation Agency (JICA).

## References

[1] Yamada. M., and Fukuda, T, An Improved Sight-Line Displacement Analyzer and Its Application to TV Program Production, SMPTE Journal P.22, Jan. 1990.
[2] Norman D. A. and Draper S. W., User Centered System Design: New Perspective on Human-Computer Interaction, Cognitive Engineering, 1986.
[3] Instruction Manual of the EMR-8.
[4] Frame by Frame Method, www2.cecomet.net.
[5] Sreenivasan. B., Stephens. R., Analysis of Substitution Test Performance Using Eye Movement and Video Data, Vol. 9, No. 3, pp. 179-182, 2002.

# Development of onboard ship manoeuvring simulators and their application to onboard training

H. Yabuki[1], T. Takemoto[2], T. Ishiguro[3] & H. Kamiirisa[4]
[1]*Tokyo University of Marine Science and Technology, Japan*
[2]*National Institute for Sea Training, Japan*
[3]*IHI Marine United Inc, Japan*
[4]*Akishima Laboratories, Mitsui Zosen Inc, Japan*

## Abstract

The authors developed two types of onboard ship manoeuvring simulators and a new onboard training method utilizing an onboard Ship Manoeuvring Simulator (SMS) that makes practical onboard training for cadets more successful and efficient. This paper describes the outline of the developed simulators and the results of an experiment conducted on a training ship that aimed at assessing the feasibility and the effectiveness of the proposed training method. Based on the results of the experiment, the authors propose an optimal combination of onboard SMS training with real training on a training ship and designed another onboard SMS to overcome the limitation of the first onboard SMS.
*Keywords: onboard ship manoeuvring simulator, onboard training, maritime education and training.*

## 1 Introduction

New maritime education and training methods that will improve the quality of onboard training are desired since the supply of able young officers is strongly requested from the maritime community in Japan. Combining classroom simulator training and onboard training was found to be effective by Murata and Kobayashi [1]. Use of an SMS makes it possible to provide training using the same scenario repeatedly and cadets can master each technical element for ship handling (elemental techniques [2]) one by one. On the other hand, onboard training offers a unique opportunity for cadets to master integrated ship-handling techniques that take into consideration the effects of such external disturbances as wind and tide, and to develop an ability to make appropriate and quick decisions in ship handling, which is indispensable for deck officers [3]. From this point of view, the authors developed two types of onboard SMS and proposed a practical onboard training method for cadets that combined simulator training with onboard SMS (onboard simulator training) and real training on a training ship (onboard training). The first onboard SMS was a compact type simulator which was installed in a lecture room of the 5,884 G.T. training ship Seiun Maru. For the effective operation of the proposed training method, it is necessary to assess the effectiveness of onboard simulator training for all elemental technique items and determine training items suitable for simulator training. The authors performed an onboard experiment using Seiun Maru to compare the outcome of onboard simulator training and that of real training. The results indicated that the training with the onboard simulator was effective. However, the real training was more effective than the simulator training for certain ship-handling skills apparently because the real equipment was not used for the compact type onboard SMS. To overcome the limitations of the compact type SMS, we designed another onboard SMS utilizing the real equipment on the training bridge of the 6,000 G.T. training ship Ginga Maru, which was launched in June, 2004.

## 2 Outline of the first onboard SMS

The first onboard SMS was developed for the purpose of supporting a practical onboard training for cadets. The original model of the onboard SMS was the compact-size SMS "IHI-SMS-EC110". The function of the onboard SMS is almost the same as that of a full-size SMS.

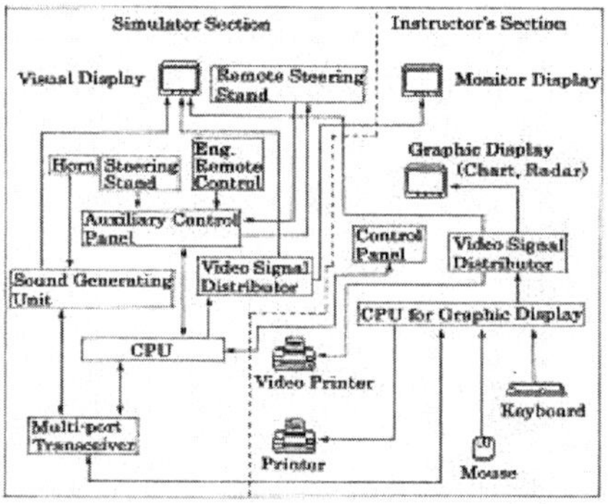


Figure 1: System configuration of the first onboard SMS.

A precise hydrodynamic mathematical model of Seiun Maru and the sea area database where the ship operates during the onboard training were installed in this simulator. The simulator is composed of the simulator section and the instructor's section shown in Figure 1. This simulator is designed so that all operation for training can be carried out by the auxiliary control panel in the simulator section. Therefore, cadets can use the simulator by themselves at the time of their demand without the assistance of instructors. The instructor's section is composed of the instructor's monitor, graphic display and control panel. The instructor's section allows users to produce a training scenario, monitor a visual display images, set environmental conditions and record the result of training. The original compact-size simulator is designed for the trainee's individual training. The developed simulator can also be used to the team training by using the portable box type remote wheel stand.

# 3 Onboard experiment

## 3.1 Method

The experiment was performed using the first onboard SMS and Seiun Maru. In the experiment, we chose anchoring practice as the training item for cadets, since it requires integration of various ship-handling techniques. This training is provided in the middle of their 1-year onboard training term. The trainees were 33 cadets of universities of mercantile marine and their previous onboard training experience was approximately 4 months. The cadets' task was to weigh anchor at one anchorage and put the ship to anchor at another pre-designated anchorage. The cadets did the task in a team that consisted of 3 cadets each of whom, in turn, played 3 roles of Captain (Capt.), First officer (1/O) and Third officer (3/O). The cadets were divided into two groups of A and B, and the group A cadets went through the simulator training first and then the real onboard training, and the opposite was the case for the group B cadets. Group A consisted of 17 teams and group B consisted of 16 teams. The procedure of the experiment was as follows:

(1) All of the cadets had 9 hours of explanatory lectures on the outline of the practice, manoeuvrability of the test ship, the procedure of anchoring, planning of ship handling and the bridge teamwork.
(2) The cadets made their ship-handling plans and the instructors (Captain or Senior Professor who has the experience of Captain) checked them and gave appropriate advice.
(3) Group A had the onboard simulator training using the same scenario as in the real practice.
(4) Group A and B had the real anchoring practice using the test ship.
(5) Group B went through the same simulator training as group A.

In the experiment, the ship-handling skills of the cadets in the real training were scored by the Captain or Senior Professor according to a checklist and the Chief Officer did the same scoring in the onboard simulator training. Each of the evaluation items was related to a small technical element of total ship-handling techniques (items of elemental technique [2]), and the instructors graded each item as "good (3 points)", "fair (2 points)" or "poor (1 point)". The detailed evaluation items on the role of Capt. are shown in Table 1. The obtained scores were converted to ability rank scores given in percentage for each elemental technique using the method proposed by Arai et al. [4].

Table 1: Details of evaluation (Capt.).

| Elemental Technique | Evaluation Item |
|---|---|
| Planning | Use of marks for ship-handling, Standard of speed control, Proper alteration of maneuvering plan according to external disturbance, Approach to anchorage, etc. |
| Positioning | Use of heading marks to measure deviation from course line, Use of beam marks to measure distance to anchorage, Estimation of external disturbance, Difference between actual anchor position and planned anchor position. |
| Maneuvering | Course setting according to ship's speed, ship's position & external disturbance, Speed control for course keeping, Speed control according to ship's position & external disturbance. |
| Communication | Helm order, Order to mates, Communication to eng. room and bow. (Timing, Clear voice, Correct term) |
| Management | Prior information to eng. room & bow (Timing of S/B eng., etc.), Actual state information to eng. room & bow (Distance to anchorage, etc.), Manner & self-possession as commanding officer, Ability that get the picture in the bridge, Attitude as commanding |

## 3.2 Results

### 3.2.1 Effects of the prior onboard simulator training on the real training

We compared the ship-handling technique rank of group A (cadets with prior onboard simulator training) with those of group B (cadets without prior onboard simulator training) for each elemental technique in the real anchoring practice. The comparison results on the role of Capt. are shown in Figure 2. The vertical axes show the mean value of ship-handling technique rank (ability rank scores [4]) of each group. In general, the ability rank scores of group A are higher than those of group B for all elemental techniques. The evaluation results indicate that prior onboard simulator training is useful for cadets to prepare for their real anchoring practice. This result is almost the same as that of classroom simulator training evaluation conducted by Kobayashi et al. [5] qualitatively. Figure 3 shows the deviation of the actual anchor positions for both groups from the pre-designated position in the real anchoring practice. The anchor positions of group A are closer to the target position than those of group B on average and the group B anchor positions are more widely scattered around the target than the group A anchor positions. This indicates that prior onboard simulator training is effective in improving the integrated ship-handling technique of the cadets. Therefore, we can conclude that prior onboard simulator training is effective to improve the ship-handling technique of cadets.

With respect to the "positioning" technique, the ability rank scores are almost the same for both groups. This may be because it was difficult for the cadets to estimate the effect of wind and tide accurately by means of bearing observation of a heading mark, and only one practice session with the onboard simulator was not enough to improve the skill. For the mastery of this kind of advanced technique, repeated practice by actual training ship seems to be effective.

The details of the evaluation results on the "manoeuvring" technique are shown in Figure 4. The ability rank scores of group A are higher than those of group B for all the evaluation items except item F. The ability rank score differences are the largest for evaluation items C and E. It seems that the cadets tried to master the techniques for adjusting her course and for controlling her speed according to the obtained position (C, E) in the prior simulator training since the instructors explained the importance of these techniques for the accurate anchoring in the briefing. On the other hand, no such large group difference is observed with respect to the technique related to adjusting her course according to the external disturbance (F). Perhaps, the reason is that it was difficult for the cadets to master this technique in the prior simulator training, since the wind that existed in the simulator scenario was not strong enough for the novice cadets to realize its effect. This technique will be improved by introducing a strong external disturbance in the simulator training scenario.

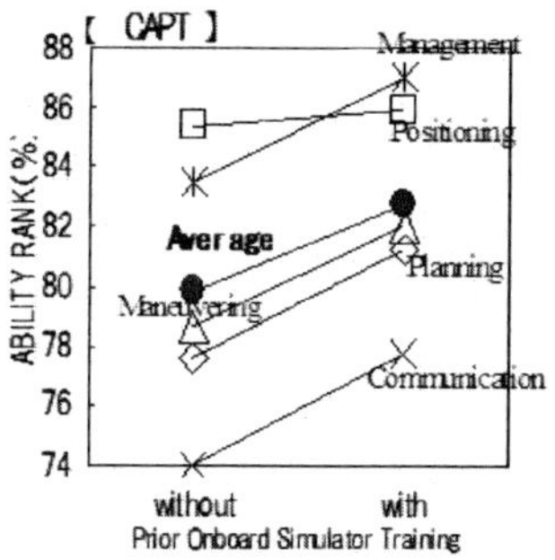


Figure 2: Evaluation result of onboard training.

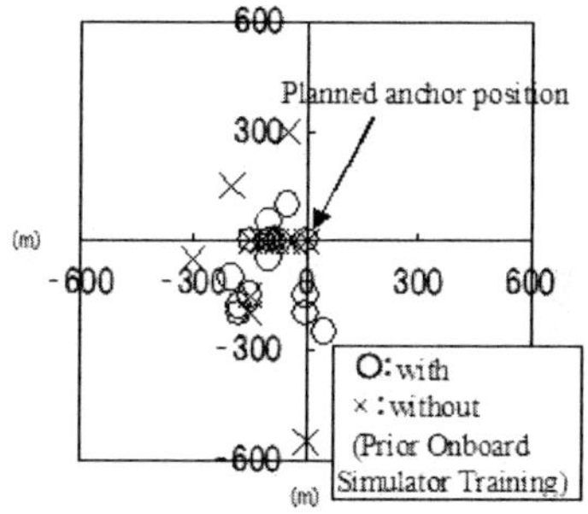


Figure 3: Comparison of anchor position.

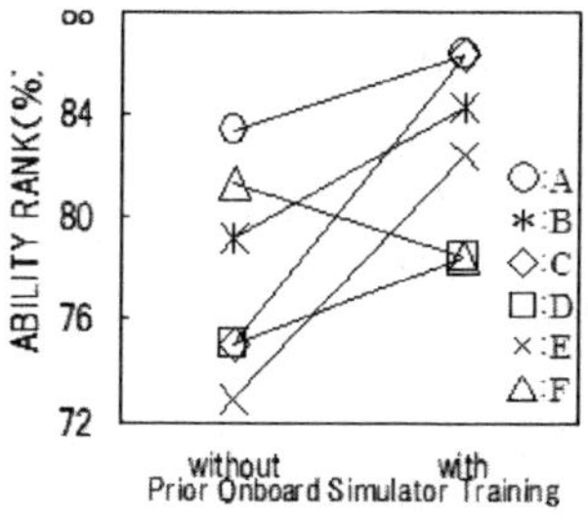


| Mark | Evaluation Item (Maneuvering) |
|---|---|
| A | Course setting according to ship's speed |
| B | Speed control for course-keeping |
| C | Course setting according to ship's position |
| D | Speed control according to external disturbance |
| E | Speed control according to ship's position |
| F | Course setting according to external disturbance |

Figure 4: Evaluation results of onboard training (manoeuvring).

Figure 5 indicates that all the items except D (self possession as a commanding officer) improved after onboard simulator training. Obviously beginners always feel stress during their actual ship handling but it is difficult to overcome this pressure in the simulator training simply because it lacks reality. This result indicates that the real onboard training is indispensable for the mastery of integrated ship-handling techniques.

### 3.2.2 Effectiveness of the real training

We made the same comparison described in 3.2.1 on the onboard simulator training to study the effectiveness of real training. Figure 6 shows the comparison results of the ability rank scores of the two groups. It can be seen from the figure that the ability rank scores of the cadets with real onboard training (group B) are higher than those of the cadets without real onboard training (group A) for all elemental techniques. The average ability rank score difference between group B and A is 14% and this figure is bigger than that of the evaluation results on the real training. Figure 7 shows the details of the evaluation results on the "manoeuvring" technique of the Capt. The ability rank scores of group B are higher than those of group A for all the evaluation items. With respect to the techniques for adjusting her course and for controlling her speed according to the measured position (C, E), the ability rank score differences between the two groups are quite large. These results are almost the same as those of the real training evaluation qualitatively. There is little difference between the two groups on the techniques for controlling her speed and for adjusting her course according to external disturbance (D, F). These results are almost the same as in the case of the real training evaluation. This is probably because these techniques can only be mastered after a considerable amount of ship handling experience. The detailed evaluation results on the "management" technique are shown in Figure 8. The ability rank scores of group B are higher than those of group A for all evaluation items and the differences between the two groups are large compared with those in the real training evaluation results shown in Figure 5.

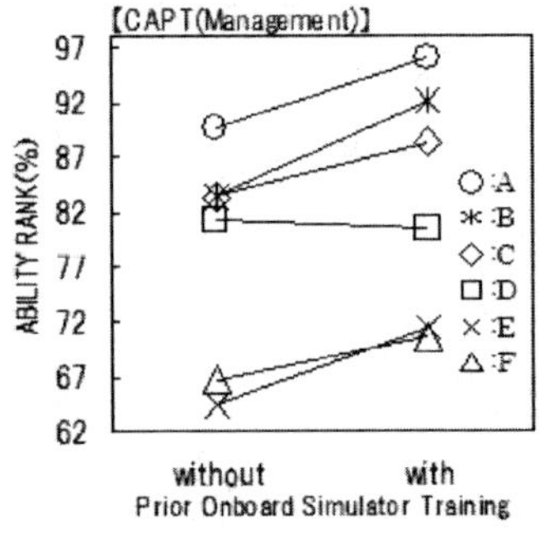


| Mark | Evaluation Item (Management) |
|---|---|
| A | Advance information to engine room & bow. (planned anchor, planned depth of water, timing of S.B engine) |
| B | Actual state information to engine room & bow. (distance to anchorage) |
| C | Clear voice order as Commanding officer |
| D | Self-possession as commanding officer |
| E | Ability that get the picture in the bridge |
| F | Attitude as Commanding officer |

Figure 5: Evaluation results of the "management" technique.

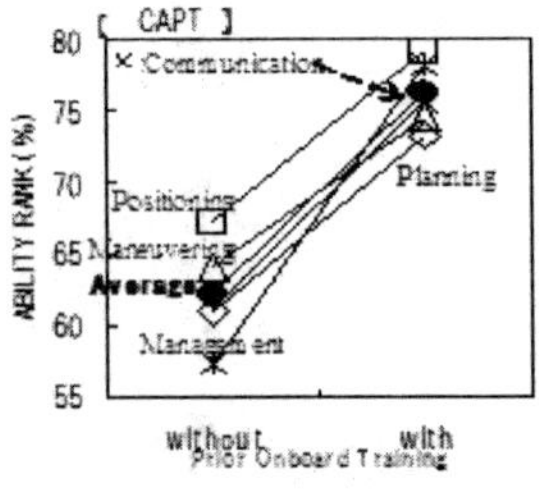


Figure 6: Evaluation results of onboard SMS training (manoeuvring).

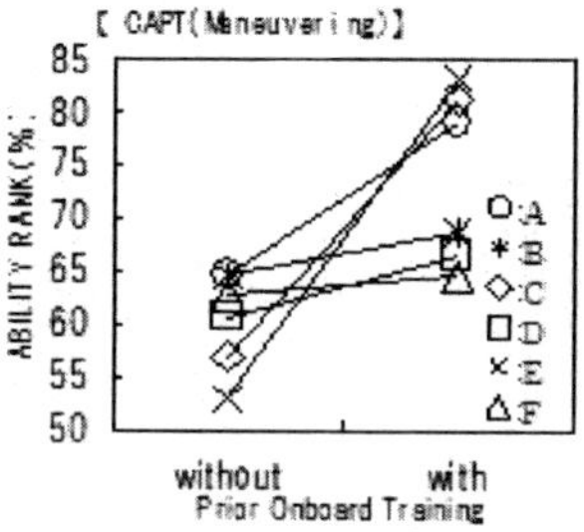


| Mark | Evaluation Item (Maneuvering) |
|---|---|
| A | Course setting according to ship's speed |
| B | Speed control for course-keeping |
| C | Course setting according to ship's position |
| D | Speed control according to external disturbance |
| E | Speed control according to ship's position |
| F | Course setting according to external disturbance |

Figure 7: Evaluation results of onboard SMS training.

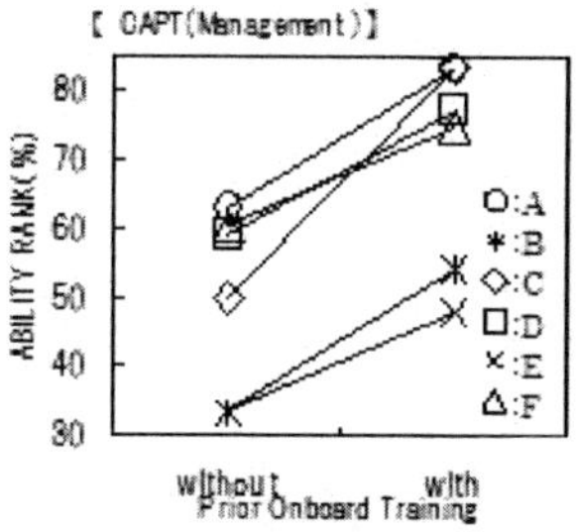


| Mark | Evaluation Item (Management) |
|---|---|
| A | Advance information to engine room & bow: (planned anchor, planned depth of water, timing of S.B engine) |
| B | Actual state information to engine room & bow: (distance to anchorage) |
| C | Clear voice order as Commanding officer |
| D | Self-possession as Commanding officer |
| E | Ability that set the picture in the bridge |
| F | Attitude as Commanding officer |

Figure 8: Evaluation results of onboard SMS training (management).

For the technique of self-possessed commanding (D), the ability rank difference between the two groups is large. The evaluation results shown in Figure 8 may indicate the advantage of real training over simulator training on the development of the ability of appropriate and brisk commanding in ship handling. We consider that the real training is more effective than the onboard simulator training for cadets to master the integrated ship-handling techniques and onboard training is indispensable to train competent seafarers.

# 4 Application of onboard simulator training to onboard training

From the results of the experiment described in the previous sections, one can conclude that prior onboard simulator training is effective for the improvement of such techniques as manoeuvring, management and bridge teamwork. Real training, on the other hand, was found to be indispensable for developing integrated ship-handling technique. The authors developed a training procedure shown in Figure 9 for the effective operation of the proposed training method that combined onboard SMS training and real training.

The merits of this training procedure are summarized below.

(1) Simulator training replicating actual training, given prior to the real ship handling training, is expected to improve cadets' ship-handling techniques.

(2) Since an SMS is installed onboard a training ship, both SMS and real ship

training sessions can be given with a little lapse of time between them, making the training scheme highly effective.

(3) The real training can be performed smoothly and efficiently because cadets can confirm their ship-handling techniques and improve them by the prior SMS training.

(4) Instructors can evaluate ship-handling techniques of cadets both in the SMS training and the real training using the same check list and can give proper advice based on the evaluation results, which will help the cadets learn their ship-handling techniques systematically.

(5) The explanation of the suitable training items for SMS training and those for real training by instructors in the briefing will assist the cadets to understand the important training items in each training session.

(6) Cadets can confirm their ship-handling plan in the SMS training prior to the real training and can revise it according to the advice of instructors.

(7) Extreme external disturbances such as wind or tide included in the prior SMS training scenario can help cadets learn to take these factors into consideration and to control the ship appropriately.

(8) Any ship-handling techniques of cadets that are not satisfactory can be focused on in further supplemental SMS training sessions.

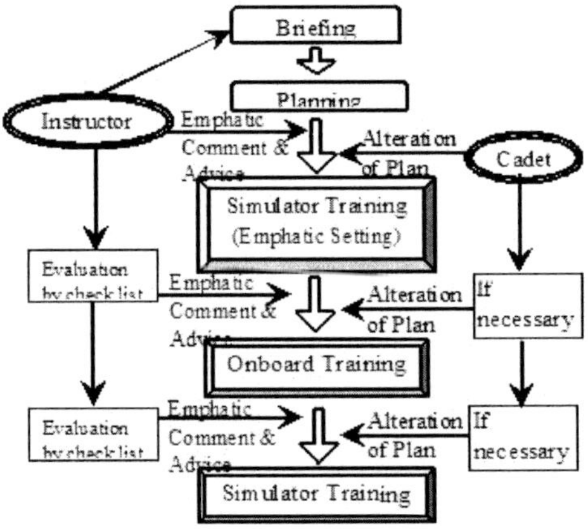


Figure 9: Proposed onboard training procedure combined with onboard SMS.

## 5 Development of the second onboard SMS

Based on the results of the experiment described in Section 3, the authors developed another onboard SMS and installed it on the training ship Ginga Maru. The function of the simulator is as good as that of a full mission SMS. The simulator was designed to utilize the real equipment on the training bridge of Ginga Maru to overcome the limitations of the first onboard SMS of Seiun Maru. The equipment installed in the training bridge of Ginga Maru, which is arranged under the navigation bridge, is almost the same as the equipment in the navigation bridge and cadets can manoeuvre the ship on the training bridge. This makes it possible to practice, using the simulator, such techniques as position fixing and nautical instrument operation, which was difficult with the compact-size SMS of Seiun Maru.

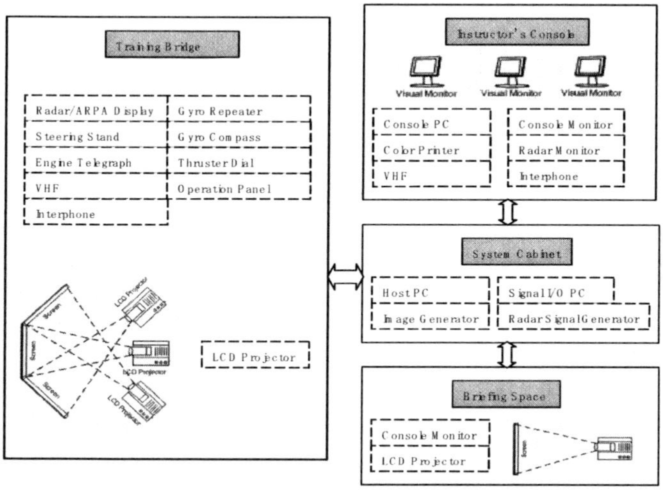


Figure 10: System configuration of the second onboard SMS.

The system configuration of the simulator is shown in Figure 10. The simulator section is installed on the training bridge. The visual system is composed of three sets of liquid crystal projectors and 85-inch wide screen and the range of vision is 135 degrees. The real equipment on the training bridge such as Radar/ARPA, Steering stand, Bearing compass, Engine telegraph and VHF telephone are used as the equipment of the simulator. The instructor's console is composed of a console PC with LCD monitor, three visual monitors, a Radar/ARPA monitor and training recording devices. A 100-inch wide liquid crystal projector, a console PC with LCD monitor and other devices are installed in the briefing space that is located in the exercise room. In addition to the simulator, a TV camera and microphone system for the simulator training evaluation are installed in the training bridge, instructor's console and briefing space. When briefing or debriefing in the exercise room, simulator screen images and radar images can be displayed on the 100-inch projector by connecting the control PC of the instructor's console with the one in the navigation exercise room.

A unique function of this simulator is the real ship-handling replay function. The manoeuvring data of Ginga Maru such as position, course, speed, rudder angle, engine motion and the target ship's AIS information can be collected using her Local Area Network (LAN) system. The simulator can replay the real ship handling of its own ship and the movement of the target ship in a training area on the screen in the exercise room based on the actual data. This function of the simulator will be effective for the evaluation of the real ship handling of the cadets and will assist them to enhance their ship-handling skills.

We are currently planning to access the effectiveness of onboard training with this new simulator, which uses the actual nautical equipment and has an additional and innovative "replay" function.

## 6 Conclusions

Results obtained in this study are summarized as follows.

(1) It is confirmed that effective training on a training ship can be achieved by combining onboard SMS training and real training.

(2) Prior onboard SMS training is helpful and effective for cadets to improve their ship-handling techniques. However, onboard training is indispensable for cadets to master the integrated ship-handling technique since simulator training is difficult to provide the "reality" that real ship handling has.

(3) In the briefing, instructors should provide the cadets with the information on the important training items in the SMS training and those in the real training. This will make onboard SMS training and real training more effective.

(4) As for the application of the proposed training procedure described in the Section 4, it is important to make a proper training scenario after selecting the suitable training items for the SMS training and those for the real training. Proposed training procedure can be applied to such practices as collision avoiding manoeuvre, route navigation and approaching manoeuvre in addition to the anchoring practice.

## References

[1] Murata, S. & Kobayashi, H., Comparative Studies between the Onboard Training and the Simulator-used Training. *Proceeding of 11th International Navigation Simulator Lecturer's Conference,* 2000.

[2] Kobayashi, H., Development of Ship Handling Technique into Elemental Techniques and Proposed of the Education/Training Method Utilizing a Ship Handling Simulator. *The Journal of Japan Institute of Navigation, Commemorative Issue of 50th Anniversary,* pp. 103-112, 1998

[3] Arai, Y. & Fujii, T., The Utilities and Possibilities on the Ship Manoeuvring Simulator Training. (Japanese) *Navigation, Japan Institute of Navigation,* No.127, pp. 28-37, 1996

[4] Arai, Y. et al., Study on the Grading of the Bridge Simulator Training for the Deck Officer. (Japanese) *Review of the Marine Technical College,* No. 40, pp.1-30, 1997

[5] Kobayashi, H. et al., Proposal for Educational and Training Curricula Using Ship Handling Simulator. (Japanese) *The Journal of Japan Institute of Navigation,* Vol. 96, pp. 119-125, 1997

# The Intelligent Tutoring System of an Engine Room Simulator

H. Sugita[1], T. Nakazawa[2], X. F. Hu[3] & T. Ishida[1]
[1]*Faculty of Maritime Sciences, Kobe University, Japan*
[2]*World Maritime University, Sweden*
[3]*Shanghai Maritime University, China*

## Abstract

This paper describes an Intelligent Tutoring System (ITS) used for the DIS-based real-time Engine Room Simulator (ERS) at the Faculty of Maritime Sciences of Kobe University. In this ERS system, some specific models of ITS can manifest almost all the behavioural features of the real systems on board ships especially those relevant to the MET (Maritime Education and Training) goals. Its evaluation models can contain the appropriate handles, to enable a knowledgeable communication with the learner about the model contents. Therefore, the ITS can provide a basis for generating articulate simulation models to successfully evaluate the students behaviours and competences. The evaluation methods are especially described in detail in the paper. The evaluation methods are divided into three types: Type A, Type B and Type C according to the different interaction relationships among evaluated objects. Type A is used mainly for a linear Node Series, Type B is used mainly for a nonlinear Node Series, and Type C is used only for malfunction simulation.
*Keywords: maritime education and training, engine room simulator, intelligent tutoring system, evaluation method.*

## 1 Introduction

The steady increase in Information Technology (IT) and computing power has in fact given marine simulators a solid position, within the area of MET, as indispensable tools. However, some studies have shown that marine simulators are only effective when proper guidance and evaluation are provided [1, 2, 3, 4]. Therefore, the Intelligent Tutoring System (ITS) and training functions are required to provide such guidance and evaluation.

Teaching trainees to act and think in a logical manner will provide them with the correct attitude to cope with unexpected problems. It has been shown that trainees who were trained in strict logical thinking performed significantly better compared to trainees who were not encouraged to solve problems logically in ERS training tasks [5]. In this paper, the training task and evaluation methods are described in detail, respectively. The training task is designed based on the Systematic Approach to Training (SAT) method. The evaluation methods are divided into 3 types: Type A, Type B and Type C according to the different interaction relationships among evaluated objects. It can avoid the human effect in evaluation, and can give a satisfactory score to realize automatic evaluation and self-training.

## 2 Training task

Simulator training can be used to provide a stimulating and challenging environment to the trainees. Providing a challenging and stimulating environment does not only involve the hardware, creating correct and challenging training scenarios is also an important factor. In this section a training method is given to create consistent and appropriate training scenarios.

### 2.1 Systematic Approach to Training

The Systematic Approach to Training method (SAT) is a well-known method for defining and implementing training programs originated from the nuclear industry [5, 6, 7, 8]. Well-trained personnel are recognized as an effective means for prevention of accidents. The SAT method expresses the view that the training and the design of training courses is a cyclic process. The training program is constantly revised during the whole life cycle of a plant. Training demands change during time and training courses have to reflect these changes.

The SAT method recognizes five sequential steps in the design of a training program:

- analysis of task and training needs;
- design of training program;
- development of training material;
- implementation of training;
- evaluation of training effectiveness.

### 2.2 ERS training task analysis

Task analysis is defined as: “A systematic examination of a task resulting in a time oriented description of tasks performed by an operator, showing the sequential and simultaneous activities”. The advantage of a task analysis is that it provides the training course designer with information about the training task in a structured manner. There are many different methods to analyze a task [5,13,14,15,16,17,18]. During a task analysis the following aspects of a particular task can be analyzed and quantified:

- what is the desired final behaviour;
- what are the important conditions under which behavior will occur;
- what are criteria for acceptable performance;
- what to train;
- how to train;
- how well to train;
- how much time to spend on training.

# 3 The final evaluation

With regards to MET, the direction in which simulator-based education and training appears to be heading these days, the time to develop appropriate strategies to evaluate trainees is long overdue.

# 4 The methodology

The steady increase in computing power has in fact given simulation a solid position within the area of educational systems. However, several studies have shown that simulations are only effective when proper training and evaluation methods are provided. In order to realize such a goal, automating tutoring and training functions require the simulator models to be articulate [9]. Two further requirements follow from this. Firstly, a specific simulation model should manifest all the behavioral features of the real system as far as those are relevant to the educational goals. Secondly, a simulation model should contain appropriate handles, by means of which these features are indexed, to enable a knowledgeable communication with the trainee about the model contents.

Automated handling of tutoring and training function in ERS training system requires the availability of articulate domain models. In this paper the qualitative models are developed to realize this purpose. The result is a highly structured subject matter model that enables the evaluation of trainee behavior by means of an adapted version of the evaluation algorithm.

More specifically, the ERS training system has to diagnose and evaluate the trainee's problem solving behavior [10]. Trainees should acquire problem-solving skills such as predicting or 'postdating' the behavior of systems using qualitative terms. Hence, the trainee's problem solving behavior consists of a set of inferences about the behavior of these systems. The way the trainee interacts with the learning environment reflects this problem solving behavior. The ERS training system therefore has to monitor this interaction and diagnose deviations, with respect to some standard, in terms of problem solving errors made by the trainee.

In this paper, the model-based evaluation method [11, 12] is applied to diagnose and evaluate the trainee behavior.

## 4.1 The model-based evaluation method

It is now becoming common in many countries to use the simulator as a testing tool for granting certificates. For the first time, government officials responsible for certifying maritime officers may now require officers to demonstrate on-the-job skills required for licensing officers using simulator testing instead of the traditional oral examination part for a particular certification. The question is "how much do we know about the effectiveness of training and evaluation on the simulator?" In this paper, the Intelligent Tutoring System (ITS) based on the model-based evaluation method and expert system is described as the supervision and evaluation system. The Conceptual Framework of ITS is shown in Figure 1.

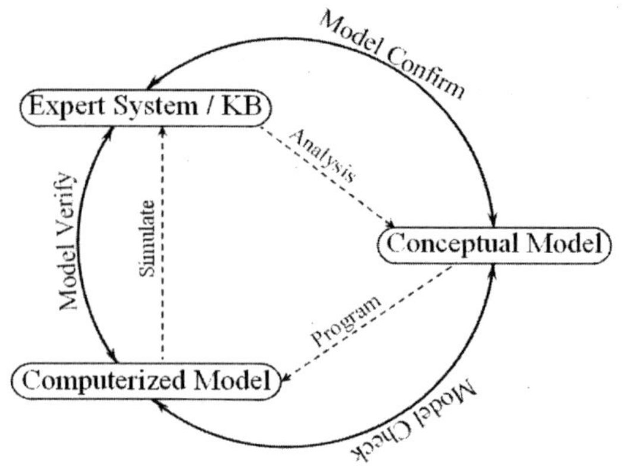


Figure 1: The conceptual framework of ITS.

ITS can monitor and control trainees' terminals on line. According to the status and items selected by Instructor workstation, one of experiment items will be produced by ITS. After that, trainee can begin operating on software and/or hardware. ITS will record the operation step by step. The records include trainee's name, commenced time, completed time, running mode, condition and contents of operating. Based on the correctness of operation, a score is given by ITS system. Result of operation can be printed through ITS station computer.

### 4.1.1 Operating data acquisition

In order to realize the functions of ITS, the operation signals from both hardware and software should be sent and collected. Figure 2 shows the mining method of

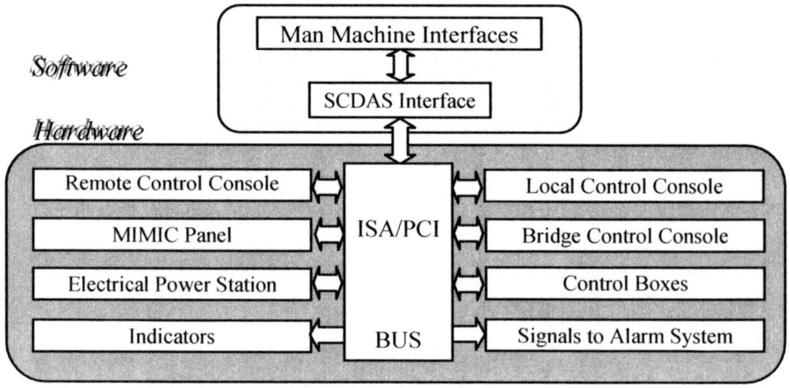


Figure 2: Data acquisition and control system.

data from hardware. All the data are then translated to the database (shown in Figure 3). It can be divided into several bases according to their different functions in ITS system (shown in Figure 4).

### 4.1.2 Some working definitions

For benefit to describing and to comprehend the evaluation methods, some working definitions are sketched out.

Definition 1: *Operation Object* is a Man-Machine Interface (MMI) or a functional area on a hardware panel/console. Operation object can be described as an aggregation $O\{W_i, S_j\}$ based on a special sequence.

Where, $W_i$ is workstation. $(i=1, 2, \dots, 8)$

$S_j$ is subsystem of workstation. $(j=1, 2, \dots, n)$

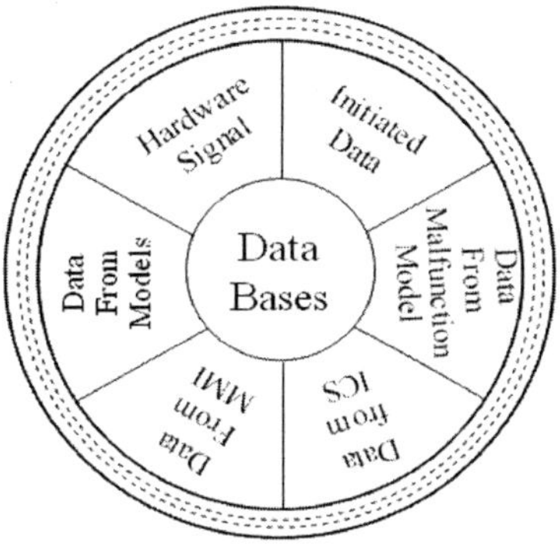


Figure 3: The data control system.

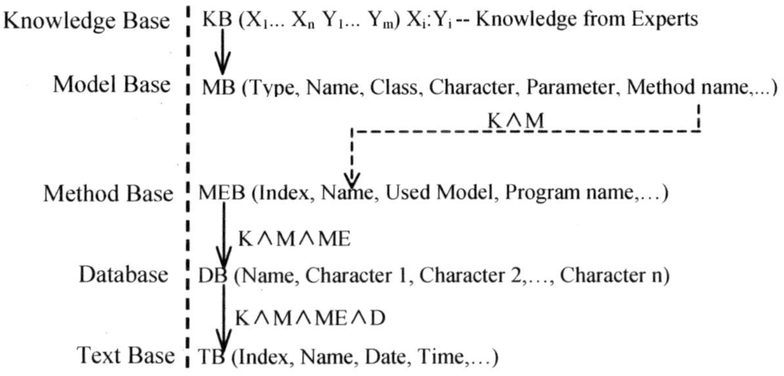


Figure 4: The relationships among databases.

Definition 2: *Evaluation Node* is an operational switch, push-button, pump, heater, cooler, valve or isolated equipment etc. in an operation object $O_i$. Evaluation Node can be described as $N\{(O_i, (H/S)_i, (A/D)_i, V_i, F_i) | i=1, 2, \dots, n\}$. Where, *H/S* is to describe the characteristic of an evaluation node. *(H=Hardware, S=Software)*; *A/D* is to describe the value characteristic of an evaluation node. *(A= analog signal, D=digital signal)*; *V* is the value of an evaluation node; *F* is the flag of an evaluation node. *(F=True* means the value has been changed; *F=False* means the value has not been changed*)*.

Definition 3: *Node Series* is a series of interacted evaluation node $N_i$, which are connected together to realize some special functions according to a functional relationship. Node Series can be marked as $S[N_1, N_n]$, $(N_i \in S[N_1, N_n])$.

### 4.1.3 Description of evaluation methods

According to the different relationships and illation and search method among Evaluation Nodes $N_i$ in a Node Series $S_i$, the evaluation methods can be divided into 3 types: Type A, Type B and Type C.

Type A is to describe the linear relationship among Evaluation Node in a Node Series $S_i$ (shown in Figure 5). $N_i$ is only influenced by $N_{i-1}$. The final score of a Node Series is described as:

$$Y = \sum_{i=1}^{n} C_i \cdot f_i \cdot w_i \tag{1}$$

where, $w_i$ is the weighting factor of $N_i$.

A matrix $M_A$ can describe the whole relationship of the Node Series $S_i$:

$$\begin{array}{cc} & \begin{array}{cccc} X & N_{i-1} & N_i & C_i \end{array} \\ M_A = & \begin{bmatrix} 0 & 0 & 0 & 0 \\ 0 & 0 & 0 & 0 \\ 1 & 0 & 1 & 1 \\ 1 & 1 & 0 & 1 \\ 1 & 1 & 1 & \alpha \end{bmatrix} \end{array} \tag{2}$$

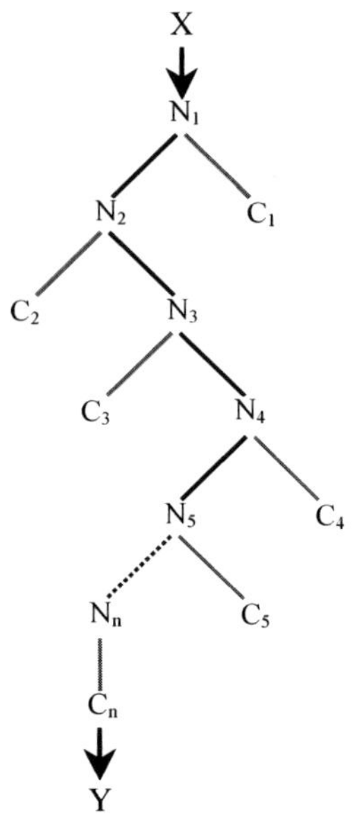


Figure 5: Illation and search tree A.

where, $\alpha = [0\ ,\ 1]$. (3)

Type B is to describe the non-linear relationship among Evaluation Node in a Node Series $S_i$ (shown in Figure 6).

$$Y = F(X) \tag{4}$$

$$f(\bullet) = A \cdot B \cdot C \cdot D \tag{5}$$

$$B = \sum_{i=1}^{n} (b_i \cdot f_{bi} \cdot w_{bi}) / \sum_{i=1}^{n} (b_i \cdot w_{bi}) \tag{6}$$

$$C = (c_1 c_2 \ldots c_n) \cdot w_c \tag{7}$$

$w: Weighting\quad Factor$

$$\begin{array}{cc} & \begin{array}{cccccc} X & A & B & C & D & Y \end{array} \\ M_B = & \begin{bmatrix} 0 & 0 & 0 & 0 & 0 & 0 \\ 1 & 0 & 0 & 0 & 0 & 0 \\ 1 & 1 & 0 & 0 & 0 & 0 \\ 1 & 1 & 1 & 0 & 0 & 0 \\ 1 & 1 & 1 & 1 & 0 & 0 \\ 1 & 1 & 1 & 1 & 1 & 1 \end{bmatrix} \end{array} \tag{8}$$

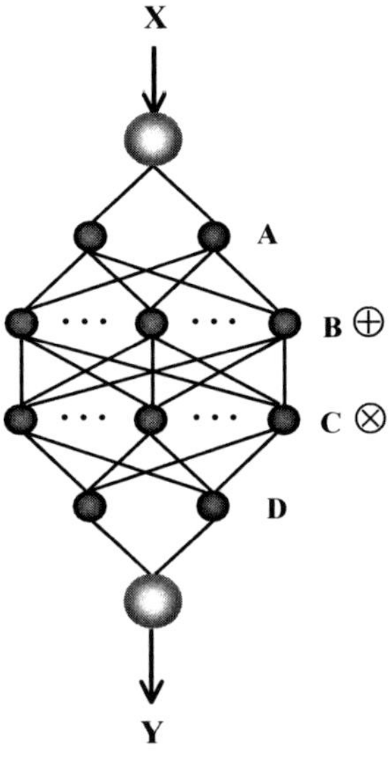


Figure 6: Illation and search tree B.

Type C is only used for malfunction simulation (shown in Figure 7). Each malfunction is provided with up to eight choices for trainee to select. Each choice has an operation description and a preset score according to the expert system. If selected operation is correct to the simulated malfunction, the preset score will be counted in; otherwise the preset score will be discounted. Some incorrect operation choices can even result in other consequent malfunctions. It means if these incorrect operations are selected, other critical malfunctions will occur afterwards and the assessing score will be very low. The following equations (9)–(13) are used for the descriptions of Type C in detail:

$$C=\{C_1 C_2 \cdots C_n\} \quad (9)$$

$$d_i = \sum_{k=1}^{8} s_{ik} \cdot f_i \quad (10)$$

$$f_i = \begin{cases} 0 & not\ selected \\ 1 & seleted \end{cases} \quad (11)$$

$$Y = \sum_{i=1}^{m} \overline{d_i} \cdot w_{di} \quad (12)$$

$w_{di}$ : *Weighting Factor*

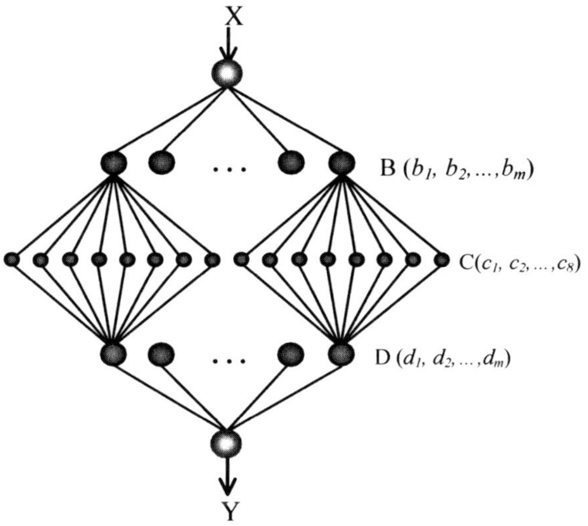


Figure 7: Illation and search tree C.

$$M_C = \begin{bmatrix} d_1 \\ d_2 \\ \cdot \\ \cdot \\ \cdot \\ d_m \end{bmatrix} = \begin{bmatrix} c_{11} & c_{12} & \cdot & \cdot & \cdot & c_{1n} \\ c_{21} & c_{22} & \cdot & \cdot & \cdot & c_{2n} \\ \cdot & \cdot & \cdot & \cdot & \cdot & \cdot \\ \cdot & \cdot & \cdot & \cdot & \cdot & \cdot \\ \cdot & \cdot & \cdot & \cdot & \cdot & \cdot \\ c_{m1} & c_{m1} & \cdot & \cdot & \cdot & c_{mn} \end{bmatrix} \quad (13)$$

Based on three kinds of aforementioned evaluation methods, the final score of training operation can be given according to the flowchart of Fig. 8. A fuzzy assessment combined with an expert system, refinement and explanation strategies is affiliated to evaluation module in order to get a convincing result.

#### 4.1.4 The applications of evaluation method in MET

In this DIS-based real-time ERS at the Faculty of Maritime Sciences of Kobe University, there are too many simulated machinery models and MMI. Here, only an example of the application in MET training is described. In this exampled MMI (shown in Figure 9), there are 3 Node Series: $S_1[N_1, N_{16}]$ for HTFW system, $S_2$ $[N_1, N_{12}]$ for LTFW system and $S_3[N_1, N_{13}]$ for seawater cooling system. The main information of this exampled MMI is listed in Table 1.

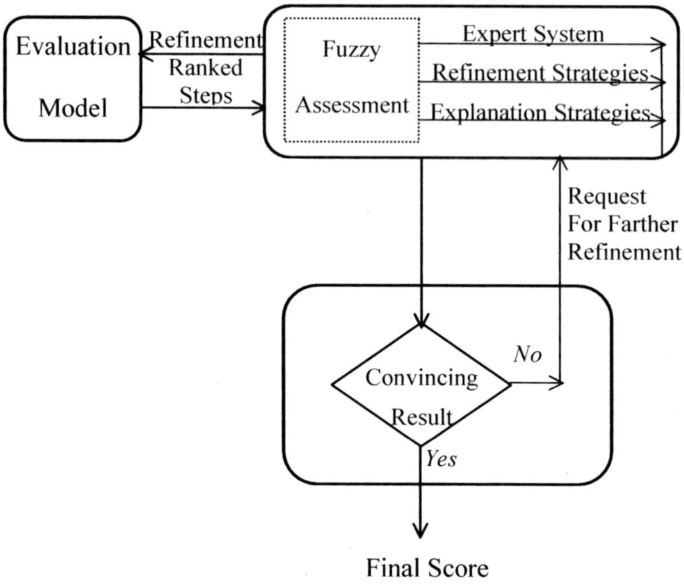


Figure 8: Final score analysis flowchart.

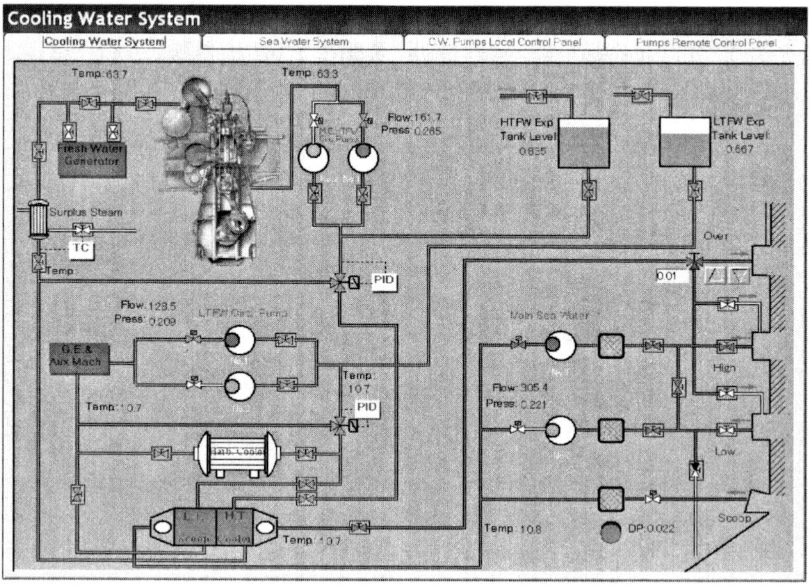


Figure 9: A MMI of cooling water system.

Table 1: Main information of the exampled MMI.

<table>
<tr><th>Workstation</th><th>Subsystem</th><th>Node Series</th><th>Node Number</th><th colspan="2">Evaluation Method</th></tr>
<tr><td rowspan="4">AM01</td><td rowspan="4">AM01002</td><td>1</td><td>16</td><td>A</td><td rowspan="2">B</td></tr>
<tr><td rowspan="2">3</td><td rowspan="2">13</td><td rowspan="2">A</td></tr>
<tr><td rowspan="2">B</td></tr>
<tr><td>2</td><td>12</td><td>A</td></tr>
</table>

In each Node Series, Type A is used for evaluation. On the other hand, Type B is used for the interaction influences between $S_1$ and $S_3$, $S_2$ and $S_3$. In the fact, $S_1$ is also influenced by Main Engine system (in ME workstation), AM01004 subsystem (Fresh Water Generator subsystem), AM02003 subsystem (Preheating System in AM02 workstation) and AM01015 subsystem (HTFW PID controller system). Consequently, the different Node Series can be collected according to the logical relationships with Type A, Type B or Type C.

## 5 Conclusions

Along with the development tendency of intelligent ships, the requirements to marine engineers are also rising. Consequently, a DIS-based real-time ERS is developed to suit for those development tendencies at the Faculty of Maritime Sciences of Kobe University. It can realize the opening structures and compatibility, and provide a realistic environment for trainees in catching the engine room technology.

On the other hand, the evaluation methods of the DIS-based real-time ERS are also described in detail. The evaluation methods are divided into 3 types: Type A, Type B and Type C according to the different interaction relationships among evaluated objects. The application of evaluation methods in DIS-based real-time ERS is exemplified. It can avoid the human effect in evaluation, and can give a satisfactory score to realize automatic evaluation and self-training.

## References


[1] Sebzalli Y.M., Li R.F., Chen F.Z., Wang X.Z., Knowledge discovery from process operational data for assessment and monitoring of operator's performance, *Computers and Chemical Engineering*, Vol.24, pp. 409-414, 2000.

[2] Hulst, A. van der, Cognitive tools, *Ph.D. Thesis*, University of Amsterdam, 1996.

[3] Kamsteeg P., Teaching problem solving by computer, *Ph.D. Thesis*, University of Amsterdam, 1994.

[4] Twidale, M.B. Coping with the variety of student actions in simulations, *Proc. of EARLI Conference*, Aixen Provence, 1993.

[5] Kuilenburg, R.F. van, Stapersma, D., Task Analysis of on board duties, a way to a better simulator? *Proc. of the 5th International Conference on Engine Room Simulators*, Singapore, pp. 245–261, 2001.

[6] Persensky, J.J., Development of a training regulation for nuclear power plant personnel, *Proc. of the 1st Mid-Central Ergonomics/Human-Factors Conference*, Cincinnati, Ohio, pp. 361–366, 1984.

[7] Whan, G.A., Long, R.L., Nuclear power manpower and training requirements, *Applied Ergonomics*, Vol.16(4), pp. 306-315, 1985.

[8] Hanauer, S.H.: The human factor in nuclear power plant safety: Progress since three mile island, *Progress in Nuclear Energy*, Vol.10(3), pp. 299-347, 1982.

[9] Rodríguez, G., Merino, P., Gallardo, M., An extensión of the ns simulator for active network research, *Computer Communications*, Vol.25, pp. 189-197, 2002.

[10] Russell P. A., The Use of Simulators to Train and Access Distance Learning Students, *Proc. of the 5th International Conference on Engine Room Simulators*, Singapore, pp. 306-313, 2001.

[11] Hamscher, W.C., Console, L., de Kleer, J. (eds), Readings in Model-Based Diagnosis, Morgan Kaufman*n*, San Mateo, CA, 1992.

[12] de Koning, K. Bredeweg, B. Breuker, J., Wielinga, B. Model-based reasoning about learner behaviour, *Artificial Intelligence,* Vol.117, pp. 173–229, 2000.

[13] Takahashi, M., Nakanishi, T. Miyoshi, I., Fujikura, T.: An evaluation of the road traffic system simulator PIMTRACS, *Mathematics and Computers in Simulation*, Vol.59, pp. 45-56, 2002.

[14] Naedele M., An approach to modeling and evaluation of functional and timing specifications of real-time systems, *The Journal of Systems and Software*, Vol.57, pp. 155-174, 2001.

[15] Kemeny A., Panerai, F., Evaluating perception in driving simulation experiments, *TRENDS in Cognitive Sciences*, Vol.7(1), 2003.

[16] Schaelicke, L.: Evaluating the impact of the simulation environment on experimentation results, *Performance Evaluation*, 2005.

[17] Houston, D.X., et al. Behavioral Characterization: finding and using the influential factors in software process simulation models, *The Journal of System and Software*, Vol.59, pp. 259-270, 2001.

[18] Spector, J.M. et al.: Models and simulations for learning in complex domains: using causal loop diagrams for assessment and evaluation, *Computers in Human Behavior*, Vol.17, pp. 517–545, 2001.

# Reducing intercultural communication barriers between seafarers with different cultural backgrounds

Y. Q. Wang[1,2] & P. Gu[2]
[1]*Foreign Languages College, Dalian Maritime University, China*
[2]*School of International and Community Studies,*
*Royal Melbourne Institute of Technology, Australia*

## Abstract

The safe operation of vessels depends on effective and efficient maritime communication, which requires seafarers to communicate linguistically, cross-culturally, and interpersonally. This study investigated cross-cultural communication barriers and factors involved in maritime communication. Chinese and foreign seafarers, pilots, shore staffs, "seafarer" students and maritime educators were invited to participate in the study. Both quantitative and qualitative research approaches were used. The results showed that linguistic competence, cross-cultural competence, interpersonal relationship competence, and psychological quality, were all indispensable and worked together to contribute to the success of maritime communication. These findings can shed light on maritime education and training. In order to make seafarers cross-culturally more competent, the cultural aspects should be incorporated into the maritime English teaching curriculum.
*Keywords: cross-cultural communication, communication barriers, cross-cultural competence, interpersonal relationship, maritime communication.*

## 1 Introduction

Maritime communication competence includes linguistic competence and cross-cultural competence. However, in maritime English teaching, the cross-cultural aspects are not given adequate attention. Usually it is the language per se that is taught, while the cultural aspects of communication are seldom touched upon. The present English teaching curriculum for non-native speakers is inadequate to meet the needs of the globalized shipping industry. The Maritime English teaching process should be optimized to make students linguistically and cross-culturally more competent. This paper focuses particularly on cultural barriers and factors involved in maritime communication that could inform teaching practices.

## 2 Theoretical background

### 2.1 Cross-cultural communication and cross-cultural barriers in the maritime context

Kramsch [1] states that cross-cultural communication refers to the meeting of two cultures or two languages across the political boundaries of nation. Any interaction between people with different cultural identities is cross-cultural communication. Communicative competence is seen in terms of cross-cultural understanding, intercultural and critical communicative competence [2]. DeVito [3] maintains that nonverbal messages and their meaning, such as the appropriate use of time and space, touch, eye contact, eye avoidance, facial expressions, body language, body distance, paralanguage and silence, etc. all contribute to successful communication.

With their varied cultural backgrounds, "ships' crews have never been so nationally, culturally, or linguistically diverse" [4]. Although in maritime communication, to a large extent, technical terms are used, it is cross-cultural communication in the maritime context and very often involves at least two cultures. In previous studies on maritime communication, the focus was mostly on the training of linguistic competence and the importance of English [5]. Attention was paid to the formation of cross-cultural competence [6], cultural differences [7], and multilingual crews [4]. However, few studies have been conducted on cross-cultural communication barriers and cultural factors.

According to Jandt [8], cross-cultural communication barriers involve anxiety, assuming similarity instead of difference, ethnocentrism, stereotypes and prejudice, nonverbal misinterpretations and language. In the maritime context, communication barriers may lead to disastrous consequences.

### 2.2 Teaching of target language and target culture

Language and culture are two aspects of an entity and are interdependent. As "second language learning is often second culture learning" [9], the cultural aspects must not be neglected in teaching. Since the goal of language teaching is to help language learners communicate accurately and appropriately in the target language, both linguistic forms and the context in which communication takes place should be taught. In maritime education, besides teaching the language itself, language teachers should also acquaint students with the target culture. This will help to reduce cross-cultural communication barriers, and make them communicate competently both linguistically and cross-culturally.

# 3 Current study

## 3.1 Methodology

### 3.1.1 Research design

The questionnaire designed for the current study covered participants' personal information, and surveyed cross-cultural barriers and factors involved in maritime communication, and suggestions for maritime education. The aim was to address the following three research questions:

1. What cross-cultural communication barriers exist in maritime communication?
2. What cultural factors are involved in maritime communication?
3. What is their significance for maritime English curriculum development?

The questionnaire had 18 multiple-choice statements, eleven of which had a choice for open-ended answers in case some factors had been left out. Four statements were on cross-cultural communication barriers and the occurrence of misunderstanding and conflicts caused by the barriers. Five statements were on participants' views on cultural factors. There were three questions for narrative answers:

1. In your communication with seafarers from other countries, what kind of barriers have you encountered?
2. As far as communication is concerned, what do you suggest should be included in the curriculum for pre-service training for seafarers apart from language?
3. What do you think could be done to improve communication at sea apart from English language teaching to marine navigation and engineering students?

These questions aimed to obtain from experienced seafarers suggestions on maritime education and training. There were two versions of the questionnaire, one in English and the other in Chinese. The statements and questions for both versions were identical.

### 3.1.2 Methods

The survey was conducted in China and Australia from November 2004 to March 2005. Sampling was targeted at seafarers with experience of being multi-national crewmembers, and staff interacting with foreign ships' crews. Electronic and hard copies of the questionnaire were distributed to those available, and responses were received in the same way. In total 112 responses were received.

For the narrative answers, five categories of barriers to communication were determined. These were labelled as language barriers, cultural barriers, psychological barriers, personality and interpersonal relationships. The labelled categories of qualitative data were added to SPSS database as variables. Each mention in the narrative of an item from a particular category was labelled as stated. Both the quantitative and qualitative data were analysed using SPSS 12.0.1 for windows to obtain frequency distributions. The open-ended responses were absent from the database as relatively few specified responses were obtained. They were included in the findings of the research paper.

## 3.2 Participants

In total 112 people participated in the study. More than half were seafarers, most of whom were ships' officers. The others were pilots, shore staffs, maritime educators, teachers at Dalian Maritime University and Australian Maritime College (AMC), who were also ships' officers, and "seafarer" students registered at AMC for the advanced diploma of ships' Masters. The shore staffs were mostly Chinese marine surveyors. A large proportion of participants (63.4%) had been a multinational crewmember. The participants were from nine nations, mostly from China and Australia. More than half (56.3%) had more than five years' at-sea service and 58.9% of them been in higher education.

## 3.3 Findings

### 3.3.1 Cultural barriers in the maritime context

The results of the study indicated that cross-cultural communication barriers do exist in maritime communication, and that they lead to communication failure. As Table 1 shows, the majority of respondents believed that language barriers occurred either most frequently, frequently or sometimes. This indicates that language barriers constitute the biggest obstacle in maritime communication. With regard to cultural barriers only 4.5% thought these occurred most frequently, while a large percentage believed they occurred either frequently or sometimes. Personality also plays its part in communication, as 6.3% thought personality problems arose most frequently, 16.1% thought it arose frequently and 35.7% thought it arose sometimes. Interpersonal relations problems showed similar frequencies to personality, although less saw it as most frequent and more saw it as rare. Opinions differed greatly as to psychological barriers, as 8.9% thought it frequently caused communication failure and 25% thought this happened sometimes, while 41.1% thought this rarely happened. A relatively small proportion (11.6%) believed other factors like age differences, cultural differences and unclear speech resulted in communication failure.

Table 1: Barriers causing communication failure.

| | NS | MF | F | S | R | N | T (%) |
|---|---|---|---|---|---|---|---|
| Language barriers | 6.3 | 26.8 | 33.0 | 23.2 | 10.7 | | 100 |
| Culture barriers | 14.3 | 4.5 | 26.8 | 33.0 | 18.8 | 2.7 | 100 |
| Psychological barriers | 19.6 | 2.7 | 8.9 | 25.0 | 41.1 | 2.7 | 100 |
| Personality | 17.0 | 6.3 | 16.1 | 35.7 | 18.8 | 6.3 | 100 |
| Interpersonal relations | 19.6 | .9 | 17.9 | 33.0 | 25.9 | 2.7 | 100 |
| Other factors | 68.8 | .9 | 2.7 | 8.0 | 7.1 | 12.5 | 100 |

NS = Not Stated MF = Most Frequently F = Frequently S = Sometimes R = Rarely N = Never T = Total.

These communication barriers can lead to the cross-cultural conflicts and misunderstandings which occur at work, when exchanging ideas, in both everyday life and during emergencies. Cultural barriers leading to misunderstanding include not knowing other nations' customs and habits, ways of thinking, ways of expressing ideas, rules of behaviour, social values and body language. Speed of speaking English, cultural differences in showing agreement, loss of face concern, not understanding crewmembers' cultural, historical and social background cause misunderstanding as well.

A high percentage (58%) of the participants responded to the question: What kind of communication barriers have you encountered in your communication with seafarers from other countries? The vast majority (91%) reported having had language barriers, 23% cultural barriers, and 9.5% other barriers. As to cultural barriers, the most frequently mentioned were lack of knowledge of social customs of other nations, cultural differences and cultural preferences, disrespect of officers for ratings, reluctance to admit incomprehension of a message, which caused great difficulty in radio communication. Next was lack of consideration for the other communicator such as speaking fast and using difficult words. Misunderstanding of body language was also a barrier causing conflicts.

In conclusion, the findings indicate that in maritime communication, apart from language barriers, cultural barriers constitute the biggest obstacle. They result in distrust, conflicts, misunderstanding and even communication failures. In addition, great differences in opinion existed between Australian seafarers and pilots and Chinese seafarers. The former were more concerned about cultural barriers while the latter were more concerned about language barriers. The cause would be worth studying in the future.

### 3.3.2 Cultural factors involved in maritime communication

When asked about their opinions on important cultural factors in maritime communication, an overwhelming majority of the respondents agreed that verbal communication was important (see Table 2). More than half agreed that cultural knowledge, appropriate ways of using English and nonverbal communication were important. Only 3.6% believed that factors like use of hand signals were important.

Table 2: Opinions on important factors in maritime communication.

| | NS | SA | A | U | D | SD | T (%) |
|---|---|---|---|---|---|---|---|
| Verbal communication | 1.8 | 53.6 | 42.0 | 2.7 | | | 100 |
| Nonverbal communication such as facial expressions, body language and gestures, etc | 12.5 | 21.4 | 36.6 | 22.3 | 5.4 | 1.8 | 100 |
| Knowledge of each other's customs, habits, social values, ways of thinking, etc. | 11.6 | 11.6 | 44.6 | 29.5 | 1.8 | .9 | 100 |
| Appropriate ways of using English | 13.4 | 15.2 | 42.9 | 22.3 | 5.4 | .9 | 100 |
| Others | 83.9 | 3.6 | | 3.6 | 1.8 | 7.1 | 100 |

NS= Not Stated SA = Strongly Agree A = Agree U = Uncertain D = Disagree SD = Strongly Disagree T = Total.

Table 3 shows respondents' opinions on necessary cultural knowledge. Most respondents agreed that knowledge of other nations' rules of behaviour, ways of thinking, religions, cuisine culture and eating habits were necessary for multinational crewmembers to live and work harmoniously. Accepting other people's cultures, having empathy and sanitary practice were also necessary. Knowledge of other nations' native languages and dressing habits were regarded as less important.

Table 3: Opinions on cultural knowledge.

| | NS | SA | A | U | D | SD | T (%) |
|---|---|---|---|---|---|---|---|
| Some of their native language | 9.8 | 18.8 | 30.4 | 16.1 | 18.8 | 6.3 | 100 |
| Their religion | 9.8 | 17.0 | 47.3 | 20.5 | 5.4 | | 100 |
| Their ways of thinking | 8.9 | 17.9 | 51.8 | 18.8 | 2.7 | | 100 |
| Their dressing habits | 12.5 | 8.0 | 30.4 | 24.1 | 15.2 | 9.8 | 100 |
| Their cuisine culture and eating habits | 11.6 | 11.6 | 50.0 | 20.5 | 4.5 | 1.8 | 100 |
| Their rules of behaviour | 8.0 | 26.8 | 53.6 | 10.7 | .9 | | 100 |
| Others | 70.5 | 5.4 | 2.7 | 10.7 | 1.8 | 8.9 | 100 |

NS= Not Stated SA = Strongly Agree A = Agree U = Uncertain D = Disagree SD = Strongly Disagree T = Total.

Table 4 gives respondents' opinions on attitudes in communication. Most of them believed that for multinational crewmembers to work and live harmoniously, mutual respect for each other's religions, customs and opinions, and appreciation for each other's work achievements were important. They also believed that multinational crewmembers must mind their wording and be tactful when pointing out a mistake at work.

Table 4: Opinions on attitudes in maritime communication.

| | NS | SA | A | U | D | SD | T (%) |
|---|---|---|---|---|---|---|---|
| respect each other's religion | 7.1 | 49.1 | 40.2 | 3.6 | | | 100 |
| respect each other's opinions | 8.0 | 33.9 | 48.2 | 8.9 | .9 | | 100 |
| respect each other's customs | 10.7 | 42.0 | 41.1 | 5.4 | .9 | 10.7 | 100 |
| appreciate each other's work achievements | 10.7 | 29.5 | 46.4 | 13.4 | 10.7 | 29.5 | 100 |
| mind their wording and be tactful when pointing out a mistake at work | 11.6 | 31.3 | 46.4 | 8.0 | 2.7 | | 100 |
| others | 67.9 | 5.4 | 6.3 | 9.8 | .9 | 9.8 | 100 |

NS= Not Stated SA = Strongly Agree A = Agree U = Uncertain D = Disagree SD = Strongly Disagree T = Total.

Most respondents considered it important for seafarers with different cultural backgrounds to have cultural awareness and knowledge of cross-cultural relations. In conclusion, cultural knowledge of other nations, understanding of body language, cultural awareness, knowledge of cross-cultural relations, right attitudes toward other cultures and peoples are all important factors involved in maritime communication, and need attention.

### 3.3.3 Participants' suggestions

For seafarers' pre-service training and maritime education, the participants offered valuable suggestions. It was suggested that students and seafarers have cross-cultural competence, including cultural adaptability, patience and tolerance, good manners and social etiquette, sincerity and affinity, respect and mutual understanding, and the ability to analyse and handle interpersonal relationship. It was also suggested that the following aspects be introduced: cultural differences, world religions, international tension, conflict resolution, nonverbal communication such as standard hand signals for port use, understanding body language and their different use in different cultures, different communication modes, and general understanding of officer/rating relationships in different cultures. It was also recommended that attention be paid to cultural differences when forming multinational crews. Cultural differences between multinational crewmembers should not be too great. Within crewmembers, there should not be a dominant nationality, in order to avoid clashes. In addition, it must be noted that Chinese marine surveyors all suggested offering psychological training to students, especially training them to be open-minded and confident.

### 3.4 Limitations of the study

The study had its limitations. Due to time constraints and distance from the possible participants, no pilot survey was carried out. The survey took place only in China and Australia, so the opinions received did not include those from other parts of the world. Additionally, the scope of the respondents' ethnic backgrounds was very limited. If the research had been conducted otherwise, by observing real at-sea communication, or by interviews, more data might have been obtained. Further study is therefore needed to follow up this research.

## 4 Recommendations

In accordance with the research findings, in maritime English teaching equal importance should be attached to different aspects of maritime communication. More attention should be given to cultural aspects. To make students and seafarers cross-culturally more competent and to reduce cross-cultural communication barriers, the research suggests that maritime education and training should include culture teaching and training in the curriculum. Such courses as cross-cultural communication, interpersonal relationship, and cross-cultural conflict resolution should be offered to students. Students should have cultural training and psychological training to make them cross-culturally more competent, psychologically stronger and more adaptable to different cultures. In addition, auxiliary means of communication should be employed to assist in communication. Standard sign language for maritime communication should be framed, decreed and enforced by the International Maritime Organization.

## Acknowledgements

We would like to thank Mr Michael Julian, who helped distribute the questionnaire to harbours in Australia, which contributed greatly to the study and Mr Ulf Schriever for inviting colleagues and students at the Australian Maritime College to participate in the study. The assistance of our colleagues and alumni in China is also appreciated. Our final thanks go to Prof. Don Webb at the Royal Melbourne Institute of Technology, Australia, who offered suggestions to improve the paper.

## References

[1] Kramsch, C. Language and culture. Oxford University Press: Oxford, pp. 81, 1998.

[2] Crozet, C. & Liddicoat, A. J. Teaching Culture as an Integrated Part of Language Teaching: An Introduction. *Teaching Languages, Teaching Culture*, Series Number 14, ANU Printing Services: Canberra, pp. 2-3, 1997.

[3] DeVito, J. A. Interpersonal Communication. Addison Wesley Longman Inc: United States, pp. 226-246, 1998.

[4] Sampson, H & Zhao, M. Multilingual crews: Communication and the Operation of Ships. *World Englishes*, Vol.22, No.1, pp. 31-43, 2003.

[5] Schriever, U. Communication at Sea: A Maritime Education Perspective: A dissertation submitted in partial fulfilment of the requirements for the degree of Master of Education, Faculty of Education, University of Tasmania, Australia, 2000.

[6] Yakushechkina, Y. Maritime English Training for Non-native Speaking Mariners. http://bell.mma.edu/~iamu2002/Papers/YakushechkinaPaper.doc.

[7] Winbow, A. The Importance of Effective Communication. Paper presented at International Seminar on Maritime English, Istanbul, Turkey, 2002.

[8] Jandt, F. E. Intercultural Communication. Sage Publications Inc: California, pp.51, 2001.

[9] Brown, H. D. Learning a Second Culture, *Culture Bound, ed. J.M.Valdes*, Cambridge University Press: Cambridge, pp.33, 1996.

# Multicultural crews and the culture of globalization

G. Benton
*The California Maritime Academy, USA*

## Abstract

Economic and geo-political forces have created the conditions through which the maritime industry has assumed its current profoundly internationalist character. Therefore, much work has been done to address the problems that arise from multilingual and multiethnic crew compositions, primarily in regards to communication and the emergent significance of Maritime English as a field of study. Less emphasis, however, has been given to "cultural literacy" and the importance of understanding culturally-motivated interpersonal dynamics as they may impinge upon shipboard operations. Potential conflicts that may surface because of multicultural crews extend beyond issues of safety due to communication barriers, to issues of maritime security, cohesion among crew members, damage to morale, and perceptions of leadership support. This paper seeks to identify problems that may arise, and to suggest what can be done from the vantage point of the maritime university. It could be argued that a solution cannot arise from a simplistic mandate to "tolerate" other customs and cultural practices, but rather to embed knowledge of cultural difference in the maritime classroom, thus making the study of the cultures of globalization a core component of the maritime curriculum. Of the many obstacles facing the 21st-century mariner, among them will be the need to manage cultural differences between crew members. The educated mariner will need to be able to understand the similarities and differences among people and to develop the capacities to solve problems. This could be accomplished through the implementation of a general education program that emphasizes critical thinking skills and knowledge about diversity and trans-cultural interactions. Finally, the question of globalization and cultural difference is not only a concern of the maritime community. In a world engaged with global affairs in regards to trade, national security, the environment, health, and justice, issues of multiculturalism impact many aspects of many trans-national operations. This paper will conclude with the suggestion that it is possible to turn the object of inquiry inside out. Through an analysis of the way the maritime industry deals (both successfully and unsuccessfully) with such issues, the study of shipboard life might prove useful to social scientists and scholars of globalization.
*Keywords: culture, multiculturalism, globalization, maritime education, curriculum reform.*

# 1 Introduction

Economic and geo-political forces have, for some time now, created the conditions through which the maritime industry has assumed its current profoundly internationalist character. As noted by Trenker and Cole, "over the past 25 years or so, 80% of the world's merchant ships have become multilingual and multiethnic in crew composition" [1]. Furthermore, according to Badawi and Halawa "one in ten ships operates with crews composed of five or more nationalities" [2]. Much excellent work has been done to address the problems that arise from such heterogeneity, primarily in regards to communication and the emergent significance of Maritime English as a field of study. However, less emphasis has been given to "cultural literacy" and the importance of understanding culturally-motivated interpersonal dynamics, as they may impinge upon shipboard operations.

The text of the STCW Resolution 22 of 1978 is taken as a starting point. This calls for an emphasis on "the importance to safety of good human relationships between seafarers on board." Certainly safety is the foundational concern of all maritime operations. What is more ambiguous in the resolution, however, is what exactly constitutes "good human relationships". How are these fostered, especially between seafarers of different backgrounds, ethnicities, and nationalities? Bracketing momentarily the issue of effective communication via a standardized Maritime English platform, what *cultural* differences may impede good human relationships, and what might be done to prevent or minimize these impediments? Potential conflicts that may surface because of multicultural crews reach beyond issues of safety due to communication barriers, and extend to issues of maritime security, cohesion among crew members, damage to morale, and perceptions of leadership support. This paper seeks to identify problems that may arise, and to suggest what can be done from the vantage point of the maritime university. It could be argued that a solution cannot arise from a simplistic mandate to "tolerate" other customs and cultural practices (or worse, to just ignore them), but rather to embed knowledge of cultural difference in the maritime classroom, thus making the study of the cultures of globalization a core component of the maritime curriculum.

# 2 The culture of globalization and the globalization of culture

Culture, in its broadest sense, is "the set of distinctive spiritual, material, intellectual and emotional features of society or a social group that encompasses, in addition to art and literature, lifestyles, ways of living together, value systems, traditions and beliefs" [3]. In addition, culture gives people a "sense of who they are, of belonging, of how they should behave, and of what they should be doing." [4]. Although, there are many disagreements between various factions of cultural theorists, generally speaking, when cultures are isolated and homogeneous, the societies they engender are relatively stable, because there are clearly delineated roles and behavioural expectations of all participants. When cultures collide and combine the potential for social and political destabilization increases. There have always been contact zones between disparate cultures, of course, but this has dramatically accelerated in the present era of globalization. This is marked by "the inexorable integration of markets, nation-states and technologies to a degree never witnessed before – in a way that is enabling individuals, corporations and nation-states to reach around the world farther, faster, deeper and cheaper than ever before... This process of globalization is also producing a powerful backlash from those brutalized or left behind by this new system" [5]. If globalization is the preferred term given to describe the current historical moment, which is characterized by an accelerated movement of good and services and people across the globe that began to fully take shape in the 1970s (a decade, not coincidentally, that saw the international institutionalization of STCW regulations), globalization also, then, impacts the formation and dissemination of "culture". For John Tomlinson, "culture has long had connotations tying it to the idea of a fixed locality. The idea of 'a culture' implicitly connects meaning construction with particularity and location" [6]. In addition, as John Clifford writes, "Dwelling was understood to be the local ground of collective life, travel a supplement; roots always precede routes" [7].

Herein lies the crux: culture is generally assigned a fixed, local particularity, therefore globalization, with its complex tendrils of connectivity, weakens the ties of culture to place. Different cultures are being introduced to one another on a scale never seen before (the globalization of cultures); conversely, this internationalism and cosmopolitanism produces a new culture of hybridity and heterogeneity (the culture of globalization). The potential tensions within this dialectic are worth exploring, particularly within the narrower objectives of maritime education and training.

## 3 Complexities of cultural heterogeneity

Seafarers have traditionally been vehicles by which culture is transmitted and transmogrified across space, but now it is the ship itself which may be the site of complex cultural exchanges and negotiations. There is, of course, a long and colourful history of the use of multicultural crews on ocean-going vessels, and if one is to believe the nineteenth-century American novelist Herman Melville, this cultural heterogeneity is what makes the seafaring life so vibrant and fulfilling. Yet, if indigenous culture gives people a sense of identity, it also "impacts behaviour, morale, and productivity at work as well, and includes values and patterns that influence company attitudes and actions" [8]. On a macro political level, Samuel Huntington has written that perhaps "the fundamental source of human conflict in this new world will not be primarily ideological or primarily economic. The great divisions among humankind and the dominating source of conflict will be culture...Global politics is being reconfigured along cultural lines. Peoples and countries with similar cultures are coming together, peoples and countries with different cultures are coming apart" [9].

These conflicts may be evident on a micro level as well, as evidenced by the findings of maritime scholars Badawi and Halawa. In their paper "The Problem of Cross Cultural and Multilingual Crews," they note that "an individual's cultural background can affect his communicative skills as well as his learning potential and capabilities" [10]. The central purpose of their work is to enlarge the concepts of communication to include not just the vocabulary and grammar of a language, but the *social* aspects of communication as well, including the context of an utterance, the speed of a delivery, and the nuances of body language. Added to this could be the communicative barriers put in place by cultural differences (i.e., in regards to the collectivist culture of Asian countries vs. the more individualistic cultures of Western countries), but also in relation to different but integrated beliefs and values, that can be organized via anthropological typologies: kinship systems, religious systems, ethics systems, political systems, health systems, and recreational systems.

Before it is possible to structure courses and contextualize the instruction of heterogeneous cultures of globalization, it is important to acknowledge that the term "multiculturalism" itself is freighted with complications, and this concept revolves around two important but antithetical positions. On the one hand, the teaching of cultural differences may embrace a particularistic vision that stresses the affiliations with one's local culture – a type of ethnocentrism or ethnic loyalty that often works to build group solidarity. On the other hand, the teaching of cultural differences may stress the unificatory nature of globalization under the title "cosmopolitanism" – from the Greek language, to be a citizen of the world, a member of humanity as a whole. According to E.D. Hirsh, "the issue about multiculturalism that we need to decide is this: Do we define ourselves as belonging to a particular 'ethnos' or do we define ourselves as belonging to a broad 'cosmopolis'? ... It is possible, of course, to hold a kind of dual citizenship, to be part of both one's particular ethnos and the larger cosmopolis" [11]. The difficulty begins only when one asserts the mutual exclusivity of one over the other, and this is precisely the difficulty that might impact shipboard relations as indeed it might impact any trans-national or multinational workplace.

How then is it possible to recognize, understand, tolerate and even celebrate cultural diversity, while simultaneously espousing a cosmopolitan stance that ensures the polyglot community works smoothly and efficiently toward a common goal? An answer may be found in the work of James Banks, who argues a new kind of citizenship is needed for the twenty-first century. He describes a multicultural citizenship which recognizes and legitimizes the rights and needs of citizens to maintain commitments to their cultural communities and to the national and global civic cultures [12].

While much of the cross-cultural negotiations must inevitably be sorted out from within the experiential arena of the workplace, much valuable information can be, and should be, acquired in the classroom. Luo Weihua makes this very clear: "Globalization directly influences maritime industry needs and in turn has immediate impact on Maritime Education and Training. The process of globalization dictates higher requests to a level of knowledge of languages and [the] skill[s] to apply it. The knowledge of vocabulary is not sufficient to work in multinational crew[s]. Globalization of the shipping industry ... demand[s] a high level of education, training, and certification of seafarers" [13].

## 4 General Education, the Maritime University, and the 21st-century mariner

Of the many obstacles facing the 21st century mariner, among them will be the need to manage cultural differences between crew members. The educated mariner will need to be able to understand the similarities and differences among people, and to develop the capacities to solve problems that arise precisely from these differences. It is relatively easy to simply call for modifications in academic curricula. However, it is much more difficult to implement such changes because of several mitigating factors. One of the first hurdles to overcome is to find a place within educational models for cross-cultural analyses and the study of the cultures of globalization.

At The California Maritime Academy cadets are required to take courses designed to educate them in multiple cultures, and the Academy is moving even further in this direction through the strengthening of a general education program. "General Education", a term widely used in traditional American universities, is designed to provide knowledge, skills, experiences, and perspectives which enable students to make connections among disciplines, and expand their capacities to take part in a wide range of human interests and activities, as well as confront the personal, moral, and social problems that are an inevitable part of human life. This programme goes beyond rudimentary instruction in basic skill sets to emphasize, in the words of Jerry Graff, "knowledge of history and culture and of science and mathematics; skills such as logical and critical thinking and communication; and knowledge about diversity and intercultural skills" [14].

California Maritime Academy, as many other maritime universities, offers a curriculum and faculty that challenge students to attain intellectual achievements. Its academic departments, with their programmes of majors and minors, are primarily responsible for developing the highly detailed and specialized skills and knowledge called for in today's world. In order to be a learned, successful, and valuable participant in the rapidly changing global community, students need more than a professional or vocational training. Courses required for a major may prepare the student for a vocation, while general education programmes help students see the place of their specialized knowledge in their total education by demonstrating that knowledge is not isolated, there is always more to learn, and the project of education is a lifelong commitment.

Granted, the call to expand the maritime-based curriculum in such a way faces many internal and external challenges, including financial expenditures, availability of qualified instructors, and the integration of additional courses into traditionally unit-heavy fields of study, but the benefits are significant and long reaching. There are many who feel that a general education program is impractical, irrelevant, or unnecessary, and that only the major or professional preparation is of value. However, as argued by Ernest Boyer, "rather than divide the undergraduate experience into separate camps, general versus specialized education, the curriculum of a college of quality will bring the two together" [15]. Complex learning outcomes therefore, must be developed across the curriculum in order to integrate, both vertically and horizontally, specialized and general knowledge.

A statement released last year by the Association of American Colleges and Universities (AACU) called on its member institutions to focus on five valued sets of educational outcomes and to concentrate on assessing them. The outcomes are: (1) analytical, communication, quantitative, and information processing skills; (2) understanding inquiry practices of the natural sciences, social sciences, humanities, and arts; (3) intercultural knowledge and collaborative problem-solving skills; (4) proactive sense of responsibility for individual, civic, and social choices; and (5) habits of minds that foster integrative thinking and the ability to transfer knowledge and skills from one setting to another [16]. It is the third set which resonates with the concerns of this paper, and it is important to note that the AACU explicitly links "intercultural knowledge with 'problem-solving skills'", the latter term of which has been highly valued in Maritime Education.

Indeed, the study of intercultural knowledge may even be considered a meta-framework with the potential for integration across curricula, precisely because it is so oriented toward problem-solving skills. The "problem" of cross-cultural exchanges itself can be foregrounded in order to teach leadership skills, crisis management, and group dynamics. A foundation of "multicultural literacy" (the ability to identify, recognize, and interpret multiple cultural manifestations) helps to produce an educated citizen of the twenty-first century, a citizen who is able to develop a delicate balance of cultural, national, and global identifications.

## 5 Conclusion

Ultimately, the issue of globalization and cultural difference is one that transcends that of the maritime community. In a world engaged with global affairs in regards to trade, national security, the environment, health, and justice, issues of multiculturalism impact many aspects of many trans-national operations. The deepening ethnic texture of nations such as the United States, Canada, Australia, Germany, the United Kingdom and Japan make the study of multiculturalism an imperative. The vast amount of material produced by, and used in, business administration departments, points to the importance of understanding cultural differences in order to effectively manage and provide leadership. Even the American National Aeronautics and Space Administration, concerned about Shuttle/Mir Space Station multicultural crews, conducted a 4 1/2 year psychosocial study to provide quantitative data on interpersonal relationships. Their findings suggest strategies that should help build stronger, more productive working relationships among crew members and among people of different cultural backgrounds [17].

Cutting-edge theorists of cultural formations like David Hawk of the New Jersey Institute of Technology and Satu Teerikangus of Helsinki University of

Technology, even propose to reorganize conceptions of culture in order to "renegotiate human futures". "A key characteristic of a culture of the future," they write, "is that it can help a social group effectively respond to change by learning to embrace, then create it. In this way culture turns from being a by-product of core, historic values, and becomes a vehicle for design of the values that better match the challenges of the 21st century" [18]. Their work suggests that culture, and the collision of cultures that are experienced today, can be realigned such that, the energies harnessed from such an integration, may transform the political and economic landscape of the world.

Those who work and do research in maritime universities, therefore, are in an exciting position when confronted with the challenges posed by the culture of globalization. On the one hand, it is important to make use of the scholarship that is being produced in academic fields such as international business, sociology, political science, global studies, and cultural studies, and apply it to maritime majors. On the other hand, the very existence of multicultural crews provides a ready-made laboratory to study the effects of multiculturalism and to disseminate that information to others. In other words, it is possible to turn the object of inquiry inside out. Through an analysis of the way the maritime industry deals (both successfully and unsuccessfully) with such issues, the study of shipboard life might prove useful to social scientists and scholars of globalization. This process can be fostered by the free and frank exchange of ideas between academics and industrialists, and by intensifying efforts to exchange students from one maritime university to another, to make the environment these students learn in as richly diverse as the world they will soon enter.

## References

[1] Trenkner, P., Cole, C. Profiling the maritime English instructor. *Proc. of the 4th General Assembly of the International Association of Maritime Universities.* Alexandria, Egypt. CD-ROM 2003.

[2] Badawi, E. El Sayed A., Halawa, A. M.: Maritime communication: the problem of cross cultural and multilingual crews. *Proc. of the 4th General Assembly of the International Association of Maritime Universities.* Alexandria, Egypt. CD-ROM 2003.

[3] United Nations Educational, Scientific, and Cultural Organization (UNESCO). Universal Declaration on Cultural Diversity website. http://www.unesco.org/education/imld_2002/unversal_decla.shtml 2002.

[4] Harris, P. R., Moran, R. T. *Managing Cultural Differences,* Gulf Publishing: Houston, Texas, pp. 4-5, 2000.

[5] Friedman, T. L. *The Lexus and the olive tree: understanding globalization.* Random House, New York, p. 9, 2000.

[6] Tomlinson, J. *Globalization and culture.* University of Chicago Press, Chicago, pp. 27-29, 1999.

[7] Clifford, J. *Routes: travel and translation in the late twentieth century.* Harvard University Press, Cambridge, Mass, p. 3, 1997.

[8] op. cit. [4].

[9] Huntington, S., *The clash of civilizations and the remaking of world order.* Simon and Shuster, New York, 1996.

[10] op. cit. [2]

[11] Hirsch, E.D. Toward a centrist curriculum: two kinds of multiculturalism in elementary school. The Core Knowledge Foundation. http://www.coreknowledge.org.

[12] Banks, J. Teaching for multicultural literacy, global citizenship, and social justice. Cultures in Counterpoint. Charles Fowler Colloquium. 2003 http://lib.umd.edu/PAL/SCPA/fowlercolloq2003bankspaper.html.

[13] Luo, W. Maritime English Education in the context of globalization. ESP in Multilingual and Multicultural Contexts. http://home.planet.nl/~kluij 016/11WeihuaDAG2.htm.

[14] Graff, J. What is a Generally Education Person? Association of American Colleges and Universities. *Peer Review* http://www.aacu.org/peerreview /previous.cfm 2004.

[15] Boyer, E. *College: the undergraduate experience in America.* HarperCollins: New York, 1988.

[16] op. cit. [14].

[17] Psychosocial effects of long-duration space flight analyzed in shuttle/Mir studies. *Space Life Science Research Highlights.* Office of Biological and Physical Research, National Aeronautics and Space Administration http://spaceresearch.nasa.gov 2000.

[18] Hawk, D., Teerikangas, S. Negotiating with our future cultures. *Proc. of the 45th Annual Meeting of the International Society for the Systems Sciences.* Asilomar, California http://www.isss.org 2001.

# European maritime Post Graduate Programmes for former seafarers

C. Ketchum & M. Pourzanjani
*World Maritime University, Malmö, Sweden*

## Abstract

While today many national maritime education and training systems offer opportunities for students to also qualify for a career in the maritime sector ashore, following their sea experience, there is a need for furthering this trend and organising it at a European level. It is believed that such a move would also help to promote the seafaring profession and maritime education. Under the European Commission Sixth Framework Programme, Maritime Transportation Coordination Platform, a study was commissioned in 2004 to survey Master's Level Post Graduate Programmes that are currently available to former seafarers leading to increased employment opportunities in the maritime sector ashore. In addition, the study proposed a common framework for a flexible European Masters Programme leading to the main sectors of the maritime industry.

This paper discusses the findings of this study that include an examination of ship to shore career paths and the current maritime job market ashore. In examining the currently available MSc programmes, criteria are discussed for the inclusion of programmes in a proposed European Commission website that would serve as an online catalogue to make the information more readily available to seafarers. Finally, the common framework for a new European MSc Programme is detailed including programme structure, mode of delivery, subject content and quality standards.
*Keywords: European Commission, seafarer, Master's Programme, maritime jobs ashore.*

## 1 Introduction

In response to the Communication of the European Commission on the training and recruitment of seafarers [1], the Council of Ministers adopted specific conclusions, on 5 June 2003, on improving the image of Community shipping and attracting young people to the seafaring profession. In this context, it invited the Commission to consider a European-level campaign for promoting the seafaring profession and maritime education.

In the above mentioned Communication, the Commission deemed that one of the ways to promote the profession and attract more European officers to it, would be to enhance the quality of maritime studies while securing post sea job possibilities for former seafarers in the maritime cluster.

While today many national maritime education and training systems offer opportunities for students to qualify also for a career in the maritime sector ashore, following their sea experience, there is a need for furthering this trend and organising it at the European level. It is worth noting that the METNET research programme [2] also made proposals in this direction.

The European Commission, under the Sixth Framework Programme, Maritime Transportation Coordination Platform (MTCP), commissioned a "Study on European Maritime Graduate and Post Graduate Programmes for Former Seafarers" [3] with the overall goals of the study to pave the way to: Bring in more people to the seafaring profession and keep them in the maritime cluster by offering them the possibility for post sea careers in the shipping industry ashore or other maritime related activities.

- Improve the employability and professional mobility of Maritime Education and Training graduates.
- Promote the quality of maritime education and training and consider upgrading study programmes and widen specialization of former deck and engineer officers.

To support these goals, the study focused on three primary objectives:

- An examination of Ship to Shore Career Paths.
- Assessment of existing Post Graduate Programmes within the European Union, relevant to former seafarers.
- Proposal for a common framework for a EU Post Graduate MSc Programme for former seafarers.

## 2 Examination of ship to shore career paths

### 2.1 Transitional education

Master Mariners, Chief Engineers and other seafarers seeking employment ashore have traditionally been tapped for a host of maritime sector jobs. The European Commission Maritime Transport Website [4] identifies the following three categories of available fields:

- Maritime related Administrations and Authorities *(Port authorities (pilotage services, towage services, harbour masters' departments etc); Port State control; Regional and national administrations (ship management, vessel traffic services, ship survey etc), International organisations).*

- Maritime industry *(Shipping Companies; Manning companies; Offshore Industry; Marine insurance Companies; Classification societies; Maritime legal and financial services;).*
- Maritime Education and Training Institutions.

Advances in maritime and related industry technology combined with increasing international regulations and corresponding domestic legislation demand mariners greatly expand their knowledge base to take up employment ashore. Lloyd's List recently noted, "Shore side management requires different skills to those involved in a running of a ship at sea, and it is idle to pretend otherwise. So there is a demand for the right kind of 'conversion' courses" [5].

The key to a successful career shift ashore focuses on obtaining the right transitional education. Depending on the type of job the mariner is pursuing, this will require either specialized training or an advanced degree such as a Master of Science. For example, on the job training provided by the employer is often the case for a Chief Engineer who becomes a Marine Superintendent or a Master Mariner who takes on the role as the Designated Person Ashore. A short course or diploma, potentially accomplished through distance learning, is typical for a Ship Surveyor, Port State Control Inspector or Ship's Agent. An advanced degree is an essential element for those seeking employment in the Maritime Law, Logistics, Naval Architecture or Trade and Finance sectors.

In considering the development of a European Masters programme for former seafarers, the study noted that those seeking employment in the areas where an advanced degree is not required would potentially find their opportunities for advancement or sector mobility increased if they did possess a degree. As will be discussed later, a EU MSc programme development should concentrate on incorporating a variety of common elements from a number of maritime sector jobs to offer the graduate the broadest range of employment and advancement opportunities. Figure 1 illustrates this concept.

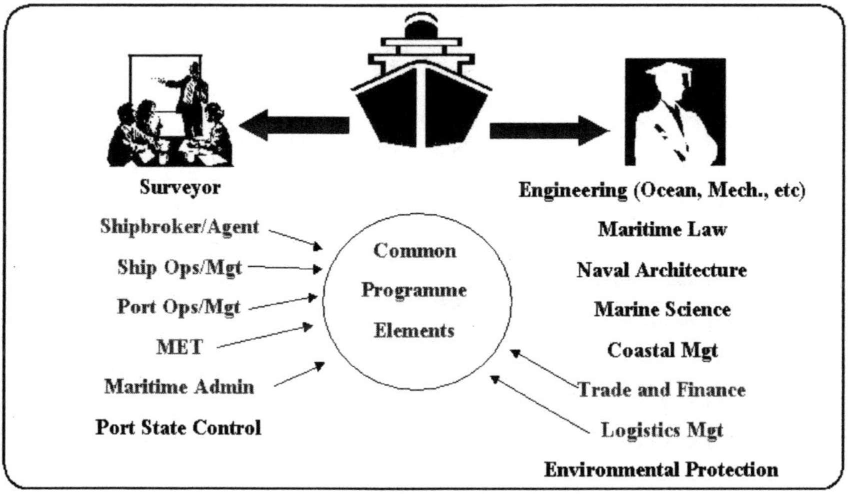


Figure 1.

### 2.2 The job market

The previous section identifies various fields and associated job opportunities that are well suited for former seafarers. In this context it should also be noted that seafarers' industry, technical and managerial experience make them not only well suited for a range of shore side maritime sector jobs, but in many cases this experience is a prerequisite. In particular, such jobs include Marine and Technical Superintendents, Ship Surveyors, Fleet Managers and Training Managers. Other jobs that greatly benefit from having incumbents with previous sea experience include Harbour Masters, MET Lecturers, and editors of nautical publications such as sailing directions. The seafarer's experience, especially that of top rank officers like Masters and Chief Engineers, would, at the very least, enhance most other maritime sector jobs as well.

## 3 Existing Post Graduate Programmes

### 3.1 Scope and methodology

The primary aim of the study was to evolve a flexible European postgraduate programme leading to the main sectors of the maritime industry. In undertaking the task of cataloguing existing PG programmes, the study established the following criteria:

- Programmes were selected that target seafarers and are geared specifically toward the maritime industry (many of these programmes also target/accept non-seafarers).
- Highly specialised programmes such as Maritime Law, Naval Architecture and Marine Science were typically excluded because they generally focus on a limited industry sector. Exceptions to this include several programmes from institutions that are centred on the maritime industry vice institutions that provide a maritime related programme as merely one of a host of varied specialisations within a specific discipline.
- PhD and similar level programmes were not considered as falling within the scope of this study.
- Programmes were only considered if they were taught in an international environment. This generally means that the programme is offered in English and open to international students.

Prospective programmes were identified by a review of professional maritime publications such as Lloyd's List, by consulting with maritime education and industry professionals, and by Internet search.

Many of the potential programmes had all the required information on their institution's web site. An attempt was also made to contact all the programme directors to obtain any information not available on their web site as well as to obtain data on demand for their respective programmes.

### 3.2 Review of existing programmes within the EU

EU PG programmes meeting the above criteria were catalogued, including extended contact information and correspondence received from various the programme directors as well as hyperlinks to the institutions' websites and a collection of electronic prospectus and course information where available. The following is an overview of common attributes identified in the various programs:

- **Structure**: All of the programmes identified are taught, with resident requirements and many are completed within one year. A few of the programmes, such as the Master of Arts programmes at Greenwich and the Master of Maritime Affairs programme at the World Maritime University span two years [6]. The MBA in Shipping and Logistics offered by the Copenhagen Business School is established as a two-year part time program. The MSc in Maritime Economics and Logistics at Erasmus University in Rotterdam is a one-year full time programme but offers an option of completing the program in 2-3 years as a part time student.
- **Subject Content**: The subject content varies by specific programme. However, elements common to a majority of the programmes that are shipping business and management related and even in a number of other programmes include courses in Maritime Law, Logistics, economics and finance.
- **Quality Standards**: All programmes maintain at least a European recognized accreditation and include internal quality monitoring programmes.
- **Mode of Delivery**: Courses are generally taught in a lecture format. Additionally, field studies are a key element of many of the programmes. Given the nature of shipping related activities, these field studies appear to be particularly important to give students first hand exposure to the industry and to exchange ideas with those already in the field. Most of the programmes also require a research project or dissertation as a final requirement for graduation.
- **Course Demand**: Although requests were sent to all the identified institutions, only a few replied with data on actual applications and acceptances for their respective programmes. For those institutions supplying this information, it can be seen that in general, applications were 2-3 times that of actual acceptances. Course acceptance/enrolment ranged from 7 for the University of Plymouth's Coastal and Ocean Policy MSc to 105 for the World Maritime University MSc in Maritime Affairs. Specific data on how many of the students were seafarers was generally hard to obtain except for WMU who reported 41 of their recent class were former seafarers.

At this point, the study strongly recommended to the European Commission that they publish an online catalogue, similar to the one produced for the study. The study noted that the extent of information contained in this catalogue is not easily available to EU seafarers. An online catalogue would not only provide convenient access to the identified programs but also serve as a career development tool by showing the seafarer what types of programmes and related jobs are available in the maritime industry. In addition to static information, the catalogue could be interactive and have a means for other potential institutions to apply to have their programmes listed as well as for those already on the site, to update their information.

After review of this recommendation in April 2005, the European Commission, Directorate General for Energy and Transport (DG TREN) began an initiative to design and place this type of catalogue on their Maritime Careers Website [7]. In addition to listing EU Programmes meeting the criteria identified above, the Commission also hopes to have a section were similar National Programmes might be listed. When completed, the Commission plans advertise its existence in industry websites and publications such as Lloyd's List and others to ensure the widest possible dissemination to seafarers.

# 4 Post Graduate Programme common framework

## 4.1 Programme structure and mode of delivery

A flexible programme structure will be critical in order to attract and benefit the greatest number of students as well as foster the interest and support of the industry. As we have seen, the preferred structure of currently available programmes is that of a full time resident programme for typically one year. The second alternative currently available would be part time students in the same programmes but taking 2-3 years to complete, noting that the part time student would still have residency requirements during the individual courses. A third option is that of a complete distance-learning programme that could be completed via the Internet. At the Master's Level, The Open University [8] in the UK is presently doing this successfully (although they do not offer any maritime sector specific programmes). Within the European maritime sector, quality distance-learning programmes abound for certificate and diploma award. These include courses and programmes offered by Lloyd's Maritime Academy, The Institute of Chartered Shipbrokers, the Nautical Institute, DNV and other classification societies.

In considering which of the above structures, or mix of structures, is best suited for a European postgraduate programme, the study identified a number of factors:

- **Coalition Concept**: The proposal is for the programme to be implemented by a coalition of 5 EU Universities, with the potential for other Universities or Colleges to join the coalition in the future. In this light, will the programme be administered in its entirety from each member Institution? Is there a possibility that certain courses and related activities be conducted at individual locations and others possibly combined? Might some institutions specialize in and thus coordinate certain programme elements?

- **Mode of Delivery**: The mode of delivery is an extremely important factor. The modern maritime industry is both global and dynamic. As has been seen, programs currently offered within the EU use a combination of classroom lecture, field study and research. The highly interactive nature of these modes of delivery is essential to enable the student to get the most out of many of the courses that are envisioned for this programme. Classroom lectures expose the students to contemporary issues and afford them the opportunity to draw on the experience and knowledge of not only the lecturer, but fellow students as well. The field study allows the student to gain first hand knowledge and insight from various leaders in the industry. Research affords the student the opportunity to demonstrate independent thought and understanding as well as serve as a basis for future analytical thinking that may be required during employment. These modes of delivery are considered particularly important for seafarers who are seeking employment ashore for possibly the first time. Senior Officers like Masters and Chief Engineers bring a tremendous amount of practical, technical and general managerial experience to the shore side industry. However, the world of a ship is an isolated one and officers may have had little opportunity to practice sound management, business and interpersonal skills on a corporate level. In order for this programme to be competitive within Europe and Internationally, these three primary modes of delivery should be incorporated where appropriate. That being said, it is also very possible to have some individual courses within the programme adequately covered through distance learning.
- **Student IT Requirements**: Computer and other IT requirements of the student need to considered in the development of residence course work and especially any distance learning modules. Many advanced software programs and associated hardware exist to facilitate distance learning including provisions for live, interactive audio and visual lectures conducted over the Internet. While this holds great potential for advanced learning, it may also require serious additional investment by many seafarers as well as by coalition institutions to participate. Although the details of this type of delivery will be worked out and agreed upon by the coalition, it is expected that the initial programme will have only basic IT requirements such as a standard computer with Internet connection, email and word processing and spreadsheet software.
- **Student Time Requirements**: It is foreseen that a part time programme of study would afford students an opportunity to potentially begin their studies prior to completely leaving the sea. In addition, those seafarers already employed ashore would be able to participate in the programme without leaving their current jobs. This in turn might foster sources of funding for the programmes from either employers or seafarers themselves if the study being done is alternating with periods of paid and productive employment.

- **Programme Funding**: The coalition of Universities involved in this programme will be tasked with identifying its actual funding source(s). This being said, the programme should operate in a manner similar to other currently available programmes. These consist of three main sources; students personally securing tuition costs, corporate/industry sponsorship of employees, or Foundation grants for particular groups of individuals [9]. This funding strategy will provide a level of transparency and competitive quality for the programme. Additionally, industry participation is essential to provide relevant input into programme development and revision, as well as serving as a channel through which graduates can seek employment.

With the above in mind, the study suggests that a flexible and competitive EU MSc programme structure would be a part time program that runs over two years. Based upon the current standards and practices of the academic community and the industry, the primary mode of delivery would be via classroom lecture supplemented by field study and research assignments. Some modules or courses would certainly lend themselves to distance learning, which would reduce residence periods at the University. One option for this delivery method would be a course in which a student obtains study material and works through it individually. Assessment would then be completed by the submission of assignments submitted by mail or electronically, or an exam administered at the respective University on a testing day. In this sense, several exams for different courses could be given over the course of a week. This method is typical maritime industry practice for the award of certificates and diplomas. A second option would be similar in that study material would be given to the student who would work through the material independently. At some point, an actual residence period would be scheduled and the knowledge gained by the student would be expanded through, for example, a week of formal lecture followed by an assignment or exam. The advantage here is that lecture and class interaction are not forsaken even though the bulk of the actual studying could be done in a non-resident status. This later method could be applied to more courses than the former because the key academic elements would be preserved. In fact, this method is presently used in the two year *MBA in Shipping and Logistics,* offered by the Copenhagen Business School.

## 4.2 Subject content

The study recommended that the content of a EU MSc programme should focus around *Maritime Management and Safety*. Maritime Management is an element common to a majority of the currently available postgraduate programmes. Maritime Safety is an important area presently lacking in many of the available programs. Combined, these elements are consistent with providing the graduate with the broadest range of employment opportunities. Within this general content it was also suggested that elective courses be offered to allow a student to further focus in the shipping, port or government sectors or others as may be decided upon by the University coalition in communication with the maritime industry.

Within this broad framework, the following specific elements were recommended as potential core courses of the programme:

- **Maritime Law and Conventions:** In order to be a player in the global shipping and maritime cluster, it is imperative to be conversant with the complex body of maritime law and maritime conventions.
- **Maritime Economics:** Given the global nature of the maritime industry, a thorough understanding of maritime economics is essential for those seeking management level positions in this sector.
- **Logistics and Supply Chain Management:** The total cost and efficiency for transportation and delivery of goods from place of manufacture to final consumer is the keystone of almost every aspect of modern transportation. In today's global economy, this is combined with the idea of goods being manufactured from components that may originate in many different areas of the world.
- **Maritime Finance:** A solid grasp of financial and risk concepts is fundamental to almost any managerial position. This element will seek to supply students with a solid practical understanding of accounting principles, budgeting, investment analysis, and performance measures.
- **Maritime Safety:** Dealing with operational maritime safety is a key competence of every seafarer. It is therefore desirable to strengthen and widen this expertise through providing further safety related education. The focus hereby is on the management aspect of safety.

Other required and elective courses would follow that might include topics such as ship (or port) operations and management, Maritime Security, Ship Brokering and Chartering, Contemporary Maritime Issues, and Maritime technology, just to name a few.

### 4.3 Quality standards

One of the specified mandates in developing a EU postgraduate program was to consider the Bologna Declaration [10]. A goal identified in the Declaration that is particularly relevant here is "the objective of increasing the international competitiveness of the European System of higher education". In this sense, the proposed programme should not only be competitive with other European programmes, but also be recognized (and even eventually admired) Worldwide. The study urged the implementing coalition to insure the programme has the highest quality standards including appropriate transparency, accreditation, and internal and external quality assessment. This ideal is also in direct support of the Bologna Declaration objective to promote "European co-operation in quality assurance with a view to developing comparable criteria and methodologies."

## 5 Conclusions

The Initial coalition of five universities for development of the programme was formed during the first quarter of 2005 and includes Gdynia Maritime University, Technical University of Catalonia (Spain), Norwegian University of

Science and Technology, Universities of Glasgow and Strathclyde and the World Maritime University.

As discussed earlier in this paper at the end of Section 2, a EU Social Fund sponsored programme on Career Mapping for the Maritime Industries, led by Southampton Institute and NUMAST, is currently underway. The results of this study will be crucial in providing justification for the EU MSc Programme development initiative. In addition, as also discussed, this study will provide additional insight for curriculum development.

The Commission and the coalition are optimistic that this will begin soon after the completion of the EU Social Fund Career Mapping Study, sometime toward the end of 2005 with the actual programme implementation as early as 2007. Once the initial programme is established, guidelines will be established to permit other universities to join the coalition as well.

The development of an EU MSc Programme, tailored specifically for former seafarers to assist them in a transition toward employment in the maritime sector, certainly holds promise to promote the seafaring profession within Europe. In this light, it may also inspire those contemplating a seafaring career to plan on a career that does not just stop with the ship. They may now envision a career that includes postgraduate education and secure and rewarding employment prospects ashore afterwards.

## Disclaimer

The views expressed in this paper are the personal views of the authors and not necessarily those of the employer of the authors.

## References

[1] Document COM/2001 (188) Final, adopted in April 2001.
[2] Thematic Network on Marine Education, Training and Mobility of Seafarers.
[3] Commissioned under MTCP Work Package 2.3 Human Resources, April 2004. The final draft of the study was delivered in April 2005.
[4] European Commission (2005), *Career Prospects Ashore*, retrieved 19 January 2005 from http://europa.eu.int/comm/transport/maritime/careers/prospects_en.htm.
[5] Lloyd's List (2005, 5 January) *Ageing Supermen.*
[6] A 9 month accelerated programme is also available at WMU for students with advance standing.
[7] See: http://europa.eu.int/comm/transport/maritime/careers/prospects_en.htm.
[8] See www.open.ac.uk.
[9] Examples include Copenhagen Business School students who are mainly sponsored by their employers and WMU students, most of who receive scholarships from participating foundations.
[10] The European Higher Education Area, Joint Declaration of the European Ministers of Education, Convened in Bologna on the 19th of June 1999.

# A network of experts for sharing MET knowledge: it works!

S. Ahvenjärvi
*Sector for Technology and Maritime Management,*
*Satakunta Polytechnic, Rauma, Finland*

## Abstract

This paper describes the NetOSKAR project and the experience gained from establishing and running an international network of maritime training professionals for the development of a knowledge assessment tool on STCW-95 subjects. At the present, the network consists of training professionals in MET institutes in five different countries. The goal is to build a large database of multiple-choice questions for testing knowledge on STCW-95 subjects. Each specialist, i.e. question producer, has access to the internet-based development tool and can enter new questions into the question database. Other specialists on the same STCW-95 subject will check and comment on the questions. After this quality control the new questions are approved and become available to all members of the network. This activity, the NetOSKAR project, was begun in 2003. The project is managed by Satakunta Polytechnic, Finland and the other partners are Svendborg International Maritime Academy from Denmark, the Technical University of Catalonia from Spain, the Maritime University of Szczcecin from Poland, Escola Náutica Infante D. Henrique from Portugal and the University of Turku from Finland. At the moment, there are 21 question producers with about 1000 new questions added yearly to the database.

There is great potential in this kind of activity. A network of MET experts could, for example, develop and share complete e-learning modules on STCW-95 subjects. In the future, the NetOSKAR project will be extended by inviting MET institutes all over the world and new training professionals to join the network. New forms of sharing knowledge will also be developed.
*Keywords: knowledge assessment, training of seafarers, e-learning, network of experts.*

# 1 Introduction

Seafaring and professions related to shipping are international. STCW-95 by IMO sets the same minimum requirements for training and education of seafarers all over the world [1], making the requirements for different licences virtually the same all over the world. The system introduced by IMO for auditing maritime training and education (MET) institutes also aims at ensuring the quality of seafarers' training. A well-educated and skilled personnel is the most critical resource for safe and efficient shipping. It is a well-known fact that the majority of all accidents related to sea transportation are caused by the so-called "human factor."

The knowledge and skills of the seafarers and those aiming to become seafarers must be controlled. Knowledge assessment is carried out by teachers at maritime education and training institutes, by maritime officials in connection with issuing licences, by ship masters and shipping companies and even by manning agencies. This universal need for controlling the knowledge of seafarers along with the common STCW95 standard, form the necessary basis for the development of general-purpose knowledge assessment aids. A large question database on STCW-95 subjects is such an aid. The idea is not new. There are some commercial products on the market available for this purpose. Also, the US Coast Guard exam question database is available at their homepage [2]. The USCG database is quite extensive, but it is said that the language of many questions is too difficult for persons who do not speak English as their native language. The questions should reflect the knowledge of the STCW-95 subject concerned rather than English language skills. There are some differences between the existing tools regarding the STCW-95 coverage, technology used and question formats. A comparison between some features of the existing question databases is described in [3].

A national OSKAR project for developing a computerised tool for the assessment of the knowledge of seafarers was introduced in Finland in 1996 [4]. Satakunta Polytechnic was the responsible leader and five major Finnish shipping companies were the partners in this project. The aim was to build a question database on STCW-95 subjects through co-operation between teachers of Satakunta Polytechnic and experienced maritime professionals of the shipping companies. As a result, a question database of more than 4000 multiple-choice questions was created, with half of the questions being in the Finnish language. After the start-up phase, new partners were invited and later on partners from Estonia and Denmark joined the project. Experience gained from the OSKAR project was very positive.

In autumn 2003 this activity reached a new phase when the new two and a half year NetOSKAR project was started [5]. The main goal of NetOSKAR is to expand OSKAR into a truly international network of maritime training experts for the development and maintenance of the question database. The experience gained from a shop floor level co-operation of training specialists during the NetOSKAR project has been very encouraging. Joint development of the question database with colleagues from other MET institutes gives teachers excellent opportunities to learn from each other, to compare course content, subject priorities and to compare teaching methods and resources in detail enables individual teachers to get new ideas to develop their own work. As stated, bringing people together can be done easily and cost-effectively by utilising the Internet. However, it is also important that the question producers periodically be brought together to meet each other at project workshops. This co-operation of MET institutes has great potential.

# 2 The NetOSKAR project

## 2.1 Experience from the pilot project

Beginning in 1996 through 2003 Satakunta Polytechnic, in co-operation with five Finnish shipping companies, developed a computer-based tool for assessing the knowledge of sea personnel. The NetOSKAR project, which started in autumn 2003, utilized the experience gained from the OSKAR project as much as possible. A pedagogical evaluation of the method was carried out in the beginning of the new project. This study confirmed that a large question database is a good tool for assessing the knowledge of seafarers. The questions in the database are multiple-choice type with four answer alternatives. While there was no reason to change the format, it was determined that the quality of the questions is critical. The questions should be written in clear and easy English (or Finnish) language and so that they measure essential knowledge. The difficulty of the questions may vary, but the information content must be absolutely correct.

It was also learned from the OSKAR project, that the idea of building and maintaining a question database in co-operation with professionals is a good idea, although it might take some time for a teacher to see the development of new questions as part of his/her normal work. Only when the teacher realises the benefits of using the question database, producing new and relevant questions becomes a natural thing and part of the normal work routine. The students generally do not oppose the use of multiple-choice exam questions, since the exam results became available much faster than from traditional written exams. It became obvious that a question database can be utilised in different ways as a part of training. A question database can be used by students as a self-education tool. A quiz can be used by a teacher to raise the student's motivation. Also, tests used before and after the training can be used to control the efficiency of the training. Thus a question database is much more than just a tool for the assessment of knowledge.

## 2.2 Goals of the NetOSKAR project

The primary goal of the NetOSKAR project was to establish an international network of maritime training and education experts for the development and maintenance of the question database. The number of member organisations shall be at least 25 by the summer 2006. While the membership of the

NetOSKAR network is agreed upon at the organisational level, the actual development work and the exchange of knowledge is done at the shop-floor level among individual experts.

Other recent goals were to improve the database itself by creating 2500 new questions, establishing and testing new quality assurance procedures and by grouping questions into categories according to STCW-95. Also accomplished was the need to test the technology and procedures for a productive and efficient operation as an international network. It was quite clear from the beginning that the Internet should be utilised as much as possible and therefore the platform software was changed to Moodle [6] from the original 'Create a quiz' [7], which used in the OSKAR project. This affected the structure of the database and the instructions for the developers and users.

### 2.3 Organisation of the project

The responsible leader and the operative coordinator of the NetOSKAR project is Satakunta Polytechnic from Finland. The other MET institute partners are Escola Náutica Infante D. Henrique from Portugal, Maritime University of Szczecin from Poland, Svendborg International Maritime Academy from Denmark and Universitat Politècnica de Catalunya from Barcelona, Spain. Two shipping companies, Silja Line and Finstaship from Finland represent the shipping companies. University of Turku from Finland was the assistant coordinator of the project, responsible for coordination of the internal reporting. The project received 2,5 years financing from the Leonardo da Vinci programme of the European Union [8]. The total budget is €387,000 (approximately 464 000 USD). The project was started in the end of 2003 and it will end in March 2006. The Internet is the primary means of communication among the parties. Also, six workshops are arranged during the project. Each partner will host at least one workshop. The main topics of discussion for the workshops are discussions about the content of the database and discussions about the project and the network activities.

### 2.4 The question database and the development tool

The question database is divided into 100 categories according to functions of the STCW-95. As mentioned, all questions are multiple-choice with four answer alternatives. The questions may contain multimedia elements, i.e. sounds or pictures associated to the question. Each question may have one or more correct answer alternatives. This reduces the possibilities of guessing. All questions are written in English. Special attention has been paid in keeping the language as simple as possible.

The software platform is Moodle. Moodle is actually a course management system designed to help educators create online courses. The Moodle software is used all over the world by universities, schools, companies and independent teachers. There were several reasons why Moodle was selected for NetOSKAR. First, it is technically suitable for NetOSKAR. Moodle offers all the basic features necessary for development and maintenance of the question database.

Also it can be used to manage the network activities. Actually it is not only a quiz software but a complete course management system (CMS). For teachers running online courses the use of NetOSKAR questions as part of their courses is very simple. The use of Moodle is very easy and does not require any knowledge about the technical details of the software or the database. Moodle is written in a scripting language called PHP, and stores most of its data in a database. The recommended database is MySQL. Today Moodle has a very large and diverse user community with over 50 000 registered users speaking 60 languages in 120 countries [6], so technical support is available virtually anywhere in the world. And last but not least, Moodle is cost-effective as it is an open source program and totally free to use.

Social construction-ism is the core theory behind Moodle. Most CMS systems have been built around tool sets and being tool-centric. Moodle is learning-centric. Social construction-ism is based on the idea that people learn best when they are engaged in a social process of constructing knowledge through the act of constructing an artefact for others. Learning is seen much as a process of negotiating meaning in a culture of shared artefacts and symbols [9].

A customised version of Moodle has been developed for NetOSKAR. The Moodle software has been complemented with various features for supporting the quality assurance and maintaining the database. The NetOSKAR question database itself is of the standard format and is compatible with any Moodle installation. Moodle software is being developed by a large international community of developers. Software updates and additional features are introduced constantly. For example, software modules for exporting questions and converting them into other formats are being developed, yet not available at the moment (summer 2005).

## 2.5 Quality assurance

The most important matter regarding the usability of the question database is the quality of the questions. Creating efficient quality control procedures was one of the goals of the NetOSKAR project. The quality of a question is defined by several factors. The most important factor is the correctness of the information. This means that the correct answer alternatives must actually be true and that the false alternatives must be false. Also the claim or the question and the answer alternatives must be unambiguous. The language must be correct and not too difficult. The question should not be too easy, i.e. the correct answer should not be obvious. Also, a good question tests essential knowledge. The quality of images must also be taken into account and other potential error sources. So, assuring the quality of a question means taking into account many aspects.

The management of the quality of the questions is based on a life-cycle approach. It means that the quality is controlled during the whole lifetime of the question. The block diagram of this life-cycle principle is shown in Figure 1. In the beginning, the quality is controlled by the author of the question. At this phase the question should also be tested using a group of students. At the next phase, the question is checked by another specialist of the STCW-95 subject from another member organisation. Finally, the question becomes "official" and it is published. During its lifetime, the question may be commented on by any user of the database. Moreover, the validity of the question will be checked every three years and continue until the subject has eventually changed so much that the question has to be removed from the database.

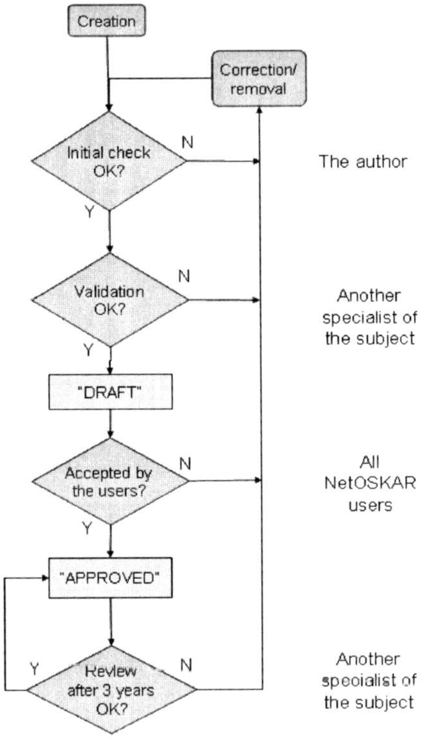


Figure 1: The life cycle of a NetOSKAR question.

### 2.6 The network of users and developers

As mentioned above, one of the main goals of the NetOSKAR project is to establish a network of MET specialists to develop and maintain the question database. Exchange of knowledge in the form of multiple-choice questions becomes more beneficial for each individual member as the network grows. At this moment the network consists of 21 teachers from five European MET institutes. In the future, the NetOSKAR community should consist of hundreds of teachers from MET organisations all over the world. Shipping companies and maritime authorities can also join the network and have access to the question database. Actually there will be two different member categories in the NetOSKAR network. Firstly, the development and maintenance responsibility is shared by the MET institutes, i.e. by the individual teachers in these organisations. These primary members form the first level of the NetOSKAR network. Secondly, there are the shipping companies, national maritime authorities and other users of the database who do not have any development responsibility. They join the network via a local primary member and they form the second level of the network.

The development of questions is carried out by small, specialist teams. These teams are small groups or pairs of specialists on a particular STCW-95 subject from different organisations. The author of the question is the primary producer, then one of his colleagues in another organisation has the main responsibility of controlling the quality of the question. He can be called the secondary producer of the question. All other teachers on the same subject can participate in the development work by providing their comments and suggestions. The primary and the secondary producer maintain direct contact with each other during the development process. The discussion about the contents and the form of the questions is carried out via e-mail, by using the discussion forum of Moodle or by face-to-face at the workshops. During the NetOSKAR project, the question producers met each other twice a year at the workshops. See Figure 2.

Figure 2: From the workshop at Lisbon in November 2004.

# 3 Experience

## 3.1 The technology

An internet based development platform was the right choice for this kind of activity. Moodle offers all the basic tools and functions necessary in NetOSKAR to support network-based operations. It is also easy to use the question database for online courses. This feature is convenient for teachers and those who are responsible for training of personnel in companies.

Presently the possibility to convert questions into other formats is limited, but tools are under development by the Moodle community. Some special features have already been added to Moodle by the NetOSKAR project in order to make management of the question database more efficient. In conclusion, the selected software platform suits quite well for NetOSKAR for the reasons mentioned.

### 3.2 The network

The most valuable feature of NetOSKAR is the network of MET specialists. It is said that sometimes the process is as important as the product of the process. This is the case with NetOSKAR. It has been very fruitful to get specialists from different MET organisations to work together. Personal contacts with colleagues in another MET institute are valuable, but working together and discussion about the knowledge assessment is even more so. When two teachers share opinions about assessment of the knowledge on a particular STCW-95 subject, they have to discuss many things: what is important and what is not; what the students are supposed to know after the training; why some matters should be weighted more than the others; what is the correct terminology; what are the important concepts; and even about how the subject should be taught. This is really the core of training seafarers. This kind of co-operation is inspiring, eye-opening and can help individual teachers in the development of their own work. This kind of grassroots level co-operation between individual teachers may be as fruitful in the development of the quality of a maritime education and training program as the co-operation on the organisational level or even the work carried out by international committees to develop new rules and standards for training. A community of hundreds of teachers working together and sharing knowledge and exchanging opinions is a huge resource and a powerful tool in the development of the training of seafarers. The larger the NetOSKAR network gets, the bigger are the benefits of the membership for the organisations and for individual teachers.

### 3.3 The project

The goals of the NetOSKAR project were quite realistic and the progress has been according to the plan. Perhaps the biggest challenge is the limited time to complete the project. Development and testing of the technology and the procedures takes time. The most time consuming phase is the establishment of the network itself. Everything should be up and running within 30 months from the beginning. The "critical mass", i.e. at least 20 new member organisations must be reached to ensure the continuity of NetOSKAR. From the project leader's point of view, the co-operation between the partners has been very fluent and fruitful. All members of the NetOSKAR project have made excellent contributions to achievement of the targeted goals.

## 4 Conclusions

The NetOSKAR project for establishing an international network of maritime education and training experts in order to develop and maintain a database of questions on STCW-95 subjects has been described in this paper. Development of new questions is carried out by small teams or pairs of specialists on a given STCW95 subject. The experience gained from the grassroots level co-operation among training professionals has been very encouraging. Exchange of opinions and experience with colleagues via the internet and during workshops can give new, fresh ideas and help individual teachers in developing the course content and training procedures. The development platform of the NetOSKAR question database is Moodle, which has proven to be the correct choice. Moodle supports network-based operations, it is widely used around the world and it is very cost-effective. Control of the quality of the questions is crucial. In NetOSKAR quality control of the question occurs during its whole lifetime. The critical question and challenge for the future of NetOSKAR is to get new member organisations to join the network in order to reach the "critical mass". One possible solution to this would be to integrate NetOSKAR with existing co-operation networks between MET institutes.

## References

[1] International Maritime Organisation IMO, *STCW 95,* IMO, London, 1997.

[2] US Coast Guard, deck and engine exam questions at http://www.uscg.mil/stcw/index.htm.

[3] Islam E.A. *Improvement of the Existing Examination and Evaluation System for Competency for Graduates of the IAMU Member Maritime Universities/Faculties,* IAMU Journal, Vol. 1, 2000, International Association of Maritime universities.

[4] Satakunta Polytechnic, the web site of the OSKAR pilot project, Rauma, Finland, http://www.spt.fi/oskar.

[5] Satakunta Polytechnic, NetOSKAR web site, Rauma, Finland http://www.netoskar.fi.

[6] Moodle community web site at http://moodle.org/.

[7] PC Shareware Inc., the home pages, Fredericksburg, Virginia, USA, http://www.pc-shareware.com/quiz.htm.

[8] European Commission. Information on the Leonardo da Vinci programme at http://europa.eu.int/comm/education/programmes/leonardo/leonardo_en .html.

[9] Cole, J. *Using Moodle*, O. Reilly Community Press, http://www.oreilly .com/ pp. 1-5, 2005.

# Cooperative learning and teamwork effectiveness: impacts of education period on cadets

E. Asyali, O. Saatcioglu & A. G. Cerit
*Dokuz Eylül University School of Maritime Business and Management, Turkey*

## Abstract

The maritime industry is a multinational industry where participants of several languages and cultures operate in a global teamwork environment. Seafarers' operating procedures are totally based on a teamwork infrastructure and climate. By the introduction of Safety Management Systems, shore-based human resources are also included in the wider system of the maritime teamwork of the company where information and communication technologies have accelerated this integration. Goals and tasks for the team, team composition, team-player styles, phases of team development, communication and interpersonal skills, decision making, leadership, and evaluation of team performance are the key elements in developing the structure of the teamwork based systems.

Training and development is the main instrument in preparing the human resources for the teamwork climate of modern organizations. Education methodologies that support the characteristics, which encourage teamwork and cooperation, are widely applied in maritime education. Cooperative learning and problem-based learning are among those approaches.

This study analyzes the effects of cooperative learning dimensions among the cadets in a maritime higher education institute with regard to teamwork effectiveness. An empirical study has been realized to measure the effects of cooperative learning dimensions on 1) individual performance in groups and 2) effective team members. To comment on the impacts of the education period on these dimensions, the study aims to realize a comparative analysis among the cadets of a senior class, before and after a simulator based bridge team management course.

*Keywords: maritime education, teamwork, cooperative learning, bridge team management.*

# 1 Introduction

In response to the demands of global competition and the increasing use of knowledge to create products and services, organizations have been moving toward a form of work that organizes employees into teams rather than a rigid management hierarchy [1]. As a result teams and teamwork have received an increasing amount of attention and popularity over the last two decades.

The workplace in the maritime industry has been changing in recent years. In the shipping industry, masters, mates, helmsman, pilots, and in a wider approach, the engine room team, must coordinate their activities to realize safe, efficient and environmental sound voyages. This coordination needs teamwork skills. The ability to work together requires some people skills such as communication, teamwork, leadership, the ability to learn, and ability to adapt to changes. But the existence of these necessary skills among students is questionable [2]. Lecturers need a mean to provide these skills to the students [3]. Active learning strategies such as cooperative learning and simulator-based learning can be effective tools in higher maritime education to provide these skills.

# 2 Teams and teamwork

Although we use terms "teams" and "groups" interchangeable in our daily life, there is a need to make a distinction between these two terms. As opposed to a group, a team has clearly defined goals and performance objectives for which members are individually and collectively accountable. Also a team requires special training and time to develop before reaching peak performance [4]. There are many definitions for teams. Dessler [5] and Daft [6] define teams as a unit of "*two or more people*" who "*interact*" and "*coordinate*" their work to accomplish a specific "*goal*". Salas et al. [7] define a team as "A distinguishable set of two or more people who interact dynamically, interdependently, and adaptively towards a common and valued goal/object/mission who have each been assigned specific roles or functions to perform". Examples of teams that fit these definitions include military command and control teams, operating room and emergency room teams, cockpit crews, medical emergency teams, intensive care units, fire rescue teams, management teams and engine room and bridge teams in the shipping industry.

The next term that we have to clarify is teamwork. Teamwork is defined as those behaviors that facilitate effective team member interaction. Hoegl and Gemuenden [8] examined the Teamwork Quality (TWQ). The required teamwork behaviors vary depending on the team's task, but recent research suggests that five teamwork behaviors such as team leadership, team orientation, mutual performance monitoring, back-up behaviors, and adaptability have been observed in all types of teams [9]. Teamwork Skills refers to competencies that individual team members must possess in order to perform the necessary teamwork behaviors.

## 3 Bridge team training

In complex and high risk working environments where cooperation among workers is needed, teamwork plays an important role in ensuring safety and avoiding errors. Teams make fewer mistakes than do individuals, especially when each team member knows his or her own responsibilities and also those of other team members. However, teamwork is not an automatic consequence of placing people together in the same room; it depends on a willingness to cooperate toward shared goals [10, 11].

A "bridge team" is a type of "command team" which is created by the organization to attain specific goals through members' joint activities and interactions. These types of vertical teams are composed of a manager (master) and his or her subordinates (mates, helmsman, etc.) in the organization's formal chain of command.

According to Australian Transportation Safety Bureau (ATSB) and Canadian Transportation Safety Board (TSB Canada) data, 25% and United Kingdom Marine Accident Investigation Board (MAIB) data, 23% of causal factors of shipping accidents are associated with "Management Group Factors". These consist of fatigue, communications, bridge resource management, procedures, manning, business management, and watch handoff [12]. This study shows that weakness in bridge organization and management has been an important cause for marine casualties worldwide. Bridge Resources Management (BRM) and Bridge Team Management (BTM) courses have been performed in all nautical schools for many years. BRM/BTM focuses on bridge officers' skills such as teamwork, teambuilding, communication, leadership, decision-making and resource management [13]. Cross-checking of individual decisions, making roles and responsibilities clear to team members, involving all team members in problem solving and decision making, and making team members clearly understand the chain of command will improve safety and can help detect errors, and correct and respond them as early as possible in both routine and emergency operations.

Simulator–based training has become a popular technique and a powerful training tool for training teamwork skills in high risk industries such as aviation, health care, maritime, and nuclear power production. Beaubien and Baker [9] mentioned that there is no direct relationship between the level of simulation fidelity and teamwork training effectiveness.

## 4 Cooperative learning

The use of active learning strategies, such as Cooperative Learning, is growing at a remarkable rate in all disciplines. Cooperative learning (CL) is the instructional use of small groups so that students work together to maximize their own and each other's learning [14]. CL is the concept of teamwork applied within a practical educational setting and provides a highly relevant and effective model for the higher education institutions for teaching and developing teamwork skills for future workforces.

A real and effective application of the CL method has many benefits both to students and to the education outcomes of higher education institutions. Researchers commonly report student gains in problem solving skills [15]. Also by eliminating the competition and working together, students will learn more in a shorter time frame while developing social and teamwork skills [16]. CL also results in greater transfer of what is learned within one situation to another [14].

### 4.1 Elements of the cooperative learning model

CL should be well structured and include five essential components or principles for small-group learning to be truly cooperative [17]. These components are Positive Interdependence, Face-to-Face Promotive Interaction, Individual Accountability/Personal Responsibility, Teamwork Skills and Group Processing.

### 4.2 Formal learning groups

Cooperative learning can be structured in many different ways. Formal Cooperative Learning (FCL) groups that are used to teach specific content and problem-solving skills are probably the most difficult to implement, but they have the greatest potential for affecting positive change [18].

FCL groups that encourage teamwork and cooperation are built in Bridge Team Management (BTM) Courses. Leadership in emergencies, effective internal and external communication, situational awareness, voyage planning, teamwork, error trapping, and relationship with pilots are the main subjects that are covered. In formal cooperative groups in BTM courses, instructors accomplish the following tasks: Specify the objectives for the lesson, Make a number of instructional decisions, Explain the task and the positive interdependence, Monitor students' learning and intervene within the groups to provide task assistance or to increase students' teamwork skills, Evaluate students' learning and help students process how well their group functioned. Self-assessment plays a vital role in the learning process as students can develop a realistic sense of their own strengths and weaknesses [19]. The instructor provides time and a structure for members of each learning group to process how effectively they have been working together. This type of "Student Facilitated Debrief" technique is found an effective tool for simulation assessments [20].

## 5 Objective and hypothesis

One of the most important expectations from maritime students is to be able to work in teams. Maritime education should be considered as an important tool for developing effective team members in maritime industry. Applications supporting teamwork should be made use of in maritime education. The main objective of this study is to analyze the effectiveness of the CL strategy to develop teamwork skills during the BTM course among senior class students of a Nautical Science Department.

The main hypothesis of the study can be formulated as follows:

**$H_1$**: Perceptions of senior deck students on CL dimensions; team member roles and required skills in teamwork are different before and after simulator-based training.
51 sub-hypotheses are developed to test this hypothesis (See Table 1).

# 6 Methodology

## 6.1 Questionnaire development

A questionnaire is applied to the senior class students before and after the simulator based bridge team management course. Formal CL groups are used to analyze the effectiveness of application of CL strategy.

To realize the objectives of the research, a questionnaire consisting of 3 parts is developed. A previous study by the authors made use of a similar questionnaire where the questions were derived from research about teamwork and cooperative learning [21].

A Likert-scale is developed as "1 = strongly disagree, 5 = strongly agree".

The questionnaire made use of some of the scales that were developed and used by other researchers. The cooperative learning scale developed by Johnson and Johnson [22], and used by Ghaith [23], was applied. Ghaith [23] used a modified version of Johnson and Johnson's [22] Classroom Life Measure in order to assess the connections of cooperative learning to learner's perceptions of social support, feelings of alienation from school, and academic achievement. Group interaction and attitudes toward CL scale was adapted from Veenman et al.'s study [24]. Pupil Perceptions of Cooperative Learning scale for pupils from grades 4 to 8 was developed by Veenman et al [24] to gather information concerning pupils' preferences for learning in groups, the potentially positive and negative outcomes of cooperative learning and other aspects of cooperative learning. On conceptual backgrounds, Veenman et al. [24] had developed two scales. The scales were attitudes toward CL and group interaction. Annett et al. [25] developed a team process model in which three processes, namely behavioral, cognitive and affective processes were defined. Behavioral process consists of communication and coordination. Annet et al.'s [25] variables were adapted to maritime undergraduate education to assess coordination in groups. Statements for *group processing, teamwork skills, individual performance in groups* and *effective team member* were developed through literature survey and their reliability was again tested in the authors' previous study [21].

## 6.2 Sample

The research was carried out in the spring of 2005 among the senior class cadets of the Nautical Science Department of Dokuz Eylul University School of

Maritime Business and Management. The population of the class is 40 and 39 questionnaires were received before implementation of simulator-based training. Thirty-two questionnaires were received after simulator-based training.

### 6.3 Data analysis and procedures

The research covers a comparative analysis. The analysis is maintained by SPSS (Statistical Package for the Social Sciences) program. Means and standard deviations are obtained and t-test is applied to finalize the hypotheses test.

### 6.4 Evaluation and results

The means of the findings and the results of the comparative analysis are given in Table 1. The variables are tested for bridge teams before and after the simulator based training and as can be noted from the results, 16 sub-hypotheses out of 51 variables have been supported. The determinants that are perceived different from the sample are given below:
*Our job is not done until everyone in the group has completed the assignment, Our grade depends on how much members learn, I have to make sure that the other members learn if I want to do well on the assignment, We cannot complete an assignment unless everyone contributes, The lecturer divides up the material so that everyone has a part and everyone has to share, I have to find out what everyone else knows if I am going to be able to do the assignment, I am self-confident, Performance of each member is assessed and the results are given back to the member, We keep to planned time / event schedule, I have high motivation, I achieve better success, I am more productive, We always divide tasks equally, I improve my own learning, I am satisfied with structure of the group. (e.g. size, member), I always do my best when working in groups.*

The supported sub-hypotheses can be grouped under the following main areas of cooperative learning components: positive interdependence in groups, group processing and individual performance in groups.

Regarding the answers to the statements, the highest frequencies obtained before simulator based training are, *satisfaction with the problem solving skills (4.26), satisfaction with the communication skills (4.20) and satisfaction with the decision making skills (4.20).* The corresponding highest frequencies after the simulator based training are as follows: *satisfaction with the problem solving skills (4.48), not being able to complete an assignment unless everyone contributes (4.41) and sharing work according to prearranged plans (4.34).*
Regarding the answers to the statements, the lowest frequencies obtained before simulator based training are: *We always divide tasks equally (2.51), We always talk about things that have nothing to do with the task* (2.57), *The lecturer divides up the material so that everyone has a part and everyone has to share (2.84).* The corresponding lowest frequencies after the simulator based training are as follows: *We always talk about things that have nothing to do with the task (2.20); I always have problems completing a task when working with other students in a group (2.65).*

Table 1: Results of the comparative analysis.

| | Before | | After | | t | p |
|---|---|---|---|---|---|---|
| | Simulator | | based training | | | |
| Variables | Mean | SD | Mean | SD | | |
| 1. We try to make sure that everyone in the group learns. | 3.62 | 1.33 | 3.63 | 1.36 | .030 | .976 |
| 2. Our job is not done until everyone in the group has completed the assignment. | 3.36 | 1.34 | 4.03 | 1.12 | -2.253 | **.027** |
| 3. We all receive the same grade. | 3.58 | 1.42 | 2.94 | 1.26 | 1.961 | .054 |
| 4. Our grade depends on how much members learn. | 3.16 | 1.34 | 3.79 | 1.07 | -2.019 | **.048** |
| 5. I have to make sure that the other members learn if I want to do well on the assignment. | 3.24 | 1.47 | 3.94 | 1.27 | -2.134 | **.036** |
| 6. We cannot complete an assignment unless everyone contributes. | 3.13 | 1.41 | 4.41 | .88 | -4.600 | **.000** |
| 7. The lecturer divides up the material so that everyone has a part and everyone has to share. | 2.84 | 1.46 | 4.19 | .78 | -4.904 | **.000** |
| 8. We have to share all materials in order to complete the assignment. | 4 | 1.16 | 4.19 | 1.09 | -.691 | .492 |
| 9. Everyone's ideas are needed if we are going to be successful. | 4.03 | 1 | 4.23 | .96 | -0.841 | .403 |
| 10. I have to find out what everyone else knows if I am going to be able to do the assignment. | 3.49 | 1.21 | 4.09 | 1.03 | -2.246 | **.028** |
| 11. I am self-confident. | 3.23 | 1.44 | 4.13 | .87 | -3.224 | **.002** |
| 12. Performance of each member is assessed and the results are given back to the member. | 2.74 | 1.31 | 3.63 | 1.21 | -2.914 | **.005** |
| 13. Performance of each group is assessed and the results are given back to the group. | 3.46 | 1.23 | 3.75 | 1.27 | -.968 | .336 |
| 14. We identify helpful and unhelpful member actions. | 3.34 | 1.25 8 | 3.84 | 1.11 | -1.753 | .084 |
| 15. I send correct information to the right individual at the right time. | 3.61 | 1.19 8 | 3.94 | .669 | -1.461 | .149 |
| 16. I receive correct information from the right individual at the right time. | 3.53 | 1.1 | 3.53 | .92 | -.020 | .984 |
| 17. I discuss situations/options with appropriate members of the group. | 4 | .95 | 4.00 | .92 | .000 | 1.00 |
| 18. I raise possible options for discussion. | 4.16 | .834 | 4.13 | .92 | .156 | .877 |
| 19. I share work according to prearranged plan. | 3.89 | 1.11 | 4.34 | .83 | -1.888 | .063 |
| 20. We rearrange plan to balance work load. | 3.67 | 1.28 | 3.88 | 1.10 | -.725 | .471 |
| 21. We keep to planned time / event schedule. | 3.41 | 1.29 | 3.97 | .97 | -2.081 | **.041** |
| 22. I have high motivation. | 3.28 | 1.39 | 4.16 | .82 | -3.286 | **.002** |
| 23. I achieve better success. | 3.38 | 1.31 | 4.03 | .86 | -2.495 | **.015** |
| 24. I am more productive. | 3.13 | 1.51 | 4.13 | .72 | -3.603 | **.001** |

Table 1: Continued.

| | Before | | After | | t | P |
|---|---|---|---|---|---|---|
| | Simulator based training | | | | | |
| Variables | Mean | SD | Mean | SD | | |
| 25. We always divide tasks equally. | 2.51 | 1.41 | 3.88 | 1.13 | -4.419 | **.000** |
| 26. The group identifies norms. | 3.03 | 1.46 | 3.61 | 1.28 | -1.739 | .087 |
| 27. We always talk about things that have nothing to do with the task. | 2.57 | 1.16 | 2.20 | 1.24 | 1.204 | .233 |
| 28. I improve my own learning. | 3.37 | 1.26 | 4.09 | .69 | -2.789 | **.003** |
| 29. I am satisfied with physical climate. (e.g. Lighting, heating, equipment) | 3.74 | 1.3 | 3.63 | 1.34 | .353 | .726 |
| 30. I am satisfied with structure of the group. (e.g. size, member) | 3.24 | 1.42 | 3.88 | 1.19 | -2.048 | **.044** |
| 31. I like to work on a task with other students. | 3.63 | 1.23 | 3.84 | 1.19 | -.702 | .485 |
| 32. I like to explain things to someone of my group. | 3.83 | 1.09 | 3.90 | .98 | -.290 | .773 |
| 33. I like someone from my group explains something to me. | 3.94 | .99 | 3.65 | .99 | 1.217 | .228 |
| 34. I like to hear the other members' ideas. | 4.06 | .96 | 4.03 | .91 | .107 | .915 |
| 35. The other members in the group always listen to me. | 3.51 | 1.01 | 3.97 | .88 | -1.936 | .057 |
| 36. I always tell other students that they did something good. | 3.66 | 1.25 | 3.97 | 1.11 | -.852 | .398 |
| 37. I always do my best when working in groups. | 3.54 | .95 | 4.03 | 1.02 | -2.022 | **.047** |
| 38. I always have problems completing a task when working with other students in a group. | 2.85 | 1.07 | 2.65 | 1.20 | .736 | .464 |
| 39. I am familiar with my strength and weakness in a group study. | 3.83 | .785 | 3.94 | .814 | -.543 | .589 |
| 40. I understand the different roles played by group members. | 3.76 | 1.1 | 3.94 | .93 | -.672 | .504 |
| 41. I understand how to work with people who have a style of work different from my own. | 3.63 | 1.21 | 4.03 | .89 | -1.510 | .136 |
| 42. I know how to work cohesively with a group of people toward a common goal. | 3.8 | 1.13 | 4.13 | .89 | -1.303 | .197 |
| 43. I know how to carry on multiple responsibilities for a project. | 4.03 | 1 | 4.26 | .89 | -.969 | .336 |
| 44. I am satisfied with my leadership skills. | 4.14 | .94 | 4.16 | 1.04 | -.076 | .940 |
| 45. I am satisfied with my decision-making skills. | 4.20 | .93 | 4.23 | .81 | -.120 | .905 |
| 46. I am satisfied with my communication skills. | 4.20 | .79 | 4.29 | .74 | -.475 | .636 |
| 47. I am satisfied with my conflict-management skills. | 3.94 | 1.05 | 4.20 | .93 | -1.036 | .304 |
| 48. I am satisfied with my problem-solving skills. | 4.26 | .95 | 4.48 | .68 | -1.103 | .274 |
| 49. I am satisfied with my brainstorming skills. | 4.17 | 1.07 | 4.26 | .97 | -.344 | .732 |
| 50. I have gained the skills in higher education. | 2.89 | 1.43 | 3.35 | 1.23 | -1.421 | .160 |
| 51. I have been taught these skills at school. | 2.83 | 1.56 | 3.42 | 1.18 | -1.747 | .086 |

# 7 Conclusion

As the organizations have been moving toward a form of work that organizes employees into teams, education institutions must adapt themselves for these new requirements. Cooperative learning is an effective tool to fulfill these needs. This study analyzes the effects of cooperative learning dimensions among the cadets in a maritime higher education institute. Comparative analysis among the cadets of a senior class, before and after simulator-based bridge team management course, shows a statistically significant increase in positive interdependence in groups, group processing and individual performance in groups. "Positive interdependence" triggers cadets to improve their teamwork skills and be an effective team member. Satisfaction with the problem solving skills, not being able to complete an assignment unless everyone contributes, and sharing work according to prearranged plans are found to be improved after the simulator based bridge team training where cooperation and planning is important.

Limitations and further study. The study was conducted in only one institute so the number of students was limited. Further studies can be performed in other institutions and also in other disciplines.

# References

[1] Naisbitt, J., Aburdene, P., *Megatrends 2000: Ten New Directions for the 1990's*, Avon Books: New York, 1990.

[2] Shullery N.M., Gibson, M.K., Working in groups: Identification and treatment of students' perceived weaknesses. *Business Communication Quarterly*, 64(2), June, pp.9-30, 2001.

[3] Fellers, J.W., People Skills: Using the cooperative learning model to teach students 'people skills'. *Interfaces*, 26, 5 September, pp. 42-49, 1996.

[4] Katzenbach, J.R., Smith, D.K., *The Wisdom of Teams: Creating the High-Performance Organization*, Harvard University Press: Singapore, 1993.

[5] Dessler, G., *Management, Principles and Practices for Tomorrow's Leaders*, Third Edition, Pearson-Prentice Hall: New Jersey, 2004.

[6] Daft, R. L., *Management*, Fifth Edition, Dryden Press: FL, 1996.

[7] Salas, E., Dickens, T.L., Converse, S. & Tannenbaum S.I., Toward an understanding of team performance and training. In R.W. Swezey and E. Salas (eds) *Teams: Their Training and Performance*, Ablex: Norwood NJ, 1992.

[8] Hoegl, M., Gemuenden, H. G., Teamwork quality and the success of innovative projects: A theoretical concept and empirical evidence. *Organization Science, INFORMS*, 12, 4, July–August, pp. 435–449, 2001.

[9] Beaubien, J. M., Baker, D. P. The use of simulation for training teamwork skills in health care: how low can you go? *Quality & Safety in Health Care,* Module 2, 2004.

[10] Smith-Jentsch, K. A., Salas, E., Baker, D. P., Training team performance-related assertiveness. *Personnel Psychology*, 49:4, pp.909-937, 1996.

[11] Baker, D. P., Gustafson, S., Beaubien, J. M., Eduardo, S., & Barach, P., Team training in health care: a review of team training programs and a look toward the future http://www.air.org/teams/publications/mtt/adv_pub_safety.pdf.

[12] American Bureau of Shipping, Corporate Technology Division, Safety Assessment and Human Factors Department, *Review and Analysis of Accident Databases: 1991 – 2002 Data Technical Report*, 2003-5.1, March, 2004, http://www.eagle.org/news/TECH/Marine/SAHF2003.pdf.

[13] Washington State Department of Ecology, *Bridge Resource Management Guide*, December 2003, http://www.ecy.wa.gov/pubs/991302.pdf.

[14] Johnson, D.W. & Johnson R.T., Making cooperative learning work, theory into practice, *College of Education*, The Ohio State University, 38:2, Spring 1999.

[15] Strom, P. S., & Strom R.D., Overcoming limitations of cooperative learning among community college student, Journal *of Research and Practice*, 26: pp.315–331, 2002.

[16] Clark, J. F., The role of cooperative education in the adult learning environment, *Creating and Sustaining Learning Communities: Connections, Collaboration, and Crossing Borders*, march 10-13, Tampa, 1999.

[17] Johnson, D.W., Johnson, R.T. & Smith, A.K., cooperative learning: increasing college faculty instructional productivity, *ASHE-ERIC Higher Education Report Number* 4. Washington, D.C.; The George Washington University, School of Education and Human Development, 1991.

[18] Smith, K. A., Cooperative learning: effective teamwork for engineering classrooms, march, *IEEE Education Society/ASEE Electrical Engineering Division Newsletter*, 1995.

[19] Boud, D., Cohen, R. & J. Sampson, Peer learning and assessment. *Assessment and Evaluation in Higher Education*, 24(4), pp. 413–426, 1999.

[20] Teel, S., Facilitating The Student Lead Debrief, *International Simulator Lecturers' Conference*, Plymouth, England, 1998, Presented Paper.

[21] E. Asyali, Saatcioglu, O., & Cerit A. G., Cooperative Learning and Teamwork Effectiveness in Maritime Education, *IAME 2005 Conference*, Limassol, 23-25 June 2005, Proceedings in CD.

[22] Johnson, D.W. & Johnson, R.T., Social interdependence and perceived academic and personal support in classroom. *The Journal of Social Psychology*, 120, pp.77-82, 1983.

[23] Ghaith, G.M., The relationship between cooperative learning, perception of social support and academic achievement. *System*, 30,3, pp.263-273, 2002.

[24] Veenman, S., Brenda, K. & Kiki, P., Cooperative learning in Dutch primary classrooms. *Educational Studies*, 26, 3, pp.281-320, 2000.

[25] Annett, J., Cunningham, D., & Mathias-Jones, P., A method for measuring team skills, *Ergonomics*, 43, 8, pp.1076-1094, 2000.

# Quantitative evaluation of consciousness improvement in BRM training

K. Inoue & H. Takahashi
*Faculty of Maritime Sciences, Kobe University, Japan*

## Abstract

In the aviation world, the introduction of Cockpit Resource Management (CRM) has been said to be the greatest success in preventing human errors ever attained in the 20th century. Human error is very likely to be made, and it is impossible to eliminate every error. CRM was introduced from the awareness that human beings are always prone to making errors, and by developing the idea that any possible error chain should be cut before the human error caused an accident. In the shipping world, especially in Japan, the accident involving "Diamond Grace", which was stranded west of Nakanose in Tokyo Bay in 1998, motivated the study of a Bridge Resource Management (BRM) training program following the model of the CRM concept. However, it is still underway and will probably take much more time for BRM to become a dependable system in the shipping world and become firmly established.

The authors, while collaborating with CRM experts, are studying how to organize a BRM training program to apply the system in the shipping world. In this paper, the authors report on the process of planning the BRM Basic Course for introduction to beginners and on the results obtained from a quantitative analysis of the effects of such planning.
*Keywords: BRM, CRM, training, evaluation.*

## 1 Bridge Resource Management

### 1.1 Objective of a BRM Training Program

Generally, an accident is likely to be caused by various factors that interact in a complex way. It is considered that an accident is usually caused not by a single event but by many trivial events that interact with each other. In other words, a human error that is connected with other errors in a chain can cause an accident. Therefore, to prevent accidents, we should find such errors quickly and should break the error chain under accurate situation awareness.

Naturally, human errors should be eliminated, and if a human error should happen by any chance, members of the team should cooperate with each other and try to cut the error chains to prevent the error from causing a real accident. The objective of the BRM training program is to improve the total performance of the team under such a concept as stated above.

### 1.2 Cutting the error chain

To cut the error chain as soon as possible and prevent the possible connection of a human error with an accident, the key point is to promote communication and teamwork between crew members. Consequently, it is indispensable to produce a friendly atmosphere in which crew members can make reports or suggestions freely, and also to try to promote a correct understanding of any information received. It should be noted that under an authoritative regime, one person's arbitrary decision, conjecture, or prejudice may lead to overconfidence, inviting confusion and finally creating a chain of errors without being able to make use of the resources that are available.

The BRM training program, in this sense, provides measures to promote the total performance of the team with serious efforts being made to eliminate an authority gradient and to improve communication. The essence of the BRM training program is to improve the quality of ship operations by fully using every resource, including human resources, and by having members cooperate with each other in a spirit of mutual reliance and respect, in the conviction that the key to safe navigation is good teamwork and communication. Consequently, it is important for each crew member, in the BRM training program, to try to understand the importance of human relations and the effects that words and behavior have on other members.

That is why the BRM training program is said to be a program that is not about to improve ship maneuvering skills on the bridge, but is about promoting an improvement of consciousness about each person's behavioral patterns.

## 2 BRM Basic Course

### 2.1 Planning the BRM Basic Course

The purpose of a BRM training program is to make each member of the team understand how he should behave as a member, namely the basic attitude required and the most desirable behavior.

The authors, in collaboration with CRM experts, are planning the BRM Basic Course as an introductory course for beginners. Also while verifying the effectiveness of the training program, they are working to establish a dependable BRM system in the shipping world. The focus in this BRM Basic Course is the efforts to eliminate an authority gradient and enhance communication.

### 2.2 BRM Basic Course in practice

The BRM Basic Course is a short one-day program planned as an introductory course for beginners. It is a combination of lectures and practice using a ship-handling simulator. In the morning, lectures aim at changing the consciousness of members so that they can understand the way of thinking and the nature of behavior under the BRM concept and utilize the results in their routine work. In the afternoon, practice using a ship-handling simulator is provided so that the change of consciousness under the BRM concept can be established in practical behavior.

Table 1: The group construction of trainees.

| Training Session | Job Experiences (Year) | Class | | Q/M | 3/O | C/O | Master | Totals |
|---|---|---|---|---|---|---|---|---|
| | 3 | 3/O | | | | | | |
| | 9 | 3/O | | | | | | |
| | 10 | Q/M | | | | | | |
| 1st | 11 | C/O | | 1 | 2 | 3 | 0 | 6 |
| | 21 | C/O | | | | | | |
| | 23 | C/O | | | | | | |
| | 7 | Q/M | | | | | | |
| | 10 | 3/O | | | | | | |
| | 22 | C/O | | | | | | |
| 2nd | 23 | C/O | | 1 | 1 | 2 | 2 | 6 |
| | 23 | Master | | | | | | |
| | 27 | Master | | | | | | |
| | 2 | 3/O | | | | | | |
| | 5 | 3/O | | | | | | |
| | 12 | Q/M | | | | | | |
| 3rd | 15 | C/O | | 1 | 2 | 3 | 1 | 7 |
| | 15 | C/O | | | | | | |
| | 17 | C/O | | | | | | |
| | 24 | Master | | | | | | |
| | | | Totals | 3 | 5 | 8 | 3 | 19 |

The BRM Basic Course was delivered at Kobe University; Faculty of Maritime Sciences and was divided into three sessions. Nineteen officers and crew from the same shipping company including Masters, Chief Officers, Second Officers, Third Officers and Quarter Masters participated as indicated in Table 1.

# 3 Evaluation of training results in the BRM Basic Course

### 3.1 Evaluation index

It is a principle of the CRM training program in aviation, which is the model of BRM, not to evaluate the progress of each member. However, if the results of training could be observed in changing the consciousness of each person, whether in CRM or BRM, we might evaluate how far and in what manner the change of consciousness has progressed in an individual or group. So, the authors have started work on developing a technique to evaluate the training results.

In the BRM Basic Course an evaluation test in the form of a questionnaire was given before and after the training to evaluate the results by analyzing variations in scores. This test evaluated nine different areas such as (1) inquiry, (2) sharing of sense of risk, (3) sharing of crisis awareness, (4) advocacy, (5) conflict resolution, (6) decision making, (7) critique, (8) leadership, and (9) followership. Five questions were prepared to cover each area for a total of 45. Among the five questions on each evaluation item there were two or three reverse questions placed at random. These answers required a selection from among the following: (1) absolutely will not, (2) perhaps will not, (3) don't know, (4) perhaps will, (5) absolutely will.

The score for each member is described as a numerical value using the following index:

Consciousness level

Consciousness level before training
= score in the test beforehand/full marks x 100

Consciousness level after training
= score in the test after training/full marks x 100

Improvement degree of consciousness

Improvement degree of consciousness
= (consciousness level after training - consciousness level before training)

Improvement rate of consciousness

Improvement rate of consciousness
= Improvement degree of consciousness/(100 - consciousness level before training)

### 3.2 Results of evaluation

#### 3.2.1 Effects of training as a whole

An evaluation was made to see if any change was observed in consciousness after BRM Basic Course training, paying particular attention to the consciousness level before and after training, as well as the improvement degree and improvement rate of consciousness. The index figures of this evaluation are shown in the average figures according to occupational classes in Table 2.

As the figures under the consciousness level before training in Table 2 show, there is not much difference in BRM consciousness by occupational class before training.

But, if we pay attention to improvement degree and improvement rate of consciousness shown in Figure 1, although a change of consciousness has been made in every class, it is clear that the training effect was remarkable in crew members of the lower occupational classes such as Third Officer and Quarter Master. Therefore, it can be said that the BRM Basic Course has had a greater impact on improving the consciousness of members in the lower occupational class and encouraged their change of consciousness regarding BRM behavior.

Table 2: The average figures according to occupational classes.

| | Consciousness level before training | Consciousness level after training | Improvement degree of consciousness | Improvement rate of consciousness |
|---|---|---|---|---|
| Q/M | 69.6 | 80.6 | 10.9 | 36.0 |
| 3/O | 71.6 | 83.4 | 11.9 | 41.8 |
| C/O | 76.0 | 80.8 | 4.8 | 20.0 |
| Master | 72.6 | 78.1 | 5.6 | 20.3 |
| Averages | 73.3 | 81.1 | 7.7 | 29.0 |

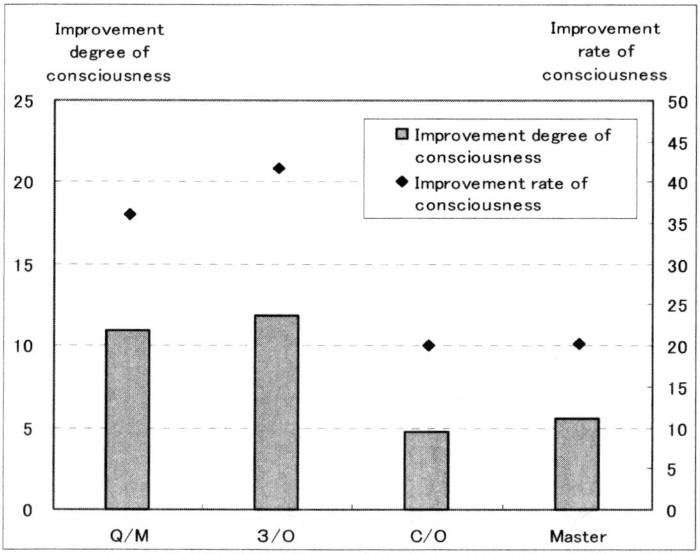


Figure 1: Improvement degree and improvement rate of consciousness.

### 3.2.2 Effect of Training from Focus Point

An evaluation was made to see which of nine evaluation items showed the most remarkable change of consciousness, paying attention to consciousness levels before and after training. The index figures in the evaluation are shown as averages according to the evaluation items in Table 3 and Figure 2.

Comparing the consciousness levels before and after training, it can be noted that the level has been raised for every item.

The average figure for consciousness level before training, taking every evaluation item and every trainee into account, is 73.30, while the corresponding figure after training is 81.05.

Considering these figures, we can observe in Table 3 and Figure 2 that the improvement of consciousness level due to training is sufficient for items 1-5. In the BRM Basic Course, the lecture and practice using a ship-handling simulator focus on evaluation items 1 to 5. As the trainees' change of consciousness for these items was deemed to be sufficient, it can be certainly maintained that the training had some remarkable results.

Table 3: Averages according to the evaluation items.

| Evaluation Items | Consciousness level before training | Consciousness level after training |
|---|---|---|
| 1 | 78.16 | 84.21 |
| 2 | 81.32 | 91.05 |
| 3 | 79.21 | 86.32 |
| 4 | 78.16 | 83.95 |
| 5 | 71.84 | 82.89 |
| 6 | 68.16 | 78.95 |
| 7 | 65.00 | 68.68 |
| 8 | 71.05 | 76.05 |
| 9 | 66.84 | 77.37 |
| Averages | 73.30 | 81.05 |

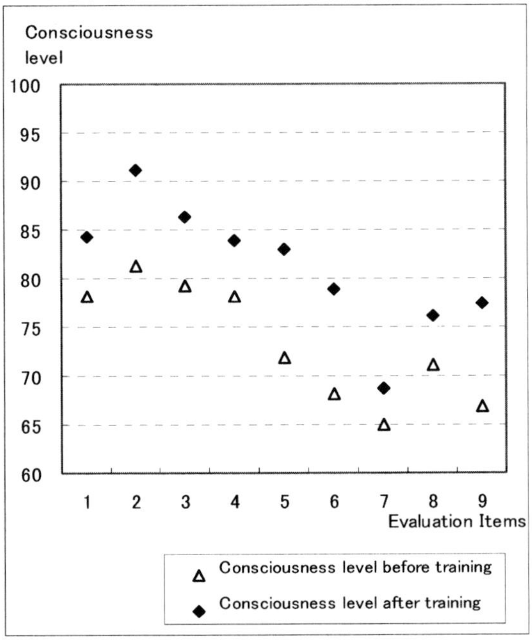


Figure 2: Averages according to the evaluation items.

Table 4: The Improvement rate of consciousness after training according to evaluation items and occupation classes.

| Evaluation Items | Q/M | 3/O | C/O | Master | Averages |
|---|---|---|---|---|---|
| 1 | 40.00 | 39.13 | 20.69 | 0.00 | 27.71 |
| 2 | 69.57 | 50.00 | 38.89 | 40.00 | 52.11 |
| 3 | 33.33 | 43.33 | 28.00 | 22.22 | 34.18 |
| 4 | 23.53 | 60.00 | 14.71 | 8.33 | 26.51 |
| 5 | 44.44 | 62.96 | 29.55 | 22.22 | 39.25 |
| 6 | 37.50 | 55.56 | 25.00 | 26.92 | 33.88 |
| 7 | -5.26 | 5.56 | 14.81 | 20.83 | 10.53 |
| 8 | 44.44 | 29.41 | -2.50 | 11.11 | 17.27 |
| 9 | 27.78 | 48.72 | 22.45 | 25.00 | 31.75 |
| Average | 35.98 | 41.80 | 20.00 | 20.27 | 29.03 |

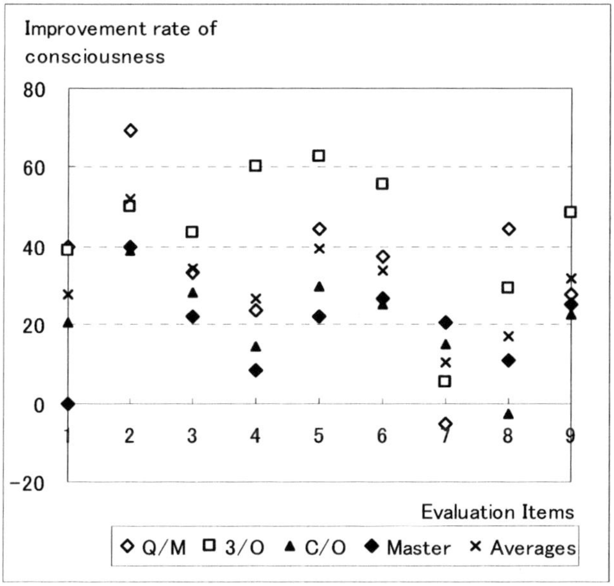


Figure 3: The Improvement rate of consciousness after training according to evaluation items and occupation classes.

### 3.2.3 Effect of training by evaluation item

Table 4 and Figure 3 show the rate of improvement of trainees' change of consciousness after training according to evaluation items and occupation classes. With younger crew members, such as Third Officers and Quarter Masters, the improvement rate of consciousness was generally higher for each evaluation item. With Third Officers, the improvement of consciousness was remarkably high for item 4 “advocacy” and item 9 “followership”. This may be because such behavior was required of younger crew members such as Third Officers and Quarter Masters on the bridge of a ship. This may be one of the main characteristics identified from evaluating the training results.

The item, for which the improvement rate of consciousness was high, regardless of the occupational class, was item 2 “sharing of sense of risk”. This is probably because everybody believes it is important to have a common sense about the technical risks involved in ship operations regardless of occupational class. On the other hand, the item for which the improvement rate of consciousness was low regardless of occupational class was item 7, “critique”. Critiques were not very common or prevalent among the ship’s crew. This is because they do not perceive the necessity of this item yet.

## 4 Conclusion

BRM training, with Masters, Chief Officers, Third Officers and Quarter Masters in a team, was performed and a quantitative evaluation was made, on the results for 19 trainees. As a result, the following was clarified:

(1) Remarkable change of consciousness was promoted. This was clearly observed in communication and in being free from authority gradient, as these are the focal points of training in the BRM Basic Course. Thus, it can be judged that the expected results of the BRM Basic Course have been duly achieved.
(2) The BRM Basic Course had a greater impact in improving the consciousness of crew members in lower occupational classes. So it can be understood that the BRM Basic Course will encourage more young crew members to improve their consciousness in BRM behavior.
(3) With Third Officers, the consciousness improvement in item 4 “advocacy” and item 9 “followership” was remarkably high compared to other crew members.
(4) The item for which the rate of consciousness improvement was high regardless of occupational class was Item 2 “sharing of sense of risk”.
(5) The item for which the rate of consciousness improvement was low regardless of occupational class was the item 7 “critique”.

It had been common knowledge in BRM training that the result of consciousness improvement for individual trainees was not evaluated. However, the authors tried to evaluate quantitatively the results of consciousness improvement in BRM training. As a result, it became possible to decide, by applying index figures, “which part of the training is useful for what, and how much.” These were not previously known. The results obtained will be as feedback to further improve the training system and the evaluation technique.

## References


[1] Inoue, K., Kuwano, T., Takahashi, T., Learn BRM from CRM. *NAVIGATION,* No.157, pp. 47-54, 2003.

[2] Inoue, K., Kuwano, T. Takahashi, T., BRM Induction Course –Awareness Reform for Error Chain Breaking, *Conference Proceedings The Society of Naval Architects of Japan,* Vol.3, pp. 71-72, 2004 (in Japanese).

# Team organization and independent learning in engine simulator laboratories

R. Jackson[1], A. Marchese[2] & S. Green[1]
[1] *The California Maritime Academy, USA*
[2] *The State University of New York Maritime College, USA*

## Abstract

This paper presents the continuing development of a teaching methodology for engine simulator lab classes in which independent learning and team organization play integral parts. The implementation of these methods has dramatically improved student learning in our steam and diesel simulator classes. We wish to share our findings as we continue to experiment with new methods to improve the program and work toward a standardized set of lessons and teaching methods for engine simulation instruction. We are not suggesting that the methods utilized by our program are the ideal way to teach for all institutions, but it is our hope that this paper will be a springboard for discussion and the sharing of ideas.
*Keywords: engine simulator, engine simulation, teamwork, instruction, assessment.*

## 1 Introduction

The California Maritime Academy utilizes part-task and full-mission engine simulators to prepare its engineering students to take an active role in industry upon their graduation from the institution. (Section 2 explains in detail the differences between part-task and full-mission simulation trainers.) To fulfil this goal the teaching methods used for training must evolve to meet the complexity and challenges of the modern marine power plant. In order to improve the methods utilized, we first determine the most important skills for our students to develop:

- teamwork;
- personnel management;

- critical thinking;
- working knowledge of instrumentation (human machine interface);
- working knowledge of engineering systems;
- working knowledge of equipment procedures.

In Sections 3-5 we examine the methods used to teach each of these skills, and determine how these methods could be improved. In Section 6 we discuss methods of assessing the students. We look to standardize teaching methods, so as to give consistent and uniform training to all students, and address this issue in Section 7. Finally, to improve our program, we need to close the feedback loop by formulating a more effective evaluation system. We aim to continually improve student learning and leave the students feeling empowered by the evaluation process. Section 8 discusses student feedback and future work on this project.

## 2 Engine simulation laboratory physical layout

Engine simulation laboratories at CMA utilize full-mission and part-task simulation training classrooms to increase the student learning experience. Each has its own inherent advantages and disadvantages and both systems utilized together can greatly enhance student training compared to either system used strictly by itself.

A part-task trainer is a software program that resides on a personal computer and all interaction takes place within the PC environment. It is very useful for classroom discussion and provides a suitable environment for the instructor to deliver lectures. Individuals also find the part-task trainer convenient to practice scenarios by themselves. Student teams can use the part-task trainer during planning sessions prior to full mission laboratory sessions greatly enhancing their chances of success. The difficulty with part-task trainers is that they do not provide the realism of a full-mission trainer and are not suitable for teaching team organization. They can also be misused where the students learn by experimentation without understanding the process or equipment. This video game mentality can be very counterproductive with the student learning bad habits and forming conclusions on misconception and poor information. Students need guidance through every aspect of their training to prevent them from forming conclusions based on a “point and click”, “try it and see” type of experimentation.

Full-mission trainers are computer-based systems with laboratory spaces which simulate control room and engine room spaces as would be found on an actual vessel. Full size cabinets are used to simulate some of the control panels and control consoles that would be present in an actual power plant. Full-mission trainers have the following advantages:

- Add a level of realism which can excite the imagination and interest of the student.
- Train the student to mentally process the complex and varied information which is provided by a modern control console with all its instrumentation and controls.

- Provide a suitable environment for teaching the following skill sets which can only be learned by the interaction in a group setting:
    - team organization and management;
    - personnel utilization for maximum effectiveness;
    - crises management;
    - critical thinking.

The disadvantages of a full-mission trainer, of course, are both its complexity and cost. In addition, full-mission trainers are not available to the students without an instructor being present.

## 3 Class design and structure

Students enrolled in the engine simulator classes at the California Maritime Academy (CMA) are equipped with experience on the school's training vessel and thus are familiar with the engineering systems of a medium-speed diesel vessel. The simulator classes must first teach the engineering systems, as a large percentage of the students taking these classes have not yet been given detailed instruction in the engineering systems of a steam or slow-speed diesel ship.

To help the students learn the basic systems, a five-step lesson plan has been developed where the students will individually, and as a group, bring the engineering plant from a dead plant condition to a full sea-speed condition. During these five steps a comprehensive start-up procedure for all engineering systems and equipment is covered.

The engine simulation courses at CMA are taught over a fourteen-week semester as weekly two-hour sessions. A two-week cycle is maintained through the first ten weeks of the course. In the first week of each two-week cycle, students learn about the individual systems and procedures used for system start-up via electronic presentations and instruction on the part-task trainers. Because assessment of the students is an important aspect of the learning process, the second week is dedicated to student testing and assessment. The students are evaluated both individually and as a group by three different evaluations (see Section 5 for details).

At the end of the ten-week simulator familiarization cycle the remaining four weeks are utilized to expose the students to common engine room casualties using the full-mission trainer. Field trips to a diesel vessel—where the students can see and experience the engine room of a power plant—also incorporated whenever possible.

## 4 Independent learning

Students are expected to take an active role in learning by preparing for each lecture and simulator session. A manual containing documentation of simulator systems, proper engineering procedures, and general engineering information is provided to each student at the start of the semester. The electronic presentations are also available (via intranet) for review before each lecture. The presentations cover the following aspects:

- Function and operation of the engineering systems that the student will encounter on the engine simulator.
- Engineering systems that are not incorporated in the engine simulator but could be normally encountered on commercial ships.
- Operational procedures for proper equipment start-up.
- Operational checks and procedures that should be performed to assure proper system operation.
- Troubleshooting techniques for various engine or system problems that could be encountered.
- Engineering safety and procedures that must be followed to maintain a safe working environment.

The electronic presentations contain illustrations of actual shipboard engine equipment for comparison with the related simulator equipment. Students are also encouraged to submit pictures from their commercial cadet cruises for addition to the class material. The addition of engine room pictures taken by students has dramatically improved the quality and depth of the presentations.

After a fifty-minute lecture using the electronic presentation, students are given training on the part-task trainer by the instructor. It is important that the students are given enough information to understand and manipulate the engine simulator, but it should be understood that the information given to the students should not be so complete that they memorize procedures rather than work through a problem set. The class time is spent talking to the students about how the engineering systems function, proper methods of equipment start-up, and system problems that can occur. The instructor should not givc an cxact click-by-click tutorial on how to work the simulator. True understanding of systems requires that the students take the time on their own to work through the procedures and find solutions to any problems that occur.

In addition to the verbal instruction, the students are given a written procedure to follow which should help them perform the procedures with practice. Students are given the written procedure electronically at the start of the course. The written procedure is designed to give the students enough information to complete their task, but is not specific about how to manipulate the simulator.

To prepare for the following assessment session, students are expected to practice simulator operation on the part-task trainers outside of normal class time. To help the students achieve this goal, the part-task trainer classroom is open until 8 p.m. in the evening six days of the week and is staffed with a student proctor who is competent with the engine simulator and can help with any problems that they might encounter.

In addition to class work, student teams are assigned emergency situations to research outside of class. Each group is required to give a verbal presentation as to how the situation could be avoided and what procedures should be followed to respond to the emergency.

## 5 Team organization

Individuals must be able to work effectively as a member of a team in order to succeed. The students should learn this as part of their training. Indeed this has been common practice with bridge simulation training for a number of years and should be just as important a segment of training for engine simulation. Those students who form strong effective groups far surpass those who do not. The difference in performance and confidence levels can be striking.

The key to successful integration of team management and interpersonal strategies is that the course instructor too must have extensive experience in managing personnel in an engineering plant environment. In addition, having specialized training in personnel management techniques would be beneficial. Each student team is made up of individuals with different strengths and weaknesses, and the instructor acts as a mentor through the process, giving them useful techniques and guidance as the course progresses.

Student progress in team building is evaluated every two weeks by the instructor during the full mission simulation. Experience has shown that most students require four to five weeks to coalesce into a team. Any group that does not form a team by the sixth week will usually be left behind academically by the other groups. At the midpoint of the course it is important that the instructor work separately with those teams that are having trouble forming and ascertain what problems exist that are preventing the group from being successful. Intervention by the course instructor can be critical to student learning and engagement at this point.

It should be noted that an important element of the team building process is that the students must be challenged by the simulator to the point where they realize they cannot succeed if they do not work together. To build effective teams takes considerable effort and cooperation among all the students. This can sometimes be difficult as one member of the team will invariably want to ride on the shirttails of the other students while others want to run the whole show. The realization that teamwork is vital to their success will prompt the students into taking the necessary steps to follow through and truly form their team. This process can be difficult and frustrating to the students in the beginning, but once their team has been formed and they see the benefit of their efforts they come to understand the necessity of the process.

In the full-mission simulator, students are divided into teams in which they are assigned titles and responsibilities as would be encountered in industry. Teams are expected to meet and discuss their operating plans for each lesson before entering the full mission simulator. Students are graded relative to the responsibility of the position they hold and their ability to work as a team. In the first few scenarios, it is vital that the students are challenged enough so that failure is assured without effective teamwork. This can be accomplished very successfully by requiring the students to bring the plant up and manoeuvre the vessel out to sea with all plant automation in full manual operation. For the purposes of this discussion, a scenario for the steam simulator will be used as an example. The student positions are broken up into the following engineering positions and examples of their duties are given:

- First-assistant engineer is in charge of the engine room whenever the Chief Engineer (course instructor) is not physically present. This individual manages all other engine room personnel and assigns them their duties. The First-assistant engineer would normally respond to engine telegraph orders and control the main engine throttles during manoeuvring.
- Second-assistant engineer is in charge of the boilers. The duties of this individual could include controlling the firing rate and combustion air flow to both boilers manually while controlling steam flow rate to the feed pump to maintain the feed water pressure at its proper level.
- Third-assistant engineer is in charge of the electrical power generation and distribution. This individual also is required to fill out the engine room logbook and bell book. As an example, this individual's other duties could include the following:
    - controlling the voltage of the main switchboard by adjusting generator excitation manually;
    - controlling the water level in the main condenser by adjusting the condensate recirculation control valve manually.
- Fireman who stands at the boiler front to light-off and secure fuel oil burners whenever boiler burner management is in manual control.
- Watertender who is required to control steam drum water level at the upper engine flat whenever water level is being manually controlled.
- Oiler whose duty is to record pressures and temperatures throughout the plant for entry into the logbook. As an example this individual's other duties could include the following:
    - controlling the D/C heater level by regulating make-up feed water
    - controlling 35# auxiliary exhaust and 150# auxiliary steam system pressures with manual steam regulating valves

The complexity of manoeuvring a steam vessel with all of the automation in manual can be challenging for the students in the beginning, but becomes second nature within a very short period of time.

As the students run through the set scenario each week the instructor watches for any mistakes that the students make in the procedures and ensures that the simulator responds in a fashion which would be appropriate for the situation. For example, if the students were to run a positive displacement pump without an open discharge valve, it might be appropriate for the instructor to trip the pump electrically after a short period of time. At the conclusion of the lab session a short debrief should be held to discuss:

- First assistant engineer's management skills
    - effectiveness as a leader;
    - manpower utilization;
    - crises management;

    - organizational skills;
- teambuilding techniques;
- scenario problems and proper corrective actions;
- performance of all students.

The number of students present during full-mission training is critical and an excessive number of students will destroy the team-building process. Due to the inherent complexity of the steam simulator, six students can be accommodated in a training session. In the case of the diesel simulator, six students would be excessive, so they are broken up into two groups with three students each.

## 6 Assessment of student knowledge/abilities

The students are evaluated both individually and as a group by three different evaluations:

- Written essay examinations which give a detailed look into each individual student's competence and understanding of the covered material.
- Testing on the part-task trainer which gives an evaluation on each individual student's competence to operate and manipulate the engine simulator. Since the testing covers a set scenario which has been laid out by the instructor at the beginning of the semester, the student has ample time to practice during the week prior to testing. The simulator software has been programmed to evaluate the student's progress automatically, and a copy of the computer snapshot is saved for later review by the instructor.
- Full-mission evaluation in which the students work through a set scenario. This portion of the evaluation tests the students' abilities to work effectively as a team, utilizing critical thinking principles and personnel management skills; and the ability to prioritize during high stress situations. An evaluation form has been developed so that the instructor has a written evaluation of each lab session which is retained for grading purposes.

The evaluation form utilized during the full-mission lab section purposefully evaluates primarily the performance of the First-assistant engineer. The First-assistant engineer is responsible for the abilities of the team as a whole. The position of First-assistant is rotated between all the students with each student being assessed twice during the duration of the course. All other participants are evaluated on their ability to follow direction and attentiveness, but this evaluation is minor compared with that of the First-assistant.

## 7 Standardized lessons

A particularly challenging aspect of the engineering programs at Cal Maritime is that the dramatic increases in the number of students in the curricula over the past five or six years have resulted in a corresponding increase in the number of instructors needed to teach all of the various simulator classes. Consequently, we have experienced many different teaching methods of many instructors. This has underscored the need for rigorous consistency among all those involved with a particular course – not only for the course material, but also for the goals of the program in general. There is a great deal of pressure on faculty to efficiently use the limited time available for simulation training, while at the same time not compromise the goals of the program, namely, that the student fully comprehends the material.

The solution to integrating the styles and philosophies of all instructors of simulator courses lies first in coordination with the program as a whole. It is therefore crucial that all instructors not only are working toward the same goals for the semester, but also that the same information is passed on to all students successfully. The primary means by which all students can be assessed equally, regardless of instructor, is through the use of standardized scenarios and course outlines. All students taking a course in the Steam Simulator, for example, should be required to perform the same assessment exercises. The full development of these standard assessments is a work in progress. The exercises currently in place accomplish the following goals (steam and diesel):

- Thorough knowledge of all ship systems and layout. Without this comprehension, trouble-shooting, team management, and casualty management exercises cannot be conducted.
- Thorough understanding of the inter-relationships between the various systems.
- Ability to bring up full electrical power on the ship, from a dead buss to normal operation.
- Ability to bring the vessel's propulsion machinery from cold iron to full-away sea voyage and back to a docking condition.
- Full utilization of all Engineering Resources at hand (personnel in the plant, as well as those on the "bridge").
- Proper adherence to laws and regulations regarding safety, etc.
- Recognition of any legitimate method the student uses to complete the exercise, as long as it poses no threat to personnel, machinery, environment, or legalities.

The exact form of these assessments is still taking shape and is largely dependent upon the faculty's familiarity with the idiosyncrasies of the simulators themselves. In all cases, any deviation from safe operating procedures is severely penalized. However, students must not be penalized for following their own system for the assessment if their system adheres to engineering principles. Experience has shown that those students who truly understand the task at hand have no trouble building their own safe procedural systems, whereas those who do not understand are bound to trying to memorize check-off lists or other step-by-step instructions. Rather than monitoring valve positions, motor status etc., it is often more beneficial from a training perspective when actual temperatures, pressures and other indicators are recorded.

Our experiences also suggest that the more engagement the student has with his/her team-mates, the more each member of the team benefits – both intellectually and socially. Therefore, scenarios and assessments are structured in such a way that the final outcome is not necessarily the most important goal of the exercise. Rather, a high score can be achieved simply by demonstrating that the aforementioned program goals have been met and by the student(s) reacting to problems encountered flexibly and in a coordinated fashion. The instructor too must be able to react flexibly to the training situation at hand, as well as be familiar enough with the simulator to ensure realistic – and thus valid – plant response

## 8 Student feedback and future work

To develop better course assessment tools, we have begun to survey students at the time of assessment (the second week of each two-week cycle). Sample survey questions are as follows.

1. Of the knowledge you have applied to today's lesson, how much has come from:
    a. Reading the manual
    b. Asking your instructor for help
    c. Asking the student proctor for help
    d. Talking with team-mates
    e. Talking with other peers
2. What did you do to prepare for the lesson? (Check all that apply.)
    a. Read the manual
    b. Practiced the part task trainer on your own
    c. Asked the student proctor for help with the part-task trainer lesson
    d. Practiced the part-task trainer with friends/team-mates
    e. Review the symbols used
    f. Get is in the full mission simulator as a team
3. Did you meet with your team to prepare for the lesson? If so:
    a. Where, and for how long did you meet?
    b. What did you discuss? (Project steps, division of labour in the simulator, etc.)?
    c. Do you feel that it helped you succeed with the lesson?
4. Do you feel that you have been given enough information to succeed with the lesson? If not, what was missing?
5. Could you confidently teach this lesson to a friend?
6. In general, do you feel the expectations of you are appropriate?
7. Do you find it difficult to treat the computer as a piece of machinery? (Does it seem more like a video game?)

We expect the responses to these questions to help us to continue to improve our teaching methodology, as well as make the students aware of what they can be doing better. Knowing now, for instance, that the students initially view the part-task trainer as a video game, we can remind them of the real-world consequences of their trial and error clicking.

# 9 Summary

It is our hope that with this paper we have opened a discussion on teaching methods for engine simulator lab classes. Engine simulation is evolving at the California Maritime Academy by empowering the students to accelerate the learning experience through teamwork and independent learning.

Team organization has the greatest potential for increasing student learning and understanding of the material. It is improved by effective instructor mentoring and guidance on techniques that promote teamwork.

To encourage independent learning, course material should be designed so that students can work independently of the instructor. Avoid detailed check-off lists which encourage students to memorize procedures. Part-task trainers must be available to the students outside of normal class time to promote individual study. The instructor should familiarize the students with the part-task trainer during the lecture to encourage its use.

Engine simulation training will continue to improve into the future due to the work being accomplished to standardize training and improvements in student feedback through the course evaluations.

# Extracts from conversations representing a social constructionist application on research

J. Horck
*World Maritime University, Sweden*

## Abstract

With practical examples from the author's conversations with an international student body the aim of this paper is to illustrate a qualitative analysis used in the social construction of reality. Constructionists focus on the meaning humans create in our world; how we *understand* it. Sometimes it is of interest to understand people's world and the meanings they put into it. Constructionists have to take words seriously because words categorize the concept of meaning.

The examples aim to give additional understanding of the challenges faced by students and teachers studying and working in an ethnic mix. The analysis does not prove anything but merely problematises phenomena in multicultural classrooms and shows the need for inductive research strategies.

The choice of research strategy is very personal. A constructivist approach is valid as long as the chosen method/strategy can be explained and justified.
*Keywords: social construction, conversation analyses, multiculturalism, classroom context, ethnicity, postmodernism, transcription and excerpt.*

## 1 Introduction

This is the fourth and last paper in a series of presentations aimed at illustrating how qualitative/hermeneutic/inductive research strategies/methods require clear systematic approaches and therefore cannot be regarded as ad hoc processes (a common argument from deductive researchers). Three examples of post-modern thinking are presented; the aim is to demonstrate a social construction research strategy; an exceptional alternative to find the meaning/consequence/impact of what people say based on experiences in their respective worlds.

Fact and identity construction is very important to understand the worlds of others. With this comes the skill to interpret words people use in an utterance. Interpretation of talk is fundamental in order to get the true meaning of utterances. Words function as building-stones for the categorization of both the phenomena and people we encounter; the basis for stereotyping.

## 2 Postmodernism

Potter [1, p.88] says that "... any contemporary discussion of ... fact construction must address the debates in postmodernism". Potter also argues, "Any definition of postmodernism is likely to provoke controversy ...", (ibid.). In short, the significance in postmodernism is focused on how things take place instead of what is perceived. Post-modern researchers try to enlighten the world on what could be described as ways in which people make sense of their social world (ethno-methodology). Postmodernism is involved in the way descriptions and arguments are produced. It also means that any descriptive language cannot be understood by only considering the words spoken, Potter [1]. "You have to understand the underlying system that gives the words their full sense and this system is only realized through the whole set of possible utterances ... ", Potter [1, p.70]. The underlying word indicates that there has been anticipation before we talk about it. This makes the post-modern society a world without originals.

People are different in experiences and perception. Fascinatingly, it is through external sources that most humans build an opinion of their world; less of experiencing. When analysing text, one has to take this into consideration. Our world is complex and sometimes also confusing. The world is mysterious. Therefore we have to ask in order to widen our knowledge.

It has become legitimate to express oneself openly. In a deregulated society, in a state of decomposition, non-authoritarian students *critically* listen to their teachers. This behaviour is encouraged in a post-modern (western) world and leads to self-assurance, predominantly in European and North American countries. For many, this behaviour can lead to conflicts between the free and rules i.e. cause confusion in a multicultural classroom. MET institutions, as an example, have to be proactive and good research is this vital.

## 3 Social construction

Social constructivists aim to find out the meaning of what humans create in this world. This we normally do by categorizing what we see, hear, read and experience. Loseke [2] records that our made categories are important because they influence our behaviour as reflected in talk and gestures. The more our categorizations do not represent truth the more disturbed will be our pre-assumptions of others (stereotyping). This can easily result in interaction-problems. Loseke [2, p.19] summarizes this by saying that research interest should be to: "... examine *how* humans create the meaning of social problems; on *what* we think about the world, on *why* we think that way, on *what happens* because we think the way we do".

The categorization of people is necessary. If we do not do it "... we would be immobilized", Loseke [2, p.129]. "It is through categorization that the specific sense of something is *constituted*", Potter [1, p.177]. We can only understand what we have constructed ourselves. If this is correct one can speculate if it is the words I read or if it is I, as a reader, which contributes to my understanding of a text. A reason for a categorization of others is also to give an identity to the ego. When a person says that a picture is beautiful others will automatically be able to categorize that person. To evaluate the truth, with the help of categorization, is problematic bearing in mind that some statements ("claims" to use a denomination by Loseke) are more truthful than others.

The person that we converse with apparently has an identity or perhaps several identities and during the conversation these identities can change and new ones added. What role does the interviewee take during the conversation and why is this role expressed as it is? Who am I? In the past this question was not a big issue because people had a genuine sense of self. But in today's post-modern era many people have difficulties in identifying themselves. The identification process comprises work of construction by each individual. Loseke [2, p.132] states, "...our reaction to other people are influenced by how we categorize them ...". Based on how we have categorized a person we treat her/him accordingly and from this treatment that person builds up an own sense of self. The building-process becomes easier if the person belongs to an identity group; this rather common. Persons like to identify themselves with others who are alike in a group; this gives confidence and assurance of the sustainability of the created image of own self.

One educational aim is to give the students a chance to change identity and find ones better self. Work and the work environment normally also trigger a change of identity. The modern human being can choose identification by numerous collective identities already established in the world. To be "assigned" a cultural group is also an identity manifestation. To change culture therefore implies a change in social values. When the group, for some reason, has been discredited and the discernment is correct to the member's view it results in the member refusing interaction (i.e. to talk) with the group because interaction is an admittance of belonging. The reason being that identity and identity changes, wherever they take place, are fundamentally accomplished through *talk*.

# 4 Analyses of transcriptions

The following four extracts are taken from relaxed conversations with: 1) a female civil servant from SE Asia and 2) a native English-speaking male seafarer. Both students have graduated with an MSc in Maritime Affairs at the World Maritime University (WMU) in Malmö, Sweden. The analyses are focussing on the phenomena that contribute to different interpretations of the meaning of what is being said.

## 4.1 Transcribing

Transcription is considered as part of the analysis. It is tedious work; listening and listening again to the conversations in order to get the transfer from spoken to written words as correctly as possible.

The following transcription-symbols have been used in this study:

| | |
|---|---|
| (.) | Break in conversation, without measuring the length of the pause |
| (//) | Overlapping in speech |

| | |
|---|---|
| indicate | Underlined words indicates these words have been stressed |
| / | The conversation (or sentence) has changed in content; often a spontaneous change |
| [ ] | My comments on the content of the sentences spoken |
| ….. | Indicates that the context has been out of interest for this research or that it has been impossible to hear or understand what have been said. |

The transcription signs are similar, with slight modification, to those used by von Brömssen [3].

Utterances like "mhm" or a tired "yes" or "no" have, in most cases, not been omitted. Spoken sentences have not been adjusted to make them more readable. When a speech *erratum* has been made this is properly indicated. To make the text more authentic, when seen in print, exclamation marks, full stops, comma signs and question marks have been added according to the transcriber's decision. The author is not a linguist but has worked for fifteen years onboard ships with multicultural crews, and for more than twenty years he has worked at the world's apex maritime university with a multicultural staff. At the same time he has addressed (facilitated) a multicultural student body.

## 4.2 Excerpts

In the following excerpts persons addressing students in class are all defined as lecturers i.e. regardless of whether they have other academic/industry status.

The two selected conversations have been chosen because the first shows how answers can be more or less reliable and the second conversation contradicts the first on the issue who can I speak to without showing extreme respect.

### 4.2.1 The female civil servant

In the following three excerpts the student comes from SE Asia. She is about 30 years old, a Buddhist with no seagoing experience. In the text IE is the interviewee and IR is the interviewer.

Excerpt 1. The topic is on how the student seeks clarification on an issue talked about during class and if she finds it disturbing when students asking questions or seek clarifications by interrupting the lecturer.

IR: You go to the professor?
IE: Nnnnn, yes if we cannot can find answer…… [after having tried many other sources] we go to the professor. (IR: You will not hesitate to) (//) yes yes.
IR: Do you hesitate to interrupt a professor during his lecture?
IE: Nnnnnnn I think quite eh / because for me / (.) I don't know is is. For me I just try to get more information first from the lecture. I will not have the (.) something in the anymore (laughing) because sometime I maybe / because of the English eh English eh is difficult for me. Sometimes, I am not sure that (.) the information that I got at that time is correct that he give me or not. Maybe I misunderstand something so I have to know and I will check with my friend that he talk like this (laughing) like this or not
IR: You will not stop him and say I didn't understand this (//) (IE: Noo). Why is it like this?
IE: Because if I stop him I will stop him all the time. (laughing heavily). I think ….. because even when when another (.) stop him too many times sometimes we talk just follow …… but when someone interrupt we will stop thinking about that and maybe the question is not relevant with the lesson. So we will loose the concent ….[concentration]. It is difficult to continue (laughing) ya sometimes not so good.
IR: Some students interfere by asking questions does this disturb you or? (//)
IE: Of course, too much (.) yaaaa

The lecturer is apparently the last source to seek clarification on something she has not understood during class. On the question, line (3), "*you will not hesitate to*" she firmly interrupts with a *yes yes*. That *yes* is apparently very strong; she has to interrupt to tell she really cannot go to the lecturer for clarifications. On the replication of the same question, line (4), IE hesitates with Nnnnnn and adds *I think* and twice changes the sentence and adds *I don't know* and makes a special reference to self, line (5). This would indicate that the first firm yes is not as firm as it first sounded. The first yes also contradicts her behaviour during this 50 min conversation where she interrupts IR 24 times i.e. an interruption about every second minute. Normally, western men have the opinion that ladies from Asia are timid and shy. This is perhaps not as prevalent as thought and neither the truth. Becker [4] states that a researcher shall not be too gullible "... because people will tell you things that aren't true from time to time". IE perhaps did not lie on purpose but her behaviour is not supporting her statement. Such behaviour does not go with a future manager. It is not good for a manager's reputation to be unclear when staff need advice etc.

IE wishes a lecture to be a one-way communication, a lecturer's monologue. She tries to "*get more information first from the lecture*", line (6). Because of her avowal of her own skill in English, considered to be weak, she at the same time is worried if she has understood everything correctly. To get the information verified she will ask a friend after the lecture; not the lecturer. Again, for the third time, the hesitation to see the lecturer is verified, line (11), with *Noo*.

On IR's question why IE cannot stop the lecturer IE answers with a joke and heavy laughing. Perhaps she is aware and wishes IR to keep the stereotyping he has of an Asian lady. During this conversation, perhaps, she realises that she shows her real self too much.

In this excerpt one can find a clear border where IE changes her identity from I to we. Between lines five and twelve there are thirteen I's and thereafter between lines thirteen and sixteen she has changed her identity to we; three we's. In the beginning she has put herself as a pure student expressing herself with I. Before turning to the role of a judge where she expresses her opinions with we, she turns into the role of a clown. She raises her voice and is funny by saying *if I stop him I will stop him all the time*, line (12). With this saying she also underestimates herself because her English is fairly good. As a judge she is saying *we will loose,* line (15), ..., *we will stop,* line (14), ... and *we talk,* line (13). By using first person plural she safeguards her opinion even if IR starts the question with *You will* ...., line (11). Her opinions are expressed with *maybe the question is not relevant* and *sometimes not so good.* The choice of the words *maybe* and *sometimes* put her opinion in shade; the door is open for any interpretation of how serious the statements really are. It looks like she does not dare to have a firm standpoint on this issue. Perhaps she, in this context, is an "animator", Potter [1, p.143], set to forward, "who says the words", an opinion she got from an earlier context expressed by others or another person, Asians presumably. One cannot tell if she distances herself from this apparently general opinion. What she says has an implication on her accountability. "You are not generally accountable for factual claims that are merely reported", (ibid.). This is an important statement to remember when analysing text.

In fact, it is a small fraction of what we know and that we have conveyed opinions on and that we categorize (as all humans do) to build on our own experiences. Loseke [2] also concludes that the categorizations we make are built on types i.e. we judge from a few of a category and allow this to be general for the whole e.g. work category/type. Still, many people are familiar only with workforces from ashore, meaning that sailors are noisy and drunken and a disturbance in society. This image or categorization that they possibly have obtained from old films/literature or old hearsay has become this person's vision of sailors. "... the best we can do is have (sic.) an image of the typical", Loseke [2, p.17]. A person should not be blamed for his categorizations. Categorizing is to see similarities among things. It is commonly human.

Loseke [2, pp.31-45] has further elaborated this idea, much of which we say and think originates from someone else, in his identification of *claims makers*. He distinguishes between five different social pressure groupings/activities that make us attentive to specific phenomena in the world. It should be noted that the truth of a statement or opinion could depend on the type of activities that is set to formulate a specific claim. The five claim makers or activities are: 1) *Cultural feeling groups* (shared values and beliefs), 2) *Popular wisdom,* 3) *Social activists (*groups of likeminded), 4) *Scientists* (evidences above politics and individual ambition) and 5) *Mass media* (packaging claims by others).

This student might be "packaging claims" that others have told her. Alas, do we really receive a true opinion from the interviewee? Perhaps not. If her answer were to be noted, using a quantitative strategy, the accountability dilemma would not be discovered.

<u>Excerpt 2</u>. The topic is on where in the classroom the student positions herself.

| | | |
|---|---|---|
| 1 | IR: | Where do you sit for instance in CP Hall: front, back or (IE: in the back) (laughing). |
| 2 | | Why you sit in the back? |
| 3 | IE: | Nnnnnnnn I don't know. Maybe my behaviour (.) but in my University [in country X] I |
| 4 | | like to sit in the front at front close to professor <u>but</u> it depend on (laughing) / I don't |
| 5 | | know. Because the seminar is not too serious sir, I think. |
| 6 | IR: | So you feel more relaxed to sit (IE: yes) in the back then (IE: yes). But if it is in a |
| 7 | | classroom? |
| 8 | IE: | Ya, if we try to get everything, (.) good [to sit] in front (laughing). |

A firm answer tells that she prefers to sit at the back. The answer is given interrupting IR. A laugh is added to the answer perhaps indicating that this is not her normal choice. On the question why she prefers to sit at the back she hesitates and starts by saying *I don't know*, line (3). IE claims her behaviour is culturally coined, but it would not be correct because then she should have chosen a front position. And this she does in adding that this is the case in her home university. In line (5) she suggests that the reason could be that seminars at WMU are not serious. This could, of course, be seen as a severe criticism of the seminars at WMU but as Becker [4, p.108] writes "Leaving cases out because they seem tasteless or politically discomforting is equally guaranteed to be a mistake". Just the mere fact that she mentions this as a reason for not sitting at the front is worth observing, especially as the explanation has not a good bearing in this context. When IR has seen IE in the auditorium she has been at the front. A guess would be that the reason for her taking the back seat is merely because then she can ask her friend directly, without being impolite, disturbing the lecturer, when there is something said that she couldn't understand. Also, when a lecturer's' English is difficult to understand a rear seat is chosen. She sometimes excuses her frank answer with a laugh; *I don't know*, line (5) and *I think,* line (5).

There is no attendance control at any lectures or seminars. Seminars are uniformly assessed as lectures in classrooms; her answer is puzzling. IE is about to give a "better" explanation by starting with *but it depend* (sic.) *on*, line (4). Now IE is about to change her mind. Normally, she would say that she likes to sit at the front because then she has more direct contact with the teacher and questions from other students will be less disturbing to her learning. To be shy would be less significant because colleagues are ignored, as if not present.

In the beginning of this extract IE takes the role of a presenter of herself and her opinions; *my behaviour*, *my University* and *I like* etc.

In line (7) she changes her role and becomes a spokesperson of the students from her country (perhaps yet all Asian students) and the footing becomes we. Still she is safeguarding her statement with *if,* line (8).

Excerpt 3. The topic is on how the student finds the assessment of herself considering that she is not active during class.

| | | |
|---|---|---|
| 1 | IR: | Do you think that the assessment of you also is negative because you don't say very |
| 2 | | much in class? |
| 3 | IE: | Yes (laughing) yaa (.) But, I think only only the same person that always talk in the |
| 4 | | class you can see. I don't know, just a few, a few students that always talk. But if none |
| 5 | | talk I will not talk for ever [?]. all the class also, it will be like that. I don't know it |
| 6 | | depend on the (.) |
| 7 | IR: | You know, if they didn't say anything (//) (IE: Nnn we will not say) it would be boring |
| 8 | | also (.) |
| 9 | IE: | No, not for me because for me it is OK because if I don't understand something I will |
| 10 | | ask later ..... maybe my question is too stupid for another [student] (laughing) I don't |
| 11 | | know. (IR: No question is stupid). No, because they already know all [everything] |
| 12 | | (laughing). |

IE starts with a firm *Yes* as an answer to the question. In the same line (3) she comes with a *But* and with this word it can be understood that the firm answer is perhaps not as firm as it sounded. In addition, IE adds *I think* signalling to IR the answer is linked to some uncertainties. In line (4) she expresses another indication on a doubt on the firm *Yes*; *I don't know*.

The rest of the answer is very non-cohesive and does not make much sense. With words expressing uncertainty IE does not clearly tell IR that her silence in class is believed to have an impact on the assessment of her. The laughing after the *Yes* also indicates that there is uncertainty in the statement. But IE is firm that any disturbance during lectures is a problem for her, even if the lecture becomes boring according to IR. The interruption of IR, line (7), indicates that she is very sure on the negative effect of any interruption of the lecturer. The raised tone of voice, line 4-5, has the same effect: it is bad for me.

On IR's remark *No question is stupid*, line (11), IE answers *No*, which would indicate that she encounters stupid questions during lectures. This disturbs her in her learning because she only wishes to listen to the lecturer. *Maybe my question is too stupid,* line (10), is a statement making the answer to the original questions something she does not wish to answer. Before entering the WMU's English Study Skills Programme IE had an IELTS level of 6.0 and made good progress. She had about a 75% average final grade in her M.Sc. i.e. she knows that she is capable and that her English is sufficient.

The many laughs in this excerpt could indicate that this question is not particularly important to her. IE did a lot to avoid a "serious" answer to this question.

Can IE be categorized such as giving sincere answers to this topic? The question is perhaps merely as Potter [1, p.139] (my brackets) elaborates in saying "... how he (here she) should act if he (here she) is to be treated as a member of the appropriate category".

In this extract IE takes the role of a worried student. She keeps expressing herself as I but when the question comes on what would be the situation in the classroom, if nobody but the teacher is talking, then she changes her footing to we, in *we will not say*, line (7). IE could well have continued with I because she has already many times said that she is not the person to interrupt the lecturer with a question or a clarification. The reason for the change could be "... to constitute the item as sensitive or controversial", Potter [1, p.144]. IE gives a signal of neutrality. Generally " ... the non-specific plural avoids these troubling difficulties with the account", Potter [1, p.162]. This is also the reason why she before a statement either says *I think* or *I don't know*.

In lines 9-12, IE expresses herself on the opinion that all the other students are persons that *already know all*. IE has taken the role of a spokesperson on all students being more knowledgeable than her. Again she has taken the backseat, being modest concerning her knowledge.

### 4.2.2 The male seafarer

In the excerpt, the student comes from an English speaking country. He is about 30 years old, a Christian with seagoing experience. In the text IE is the interviewee and IR is the interviewer.

<u>Excerpt 4</u>. The topic is on the issue if fellow students can interrupt him when they do not understand what he says.

IR Can one say that they [the fellow students] don't hesitate to stop you if there is something they don't understand?
IE Ya, ya I would say that's true.
IR They would say: Hey, [...] what is this?
IE Right, jah. Because if sometimes I speak too fast I would slow down.
IR And they openly tell you this?
IE <u>Ya</u>, ya (.)

These few lines indicate that fellow students do not hesitate to interrupt a colleague. An example of a fellow student was discussed in Excerpt 1, confirming that she does hesitate to interrupt lecturers. The obvious conclusion must be that power distance and students respect for the teacher, as an authority, is a feature, most likely, predominant in shipping circles; a good behaviour in certain contexts but a hindrance in an interactive classroom where one wishes to argue and discuss specific phenomena. Therefore, individual students (read predominantly female Asian) will feel left out and their grades might suffer from their culturally inherited behaviour. Interestingly, these students still have good grades; they are good at memorizing. At the MSc study-level the exam-questions should be of such type that they encourage independent thinking, draw upon formulating conclusions and find consequences (right or wrong is of minor interest, *arguing and critical thinking* is vital).

# 5 Conclusion

A major goal is to find what happens to a person's identity, values and perceptions in a specific context. The language used and the behaviour showed by the civil servant, demonstrates we are "all alike" when being approached on a level playing field. It shows that culture acts as a barrier for self-defence and protection against the unknown. The theatrical acting becomes less necessary when the two conversing know each other; the stereotyped categorization becomes less deviant. The discussions also show that with less power-distance (excessive respect) the outward show becomes more natural.

Fact constructions in the statements by the interviewee very much depend on the footing. "... the paraphernalia of footing is often a major resource in building factual versions", Potter [1, p.148].

In the first three excerpts there is a remarkable repetition of I: I think, I will check, I don't know (thrice), I don't understand, I will ask, I will not talk, I like, I just try, I am not sure etc. that will underscore she is rather self-centred. Her talk is principally specific for her. How she expresses herself does not have to be typical of her culture. This self-centred approach would possibly make her a good leader among likes and good for survival in a male dominated industry like shipping. When she becomes confident in English, she might be a leader also among non-nationals. An argument against this statement could be that too often, she does not give firm answers. This ego-centred behaviour is perhaps also something that throws our stereotyping of Asian females overboard.

Another phenomenon in our talk is that we often speak in single words, phrases and fragments of sentences. Conversational talk appears to be structured in a rarely consciously clear manner. Sometimes we find it necessary to "watch our language" by avoiding certain phrases or words. Because of this some statements perhaps are more truthful than others. Irony and sarcasm is another way of saying one thing and meaning another, as exemplified in excerpt 1 line 12.

We seldom make deliberate decisions when talking. And as Tannen [5] concludes, "... there's an aesthetic pleasure in communicating cryptically". These phenomena, and also that people suddenly become silent, are difficulties that one still can overcome and analyse in an effort to find the meaning and reason of talk. In excerpts one, two and three the student is expressing herself with different constructed identities. The changes are both frequent and striking. Table 1 summarises this phenomenon and illustrates how the context and the reason for the arguments labels the way she expresses herself.

Table 1: The civil servant's identity changes.

| Excerpt | Identity | Pronoun | Reason | Topic |
|---|---|---|---|---|
| 1 | Student | I, me | This is own opinion assured with "for me" | Stop teacher |
| 1 | Clown | I | Expressing own opinion being self-ironic on own behaviour | Stop teacher |
| 1 | Judge | We | Safeguarding own opinion when talking about another and others opinions | Stop teacher |
| 2 | Declarer | I, my | Statements self guarded with maybe, I don't know, I think | Seating selection in the auditorium |
| 2 | Spokesperson | We | Firm statement on behalf of others | Seating selection in the auditorium |
| 3 | Worried student | I | Safe guarded with a number of buts | Assessment |
| 3 | Students' spokesperson | We | Statement on other students | Class-room situation |

People construct themselves and create identities as expectations or views change and in a way to fit the current situation, Potter [1].

One of the powers of descriptions lies in what they fail to describe (ibid.); what has been ignored or left out. Not in any of the three excerpts has this been examined as it is both difficult and contentious.

To understand is not a single-minded operation. Questions associated with constructionism might not seem real or very important. Though, Loseke [2, p.167] summarises that "... constructionist studies nonetheless can give us very important information about the world around us". Apparently, it could give more information of the truth than a tick in a questionnaire box.

## Disclaimer

The views expressed in this paper are the personal views of the author and not necessarily those of the employer of the author.

## References

[1] Potter, J., Representing reality. Discourse, rhetoric and social construction. Sage: London, 2004.

[2] Loseke, D. R., Thinking about social problems. 2nd Ed. Aldine de Gruyter: New York, 2003.

[3] von Brömssen, K., Tolkningar, förhandlingar och tystnader. ACTA Universitatis Gothenburgensis: Göteborg, p.137, 203 (in Swedish).

[4] Becker, H. S., Tricks of the trade. How to think about your research while you're doing it. The University Press: Chicago, p.100, 1998.

[5] Tannen, D., That's not what I meant; how conversational style makes or breaks your relations with others. Virago Press: London, p.48, 1998.

# Proposal of an evaluation method using a physiological index in navigator-centered education

T. Takehara[1], K. Murai[2], L. C. Stone[3] & Y. Hayashi[2]
[1]*Graduate School of Science and Technology, Kobe University, Japan*
[2]*Faculty of Maritime Sciences, Kobe University, Japan*
[3]*English Department, Maine Maritime Academy, USA*

## Abstract

We have been researching how to evaluate navigators' arts using their physiological and behavioural information in order to make a new index of human-centered education as carried out on a training ship. We need the evaluation for specialised merchant ships such as tankers, container ships, LNG carriers, etc., because the responsibilities and actions of the bridge team-mates differ according to each ship's type. In this paper, we describe, using the frequency components of R-R interval data, responses in bridge team-mates while aboard merchant ships.
*Keywords: SNS, R-R interval, mental workload, merchant ship, team-mate.*

## 1 Introduction

In Japan, a university or a maritime technology college, not a navy or a coast guard, controls the education for merchant ship navigators. Practical on-board education is conducted on a training ship, such as a power vessel or tall ship. Specialists who have a lot of experience educate students on the ship. However, the content of the practical on-board education is not always clear to the students, because real situations include all things, not just simple linear knowledge. In real life, complex situations are difficult for student navigators to understand. We need some evaluation indices of navigational arts/skills, which can form the basis of ship handling in on-board education, and these indices must be able to evaluate human behaviours.

We have been researching how to evaluate navigators' arts/skills using their physiological and behavioural information. We are using heart rate variability (R-R interval), nasal temperature, eye movement and gravity centre as quantitative indices [1, 2]. One of our recent main studies includes findings on the characteristics of the mental workload among ship's bridge team-mates during navigational watch keeping. However, the vessels on which we always conducted the experiments were training ships, not commercial merchant ships. We need to evaluate navigators on merchant ships. The vessels are categorized according to their cargo properties (e.g., tanker, training ship, LNG carrier, etc.); consequently, the work of bridge team-mates differs according to each ship's type. Additionally, the characteristics of bridge team-mates' performances differ depending upon their nationalities.

The purpose of this paper is to determine whether we can find changes in team-mates' mental workloads on the real bridge or not by the R-R interval. We evaluated the bridge team-mates' performance on merchant ships rather than aboard training ships. The experiment was carried out in Istanbul Strait in Turkey using four kinds of vessels. We show the relationship between the bridge team-mates' performance and the characteristics of their mental workload with SNS value [3], SNS=LF/HF, which is used to evaluate the mental workload in many study fields. LF consists of the frequency components between 0.04 and 0.15 Hz, while HF consists of the frequency components between 0.15 and 0.40 Hz. SNS value is influenced mainly by the physical conditions and the postures rather than by the mental workload. The navigator's responses give credence to our evaluation. In this paper, we confirm whether the navigator's responses to handling the ship in the busy Istanbul Strait are valid.

## 2 R-R interval and SNS value

We show an outline of the R-R interval in Figure 1. In Figure 1, the electrocardiogram consists of P, Q, R, S, and T waves, and the R-R interval is time interval from a peak R to the next peak. The R-R interval fluctuates according to physical and the mental conditions such as those in Figure 2. In this study, we use a frequency component of R-R interval data as a consistent measurement.

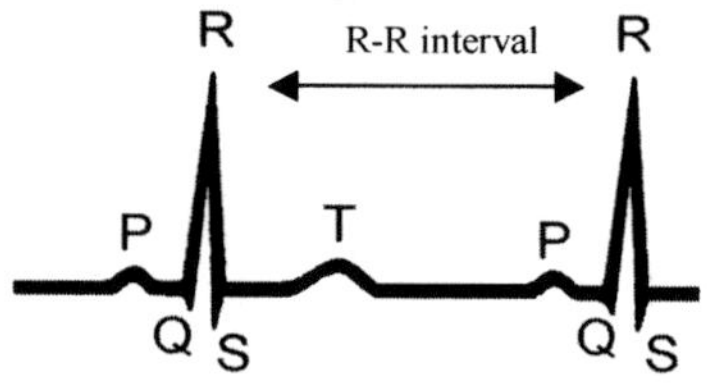


Figure 1: Outline of R-R interval.

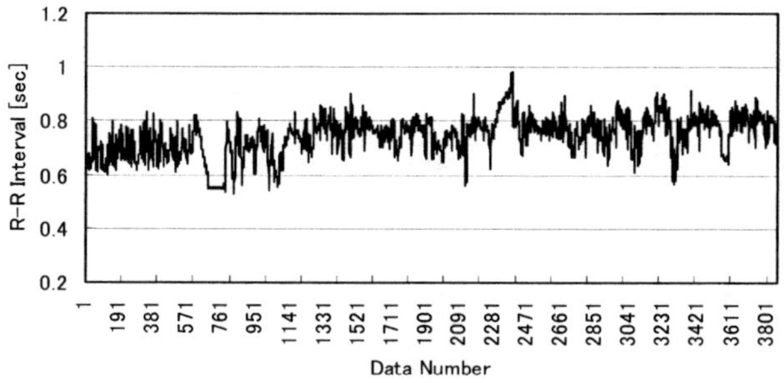


Figure 2: R-R interval data.

Our evaluation index in this study, the SNS value, can be calculated by using two frequency components of the R-R interval data. They are the Low Frequency component (LF) and the High Frequency component (HF). We calculate the SNS value by Equation (1) as follows:

$$SNS = LF / HF \tag{1}$$

LF consists of the frequency components between 0.04 and 0.15 Hz and reflects the sympathetic nervous system. HF consists of the frequency components between 0.15 and 0.40 Hz and reflects the parasympathetic nervous system. The SNS value can be used to evaluate the influence on the sympathetic and parasympathetic nervous systems simultaneously. Meanwhile, the SNS value is influenced by the physical conditions, the postures, etc. of the navigators excluding their mental workload. The recorded responses of the navigators lends credence to our evaluation [4, 5]. We tackled this problem [6], and we confirmed the responses to ship handling. However, we need more accurate research on the changes that occur in the SNS value.

## 3 Experiment

We measured the bridge team-mates' R-R interval during navigational watch keeping on four kinds of vessels in Istanbul Strait (a star in Figure 3). Istanbul Strait is the narrow channel between the Black Sea and the Marmara Sea. We got good measurements of R-R interval data for the following navigational situations: entering port, leaving port and transiting the strait.

We observed the performance of the navigators using the Work-Sampling Method every second. The results were recorded on record sheets shown in Table 1. We also recorded their conversations with an IC recorder; checked and recorded sea/wind conditions; and recorded some target information, etc. on the navigational instruments.

Figure 3: Experimental area (Istanbul Strait).

Table 1: Work-Sampling data sheet.

| | | | | | | |
|---|---|---|---|---|---|---|
| Ship Name: | | | | | Date: | |
| PILOT-Name: | | | | | Start: | |
| Age/Weight/Height: | | | | | Finish: | |
| Time | | | Event-1 | Event-2 | Whom | Remarks |
| Hr. | Min. | Sec. | | | | |
| | | | | | | |

On each Work-Sampling data sheet, we wrote the experimental vessel's name, type, length overall, gross tonnage, and dimensions. Then we recorded the names of the bridge team-mates as well as the navigational situations. They were as follows:

1) *ATLANT*: Ro-Ro Fishing vessel, 76.7 m, 2,065 tons, Pilot and Captain, Entering port.
2) *WEISSHORN*: Container ship, 157.1 m, 12,029 tons, Pilot, Captain, and Helmsman, Entering port.
3) *ANKARA*: Container ship, 167.2 m, 14,865 tons, Pilot, Captain, and Helmsman, Leaving port.
4) *PARAGON*: Bulk carrier, 180.8 m, 17,153 tons, Captain, Chief Officer, Second Officer, Helmsman-a, and Helmsman-b, Transiting the strait.

## 4 Analysis

We used the SNS value in order to evaluate the bridge team-mate's mental workload and calculated it in three steps:

1. We interpolated the R-R interval data every second with a Spline Function.

2. We calculated the spectrum of the interpolated R-R interval data by the Maximum Entropy Method (MEM) every thirty seconds.
3. We calculated the SNS value using Equation (1).

We analyzed the bridge team member's mental workload by comparing R-R interval data with the observation data, which we got using the Work-Sampling Method.

# 5 Results

We show the result of the *WEISSHORN* entering port in Table 2 and Figures 4 to 6. The bridge team-mates of the *WEISSHORN* are the pilot, captain, and helmsman. Figures 4 to 6 show the results relating to the pilot, captain, and helmsman respectively, and these Figures show the relationship between real time and the SNS value. Table 2 shows seven events from A to G at which the SNS values increase dramatically.

Table 2: Seven events when SNS value increases (*WEISSHORN*).

| | Hr. | Min. | Sec. | Events |
|---|---|---|---|---|
| A | 10 | 20 | 0 | Pilot on board |
| B | 10 | 26 | 11 | Ask the control station the distance from here to the berthing area |
| C | 10 | 36 | 43 | Talk with Captain about cranes |
| D | 10 | 43 | 15 | Go to starboard wing and give the berthing information to tug |
| E | 10 | 53 | 52 | A ferry is on the starboard and is drawing near the ship |
| F | 10 | 58 | 12 | Stop engine |
| G | 11 | 25 | 2 | Order tug to push at midship |

In Figure 4, the pilot had six events: A, B, C, D, E and G. We describe the events in comparison with Table 1.

A) The Pilot went on board.
B) The Pilot asked the control station the distance from here to the berthing area, and gave information about berthing to captain.
C) The Pilot talked to captain about cranes.
D) The Pilot went to starboard side to give the information about berthing to tugboat.
E) A ferry pulls up on the starboard side for the crew to board. If he feels there is danger of a collision with her, he has to avoid her.
G) The Pilot ordered the tugboat to push the midship of the *WEISSHORN*. Then the pilot used the tugboat and the *WEISSHORN*'s engine to change the *WEISSHORN*'s position.

Based on the results, SNS values increase when the Pilot gets information for handling the ship.

In Figure 5, the Captain had an event: F. We describe the event in comparison with Table 1.

F) The Pilot slowed the forward speed of the engine and shifted it to astern to slow down her speed. The *WEISSHORN* had to reduce her speed because she was already near the berth.

Based on the results, SNS values increase when the Captain gets the information for handling the ship. This result is similar to the result obtained from the experiment with the Pilot.

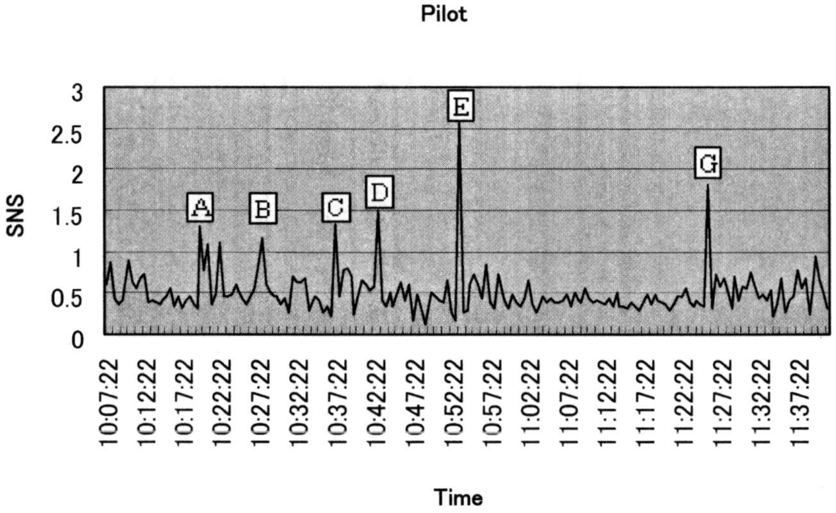


Figure 4: SNS value of the Pilot (*WEISSHORN*).

In Figure 6, the Helmsman had an event: C. We describe the event in comparison with Table 1.

C) The Pilot talked to the Master about cranes.

Based on the data, we could not find information about ship handling for the Helmsman. At that time, the Helmsman took part in the discussion with the Pilot. SNS values increase during talking, moving, etc. In this case, SNS values increase during talking.

From Figures 4 to 6, we determined that there is a tendency for SNS values to increase when bridge team-mates need to make judgments (brain work), and perform chart work (action); to give orders and to receive answers back (brain work and action). This tendency recurred in the results gotten from the *ANKARA*, the *ATLANT*, and the *PARAGON*. Moreover, these results matched those recorded aboard the training ship. In other words, we were able to confirm the efficacy of applying the SNS value to the navigators on the merchant ships.

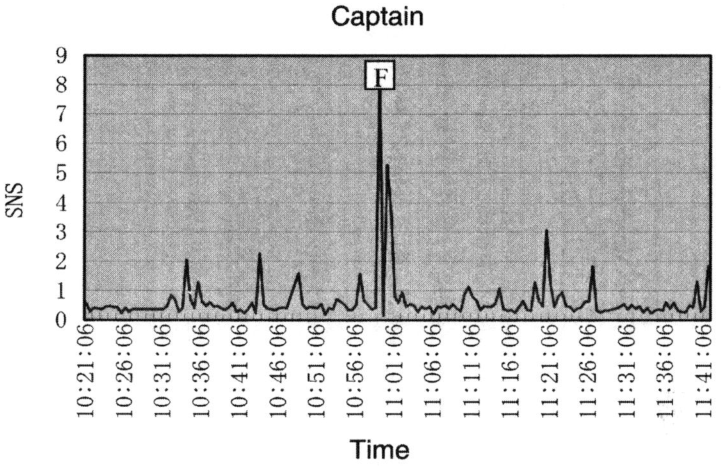


Figure 5: SNS value of the Captain (*WEISSHORN*).

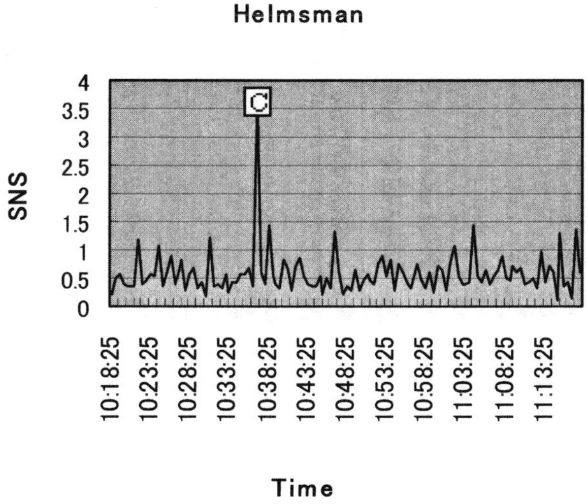


Figure 6: SNS value of the Helmsman (*WEISSHORN*).

# 6 Conclusions

We attempted to evaluate the mental workload for merchant ship bridge teammates using the R-R interval. The results showed that the SNS value was an effective tool in evaluating the mental workload of the navigators. The conclusions are as follows:

1) The bridge team-mates maintained good mental balance during their turns at navigational watch keeping. Their mental workload increased when they needed to make judgments, perform chart work, give orders and receive answers back.
2) The SNS value was a good index to represent the performance of the bridge team-mates for a merchant ship. We confirmed the same characteristics for the training ship; however, the particular performance of the bridge team-mates differs according to each vessel's type. For example, on a training ship, the bridge team-mates educate/train the students, and do not handle cargoes.
3) The SNS value sometimes increased when the navigator took actions or performed brainwork not related to ship handling.

Our future aims are:

1) to find the relationship between the performance patterns of every bridge team member and his response to the index;
2) to develop a framework for evaluating thoroughly the ship navigator's performance; and
3) to find a hybrid evaluation method using physiological indices.

## References

[1] Murai, K., Hayashi, Y. and Inokuchi, S., A Basic Study on the Body and Physiological Response to Visual Simulation of Ship Rolling, *Trans. of the Institute of the Electrical Engineers of Japan (IEEJ)*, Vol. 122-C, No. 12, pp. 2172-2179, 2002 (in Japanese).

[2] Murai, K., Hayashi, Y., Miyoshi, Y. and Inokuchi, S., A Basic Study on Navigators' Visual Observation Area and Stress Level for Ship Handling by Actual Ships and Simulator, *Trans. of IEEJ*, Vol. 123-C, No. 7, pp. 1311-1318, 2003.

[3] Kobayashi, H. and Senda, S., A Study on the Measurement of Human Mental Work-load in ship handling using SNS value, *Jour. of Japan Institute of Navigation (JIN)*, Vol. 98, pp. 247-255, 1998 (in Japanese).

[4] Murai, K., Hayashi, Y. and Inokuchi, S., A Basic Study on Teammates' Mental Workload among Ship's Bridge Team, *Institute of Electronics, Information and Communication Engineers, Trans. on Information and Systems*, Vol. E87-D, No. 6, pp. 1477-1483, 2004.

[5] Murai, K., Hayashi, Y., Nagata, N. and Inokuchi, S., The Mental Workload of a Ship' s Navigator using Heart Rate Variability, *International Journal of Interactive Technology and Smart Education (ITSE)*, Vol. 1, No. 2, pp. 127-133, 2004.

[6] Naitoh, H., Murai, K. and Hayashi, Y., A Basic Study on Characteristics of Sequential R-R Interval-II. -Fluctuation of the Heart Beat Frequency Components for Each Human Behavior-, *Review of Kobe University of Mercantile Marine*, No. 51, pp. 139-146, 2003 (in Japanese).

# Author Index